Other books by J. D. Murray

Asymptotic Analysis
Clarendon Press, Oxford 1974

Asymptotic Analysis
Springer-Verlag, New York, Berlin 1984

Nonlinear-Differential-Equation Models in Biology
Clarendon Press, Oxford 1977 (Russian translation 1983)

Mathematical Biology
Springer Verlag, New York, Berlin 1989
(2nd printing 1992, 3rd printing 1993)
Mathematics Book Club (USA) choice 1991
(Chinese printing 1998)

The Mathematics of Marriage
MIT Press, Cambridge MA 2002
(co-authored with John Gottman, Catherine Swanson,
Kristin Swanson and Rebecca Tyson)

Mathematical Biology I An Introduction
Springer Verlag, New York, Berlin 2002 (3rd edition)
(Polish translation 2006, Russian translation 2010, Chinese
printing 2016)

**Mathematical Biology II Spatial Models & Biomedical
Applications**
Springer Verlag, New York, Berlin 2003 (3rd edition)
(Russian translation 2011, Japanese translation 2016, Chinese
edition, 2nd printing 2015)

My Gift of Polio

~ An Unexpected Life ~
From Scotland's Rustic Hills to
Oxford's Hallowed Halls & Beyond

James D. Murray

Chauntecleer.com

My Gift of Polio An Unexpected Life from
Scotland's Rustic Hills to Oxford's Hallowed
Halls & Beyond
Copyright © 2018 by James D. Murray

To

Sheila, my wife of nearly 60 years,
our children, Mark and Sara, and our
grandchildren, Mazowe, Neroli and Eloise

Sheila, Nov. 2017   Mazowe, Stockholm 2017

Sara and Mark (standing), Eloise and Neroli 2016

Contents

Preface

The second quarter of the 20th century was a period of threat of another war, depression, increasing unemployment, particularly in Scotland, the introduction of disastrous medical treatments and a rigid class structure, clearly designated by accent, dialect, income, wealth and ancestry. I was born in the early part of this period, the last of six children, into a poor working class family and contracted polio as a baby. Had it not been for polio my life would have been a typical working class one of the time. This memoir is the story of how very different my life has been and how grateful I am to have contracted polio, a disease which at the time often removed you from the normal world. In my case it instead instilled in me a determination to learn and excel in whatever I wanted to do and to indulge an insatiable curiosity about everything. It launched me into a totally different, unknown and exciting international world.

I

A Rural Scottish Childhood: Moffat 1931-1946 – a Forgotten World

Hearing *"Jimmy ride a bicycle, Jimmy ride a bicycle, Jimmy ride a bicycle all the way to London"* is my first lasting memory from very early childhood. It was recited, each time the kind district nurse came to our house, as she vigorously pumped my legs up and down as I lay on my back on our large old pine table in the kitchen-living room looking up at the wooden wash drier pulley and yellow curled flypapers hanging from the ceiling. I had contracted polio, or infantile paralysis as everybody, including the doctors, called it then, when I was a baby in 1931. I was the only person in the town, or in the whole county as I was later told, who had contracted it around this time. Against the dogmatic and blinkered universally prescribed medical treatment of the time, such as no exercise, which scarred untold thousands of children until the 1940s, the local country nurse strongly believed movement and exercise were crucial. How right she was. There had been a wide variety of treatments suggested, often bizarre, dangerous, opportunistic and dishonest. Although polio existed millennia before, it was still very much a serious disease in the 20th century until the vaccines were developed. I fortunately missed the worst of these treatments such as electric shock treatment in the early part of the century. Another example was draining fluid from the skull which was still prevalent in the mid-1930s when I was a small child and which I was also thankfully spared.

I was so fortunate to get polio, the first really important positive thing that happened to me, since it changed my life forever in totally unforeseen but, as it turned out, incredibly positive ways. As a consequence of contracting polio it also resulted in the most important event in my life 27 years later as I describe in Chapter 4 and for which I have been so immensely grateful ever since.

The other major medical problem in the family happened to my sister Annie, the second eldest child, when she was a young little girl and before I was born. Practically everybody in the town had milk delivered early every morning in glass bottles left at the door. The milk came from a small farm on the edge of the town. Unfortunately Annie got tuberculosis from the milk of one of the cows. Looking back I'm surprised that no one else got tuberculosis, particularly any children, in the whole town. Annie had to spend considerable time in a sanatorium in the small town of Lockerbie, 16 miles south of Moffat. She recovered but it sadly had lasting effects, such as not being able to have children. The cow had been sold at a farm auction but was eventually traced and slaughtered.

I was born in January 1931, the youngest of six children, into a loving, respectable, poor, working class family in Moffat, officially in the Southern Uplands of Scotland although they were always known as the Lowlands. At the time we lived in a very small single floor terraced cottage called Lochan Cottage. My eldest sister, Jane was born in 1919 with another child born roughly every two years. My sisters, Jane, Annie and Marion were born first then my brothers Peter and John. For as long as I can remember my sisters were always incredibly kind, protective and warm towards me. To my brothers, who were never unkind, I was more of a nuisance than anything else although when I was older I had a closer relationship with John. Peter had been conscripted into the army in 1944 and was only at home very occasionally since he served in North Africa.

Moffat all the time I was growing up, was a very small isolated town, village rather, notwithstanding its having been a tourist mecca for the previous 250 years, with a population of around 2,000. Before the discovery, in the mid 17th century, of the "*Moffat Well*", the water of which had reputed health benefits and which was the basis for its tourist attraction, Moffat was a backward, dilapidated and very poor village. Even in the 1930's, it was sufficiently isolated that as children we made fun of the accents of children from villages 10 miles away. Of course we all spoke Lallans, the dialect of rural southern Scotland.

Moffat is nestled at the top of Annandale valley. There is a splendid panoramic view from just north of the town on the Edinburgh road looking south. Moffat is just a few miles south of a deep hidden valley known as the *Devil's Beef Tub* into which the Scottish cattle thieves, known as *Border Reivers*, used to drive the cattle they had stolen from the English across the border about 40 miles south.

The town itself was an attractive place, in a slightly severe Scottish Calvinistic sort of way, although it is now filled with lots of flower gardens placed around the incredibly wide High Street to help attract the tourist trade which now chokes the town centre with people, cars and buses.

Moffat High Street looking north, c1870. The stagecoaches stopped at the main hotel to drop the well-off and well-dressed tourists who would be taking the water of the *Moffat Well*. (Photos of Moffat are courtesy of my sister, Mrs Jane Boyd, who wrote the book, *Jane Boyd's Old Moffat*. 1998).

Moffat High Street looking north, c1880 – a more typical view with local inhabitants.

Moffat High Street looking north, 1935. The building on the extreme right of this photo is the *Star Hotel* which is the narrowest hotel I have ever known: it is only 20 feet wide with small streets on either side.

Moffat from the hill looking east at the town entrance from the south, 1890. The large old house on the bottom right has been my brother John's house for several decades now.

Moffat High Street looking south and west. Etching 1869.

Except for two rows of small trees down the middle for parking cars and the few regular buses, such as to the county town, Dumfries, and a *First World War* memorial, the town of my childhood looked like the 19th century photos except there were very many fewer people since it was no longer a tourist "health" centre.

Near the top of the wide High Street, which is about 50 yards wide by 300 yards long, is a sculpture of a ram as in the 19th century photo below, and known as the *Moffat Ram*, on top of a tall heavy sandstone rock base which, as long as I lived in Moffat, had four marble sinks around the bottom with constant running drinking water. Attached, by a heavy chain, to each sink was a large ludicrously heavy iron mug which everybody used when they wanted a drink of water: hygiene did not loom large then. It was given to the town in the late 19th century because Moffat had been a small market centre for wool. The ram sculptor forgot to give the ram any ears. At the bottom of the High Street is an old cemetery, which was a favourite place to play in when I was a young child. There are lots of large old headstones to hide behind: it was also always empty of any grownups.

The compact township, as in the photo above of the town and surrounding hills, is nestled in the hills roughly at the geographic centre of south Scotland about 50 miles south of Edinburgh and Glasgow and about 40 miles north of the English border. The "*Moffat Well*" is just over a mile east up into the hills: the tourists were carried up and down on specially designed open horse drawn carriages to partake of the water. One regular visitor in 1748 wrote that "*as the Well is quite open night and day there is a number of diseased, scrophulus, leperous people lying about who seem to be watching for an opportunity to wash their sores unseen by the two keepers*".

Moffat High Street, c1890, looking south and the *Moffat Ram* with gaslights. The *Old Kirk Yard* (churchyard) cemetery is at the bottom on the left where the tree is.

James Boswell was also a partaker of the *Well* water "*to wash off a few scurvy spots which the warmer climate of Europe had brought out on my skin*". With his regular womanizing it could well have been to drink it as a possible cure for a venereal infection. In his journal, he referred to bouts of sparring with Signor Gonorrhoea. He was a lively, heavy drinking, interesting man who aggressively tried to meet as many as possible of the renowned figures of his time. Rousseau, rather a recluse, for example, eventually agreed to see him, and clearly enjoyed his company. Boswell repaid him by seducing his mistress. In his 20s he was already very much on the make. In his journal he wrote: "*I am one of the most engaging men that ever lived*". His "*Life of Johnson*" is a major, very well researched, classic which totally changed in a major way how to write a biography. Boswell, although prone to drinking bouts and depression, was unquestionably a fascinating man.

As a child it was still possible to drink the foul disgusting water which both smelled and tasted like rotten eggs because of the sulphur in it and whatever else. An imposing building in the middle of the town High Street, called the *Baths Hall* (recently renamed the Town Hall), was built in the early 19th century by a company to exploit the water which was piped down so that visitors could take baths in the "healing" water. A hot bath cost 2 shillings and a cold one, 1 shilling: these were very large sums of money at the time and only affordable by the rich.

A luxury hotel, the *Moffat Hydropathic*, was built about 1878 on the edge of the town specifically to cater for the health tourist trade but it burned down in 1921, in suspicious circumstances, and was never rebuilt. After the *Well* "health" trade died the Baths Hall was still used by locals for many years where one could pay for a bath since many houses still had no bathrooms. This was the case in the small one floor terraced house my family originally lived in, and where I was born, shortly before moving to our real home, called *Caledonian Place*. There are two interesting, nicely written, books: *Moffat 17th to 20th Century* and *Jane Boyd's Old Moffat* both written by Jane Boyd, my eldest sister, which have many interesting old photos which describe much of the town's moderately interesting history. Jane loved Moffat and its history and lived there for practically all her life and, for most of it, with her family in the house we all grew up in. She was the accepted authority on the town's history and dealt with enquiries from people around the world seeking information on their ancestors.

Because of the *Moffat Well* the town was a well-patronised centre for the wealthier tourists who came to partake of the water or bathe in it. The stagecoaches regularly came from the cities, particularly Edinburgh and Glasgow, and parked in front of the major town hotel, the *Annandale*. In the photos, and particularly the etching, the clothes of many of the people are clearly of the wealthier, such as the two men with white trousers, the couple with their maid in her white apron, men with their bowler hats, women carrying sun umbrellas and so on. Not all were tourists in the photos: two of the, clearly, local children on the bottom right are barefooted. After the *Hypdropathic Hotel* burned down and the well no longer used and out of fashion, the town centre became very much less busy with essentially no tourists. Moffat became the rather isolated very small town as in the photos above and which I knew as a child growing up.

My family lived free in the tied 19th century house, called *Caledonian Place* in a small gravel earth yard known as the *Close* with several derelict buildings. It was in effect, part of the Moffat branch of a large sister business based in Dumfries, the county town, 20 miles south. Our family moved into the house around the end of 1931, the year I was born. My father, Peter, born in Ecclefechan in 1894 the second youngest of 12 children, ran the Moffat branch very efficiently and dictatorially. The fifty years he ran it the Moffat branch always made a profit for the company which was owned successively by one of a family called Drummond in Dumfries. The Drummonds belonged to the upper middle class society and certainly made that clear on their visits to the Moffat branch.

My father had, albeit infrequently, a frighteningly quick temper and any of the five or so workmen who crossed him were immediately fired and told to "*Git yer cairds*" (Get your cards). These were the documents associated with their job and which, if you were given them, you were fired. Generally, though, they were later rehired. My father was a very intelligent man, of surprisingly limited interests, but an exceptionally good and imaginative plumber who loved his work, continuing to do it full time until into his 70's when he had a stroke, got glaucoma and, very sadly, effectively went blind. He was very gentle, concerned about the family, genuinely warm and considerate for the last fifteen years of his life.

Murray family, c1941: in the "*Close*". My sister Marion, is top left, beside my father Peter, my mother Sarah Jane and my eldest sister Jane. Middle row: JDM and my brother John. Front row: my sister Annie hugging my eldest brother, Peter.

Plumbing covered everything then from the usual plumbing to detecting a water source in the country, to designing gravity systems of water supply, septic systems, the tanks of which had to be cleaned out manually, roofing, lead work on church roofs and much more.

Our house had four rooms: one, the "*Front room*", was only used on very rare and important occasions, the kitchen, where we all lived, and two bedrooms upstairs. The bedrooms, which I thought large, were all about 12 feet by 16 feet. The only heating regularly used was the coal fire range in the kitchen which also heated the water. It had two ovens: the top one was regularly used to dry my father's wet socks after work and which often got roasted spreading a foul wool burning smell everywhere. It was always considered my mother's fault when this happened.

Although we had neither a vacuum, fridge nor radio we felt immensely fortunate since we had a bathroom and a separate toilet, the latter being half way up the stairs and house on its own in the small *Close*. For several years we still didn't use toilet paper, only old newspapers. When, in the mid-1930's, we were able to change from gas to electricity lighting, all paid for by the plumbing business my father worked for, my father said "*We dinnae need a licht in the lavy, ye jist leave the door open tae the stairs*" (dinnae = don't, jist = just, lavy = lavatory). It was one of the few times, until he retired and mellowed, that he didn't get his own way.

Of course, like everyone we knew in the town, we did not have a phone: we only got one after the war. There were only two public phone kiosks in the town. When anyone had to get in touch with us in an emergency it had to be by telegram. These were rare and always about someone who had died unexpectedly or had had a serious accident. Telegrams were delivered by an appropriately uniformed man the site of whom approaching any house was always incredibly anxiety-making.

In practically the whole town the water pipes coming into the houses were lead. The water, which supplied the town, came from a ludicrously small tank beside a water source just north of the town but which never ever went dry but if it had the whole town would have been without water after a few hours. The water was incredibly soft and appalling for teeth. As a young child I never knew you had to clean your teeth. Repairing leaks in these lead pipes was quite an art. You had to surround the leak with molten solder. This was done by first pouring molten lead onto a small moleskin pad, which you held in the palm of your hand. You then spread the molten lead all round the pipe smoothing it as you went. I always wanted to try new things and I became adept at this lead repair technique by the time I was about 8. My father was always very patient with me when I wanted to know how to do or learn about something practical which is something I always liked doing.

JDM with our dog: in the *Close*, c1939.   JDM in the *Close*, c1944.

One of my father's regular weekly occupations was to do the "Pools", a betting pool. This was a cheap weekly activity particularly popular with the working class: it was in effect a lottery. He got a form mailed to him every week with all the premier league football matches listed which would take place on the following Saturday. He had to mark which team would win in each match. He then mailed it in with a small amount of money, usually a few, very few, shillings postal order. Although it was possible to win a relatively large amount of money he never did: in fact it was rare for anyone to do so. He only won something very very rarely and then it was something like one or two pounds at most since he never ever got the matches all right. The companies who ran the pools made large profits.

I spent a lot of time in the large, rather shambolic, workshop beside our house. The workshop also had the office where the old spinster secretary, Miss Scott, sat dictatorially and wrote out bills in elegant script with an old-fashioned nib pen she regularly dipped in the inkwell. My sister, Jane, became the secretary when Miss Scott retired. The workshop had a huge solid iron bench about 20 feet long and nearly 3 feet wide which must have weighed at least a ton. The workshop, or rather the business, also had several other old buildings in which plumbing materials were stored with attics accessed only by steep ladders. For a year I kept pigeons in a large cage in the attic of one of these buildings. Feeding wild pigeons regularly eventually made them homing pigeons so they came and went as they pleased. Keeping pigeons was very popular at the time. I remember wondering what made them so interesting: I never did find out.

Perhaps all the curiosity and desire to know how to do things sowed the seeds of my artisan practicality much much later when I did silversmithing, carpentry, leather work, renovated old houses, black and white photography and much more as described in Chapter 13. During the winter the frost caused burst pipes all over the town. Lead pipes burst easily so all plumbers had to be adept, as mentioned, at applying molten lead on them. During the war, however, lead became incredibly expensive. The lead on church roofs was often stolen by gangs of thieves - of course from Glasgow, particularly the Gorbals, which we thought of, with some justification at the time, as a den of iniquity and violence. They brought ladders with them. We also thought "Glaswegians" had a particularly ugly accent. The Edinburgh accent we thought was phoney, trying to be English. Both accents were the butt of children's jokes.

The children in our family all slept in one of the upstairs rooms, with an old brass-ended 3½foot wide bed for the girls and another for the boys. I hated it and in an attempt to try and be a little separate and have more room I slept with my head at the bottom of the bed between the legs of my brothers. I was often the last to go to sleep. My knowledge of physiology at the time was singularly limited and I didn't know that a heart had to beat continually and that you could actually hear it thumping. I would lie awake in the dark frightened by this thumping that I was sure came from something between the double brick walls of the house. Privacy was non-existent and we all accepted the crowded living as completely natural. In fact we felt quite privileged since not only did we think we lived in a large house it was also on its own in its small courtyard, the *Close*. On the south side of the *Close* was the large workshop and on the other, attached to our house two small "butt and ben" derelict houses. A butt and ben is a house with one room downstairs and one upstairs and generally an outhouse toilet.

My mother's family were highly critical and condescending to my mother because of what they deemed the height of irresponsibility to have six children when everybody else in her and my father's family generally had two at most. She bore their disapproval with dignity. They could not understand how we could live on my father's meagre wage of just £5 a week in the 1930's. Out of his wages he had to have £1 for his 30 cigarettes a day and the cost of going weekly to see a football match in the county town, Dumfries, the seat of the football team, called the Queen of the South. He seemed to me, to take neither responsibility nor interest, in how my mother coped.

Food in our house was basic. A regular and real treat for breakfast consisted of individual round bread rolls known as "*baps*" which we got directly from the old bake house up an old narrow alleyway very close to our house. The bake house was just as it was when built in the early mid-19th century and was always filled with a flour-laden delicious smelling warm atmosphere. The baker, a kind man, who later married the French teacher in the local school, enjoyed his skill particularly with the traditional long handled large flat wooden paddles used in the cavernous oven which was heated with wood. It was still the same when our own two very small children, Mark and Sarah, went for the rolls each morning when we visited my parents in the 1960's. The old 19th century bakery was made the local museum which was proposed and developed by my sister, Mrs. Jane Boyd who was awarded an MBE (*Member of the British Empire*) for her work on the history and preservation of the town and the founding of the small museum. She had also been the volunteer librarian for nearly 30 years: it was not a full time job in the town. My brother John has lived in Moffat all his life, and reluctantly became a plumber since grants to go on to higher school were not available at the time. He was also involved in starting the town museum with my sister Jane, and has also been very involved and influential in preserving the town's character and defending its beautiful countryside from outside predator businesses whose only interest is money. He was recently also awarded an MBE. It is an unusual distinction for two children from a poor working class family to be so recognised. John and his wife, Marion, also started an amateur theatre in the town and were regular actors in the plays.

Keeping our family even minimally clothed and fed on my father's wage was a constant struggle and worry about which I never heard my mother complain although we were all very much aware of it. We were regularly in debt, almost weekly, through getting food "on tick" at the Co-op, the cooperative grocery store and butcher's shop round the corner from our house. Her family was everything to my mother. In times of particular financial difficulty she would take little food saying she wasn't hungry. She would make it seem a great treat for us when she made porridge, taken with salt of course, in the evening so that we would not go to bed feeling hungry. It was not until the early 1950's that life became easier and from then until she died in the 1973 at 79 she had the comforts, and the continuing love of her family, she so rightly deserved.

My mother, Sarah Jane (sitting) with her
twin sister, Mary, c1916.

My father, Peter Murray, in his
World War I uniform, c1915.

My father survived her by several years, dying of lung cancer when he was 83 even though he had been scared by the doctor into stopping smoking which he did immediately when he was in his mid-fifties. It could well, of course, have been because of the asbestos which was regularly used in the plumbing business at the time.   My father took little part in bringing up the children although he doted on my eldest brother, Peter, whom he wanted to follow him into the trade. Peter did, eventually having his own successful plumbing business but, to my father's disappointment, in Swindon in England where his tough and dominant wife grew up. My brother, John, who eventually bought the local plumbing business for a very reasonable sum when the owner in Dumfries, a Major Drummond, decided to sell all the branches. He did not notify my father, nor my brother, that it was for sale. He had advertised it in *The Scotsman* the major newspaper in Scotland for the educated and middle class. The newspaper was generally never read by the working class. Drummond felt the new owner should be of the right social class assuming that neither my father nor brother would ever read *The Scotsman*. My brother John regularly read it and saw the advertisement. My father and John were justifiably outraged to be so treated after a lifetime of my father's total commitment to the firm. When confronted about it the owner finally agreed to sell it to John since, if he had not, my father and John were going to start their own plumbing business in the town which would certainly have made the Drummond one unsalable. John bought it and, with the scarcity of good plumbers, together with his imaginative insight in running the business it became even more successful. John, many years later, bought the large old mansion, called *Mount Charles*, which is the old period house on the bottom right of the distant country photo above of Moffat.

My father was certainly not unkind but he believed strongly in discipline and certainly unquestioned obedience. My mother, Sarah Jane Black, born in 1894 in Maxwelltown (Dumfries), and whom he married in 1917 when he was in the army during the World War I, was the backbone of the family. Although not religious my father had a strong sense of what he thought was right and wrong, and correct behaviour. When my sister Marion got pregnant, by her future husband before they were married, my father was outraged. It was not until he was well into his 70s that I learned he had an illegitimate daughter from before he was married in 1917 and who was still living.

My mother was a very kind, incredibly warm, overweight, uneducated woman of strong views and with remarkable common sense. She was generally right about people except for a slight gut antipathy to the middle and upper middle classes in town whom she thought were always putting on airs, as indeed many did, and who made her uncomfortable. Some of the more portentous in the town expected working class men they had employed to pull their forelock when they passed them.

I had a particularly close and loving relationship with my mother and her influence has been lifelong. Although I was my mother's clear favourite, her concern and deep, but undemonstrative, love for the whole family sustained us all in the difficult times we often had until after World War II. Like my father, and all my siblings, she had left school at 14, possibly earlier. Her education had been extremely limited and, although she never said so, I felt she found reading and writing a bit of an effort. What she lacked in education she made up for in her ability to judge a person's character quickly and with remarkable accuracy, an ability I have seen in few others.

24

My mother would sense the state of my father's temper from the way he walked from the workshop across the *Close* to our house, after finishing work at 5 pm. His dinner had to be on the table waiting but still hot. If he was clearly upset she would warn me not to cross him or I'd get a skelp which occasionally did happen over some minor, at least to me, behavioural infringement. His temper was always very short lived so that if you could physically avoid it in some way for a few seconds you didn't get the slap across your head, back or whatever part of you was closest. I discovered early on that quickly crawling under the old pine table in the kitchen sufficed since he couldn't reach me easily. His temper got markedly worse for two years after he was told to stop smoking which he did in one day when he was 56. He mellowed in his sixties and after he became blind from a stroke he became much warmer and tried very hard, with success, to be genuinely interested, considerate and loving. I tried to get him to learn braille but he thought it was too late. He did, however, learn to write letters to me when I was in America using a simple writing contraption I sent him that fixed onto a writing pad which kept his hand and pen between two wires so he could write on the pad without seeing it. He was the usual letter writer when I was first in America.

Moffat in the 1930's was a small town of unforgettable smells. The distinctive coal smoke from domestic fires spiralling up from the chimneys permeated the town in the winter months. Chimney fires, officially illegal and supposed to incur a fine but never did, were fairly frequent from the built up layers of soot and tar in the chimneys from burning coal. As children we would rush to the house with the fire to watch the billowing smoke from the chimney which you could hear roaring up the chimney into the sky. Cleaning chimneys was another job the plumbers did: it was filthy business. A cloth covered the fireplace and someone went up onto the roof and pushed down a round hard bristled brush so that the soot gathered in the fireplace. The covering cloths never worked very well and the soot went everywhere. The house smelled of soot for days.

The back yard to the side and back of our house beside the store buildings of the plumbing workshop was immediately adjacent to the large town gas works, again with its pervasive distinctive gas smell and an enormous gasometer, the kind which floated up and down with the amount of gas enclosed. The gas smells were fairly well contained.

Monday was washing day for our house and was the day my mother could use the very small wash house at one end of the *Close* in front of the large blacksmith's workshop which was immediately next door. The washhouse was a tiny old slated building about 6 feet wide by 10 feet long: it is the small stone, sloping roofed, building directly behind me in the cover photo. At one end of the wash house there was a large mediaeval looking cauldron-like washtub about 4 feet in diameter under which you lit a fire to heat the water: this was my job. You were enveloped in the warmth and fresh smell of the steaming tub in which the clothes were boiled after they had been vigorously scrubbed on the old corrugated iron washboard in one of the two ancient stone sinks. The clothes in the washtub were stirred and moved around with a long wooden pole which was also used to lift them out. When the large wooden lid was taken off the steam totally filled the small building, even going out the small chimney. The clothes were rinsed, called "*sihnin oot*", in the large sink and then put through the huge ringer, the mangle, with its two ancient cracked wooden rollers. It was my job to turn the handle as my mother fed them into the ringer. Finally the clothes were then hung in the yard behind our house, adjacent to the gasworks and the pervading smell of coal which was burned to produce the gas: the whiteness of the sheets was a matter of some pride.

Another smell firmly imbedded in that part of my brain is of burning horses' hooves. The old blacksmith, "Wullie" Donaldson, a small stooped man, would let me pump the large bellows when he made horseshoes for the huge Clydesdale horses that were still common in the town and the surrounding farms. It was still the era of the horse. He was a slightly gruff but very kind man who occasionally let me hammer the red hot metal on the ancient anvil and make an approximate horseshoe. I was about ten when I started going regularly to see him. He treated the horses as if they were little dogs, shouting at them, slapping them if they wouldn't immediately let him raise their hoof to put between his legs to cut parts off the hoof and to nail on the glowing red-hot horse shoe. His thick leather apron was ancient and shone as if polished. He would take the red hot metal shoe he had fashioned on the anvil and press it onto the hoof amid thick clouds of burning hoof smoke which filled the small stable-like part of the workshop used exclusively for shoeing. I could not understand how the horse could stand both the burning and having enormous 2 inch nails, also made by the blacksmith, hammered into its hoof. I always watched with trepidation since I thought the horse would eventually react to the verbal and physical abuse, the burning, hammering, slapping and shouting and lash out with the leg throwing the blacksmith out through the large window onto the courtyard impaling him on one or other of the old rusted iron farm implements which filled the small yard. It never happened. Years later, when I was a university student, I went to the blacksmith's shop to say hello to Mr. Donaldson. He told me he was retiring, since he was 70, and gave me the old hand made bone handled knife he had made and used for cutting the horses' hooves when I was a small boy. We still have it and we use it as a letter opener.

Childhood visits to my grandparents
Knowledge of my family background is scant and, from what I gathered, illegitimacy was the norm among my ancestors back to the mid-19th century which is as far back as anyone had any ancestral knowledge. My maternal grandfather died before I was born. My maternal grandmother I did know and with whom I became close as a child. The only other grandparent I knew was my paternal grandfather, an imposing distant man who was also illegitimate and who lived in the small village of Ecclefechan a few miles south of Lockerbie and close to Gretna Green of runaway marriage fame. My grandfather, born in the middle of the 19th century, had been a postman before he retired but he felt he had gentrified blood. The story in the family was that his mother, a maid, had been seduced by one of the lairds of the manor where she worked not far from where my grandfather had lived all his life. He has a rather arrogant superior look on his face in the photo below. Of course I learned about this much later and always thought it was simply another of the usual tales (and facts) that were common in the country. However, many years later in the 1970's my eldest brother, Peter, was doing some plumbing for someone in the Swindon area who was a (legitimate) child of the owner of that manor near Ecclefechan and had grown up in it. My brother said that when he first saw him walking to greet him he could have been our grandfather's brother and looked like our father's twin.

I called my grandfather Papa, the usual form in Scotland, if I actually had to address him since we were very much children to be seen and not heard. He lived with my Aunt Mina a sister of my father in a very small terrace house on the village High Street in Ecclefechan. Visits to them were always family affairs, lasted most of the day and involved a bus trip to Lockerbie with another to Ecclefechan about 6 miles farther on. My father had been born there. Although I did not know what "depressed" meant when I was a child in the 1930's it is clear in retrospect that that was what I felt whenever I heard we were going. I looked forward to such visits with gloom. Although my Aunt Mina was welcoming and hospitable my grandfather was always the same rather aloof authoritarian. My aunt generally had a nervous harassed air about her since my grandfather was a demanding man and life was certainly not easy. I never remember my grandfather other than sitting in an upright armchair, like in the photo below, on the right hand side of the large fireplace facing into the kitchen with the one small window onto the street behind him. He would greet us, never ask any questions and give us 2 shillings to divide between the three boys which I promptly said was 8 pence each just in case he thought the division should have differentials for age: I was the youngest and felt I had to look out for my interests. Solving this monetary arithmetic problem was the only thing that I think ever impressed him about me.

My parents, Sarah Jane and Peter Murray marriage photo, 1917.

My grandparents, Nanny (Annie Lind c1868-1957) and Papa (John Black, 1870-1928), c1926.

Another aspect which loomed large when we visited Ecclefechan, was that there was only a privy, or dry closet as they called it, at the bottom of the small kitchen garden. The smell wafted around you by the time you got half way down the very small narrow garden. I desperately tried not to have to go all day but never succeeded. It was the primitive kind of privy with a simple bucket and a plain plank with a hole in it. It was in a tiny wooden hut and always smelled abominably.

Across the narrow street, in front of the house, was a small river, referred to as the "burn", the Scottish word for a small river or stream. I used to think that the buckets from the privies were emptied into it daily and I would look up and down the river fully expecting to see someone doing it. I never did but I would be surprised if it was never done. Drinking water had to be carried from the old cast iron pump on the street outside, beside the small burn but in the year before World War II a few houses, including my grandfather's, managed to get the water piped directly into the house. It was the height of luxury.

As well as the boredom of visiting my relatives, Ecclefechan, or "*The Fechan*", its Celtic name, as it was always referred to by the locals, is a dreary backwater of a village with no redeeming features whatsoever. The village's only claim to fame is that Thomas Carlyle was born and buried

My grandmother, (Nanny) Annie   My grandfather, (Papa) Peter Murray
Black, Dumfries, Scotland, c1945.   Ecclefechan, Scotland, c1936.

there. He grew up in a strict Calvinist family. His father was a mason who built many houses in the village and probably the one my aunt and grandfather lived in. With such an austere upbringing his writings and gloomy philosophy of the world is not surprising. He gave up his religious belief when he was at Edinburgh University, where he went at 15, but assiduously retained the humourless unforgiving Calvinistic attitudes and view of the world for the rest of his life. I can well believe it was the basis for his vocal distaste for democracy. He held the strong belief that the abolition of slavery, abolished in England almost 50 years before, was a huge mistake. He described black people as "two-legged cattle" who could only be taught how to live in society if subjected to the "beneficent whip" of the whites. He also believed passionately (if that was possible) that

29

countries should be led by heroic leaders: his philosophy could clearly have been the basis for fascism. When he was 31 he married Jane Welsh, who also had literary ambitions. It was a peculiar marriage in which the premarital letters indicate that all she wanted was a bother-sister relationship and to which he seemed to agree in one of his letters: it has been suggested that the marriage was never consummated. When people claimed the marriage was a mistake Alfred Lord Tennyson's comment was apt: "*By any other arrangement, four people would have been unhappy instead of two*". I knew none of this as a child but oddly I heard his name every time I visited my grandfather.

Just across the street, on the other side of the burn, lived a sister of my grandfather, my Great Aunt Jean. Her house was in a very small cobbled courtyard, or "*Close*" as it was always referred to. You entered through an archway. It was the sort of small courtyard now considered very romantic which was certainly not the case then. She lived in a "*butt and ben*", that is a small terrace house with one room downstairs and one up with a privy in the small back garden. She was probably in her 80s at the time and the biggest thing in her life was that Carlyle had lived in the same courtyard. Every time I went to see her she would take me by the hand and point to the house that spanned the archway and say: "*Ye see that hoose? That's where Tommy Carlyle lived*". I thought this Tommy was just another of the numerous "*Tommys*" in the village. I always tried to be suitably impressed by this ritual. By the time I knew who Thomas Carlyle was and had read some of his work it still gives me a certain pleasure to think of Carlyle irreverently as "Tommy". The presence of Carlyle in the same courtyard was clearly very real to my great aunt. She said "*A' kent 'im weel*" (I knew him well). He was actually born in the house she had pointed out. In retrospect it is, in fact, likely she had met him as a young woman when he came to visit his parents (whom he revered and is why he wanted to be buried near them) since she must have been born in the 1850s, while Carlyle died in 1881. The Carlyle house is now a museum while the houses in the courtyard are no longer there. There is a suitably rather dour statue of Carlyle in the centre of the short village High Street.

On my mother's side, my maternal grandfather was, by all accounts, a talented drinker. I never knew him since he died in 1928 before I was born. According to the family, he accidentally killed himself when returning home drunk. He slipped on the cobbles on the slight incline up Maxwelltown to their house, which is part of the Old Bridge House (known as the "*Old Brigen'*" in (Dumfries) and hit his head on the large rock which is the corner foundation stone of the house. My grandmother, Annie Lynn Black, whom everybody seemed to know, and like, and would always refer to her as Mrs Black, lived in the house for more than fifty years, from around the beginning of the 20th century until 1957 when she died. The house, built in 1660, is the oldest standing one in Dumfries: it lies on the west side of the old mediaeval bridge, a foot bridge, built in 1431 crossing the River Nith from Dumfries to Maxwelltown. It is still known as the "*Auld Brig*" or more romantically, the "*Devorgilla Bridge*" after the mother of John Balliol, King of Scotland from 1292-96 when he was chosen and then forced to abdicate by Edward 1 of England. There's no record that he build it, however, but it sounds much more romantic. In former times the house had been an inn, a tollbooth and a Covenanters' meeting place among other things. The Covenanters were involved in developing rigid Calvinist Presbyterianism in Scotland and opposed James VI's attempts to establish the Anglican Church in Scotland which certainly could not have been worse.

As a child growing up in Moffat, 20 miles away, in a family of six children, it was among the highlights of my childhood to go and stay for a few days with my grandmother when I was about 7 to 10. About this time I remember asking my mother about my grandmother's parents. "*Nanny's illegitimate, ye ken*" (you know) she whispered to me in a low voice in case we might be overhead, although by whom I'd no idea since we were alone. She had worked on a farm and her mother was no doubt seduced there, as so many were, in spite of the all-pervading, rigid, unforgiving, self-righteous and depressing Calvinism of the time. I didn't know what illegitimate meant: it sounded very exotic and made it all the more exciting going to stay with her.

The house is the last one on the bridge on the left in the photos below. It was exactly what it is like in the photo below when I visited my grandmother. The beautiful romantic painting, 1923, is by Mrs. Chris Ferguson, the well-known artist in the Dumfriesshire and Galloway counties who lived a relatively short walk from the bridge. Although my grandmother and Mrs Ferguson both lived in Maxwelltown about the same time they were in very different social classes. They probably knew each other, at least by sight, and I am sure that they spoke together, when Mrs Ferguson was painting since my grandmother must have seen her painting and would probably have gone out to look, since, to her, the old house was hers having lived in it for so many years. She also felt very proprietorial about the bridge. Although the house when I knew it as a child and much later looked like the photo it has always had a romantic and warm feel to me which is so much more accurately represented by Chris Ferguson's painting.

The *Old Brigen' House* has windows that look across the old bridge and also down the river to the "*caul*" (a diversion of the river on one side of the river to drive machinery) the Lallans word for a weir, the noise from which was clear in the house. My grandmother always seemed to be looking out to see who was crossing the bridge and never failed to see me and wave vigorously when I climbed up the steps of the old bridge on the Dumfries side where the buses arrived from Moffat and other outlying towns and villages. She continued to wave until I reached the door. The working class in Scotland at the time was a very undemonstrative class. Touching, or hugging heaven forbid, was simply not done and generally associated with the English who were universally considered insincere. "*Ye cannae trust people like that.*" "*People like that*" (*cannae* - cannot) in Scotland also included, of course, all Catholics. My grandmother I'm sure did not know any English people. She always greeted me incredibly warmly, without a hug, at the doorstep and would promptly lead me up a short flight of stairs to the kitchen, where she spent most of her time. There she would ply me with a glass of milk and a "*piece*" which was a slice of bread with lots of jam. The milk was because the accepted wisdom of the time was that if you had polio and, as in my case a small and deformed right leg, lots of milk would be beneficial and help it grow.

The kitchen exuded warmth, and not just from the large 19th century stove on which she cooked and which also inadequately provided heat for the whole house when the fire door was open. It was always highly polished which was clearly a matter of pride. We often spent time on our knees putting on the stove black and vigorously polishing until you could almost see your face in the shining black metal. The small toilet, up extremely steep and narrow stairs, was in the roof space. There was no bath in the house but there was a communal bathhouse relatively close by, not that I ever went to it or even heard of my grandmother going to it.

At night, the noise of the river was in many ways a sinister sound to me which occasionally gave me nightmares about falling in and going over the weir. The irregular sounds sometimes seemed to be the whispered discussions of men planning some dastardly act. It did not help that the "*caul*" used to provide power for a mill on the west side added background noise of fast rushing water: it was about 100 yards down the river on the same side. It was a disused building with a sinister, rather than a forlorn, air about it. Water ran under it which conjured up a host of uses: I always rushed past it. It no longer has the same look having been renovated: it is now the *Robert Burns Centre*. Another aspect of my grandmother's house with slightly sinister but exciting connotations was a hidden staircase which went down to the lower part of the house, which at the time was another residence. The staircase was buried in a cupboard but was closed over. The frisson of the hidden staircase just added to the excitement of my visits.

I would always stay for a few days. We went out every day ostensibly to go to the local baker or butcher or newsagent but really to meet and gossip with the neighbours. Everyone knew my grandmother and they always had something to say to me although after this initial greeting it was assumed I could not hear, and certainly not understand, what was being discussed. The Scottish dialect, Lallans, the dialect in which Robert Burns wrote so many of his poems, was the language in common use. Men greeted each with "*Whit fettle, Tam?*" (How are you Tom?) or "Wullie" or "Jock" or "Rabbie" (Robert). I thought for some time that all men in Maxwelltown were called one or other of these four names. The women tended to use fewer dialect words and addressed each other more formally as Mrs, usually without their name. The gossip was of who had been blind drunk and when, who had lost their job, which couple was having problems, which children had got into bad company, who was carrying on with whom (I had no idea what that meant), who had had an illegitimate child and so on. An eviction or a suicide, or attempted suicide particularly, was grist that lasted for days. It was not until later I learned that attempting suicide was a crime under Scottish law, but succeeding got you off, of course. With suicides there was none of the "not being allowed to be buried in hallowed ground" vindictiveness. Scottish law is different to English law. For example it has three court sentences, Guilty, Not Guilty and Not Proven. Years later, as a university student I asked a visiting lecturer, a senior Scottish judge from Edinburgh, what "*Not Proven*" really meant to which he said "*Not Guilty, but don't do it again.*"

Two other of my grandmother's children, a widowed aunt and an uncle and his family also lived in Maxwelltown, in a long hideous tenement building about a 5 minute walk along the river past the sinister old mill. At least one visit was obligatory each time I stayed with my grandmother. I always went on my own. The tenements were gloomy, depressing and dark with small narrow corridors. The eldest, my Aunt Mairn (Marion) whose husband had been killed in World War I, was a younger version of my grandmother and I was always warmly welcomed. My Uncle Wullie was a kind but not a very interesting man, who was married to a small woman, called Jenny, whose voice seemed to be constantly trying to make up for her lack of height and who regularly showed disapproval, with thin pursed lips, of something, or more usually, someone.

It was a duty to visit all our relatives whenever any of my family were in Dumfries. It would have caused great offence if we didn't, and cause another extended family coldness which occasionally punctuated my growing up. One aunt, a cousin of my mother's I believe, who lived in Dumfries across the river was a small, rotund and kind woman but a continual source of embarrassment to me. She was the caretaker of the women's public toilet and sat all day in a minute room with a small high window you could not see out of, in the "Women side". I would hover awkwardly around the small building until I thought no one was watching and rush into the women's toilet to the sanctity of my aunt's small caretaker's room. The visit over I had to repeat the process in reverse. It got progressively worse as I got older and by the time I was a pupil at Dumfries Academy after I was 15, I gave up going, which, of course, caused much offence.

"Old Brigen' House" in the 1930s, Dumfries (Maxwelltown). Reproduced courtesy of the Dumfries Museum.

Painting by Mrs Chris J. Ferguson (née Stark), 1925. Reproduced with the kind permission of Mrs Ferguson's grandson Mr. James Henderson and the artist's family. Reproduced courtesy of the Dumfries Museum (Dumfries Museum DUMFM:1993.40.3).

Dumfries, as opposed to Maxwelltown, was considered another town and was officially so until 1929, even though it was simply the other side of the River Nith which is about 70 yards wide. When any of us were going to go to see my grandmother my parents usually said we were going to the *Brigen'*. I thought this was just a shortened version of bridge end but in fact *Brigen'* was the old name for Maxwelltown, the name only adopted around 1820. During these sojourns with my grandmother we rarely ventured into Dumfries except to shop for something, other than food. *Greyfriars* Church at the top of the hill with the statue of Robert Burns and the market place and Mid Steeple down the High Street were generally as far as we went. Such trips were always planned and my grandmother made it feel like it was a great adventure. Except for the occasional bus there were so few cars that the whole town seemed like one large pedestrian area. Horse drawn carts were dwindling but enough to give me the feeling that we were living in the era of my grandmother's youth.

I never thought how my grandmother lived since she only had the very small government widow's pension. I know that when my father visited her, on his weekly trips to see the football team, Queen of the South, play he always left her some money, half a crown (two shillings and sixpence), on the kitchen table which she studiously never saw until he was half way across the bridge. The ritual was completed with her shaking her fist from the window at my father until he dropped out of sight down the stone steps at the other end of the bridge.

To me, my grandmother was always the height of elegance. She seemed tall and elegantly dressed, always in black. When I waxed on about how much I liked Nanny, my mother, with a certain disapproval, would often say that she likes a *"wee dram"* (small glass of whiskey) now and again, for medicinal purposes she'll tell you. She never seemed to be ill and only moved out of her house - *"It's no fur guid, ye ken"* (It's not for good you know) in 1957 when she went to stay with my Aunt Mairn (Marion) in her tenement flat since she was clearly very ill. Leaving the old *Brigen' House* I think was really a premonition since she died a few months later. About three years after my grandmother died the house was made into a folk and historical museum called The *Old Bridge Museum*. It is not greatly changed inside to what it was like during my grandmother's time but there is no way to evoke the warmth of her presence.

Medical world

It took me several years to learn to walk because of my weak, shorter right leg which also had a birth defect of a severe knock knee. The major charity medical centre for children was the *Sick Children's Hospital* in Edinburgh, about 50 miles northeast of Moffat and which served much of southern and middle Scotland. We went, by train, once a year for my polio to be examined. I learned years later that the doctor and the volunteers, who visited and "advised" the poorer working class families on health and hygiene in the town, recommended that I should be put in a home since I could not walk and they said I would probably never be able to do so. Many of these institutions, set up by rich benefactors were essentially centres where disabled children could simply live and be fed. There were several of them around the country. My mother was totally appalled at the suggestion. I could not walk until I was almost three years old and then very awkwardly. On one of these visits to the *Sick Children's Hospital*, when I was around two, when most children could walk and run easily, the surgeon specialist in Edinburgh who saw me said to my mother: *"I've decided to cut off his leg since he'll never walk. It will be much neater"*. Specialists were considered gods, which they also firmly believed to be the case, and

36

never expected, and certainly never accepted being disobeyed. My mother, a member of the class that was always expected to agree to whatever her "betters", particularly doctors, said, picked me up and said "Ye *will nowt*" (You will not) and left with the doctor shouting at her back that he'd never have anything more to do with me and not to ever come back to the hospital.

I think my scepticism about the arrogantly assumed infallibility of so much of the medical world dates from when I first heard of that experience many years later. Later, when I was around 10 years old, another surgeon in the same hospital in Edinburgh wanted to correct the knock knee on my polio leg supposedly to make it neater but looking back I am sure it was experimental to see if the surgery would heal since the circulation in the leg is very much reduced. Such curiosity operations were not that uncommon at the time. By then, however, I had a contributory say which was unhesitatingly a definite no. Now, many years later, having seen and talked to numerous doctors and actually having carried out a lot of research in various medical areas and collaborated with many doctors, I have considerably more justification for my scepticism of much of the profession, admittedly not of any of my medical collaborators. To try and be fair, which with many in the medical profession is not always easy, a doctor's training is not generally to train them to think but rather to learn essentially by rote. When I went up to university in 1949 medicine was one of the easiest subjects to be accepted in to study, although now it is no longer the case. It's scary to think of some of the students I knew who have spent their careers as practicing doctors.

Although critical of the typical doctor I have had several excellent ones and ten surgeries nine of which were very successful, three of which were done much later by a close family friend, Malcolm Gough, the senior surgeon in Oxford in my time there, and the former President of the *Association of Surgeons of Great Britain and Ireland,* and certainly not a typical surgeon. When our daughter, Sarah, was a young teenager, staying with a friend, they were on bicycles and Sarah had an accident with a car and was severely cut on her face. She was taken to the nearest hospital where the surgeon sewed her up and told her that unfortunately her face would permanently be severely scarred. When our friend Malcolm Gough saw her two days later back in Oxford he was appalled and immediately had a young surgeon colleague redo it all. It's now impossible to see where she was injured unless you know what to look for and even then only if you look very carefully. When I required a triple heart bye pass operation many many years later I was encouraged that the surgeon (even though he looked about 20!) also had a Ph.D. which meant he could think originally: he did an excellent job of it.

The local town doctor, Dr. William Park, known as *"Poultice Wullie"*, probably did his medical training around the end of the 19th century. The few times I was taken to see him he was very kind but limited to basic remedies hence the origin of his nickname. In those days doctors' prescriptions were always written in Latin so the patient would not know what it was. He was involved in the affair which thrust Moffat into the national spotlight in 1935 when the dismembered bodies of two women were found in a small ravine about a mile north of the town. Two local women who had gone up the road for a walk (it was a regular scenic walk at the time with no traffic) saw a leg sticking out of the ground when leaning on the bridge wall looking into the ravine. The affair is a gruesome story.

A *Parsi* Indian, born of mixed parents in Bombay, qualified and worked as a doctor in India before coming to Britain to do a graduate degree in general medicine and surgery in Edinburgh after which he changed his name to Buck Ruxton. Although he had been married before in India he kept it secret and married a young Scottish woman Isabella Kerr in 1930 and they had several children. They eventually settled in Lancaster in the north of England where he was a well liked, kind and respected general family doctor. The marriage however was volatile and Ruxton, who was obsessively jealous, was sure his wife was having an affair (later, during his murder trial there was shown to be no evidence of it) so he strangled her and, to prevent their housemaid, Mary Rogerson, from learning about it before he could dispose of the body, he strangled her too.

With considerable skill and his knowledge of anatomy he professionally dismembered the bodies, drained the blood, mutilated fingerprints, removed ears and so on to try and hide the identity of the victims. He then drove up to Scotland and decided that the countryside around Moffat was a sufficiently remote and isolated place to dispose of the bodies and he decided on the small steep ravine about a mile north of the town. It turned out that he had loosely wrapped the body pieces in a Sunday newspaper that was only sold in the Lancaster and Morecambe areas which proved crucial in his detection. The bodies were eventually identified using, for the time, impressive forensic evidence, X-rays of the skulls, entomology to determine the age of the maggots in the skull and so on. Dr Ruxton was eventually arrested, in 1935, tried and hanged in 1936. The ravine where the bodies were found became known as *Ruxton's Dump*, a well-known place among the Moffat inhabitants. A very popular romantic song at the time was *"Red Sails in the Sunset."* With the same music it was adapted to:

Red sails in the sunset	from	Red sails in the sunset
Red stains on the knife		Way out on the sea
Oh Dr Buck Ruxton		Oh, carry my loved one
You murdered your wife.		Home safely to me.
Then Mary she saw you		She sailed at the dawning
You thought she would tell		All day I've been blue
So Dr Buck Ruxton		Red sails in the sunset
You killed her as well.		I'm trusting in you.

There was, for a while, a dentist in the town, whose basic philosophy of treatment consisted of pulling out any tooth that was either sore or needed a filling or was even slightly chipped. He did not have a high reputation and in retrospect was rather a sad figure. His clinic was in a small dark room, to my mind and personal experience, his chamber of horrors rather, contained his few instruments of torture. Whether or not he was, in my memory he was a large overweight man who loomed over you in the chair. He injected the gum in several places to numb the area, not infrequently missing the gum thereby getting the needle into the root of a tooth with an agonising grinding sound and shooting pain. He then left you for about ten minutes while you fantasised about what further tortures he had in store. He would return smelling strongly of the whiskey he needed to fortify himself for the extraction process of which he was far from competent, generally breaking the tooth in various pieces in the process and having to fish them out with old tweezers.

When I did learn to walk I became distinctly lopsided since, as I grew, the right leg became increasingly shorter relative to my left. It seemed to me quite natural and never really bothered me. Around the age of four, when the medical gods in Edinburgh deigned to see me again, I was fitted with a full-length unbending leg brace with a raised boot.

When it was time for me to start school at age 5, the doctor in Edinburgh decided that I should walk as little as possible since he also believed it was not good for me, and said that I must go back and forward to school in a small pushchair. So, under protest, for a few weeks I was wheeled to and fro in an old small, very basic, child's wheelchair with wobbly wheels. I was never wheeled by other than a brother or sister and even then I generally walked. By then I had no problem walking so the pushchair instead became one of the splendid communal toys used by two of my friends, one on the step facing backwards holding on to the arms, the other on a small board at the back with his upper body thrust underneath through the handle as we hurtled down the High Street from school with my right leg sticking straight out like a mediaeval battering ram. Cars were not a problem since there were hardly any, only very few each day, but at the speed we went we could all have gone flying if the pushchair had hit a hole or stone. Being seen in this game it was duly reported back to my mother who immediately decided that going to school in a wheelchair was much too dangerous and I again took to walking and running, after a fashion, just like everybody else.

Parents never ever walked their children to or from school. It was never thought of and, had it ever occurred, it would have been the basis for much teasing. Children – and dogs – wandered everywhere themselves unlike now with parents making sure their children get to school safely. I do not remember ever seeing a dog with a leash: they were also welcomed in shops; they simply followed their owner.

Early School, Moffat Life and the World War 1939-1945

I benefitted enormously from the universal and excellent education in Scotland, a tradition in Scotland for some centuries. The *Scottish Enlightenment* of the 18th century was arguably the most exciting intellectual community of the century and one which has had immense lasting effects around the world. It produced such intellectual giants as Adam Smith and David Hume. Benjamin Franklin had an active correspondence with several of them.

When I went to school at age five, there was still the lingering philosophy that education was all for the glory of God, the right God of course. Many years after I had been to university I met the old, long retired, music teacher who was probably born in the 1880's who stopped me on the High Street in Moffat the summer of 1956 and said he wanted to talk to me. He surprised me by recalling the various academic achievements I had garnered up to then, such as school certificates (including Latin he was pleased to see), prizes, a sciences degree and a recent doctorate. He then said: "*I think you're now ready for the kirk*" (kirk – church). He was completely serious and genuinely believed that only educated people, "*with letters after their name*", should become church ministers. I became a great disappointment to him.

There were two private boarding schools in the town, *St. Ninian's*, a preparatory school for children up to 12, and *Warriston*, a school up to 15, both long since closed for financial reasons. The pupils wore their own school uniforms and seemed to spend all their time in the school grounds, which were not at all large. We hardly ever saw any of them in town and certainly not in the country, the woods, or along the river, a favourite haunt of the working class children. The main public school, Moffat Academy, was a quite large early 20th century imposing sandstone building situated at the top end of the town with some older buildings behind. The school's history went back to the first half of the 17th century but in 1834 it merged with a parish school which was when it was renamed Moffat

Academy and adopted a motto: *Ready Aye Ready* (*aye* – always). We never knew what it really meant.

When I went to the academy it only had pupils from 5 to 14 years old, or 15 depending on when you were born, at which age, essentially everybody left school and tried to get a job. There was a girls' entrance and a boys' entrance both strictly adhered to. The first year teacher, a Miss Davenport was a totally devoted teacher, dearly loved by us all. She had an astonishing memory, not only for names, but also for what the children were like when she taught them many years before. Apparently I delighted in poetry which I don't remember but I certainly do remember what I thought a great injustice which was when she would not let me on the class rocking horse: she worried I might hurt myself with my right (polio) leg sticking out straight. Polio leg braces could not bend in those days: in fact, not even until I finished university when I got my first bending one.

The curriculum in all the classes was left entirely to the teachers and, by the end of that first year when we were all six, practically all of us were reading, reciting poetry, printing and reciting multiplication tables. We sang the alphabet and the multiplication tables: it was all a game. I also benefited from the very recent change in the rule about left-handed pupils so I was not forced to write with my right hand.

Practically all the teachers were women and spinsters. Miss McDonald, one of the third year teachers was always a classy dresser with immaculate elaborate hairdos. Miss Mitchell, my third year teacher, was extremely severe and a touch sadistic. Notwithstanding I learned a lot from Miss Mitchell who felt her mission was to bludgeon you into learning. The idea of actually enjoying it she would have considered heresy. I started in Miss Mitchell's class when I was 7. Without fondness, I remember most our writing, as opposed to printing, lessons. We had individual desks each with our own small white pottery inkwell in the special hole in our desks and which we had to keep filled. We had to use a basic nib pen, of course, which seemed to drop ink blotches continually and our tentative protests that it was the nib got us nowhere. The art of dipping the pen in to just the right depth came rather quickly since blots warranted a sharp painful rap on the knuckles with a wooden ruler Miss Mitchell carried as she marched up and down the aisles looking at our work. We had pages with a line of the letters in elegant copperplate script that we had to copy on the line beneath. Being left-handed I had occasional problems with smudging letters if I didn't blot them immediately after writing, which I frequently didn't do. I often ended these lessons with red-topped sore and swollen knuckles.

Until Miss Mitchell's class learning was social and fun. Singing the alphabet and chanting the multiplication tables had been such a fun game. Miss Mitchell taught us that, in her view, learning was certainly not a game. Among many things, we learned first hand about discipline, what constituted bad behaviour and, supposedly, just punishment. We were introduced to "lines" the most banal and unproductive of the milder school punishments. Several times I got my 100 lines of "I must not talk in class". Since these could be written in pencil I tied three pencils together with a small piece of wood and string so that I could write three lines at the same time. It was the year in which we were introduced to the "*tawse*", a gruesome piece of stiff leather about a quarter of an inch thick and about 18 inches long divided half way along into two whip tails: it was thick enough that it could only be bent in a large curve and it was conveniently held between two vertical pieces of wood which was part of all the teachers' desks. For a severe infraction, or what was considered bad behaviour, you were called out to the front of the class and made to hold out your hand to be hit by the teacher wielding the *tawse*. It was a fairly common punishment. Just before my time in Miss Mitchell's class its practice had had to be modified so that the teacher had to hit you perpendicularly to your palm since this required less accuracy than along your hand which could damage the veins on your arm and possibly cause them to bleed. So that you couldn't drop your hand, to reduce the pain as the *tawse* came down, the teacher often made you hold out both your hands one on top of the other since it was less easy to lower your hands with the same precision and timing. Still, as regards the *tawse*, Miss Mitchell was not in the class of Mr. Whitby, the English teacher who taught us further up the school. In his class, if you were transgressing like whispering to your neighbour, or passing a note, and, crucially, not looking at him, he would fling a piece of chalk at you. The number of the *tawse* you got was related to the number of pieces it broke into – never less than two. This usually evoked a shout of "chalk" so that one of us could perhaps catch it and reduce the number of broken pieces. He was a dreadful, idle and sadistic teacher: we learned little from him. He eventually left to become the headmaster of a small primary school in the tiny village of Beattock two miles south of Moffat.

The headmaster, the formidable Mr. Shaw, presented an awesome presence and whom we always had to refer to, in Latin, as *Domine* (Master). He very much felt part of the upper social class in town. To be sent to the headmaster was the ultimate punishment and very scary. When he gave the *tawse*, admittedly very rarely, it was generally four or six lashes; it had to be an even number so that you could have the same number on each hand changing your hands after half. I wasn't punished often, the worst, and rightly deserved, being when three of us rang the outside fire bell and the whole school was rushed out on to the playground in front of the school. It was such an enticing bell, a large antique iron one with an elegant wheel from which the rope hung practically down to the ground and easily pulled by the smallest pupil.

We never got any homework until we moved into the higher grades at age 12 to 13 when we started to have specific teachers for specific subjects. Even then it was scant and not in all subjects. The history teacher, Miss Allen, was no more than five feet in height and roughly the same in girth. She was an enthusiastic and totally pro-Scottish, anti-English historian who taught history accordingly. She dictated notes that we took down in notebooks in minute writing since we had to draw lines between the printed lines to increase the writing space to save paper as a contribution to the war effort. She would enthral us with details of the gory battles between the Scots and the English, with occasional positive asides about the French. We only heard about the great Scottish victories like Bannockburn and the folk heroes like Robert the Bruce and William Wallace. She dwelt at length on William Wallace as an illustration of the perfidy of the English because of his betrayal by the English who lured him to London to talk and where he was hung, drawn and quartered. Mary, Queen of Scots, got much sympathy but always coupled with the perfidy of Queen Elizabeth and the English. Bonnie Prince Charlie of the 1745 rebellion was another of her darlings but she wondered that he might have been a bit of a backslider and too sympathetic to Catholicism, considered as shallow, evil and, at the very least, apostasy. It might not have been the most balanced view of history but it was lively and instilled a strong sense of Scottish pride, and nationalism, in her classes. No doubt similar teachers around the country contributed to the rise of *Scottish Nationalism* which had a resurgence when I was a university student. Even then I thought that Scottish Independence was a crazy ridiculous idea.

One day when we were on average 11 years old, without warning, we were presented with a series of printed pages of multiple-choice questions some devoted to arithmetic and some to English. We had no idea why we were asked to answer them since it had never happened before and it was not exam time. We thought of it as a bit of a game and several pupils put silly answers just for fun. It turned out to be the notorious 11+ examination which was designed, we learned later, to separate us into those who should do two, one or no foreign languages from age 12 on. Those with no foreign language were destined to go into a manual trade and had to take classes in woodwork, while the girls did domestic science and learned how to cook. Those who had to do two foreign languages were considered the more intelligent. We only learned this at the end of that school year when pupils' names were read out like "George Mundell, one foreign language" or "James Murray, two foreign languages". The choices of foreign languages were French and Latin, in that order, not that either ever seemed a language since we practically never heard either spoken by the teachers.

We were encouraged by the French teacher to have a pen friend in France and I duly had one, a buxom girl a few years older than me who lived on *Belle Isle* off the west coast of France. She wrote in French and I wrote in English. The first letter I got the teacher wanted to read it out loud to the class. Shortly after she started to do so she suddenly stopped. It was because my penfriend's sister was "*enceinte*" (pregnant) which made our teacher blush and which she didn't read out but asked me if I knew what it meant. I did since I had looked it up.

School gatherings as a whole were rare. There was the yearly *Prize Giving* with a speech by some suitably respectable and distinguished guest. They were generally a litany of homilies to work hard, be honest, to trust in God and so on. One rather different occasion, however, was when the whole school had, for the first time, to have diphtheria vaccinations. Each class gathered in the domestic science building and we were duly inoculated. The same needle and syringe was used until the needle got too blunt causing more pupils to cry: only then was the needle changed.

Religious study began in earnest from age 12: it was a weekly class which was excruciatingly boring. It probably started the invidious indoctrination that, even when one reached the age of rational thought and perhaps no longer believed, left its lingering guilt-ridden Calvinism which so many Scots never get over. Among other things, it tried to instil a feeling of guilt if you ever spent time on frivolous pursuits or are just enjoying something. We had to learn by heart long sections of the King James Bible, usually the Old Testament which had enough passages which showed how the wicked are punished. Job was a favourite for class study –

what a God we thought. Although appreciation came later I must have absorbed something of the elegant and beautiful English of the King James Bible and for that I am still grateful. We all envied the one catholic who didn't have to take the class but sat at the back reading. It was not quite the rigid religion of the extreme Free Church of Scotland but it still followed the Calvinist party line of rigid sermonising, a severe and unforgiving God and a terrifying Hell. The Free Church's wayside pulpit on the road in front of the church was a glass covered notice board conveniently placed close to where we all had to pass to go to school. Just after the war when the golf course was first opened on a Sunday it exhorted us to *"Remember the Sabbath to keep it holy"*.

In the 18th and 19th century Scotland, the Calvinist church was sufficiently powerful to require sinners to sit in the penitents' chairs in church on Sundays. (The Scottish poet, Robert Burns, had to do it regularly, in a church in Dumfries and it was where he wrote *"To a louse"*: one was crawling on the head of a woman in front of him.) Years later, as a student at the University of St. Andrews, one of the Divinity students said that he would describe Calvinism to me in a nutshell:

The minister addressed the two regular drunks sitting on the penitents' chairs: *"Wullie an' Jock, ye'll gan (you'll go) tae (to) hell. And Hell is a terrible place, with burning fires, torture with red hot irons, famine and everything mare (more) awffy (awful) than ye can ever imagine."* Eventually Wullie and Jock died and sure enough they went to Hell which was indeed as awful as they had been told. They looked up to God and said: *"We didnae ken, God, we didnae ken"* (We didn't know, God, we didn't know.) to which God replied, in his infinite mercy: *"Weel ye ken noo."* (Well you know now.)

Travelling evangelists in Scotland were particularly active before the war. In the mid-1930s they put on a whole week of afternoon and early evening sermon meetings for people in the town and, like the equivalent in the USA, they tried to get rousing enthusiastic responses – without any success however. They had erected a large tent in a field a few minutes walk from the town centre towards the River Annan. It was filled every day, particularly with many children who were to be given a religious memento but only if they went to most of the week's meetings and sat in the front, which of course we did with such bribery. The mementos turned out to be cheap small lapel pieces which were a great disappointment to us all: even as very young children we felt we had been taken. The grown up people who went did so I suspect mainly out of curiosity.

The *Temperance Society* was a major part of the Scottish scene at the time. It actually had a large hotel (Temperance Hotel) for many years at the top of the Moffat High Street and for more years a small one near our home: it is now a town museum. In my final year at Moffat Academy, when I was 14 the Temperance Society decided to have a county (Dumfriesshire) wide essay competition. We were all strongly encouraged (that is, required) to submit an entry. The essay was to be: *Robert Burns (1759-1796) the National Bard of Scotland*. I thought it would be original to write about his life, and particularly his life style rather than eulogising about his well-known lyrics and accepted parlour poems. With all the burgeoning interest in sex among us I launched into Burns' unbridled enthusiasm for seduction, sex, delight in bawdy poems and mocking of the inconsistencies and hypocrisy of rural church-dominated Scottish life. I included what I thought were excellent apposite quotes such as from *Holy Willie's Prayer* about a sanctimonious, womanising, hard drinking Elder of the church confessing his weakness for alcohol and sex and whiningly asking for forgiveness:

O Lord! yestreen, Thou kens, wi' Meg-
Thy pardon I sincerely beg,
O! may't ne'er be a livin plague
To my dishonour,
An' I'll ne'er lift a lawless leg
Again upon her.

Besides, I farther maun allow,
Wi' Leezie's lass, three times I trow-
But Lord, that Friday I was fou,
When I cam near her;
Or else, Thou kens, Thy servant true
Wad never steer her.

(*yestreen* – last night, yesterday; *kens* – know; *wi'* – with; *maun* – must; *trow* – think; *fou* – drunk; *wad* – would; *steer* – ride, in a sexual sense)

Robert Burns, of course, was well known for his prolific sexual activities. He had twelve children, seven of which were illegitimate. He eventually married one of the mothers, Jean Armour after she had the first four illegitimate children. Under Scottish Law the children were officially legitimate after she and Robert Burns were married. She survived him nearly 40 years and when he died she kindly took in one of his illegitimate daughters and brought her up.

In the essay I included a few verses from one of his romping songs:

Corn Rigs are Bonie:

The sky was blue, the wind was still,
The moon was shining clearly;
I set her down, wi' right good will,
Amang the rigs o' barley:
I ken't her heart was a' my ain;
I lov'd her most sincerely;
I kiss'd her owre and <u>owre</u> again,
Amang the rigs o' barley.

Corn rigs, an' barley rigs,
An' corn rigs are bonie:
I'll ne'er forget that happy night,
Amang the rigs wi' Annie.

I lock'd her in my fond embrace;
Her heart was beating rarely:
My blessings on that happy place,
Amang the rigs o'barley!
But by the moon and stars so bright,
That shone that hour so clearly!
She aye shall bless that happy night
Amang the rigs o' barley.

Corn rigs, an' barley rigs,
An' corn rigs are bonie:
I'll ne'er forget that happy night,
Amang the rigs wi' Annie.

(*bonie* – lovely; *amang* – among; *rigs* – ridges at the top of a hill; *ken't* – knew; *owre* – over; *ain* - own)

I also wanted to show his relevance to the hard drinking rigid rural life of my childhood, although not at all in my own home, by quoting from Burns' marvellous, long, epic poem, *Tam O'Shanter*. Along with its humour, horror, pathos and incredibly beautiful evocative lines, it describes his dour humourless home life and hard drinking of the main character, Tam (Tom). Tam hallucinates and sees witches in short white nightgowns (called *cuttie sarks* in dialect) cavorting in a ruined churchyard on his ride back home from a drunken evening at the pub. In a very Scottish image of the time, his wife, waiting at home, is captured in the last three lines:

Where sits our sulky sullen dame,
Gathering her brows like gathering storm,
Nursing her wrath to keep it warm.

The quotes I included were not all of sex and drink, I included quotes from some of his beautiful poems, including one from *Tam O'Shanter*:

But pleasures are like poppies spread,
You seize the flower, its bloom is shed;
Or like the snow falls in the river,
A moment white – then melts for ever

I was enormously pleased with my essay and was sure I had been highly successful in showing how marvellous I thought Robert Burns was, not only as a great poet and observer of rural life but as a real flesh and blood man, who still spoke to us as if he were a contemporary. It was totally different to those of any of my classmates. I naively thought it might perhaps be a serious candidate to win the prize. Burns, unquestionably one of the greatest British poets, outside of Scotland and its enormous diaspora, is a little difficult to fully appreciate because so many of his lyrics and poems are in the Scottish *Lallans* dialect with colourfully descriptive dialect words: their imagery and dialect turns of phrase often do not always readily translate. Much of his work, however, has been translated into many languages, such as Russian, Chinese, French and others, including English if there are Lallans words. The only poem I read, out of curiosity, in "English" was, to me, appalling. Burns lived most of his short life, 1759-1796, in the lower part of Scotland, called the Scottish lowlands the main town of which is Dumfries, 20 miles south of Moffat. I got to know the whole area where he spent most of his life.

When I submitted my essay, to me my first attempt at a literary magnum opus, to the English teacher, it was not only not appreciated I was strongly recommended not to submit it since it was not "proper" and would greatly offend the Temperance Society committee judging the essays. "Strongly recommended" meant, of course, that I wasn't allowed to submit it. It was, however, the first piece of writing which totally absorbed me for weeks.

Burns' writings - letters, poems, songs, lyrics and much more - so impressed Lord Byron that in his journal of the 13th December 1813, after reading some unpublished poems and letters, he wrote: "*They are full of* oaths and obscene songs. *What an antithetical mind! – tenderness, roughness – delicacy, coarseness – sentiment, sensuality – soaring and groveling, dirt and deity – all mixed up in that compound of inspired clay!"*

The mathematics and science teacher, Mr. Walter Scott, was an exacting, highly respected teacher who never had to resort to the *tawse* to maintain order. He instilled in me a feeling for the elegance of mathematics and science. He talked about Pythagoras' theorem as being the most difficult and beautiful piece of mathematics we would do for several years to come. He kept referring to it for some weeks before he proved it in class to try and keep up our interest. It was such a disappointment since I thought it incredibly easy and not unusually interesting. It did not seem any more difficult nor more interesting than many of the other theorems we studied, all, of course, from the unadulterated *Euclid's Geometry* book which we used throughout all my school mathematics teaching. Mathematics seemed such a logical subject I found it surprising that many find it so difficult. I always put it down to them having had a bad teacher at school or alternatively being right handed! Left-handed people are disproportionately much better at mathematics than right-handed people.

There were no books in our house and with a family of eight daily living in the one room (the kitchen) there was little peace to read and certainly no quiet. My father only read library cowboy books in the evening as he smoked, almost chain smoking, his Piccadilly cigarettes dropping ash everywhere and filling the house with cigarette smoke. I never read much and only very occasionally went to the very small town library and then only as required. English at school was very much the in-depth study of Shakespeare and the major poets, including of course, the acceptable poems of Robert Burns, who was almost considered as a local. Again, committing to heart long passages from Shakespeare's plays, the bible and poems by major poets was a normal part of one's education. We had to read a few novels by authors such as Dickens, Thackeray and naturally Walter Scott whose large castle-like house that bankrupted him is about 15 miles north of Moffat. With the novels, each week we had to read a chapter of the assigned book and then write a brief summary of it, around 100 words. The morning before the English class there was much copying since practically everybody in the class found the books boring and irrelevant. One of our class found a Dickens book in the town library which had chapter summaries at the beginning: they were a godsend. It was in this class, however, that almost overnight my whole attitude to books and reading changed. We had to read George Eliot's *The Mill on the Floss* which absolutely captivated me and sowed the most prolific seeds of a love for reading and literature. I carried it around with me reading it whenever I was alone and not seen by friends from school. I was in great demand for the chapter summaries but I had to pretend I had only just managed to write from selected paragraphs in the chapter. To have admitted actually enjoying it would have been incomprehensible to my classmates. I certainly could not admit to having read it and had found it totally absorbing like nothing I'd ever read before. From then on I became an insatiable reader and spent hours in the small town library in which my sister Jane was the incredibly helpful librarian. My whole attitude to the world of literature and learning changed forever. Science and mathematics were just subjects that were interesting but certainly not captivating.

Moffat town life

The official church in Scotland is the *Church of Scotland* as opposed to the *Free Church of Scotland*, known as the "Wee Frees" (wee – small). In the early 1950's the Moderator of the Church of Scotland (the Moderator is the official chair of the General Assembly and serves a year) paid a courtesy visit to the Pope in Rome. The Moderator of the Free Church was asked if he would do the same to which he thundered back *"I'll no' be pawn to priest and prelate"*. Great stuff. John Knox, himself a Moderator of the Church of Scotland in 1562, would have been proud of him. His comments among most of the students (when I was a student at the University of St. Andrews) when repeated in a mock very strong Scottish accent always got a laugh. Although not specifically associated with the church, the John Murdoch's Trust epitomises a similar sentiment but one must still respect the thoughts behind it. He died in the early 20th century and directed that the residue of his Estate be used *"in instituting and carrying on a scheme for the relief of Indigent Bachelors and Widowers, of whatever religious denomination or belief they may be, who have shown practical sympathy either as amateurs or professionals in the pursuit of Science in any of its Branches, whose lives have been characterised by sobriety, morality, and industry, and who are not less than fifty-five years of age"*. Women were not even thought of. Still, it is mild compared to John Knox's 1558 tract *"The First Blast of the Trumpet Against the Monstruous Regiment of Women"* which was actually a tirade against women in royal positions, like Mary of Guise, the wife of Henry V of Scotland and mother of Mary, Queen of Scotland. *"Monstruous"* is not misspelled but from the Latin *monstruosus* (unnatural).

Until the end of the war, the *Temperance Society* was in full swing and the churches in the town still held some moral sway with the population as it did with my father. Even with such a small population there were three large protestant churches in the town, each with huge tall steeples: there are now only two. The Free Church of Scotland, practiced its rigid humourless moralistic philosophy epitomised by *"if it's enjoyable it's sinful"* although it was a philosophy generally shared, if less strictly, by the other churches. The Free Church in its beliefs is closer to the fundamental Christian Right in the USA but less rabid and certainly more literate and educated. The ministers of these churches, particularly the large official Church of Scotland parish church, St. Andrews, lived in enormous manses in large grounds. They belonged to the upper echelons of the class structure in town, socialised with them and preached, lectured and generally condescended to the rest.

During the war we had a vegetable and fruit allotment behind some old cottages, owned by the plumbing business my father worked for. It was further up the town so our father would not let us go there directly on Sunday between 10.30 am and 12.30 pm in case we would be seen and chastised for not being in church, and also my father for not sending us. The allotment was quite large and my brothers Peter and John and I worked on it regularly on the weekend. One of the large protestant churches adjoined the property with an enormous manse with its large tower behind it. It was one of the churches which was closed after the war and the large steeple removed. My brother John and his wife, Marion, managed to get the town to save the main part of the church for the amateur theatre they got started and which is still regularly used.

The large red sandstone St. Andrews Church, built in the 1880's at the southern entrance to the town, dominated our house being literally across the road and on a small rise in front of the *Close* and towered over our house. The clock's striking every 15 minutes reverberated in our house. None of our family ever went to church. My father was not a religious man but he felt it would be disrespectful for us to be seen outside on a Sunday during church services. His Calvinism, a way of life if not belief, was deep seated. When asked by the minister at my christening (the only times he went to church was for the children's christenings) what I was to be called he said *"I micht as weel ca' 'm James for the last o' the disciples"* (I might as well call him James for the last of the disciples) - my elder brothers are called Peter and John.

There were numerous pubs in the town into which only men went. One, *The Black Bull*, was very close and part of their storage buildings backed on to our *Close*. It is a long low traditional building and the oldest building in the town, dating from the mid-16th century. The sound of drunks on a Saturday night was simply an accepted feature of our life. No woman, of course, would ever step foot in a pub.

The *Black Bull* had been a popular haunt of Robert Burns, the Scottish national bard. He spent most of his life in the general area around Dumfries. It is the pub in which he scratched an epigram on a windowpane. It was first in a letter he sent to a long time close friend but whom he always addressed as Mrs. Dunlop. In it he sent her an epigram on " *a stupid, money-loving dunderpate* (numbskull) *of a Galloway laird*". He was asked why "*God had made Miss Davies so little and Mrs S- so big*". Burns knew Miss Deborah Davies, whom he described as "*the least creature ever I saw, to be at the same time unexceptionally, & indeed uncommonly, handsome and beautiful; & besides has the felicity to be a particular favorite of mine. – On the contrary Mrs S – is a huge, bony masculine, cowp-carl, horse-grandmother, he-termagent of a six-feet figure, who might have been a bride to Og, King of Bashan; or Goliath of Gath*". The epigram he sent to Mrs. Dunlop is the one scratched, somewhat modified, on the window:

Ask why God made the Gem so small
And why so huge the Granite?
Because, God meant mankind should set
That higher value on it.

The window had gone by the time I was born but the epigram was painted on the outside wall above the window.

With several siblings of my father being inveterate drunks and my maternal grandfather killing himself from falling on returning home one Saturday evening when drunk, its affect on my parents was that they never ever touched alcohol except for the one token sip of sherry at New Year from whoever came as our "*First foot*". They were so superstitious of the first person of the year who entered the house, rigidly at 00.01am, that he was always a dark haired relative or one of my brothers – fair-haired people were always considered to bring bad luck. Women were never accepted as "*First footers*". The last night of the year, "*Hogmanay*" was a festival celebrated universally in the town with groups of people going from house to house laden with bottles of liquor of one sort and another and kissing each other with abandon until dawn broke up the parties. As a teenager I loved it. Surprisingly, really drunk people were nothing like as common as one would have imagined with the bounty of free liquor. It was the closest anything came to a whole town party. Another universal partying was at Halloween when practically all houses were open to visits where there were games like trying to bite apples floating in water. Everybody made their own costumes and had to be able to do something such as sing a song, recite a poem etc. before you got your "treat", which was usually fruit. You knocked on the house doors and asked for your "trick and treat" which in America became fundamentally different in tone with "and" replaced by "or". A smaller one was *Guy Fawkes Night* which commemorated Guy Fawkes' attempt to kill King James I in 1605 by blowing up the parliament at its opening by the king. Guy Fawkes was a catholic and the evening bonfires with effigies of him, on 5th November are to celebrate his failure: it is also known as the Gunpowder Plot.

As children we spent almost all of our free time outside. A regular pastime was playing in the High Street such games as trying to hop from one side of the wide road to the other with your arms folded. Each boy (there were never any girls) tried to make one of the opposite side stop hopping by bumping against them. You dropped out if both feet touched the ground. In the coldest part of the winter, and there always seemed to be a lot of snow each year, we poured buckets of water down one of the slopes on the High Street to make enormously long ice slides. Much of the time, however, was spent along the River Annan where we built dams, for swimming in the summer, or catching fish at other times. We all learned, with varying degrees of skill, how to *guddle* (a Lallans word) or catch fish with a "*girn*". Guddling involved standing in the water downstream of a large stone under which you moved your hands up under it very gently to try and find a fish. If you found it you quickly stuck your finger in its gills and yanked it out of the water. Many of us were very good at it. A "*girn*" consisted of a thin cane a few feet long with a wire noose tied to one end. With it you tried to get the noose round a fish as it was quasi-stationary in the current and pointing upstream. You had to get it on from the back, a tricky manoeuvre since the tail moved continuously to keep the fish relatively stationary. We always ate any fish we caught. Girls never took part in any of these games and pursuits; they led their own separate lives.

Polio unquestionably had a major influence in my development. I was never excluded from the usual boyhood pastimes, playing football, fishing, bird nesting, sledding, swimming and so on. I was only very rarely teased about my polio, although occasionally I was called *Hopalong*, but never unkindly. I was fortunately treated like everybody else. I had to climb trees, build river dams, steel apples from orchards by climbing over fences and walls, get tripped and pushed in games and so on. One year when we were all around 8 years old we decided to try and get bicycles which we all managed to do within a year. They were all old wrecks of bikes which we raced on the streets and in the fields. It never occurred to me that I would not be able to ride a bicycle but I had to work out how to do it with one straight leg. I came up with the idea that as the pedal got pushed with my left leg the momentum was just enough for the pedal to be in the position where normally the right leg would push on it. I couldn't do that but I could lift my straight right leg and let it rest on the pedal until it went down with the bicycle moving until the left foot could push the peddle again. I continued riding bicycles like that until I was close to retiring since at university, and later when at the University of Oxford, everyone rode a bike. It was somewhat similar years later when I wanted to be able to drive a car. I was told there was no way I could get a driving license since I had to be able to push the brake and clutch at the same time. When I first went to America I worked out how to do it with a simple extension to the brake pedal which let me push either or both with my left foot and was thus able to get a license.

I must have felt I had to be better at doing things than my peers and the seeds of determination and perseverance probably date from this period. I became the unsurpassed expert with a catapult which I made from a near perfect Y-branch from a tree with the elastic cut from motor tire inner tubes we scrounged from the local garage. Among the children roughly my age we sometimes had competitions standing about 30ft from a vertical rone pipe (the Scottish word for the gutter taking the rain off the roof) and which you tried to hit. I quickly realised that if you stood slightly to one side and hit the wall close to it, it bounced onto the pipe. This way you increased the area that let you hit the pipe. My arrows always flew better and more accurately since I took special care to choose only very straight branches to which I fitted feathers in a slot at the back. During the war my Uncle, Jim Dickson, who ran the Army cadets kindly let me join the junior cadets. He had been a Captain in the First World War. I won the cup for the yearly 22mm shooting contest. My sled went faster since I sanded the runners to a fine polish. Although it never occurred to me these must have required some reasonable modicum of willpower, self-discipline, perseverance and thought about how to do things as well as possible, all of which seemed natural and obvious to me.

My Uncle Jim Dickson, after whom I was named, was married to my Aunt Mary, the twin sister of my mother. He was an incredibly kind man who in a later age would have gone to university and moved "up" in the world. He had left school at the usual age of 14. He was highly articulate and his writing was always elegant script. He took up the problems of the less intelligent in the town, argued for them in a wide variety of situations and wrote formal letters for them. He was the janitor in the school and during the war substituted for the physical education teacher. When he died, literally the whole town came to his funeral. Only men of course, in those days, walked to the cemetery about half a mile north of town. It was the largest funeral in living memory. The line stretched throughout the town. I've always felt privileged to have been named after him.

Fishing, or rather poaching, was one of the things that I did with my father. We would go off up the Annan Water, the small river which flowed at the bottom of a narrow steep valley and which started up the hill from a waterfall called the *Grey Mare's Tail* at the top of which is a large spectacularly situated lake, *Loch Skene*. (There is a photo of *Loch Skene* in Chapter 6.) It was about 6 miles away and we went in the plumbing van. A short walk further up the valley, close to the source of the small river, is much better known since it is the well known Dobbs Lin now internationally noted for its abundance of fossils. Although we knew of its fossils, surprisingly we never went there- we were more interested in living things.

Loch Skene was full of fish. Although fishers, which were very very few - I never ever saw one - used fishing rods, the implement of choice for us poachers was called an *otter*. This is a piece of wood about 18 inches long, with one end tapered off-centre, to which were attached several lines with hooks each with a worm. As you pulled the string, attached to the front, walking along the shore the off-centre curved front pushed the worm-bated wood further away from the shore. It was highly efficient and, of course, also illegal. Fishing in the small stream below, with numerous deep pools surrounded by steep rock formations was always by rod, hooks and worms which we got from the horse dung mounds at the blacksmith's before we went. The tastiest fish were young salmon, called parr, which are clearly distinguishable from trout by the fingertip like markings on their sides. Again it was illegal to catch them since they were bound for the large River Annan south of the town and for which a license was required to fish. On the few occasions we saw the gamekeeper we immediately hid our catch and my father and the gamekeeper, whom he knew well, would greet each other with "*Whit fettle, Tam*" (How are you, Tom) and "*Gran' Peter, an' yursel?*" (Fine Peter, and yourself?). They would talk about fishing and my father would show him a few trout we'd caught if asked. We knew that the gamekeeper knew we had been poaching for young salmon and that they were safely hidden in the bushes somewhere on the riverbank. I always had the feeling the gamekeeper was in fact sympathetic and never wanted to catch us.

My Uncle Jim, Captain James Dickson in his World War I uniform. Armistice Day, c1945.

JDM at the "cliff" 9th hole of the Moffat Golf Course, c1947.

My father understood my insatiable curiosity about everything so one time he said I could go with him on a plumbing job he had in a farm a few miles up the valley towards where we always went fishing. The farmer, who seemed incredibly old to me, was very much a traditionalist which is probably why my father took me. The farmer still only used a horse, a large Clydesdale, his only horse, to plough his land, pull carts and so on. The straightness of the ploughed furrows was a source of pride. When we arrived he was scything a very small field near the farmhouse and, as my father was doing the plumbing job (replacing a cracked sink which I already knew how to do) I stood watching the farmer scythe. He had an elegance and rhythm I can still conjure up. He must have sensed my curiosity since he asked if I would like to try. When I said I was left-handed he said: "*Y'ur lucky. It's far better to be left handed with a right handed scythe.*" For the next hour he patiently showed me, taught me rather, how to scythe, something which I've never forgotten and later often did on some of our properties. I remember the surprising tranquillity of the regular swishing and the falling hay under the scythe. Raking the field and gathering it all afterwards to make the stooks was simply work. It gave me an image of what farming had been like for centuries.

With Moffat so isolated and surrounded by empty dramatic, generally treeless, hill country almost the only inhabitants were sheep and wild goats. I always loved watching the shepherd and his sheepdog gathering the sheep and herding them into a farm enclosure or, often, into roughly circular walled enclosures which were always built of stones, gathered in the hills, and often built on the slope of a hill. The way they communicated was incredibly impressive. The stone walls are about 3 feet high which the frightened sheep occasionally tried to jump over, if the sheepdog was near, and knock the odd stone off the wall. It was an activity which had been unchanged for centuries: it never ceased to fascinate me.

Since we could not afford to have our shoes and boots repaired by the shoemaker in town my father did it using leather he bought from the shoemaker. The thick leather would first be soaked in water so it was easier to hammer the nails in. It was another of the practical skills I wanted to be able to do. I spent time in the town shoemaker's small workshop close to our house watching and helping when allowed. On one occasion he was ill and could not come in to the shop. He had promised a customer that his boots would be ready that day and, feeling responsible, he asked my father to ask me to come and get the key of the shop and do them for him, which I did being already relatively skilled. It never occurred to me that I would, many years later, have to do such shoemaking again for myself since in the US such shoemakers are rare and, with my leg brace boots, which are almost unobtainable, almost non-existent. I still have to do most repairs myself to make sure they get done properly.

A passion of some of the boys was egg collecting and swapping. We learned a lot about the birds, practically all of which had dialect names such as *whap* for a curlew and *mavis* for a thrush. I learned to identify all the eggs. I knew, for example, how many eggs each bird laid, how they were placed in the nest, how ground-laying birds tried to hide their nests by landing on the ground to give the impression that that was where the nest was and then running to where their nest actually was. Pheasant nests were particularly popular since there were often lots of eggs in each nest most of which I gleefully gathered and took home, to eat, particularly during the war years. Nests were never stripped since we knew the birds would lay more - up to their usual number - if there were still some eggs in the nest. With owls, for example, you only took one egg if there were two in the nest since that was all an owl laid. Owl egg collecting could be hazardous. First you had to climb the tree but that was not the problem. If the owl spotted you near its nest it would swoop down towards you to try and scare you: it always did. Blowing, that is extracting the yolk from the egg, was an obligatory skill involving making a small hole and sucking it out or with one small hole at either end blowing the yolk out. We always tested the eggs in water first to see if the embryo had started to form in which case they floated: these were described as *clokin'* and were useless for eating or collecting since you couldn't suck or blow the embryo out. If the shell was not cracked we put it back in the nest. A favourite place for ground nests was on the huge barren uncultivated areas along the River Annan east of the small railway line to the mainline station 2 miles south. Along with one of my school friends, Hayward Bantam, whose mother had the small tobacco shop in town, we would go nesting there. I acquired quite large collection, about 150, which I carefully kept, surprisingly, until around 2007. I offered it to the University of Oxford's *Natural History Museum*, which unfortunately was not interested, so I gave it to a couple, friends in France, who had a very young son who was clearly very interested as I had been at his age.

I'm quite sure such collecting of common birds' eggs had no lasting effect whatsoever on their population. It was very much the era of natural fertilisers which did not poison the birds. It is the astonishing predation by cats, as shown in a study many years later, which has the major effect.

It was during this time, around the age of 11, out of curiosity Hayward and I started smoking. Since so many grownups we knew seemed to be smoking all the time we thought there must be something great in smoking. Our addiction lasted about 10minutes from the few puffs from two cigarettes, which Hayward had got: it cured us both of ever smoking again. We couldn't understand how anybody could possibly smoke at all.

We were both American Indian enthusiasts and tried to simulate how they lived, not that we knew other than from old movies, but we made

59

bows, built stepping stone dams across the river and so on. It was because of this enthusiasm that I put feathers in the arrows I made which made such an enormous difference to my accuracy.

My enthusiasm for making things from nature was encouraged by a cousin of my grandfather who had spent some time in America at the end of the 19th century and had gone to the Klondike. When around 9 years old my mother took me to visit him and his, clearly better educated, very kind wife, in Glasgow where they lived in a small tenement apartment overlooking garden allotments.. They did not have any children. He gave me a soft, incredibly well made, hunter's moose jacket he had worn in the Klondike Gold Rush saying that I was the only person he knew who would appreciate it even if I would have to be grown up before I could wear it. I have treasured it ever since and still wear it in winter: it is the leather coat I have on in a family photo in the garden of our Oxford home which is in the Epilogue.

My friend, Hayward Bantam, a somewhat scatterbrained, impulsive, impractical, but fun friend, was, many years later, conscripted into the army during the Korean War and was sadly killed.

World War II 1939-45

Even as a child of seven in 1938 I was very much aware of the constant talk of war. My father had been in the First World War and in the trenches for a time, and then in the Flying Core, but not as a pilot. He only talked about it once to describe how he and some fellow Scots had fried a haggis on a shovel. My mother had sent it to him but it took weeks and was mouldy by the time it arrived. In spite of it they fried it on a shovel and ate it with relish. His other, a quote from his time in France, was French for asking a woman to go a walk with him! From the rousing stories of war and battles in our unbalanced view of history at school, in which the Scots always won against overwhelming odds, I was desperately hoping that war would be declared. The battles would, of course, be fought in the Moffat valley and would be able to be viewed by us all from the Gallows Hill, the wooded hill which overlooks the town which had been used for the gallows in early times. Propaganda was everywhere. Germany did not seem very threatening or real. After all I had an album of interesting German postage stamps which I'd been collecting for a few years and they were not very different from other countries. German stamps like many of the stamps of the time glorified one leader or another; Hitler seemed no different. The war felt totally distant in the early days. With the memory of the First World War use of poisonous gas everyone was issued with a gas mask encased in a small square cardboard box. To show us how to use them, and hopefully show that they worked, everybody in the town one day had to go outside and wear their mask when a smoke bomb was released in the middle of the High Street which was only about 100 yards up the road from our house. The smoke, to my great disappointment, did not come down even close to our house because the wind blew it north rather than south.

The war brought unexpected changes to our school life. A welcoming one was a new school arrangement by which we went to school for only half a day; the morning was for the local children with the afternoon for the evacuees from Glasgow. The evacuees, generally from the poorer areas of Glasgow, brought with them their rough distinctive Glasgow accent, head lice and scabies. There was little mixing. The combing of your hair with a minutely close-toothed comb, called a "*came*", was a daily ritual. It involved closely scraping your head and the killing of the lice with a fingernail against the comb. Scabies which spread throughout the whole town was treated with foul smelling yellow liquid which did somewhat reduce the wild itching.

The war, of course, changed much of our daily lives forever. The plumbing business relied on work in the outlying farms and houses so a van or some mode of transport was essential. When the pre-war van collapsed my father managed to get an old car, which now would be greatly sought after and worth an enormous sum. It is in the photo below with two of my sisters sitting on the hood.

During the war Moffat was an army commando training camp for some years. Their training sites, supposedly out of bounds to the town people, were fascinating playgrounds with ropes to climb up, large areas of tied ropes to crawl under, rickety hand made bridges over the river and so on. The commandos were very tolerant of us children. Occasionally they let me get up onto the brengun carriers, which are like small open tanks with armoured tracks which came into service just before the war, and ride up with them through the town. Bren guns were lightweight machine guns. It was strictly forbidden but the officers also had a lenient attitude towards the children.

Moffat was also where many Polish soldiers and their wives came to stay, temporarily, just after the beginning of the war when Poland was overrun by the German army. We children were particularly popular with the Poles since we helped them with learning English and in turn learned our few words of Polish, my first foreign words. We learned, with a good Polish accent, words like "*Dobry dzień*" (Good day), "*Dobranoc*" (Goodnight) and the numbers "*jeden, dwóc, trzy*" and so on, now the only few I remember. The soldiers and the Poles were billeted with families all over the town. For some time a young Polish couple were billeted in our bottom floor "front" room. We saw little of them since they ate all their meals in canteens in the town and did not mix socially.

Although the town was an army site with large numbers of soldiers, it was, except for one incident, left untouched by the blitz which devastated so much of London and other cities. Our one bombing was by a plane which still had three bombs left after a large air raid on Glasgow, the fires of which lit up the sky even in Moffat, about 50 miles to the south. The pilot of the plane thought he had found an army camp because he saw many white tents and tried to drop his bombs on them. It was in fact a duck farm and resulted in only a few dead ducks since he actually missed the tent area. We were all very excited and the next morning rushed out to gaze at the large craters in the ground and look for bits of shrapnel as souvenirs; they were pretty gruesome pieces of metal.

I had heard the plane but did not actually see it. I would have recognized it since I had been interested in the different German planes as well as the British ones and knew what they all looked like. I had also carved wooden replicas which adorned a small part of our attic I had made into a separate small room which I decorated with all sorts of war paraphernalia from empty hand grenades, bayonets from the First World war, commando knives one modern one which a commando gave me, rifle bullets and so on. It never really registered with me that they were actually weapons with which to kill people.

In spite of the presence of the war all around us we didn't know very much of what was really going on although the sudden efflux of large numbers of commandos presaged a raid somewhere in Europe and also the D-Day landing in June 1944. We had a small radio in our house, only recently bought, but we were not allowed to listen to it unless my father was there to switch it on for the news broadcast. We were forbidden to touch it and it was generally ignored when he was not around. Our house became a *de facto* small club for about 15 soldiers. My mother felt very sorry for them being so far away from their homes. She quickly became reconciled to the fact that they were almost all English and, surprisingly, very kind. Initially, but for only a very short time, she still had reservations. Of course, another attraction, the main one probably, was that my sisters were, in the early years of the war, all young, unmarried, reservations. Of course, another attraction, the main one probably, was that my sisters were, in the early years of the war, all young, unmarried, very nice, very lively and attractive. One of the commandos formally asked

Photo of the plumbing workshop "van" with two of my sisters, Jane (left) the eldest, and Annie, right, the second eldest, together with one of the workmen, a cousin, c1941.

my father if he could marry my sister, Annie, the second oldest, to which he replied "No". When asked why, he said: "You're English and you're a catholic." But then nobody in the family, except my sister of course, particularly liked him. They eventually got married anyway and my sister went off to London, survived the London blitz and lived there together, in Barking in east London, for the rest of their lives. Weekend evenings in our home were always lively. Some of the soldiers worked in the catering corps and we often had food which had long ceased to be available in the few shops in town.

Supplementing our food rations and getting petrol for the workshop van was a constant activity. We still got our ration of 1cwt bag of coal a week, brought on the back of old, gentle and kind Mr. Bell who went round the town on an open horse drawn cart on which the full coal bags were neatly stacked. Our "*coalhoos*" (coal house) was a small area under the stairs in the small front entrance of our house. I was fascinated and greatly impressed by the way he loaded a bag of coal (1cwt) onto his back, walk down into our house where he would lean forward almost double and tip the coal out of the bag over his head onto the floor enveloping himself in clouds of coal dust. He looked like one of the made up "black" singers in American musicals of the time.

My father would occasionally do some small extra plumbing jobs for people in the country who would pay in eggs or loads of wood for the fire. I used to go hunting rabbits with a gardener-cum-gamekeeper, an acquaintance of my father, who lived in the stable courtyard of Dumcrieff, a huge slightly down at heel period mansion just over a mile outside the town. It was owned by the Reverend Adam Forman who had married a very rich shoe heiress and had never worked in his life. He was the District Commissioner for the scouts and was justifiably much liked. He also always tipped workmen who worked on the estate and in the mansion which helped to make him even more popular.

Things got a little easier in the plumbing business towards the end of the war when Italian prisoners of war, who were interned in Lockerbie 16 miles south, were allowed out to work as labourers under my father's direction. They were an incredibly friendly group: one, a farmer, could not wait to get back to Italy. Another, an educated man who spoke very good English asked me, "as a great favour", if I could borrow a copy of Bernard Shaw's *Saint Joan* from the library for him since he had never read it. My mother and father treated these prisoners the same way they did the soldiers billeted in Moffat. They were considered poor unfortunate men who had been exploited by the dictator Mussolini for most of the war. They all absolutely detested Mussolini and all the Nazis whom they felt had ruined Italy. One of the German prisoners who came for only a few days was an unrepentant Nazi, an arrogant man. He was strongly disliked and shunned by the other prisoners. My father never had him back.

The Reverend Adam Forman of Dumcrieff, was a man of strong views as to how to live a long time. Until well into his 90's he took a daily dip in the small river which ran through the enormous grounds which surround Dumcrieff. He lived there for more than 50 years. He was always particularly kind to me and, much later, always seemed to like having me visit him when I was back on holiday from school and university. He was genuinely curious about what I'd been doing, what I was going to do, what I liked and so on. The Dumcrieff Estate and its tower were originally given to the aristocratic Murray family in the late 15th century – certainly not ancestors of my family. It is now an exclusive holiday mansion.

Mr. Forman also arranged for me to go to the first Scout Jamboree, one of the first major international events soon after the war, which was held in France in 1947. Since I was the first to become an Eagle Scout in the Moffat scout troop and one of only the very very few in the whole county, there was no problem in my being accepted as one of the Dumfries County representatives. It certainly helped of course that the Reverend Forman was also the County Commissioner of the Scouts. My close friend, George Mundell, whom I had dragged through all the required badges to become an Eagle Scout as well, also went. It was only possible for me since the Reverend Forman very kindly paid the necessary UK£5 which covered all expenses to and from France and at the jamboree. £5 was a huge amount of money at that time, being a typical weekly wage of a tradesman, as in the Moffat plumbing branch. Our last visit by Sheila and our children to see the Reverend Forman was in 1976 when he was 100 years old. Our 11-year old daughter, Sarah, presciently commented that he was exactly half as old as America, which was then celebrating its 200-year anniversary that year. He sadly died some three years later by falling down the main stairs of his huge mansion as a result of tripping over his enormously obese dog which had been overfed for years and which could barely walk.

The jamboree, the *Jamboree Mondiale de la Paix* 1947 (World Peace Jamboree) was the major world jamboree of the 20th century. It was held in the country in the small town of Moisson beautifully situated on a bank looking down on the River Seine, north west of Paris. The French government arranged everything including travel in France in special trains, food, and so on. It lasted for ten days in August. So many youth organisations on the continent were banned during the war with concern about potential radical groups. The more than 24,000 scouts were grouped into different sub-camps each named after a town or area in France; I was in *Lanquedoc*. It was the official one for handicapped scouts: I thought it was ridiculous that I had been put in a handicapped camp. The jamboree was officially opened by several Ministers of the French government with the scouts from each country marching into the camp together. At night it was lit by thousands of torches, probably around 10,000. There was an incredible spirit of brotherhood throughout the whole ten days.

Each of the sub-camps had to make some monument out of tree branches tied together. Some were incredibly impressive such as a huge one of *Notre Dame* cathedral. Everyone mixed together, ate together and played together. We somehow managed to communicate within the large number of languages. We each had a small official cloth patch with the sub-camp name: I still have it. These patches are now apparently in great demand by collectors at ludicrous prices.

JDM in his kilt and Eagle Scout uniform, 1945.

Sub-camp Official Patch for the the Scout Jamboree, France1947.

As I mentioned, I would regularly cycle to Dumcrieff to go with the Reverend Forman's gamekeeper into the woods and rough parts of his fields looking for rabbit warrens. I became an expert at catching rabbits. My job was first to cover and stake the warren holes with a strong flexible mesh. We then went to the one open hole and put down a ferret. It was an elegant, very independent but rather scary little animal, which had been kept on limited rations for the previous day or two. It was never considered a pet. It would sniff the air briefly and rush down the hole. The petrified rabbits would rush out of the other holes to avoid it and be caught in the nets I had set. I became deft at killing the rabbit quickly by grabbing its hind legs and yanking its head to break its neck. It all seemed perfectly normal.

Occasionally one of the rabbits would be too scared and would remain petrified in the den. This was a great nuisance but what, of course, the ferret hoped for. It would pounce on the rabbit and highly efficiently kill it by biting its throat. This gave rise to many oaths from the gamekeeper since we either had to dig it out or, more often, set a fire at an appropriate hole so that the wind would carry the smoke down into the den. This drove the ferret out into one of the nets. We often caught as many as six rabbits from one warren. The gamekeeper sold the rabbits to the two butchers' shops in town and occasionally to the fish shop. I would always get one to take home, where I would skin and clean it and occasionally cure the skin with which to make things, like the Daniel Boone hat in the photo in Chapter 1 and which I wore for about a year but then decided I didn't like wearing a hat. Rabbit meat was considered rather down market and not the delicacy it is so often considered now. We all liked it and ate it regularly since it was so much cheaper than other meat and which my father often got from farmer customers and friends.

A little later, when I was 14 and 15, I worked after school as a delivery boy in one of the two fresh fish shops in town, which was run by my sister Marion. It also sold rabbits brought in by locals. I delivered fish to some of the major customers, such as the local hotels. One of the major hotels, the *Annandale Arms*, used to get rabbits, cook them and then slice the meat thinly. This was then served as chicken, a great rarity on the menus of the time. I could never understand why, since chickens were as plentiful as rabbits and much easier to catch. All the chickens of course were free range, not that that made any difference then. The *Annandale Arms*, was, and still is, one of the major hotels in the town: it is the largest building in the middle of the 19th century etching in Chapter 1. It was the old coaching inn in the 19th century.

Fish was delivered each day, via the railway, in wooden boxes filled with herring or cod or halibut and so on. Mackerel, of which a few were often found still wriggling in the boxes of herring, were, along with cod, considered the most down market of the edible fish with sole and salmon the most upmarket. Mackerel was often simply given away or thrown out. I learned to fillet fish expertly. Generally it was not a strenuous job except for the weekly carting of the empty wooden fish boxes back to the railway station on a large heavy metal and wood railway pushcart. I would pile the boxes on the pushcart up to about 8 feet high and struggle with it down the High Street frequently stopping to re-pile the boxes which fell off the cart. I used to stink of fish. The idea of a daily shower or bath would have been considered ridiculous as was the wearing of underpants for boys or having more than two shirts, which, in my case, were, for me, usually well-worn hand me downs.

One of my best friends, George Mundell, had been in the Boy Scouts for some years. I was 13 when I decided to join the scouts. Again, although I didn't recognise it as such, the urge to excel again came to the fore. The one scout badge we both wanted, since we regularly roved around the local woods and hills, was the *Backwoodsman's* badge which entailed going off into the country for two nights and living off the countryside. We were immersed in the myths, which we thought truths, and the folklore of the American Indian and how we thought they lived. It was very much the 'noble savage' image. The scoutmaster, Mr. Walter Scott who was the excellent mathematics and physics teacher in the school, played his Chief's role superbly. He wrote out our instructions in elegant script on what we had to do:

Chief Whu Dun It gives greetings to his Braves! Hear, O my Warriors the counsels of the Wise!

It has come to pass that our lodges have stretched far beyond the ken of the counsellors. Our people have become many, the grass sparse, and the wild creatures few.

We must set up our lodges in another place. We must try this place next summer for a fortnight and we must train our Tenderfeet in the ways of the wild by sending them to live at weekends Away from the squaws and the braves.

You my braves are the pioneers and you must obey the directions of the wise men and report to me on what you find.

Go from here to the Laverhaye which is on the Wamphray Water nigh unto the place which the Paleface calls Wamphray. Near here is the spot where we hope to set up our lodges. You my warriors will tell me whether it is wisdom so to do. And this shall be your journey:

Go to the spot known as the Meeting of the Waters. You must picture this place for us and there find the breadth of the river Annan that we may know what obstacles lie before us.

Thence you go past the House of the High and Mighty Local Chief and make way towards Wamphray.

On your way you must report to me on the fields and the harvest that we may know the wealth and the crops and meat of these parts.

I want you to gather many leaves and make impress with sheets of carbon that I may know the timber on the way.

Proceed to the bridge ¼ mile before the school at Wamphray where the papoose of the local ones are taught.

I must know the height of this bridge above the water.

Turn left and make your way to the hills past the farm of Laverhaye.

Near there we hope to build our lodges, and near there you may rest your weary bones my braves. Report upon this spot and plan our lodges. Tell me of the water we may drink, of the water in which we may fish or swim. Tell me of the food and shelter and draw me maps with compass bearings showing me our lodges in position and the hills and space around where we may play and train our young.

Eat where you will but watch for ways by which we go so that our men may avoid the Paleface highroads – the places of danger, stink and noise, Tell us of the narrow path, hidden and secret.

Report on all your journey with maps and tales of your adventure.

Return as you will but find out if we may continue the route over the hills to Crofthead and the Selkirk Road. Let us know the distances and difficulties of this journey and the directions we must obey.

Report to me that you have returned on the Sunday evening and by sundown on the third day after you return let me have a full and detailed report from the moment you set out to your return. The times for your journey must be included.

Of course, we knew where all the various places and rivers were so off we went. We built a hut of branches in the woods of the District Scout Commissioner, the Reverend Forman. We gathered berries on our trek and on the way stole apples from house orchards - a widely accepted activity. We did have to eat, however, for the two days. Since I was very good with a catapult, I killed a rabbit which I skinned. We roasted it over a fire, which we actually managed to get going by rubbing a stick on some hard wood surrounded by dry brush; that took ages. The rabbit was quite tasty if a touch uncooked and it did us for both days. We also ate wild raspberries and gooseberries which were quite abundant in the country at the time and drank the water from the small streams. We duly wrote our detailed report in comparable style if less elegant script. Up to that time we both wanted to be woodsmen which I envisaged as spending all one's time walking around woods and enjoying oneself looking for nests, rabbit warrens and so on. The whole episode however, although fun and challenging, cured me for any further taste for the David Thoreau simple life, not that I had ever heard of Thoreau at the time.

In the town there was an Italian family, called Dicerbo, who had lived in Moffat for many years. Mrs. Dicerbo ran the fish and chip shop and never quite managed to speak completely understandable English. Mr. Dicerbo ran the ice cream shop. Every year on the last day of school before the summer holidays he would come to the school gate with his old ice cream cart and give a free ice cream to every pupil. The family was very well liked in the town. When the war began, with the spy hysteria, Mr. Dicerbo and his eldest son were arrested and sent to an internment camp to the outrage of the whole town, but protests as to how ridiculous it was were of no avail. My Uncle Jim Dickson tried to get them released. Unfortunately they had to stay interned for most of the war. Nobody could imagine a more unlikely pair of spies.

Opposite the actual fish and chip shop was an old dilapidated stone house where, on the earthen ground floor, the sacks of potatoes were stored. It was the de facto drop-in masturbation club. The potato sacks provided relatively comfortable seats.

Sex, and any discussion of it, was absolutely taboo: we weren't supposed to know what it was which, as a first approximation, was the general state of our knowledge. The very word, in fact, was not said in company other than very very occasionally with school peers. With age came the usual increasing over abundance of hormones and a fascination with sex and interest in girls. As young teenagers there was sometimes talk about how babies came about. We knew intercourse was necessary, but were rather vague about it. There was considerable disagreement as to how many times it had to be done to produce a baby. Eventually the generally accepted number was 25.

Very very occasionally when we were around 14 three or four boys with the same number of girls would go off a walk, generally up the wooded hill, the Gallow Hill, behind the school. The popular game was "dare" in which each had a turn: *"I dare Wullie tae kiss Moira"* and Wullie would go over and give the most chaste suppressed kiss – a fleeting peck is a better description - to Moira. By the 1960's with the earlier discovery of sex they'd no doubt be off together further into the woods and not heard of until reappearing dishevelled and exhausted. Pity it hadn't started much earlier.

Social Class

Because Moffat was such an attractive small town in a beautiful setting among the hills, and had been a socially elite tourist stop for so long, it was a popular place for retirees with money, often limited, or with social pretensions and often both. They generally came from Edinburgh and Glasgow but with a few English, always considered foreigners, some of whom were talked about by the locals, adding *"even so, they're quite nice."* The town had three upmarket areas in the town outskirts the most prestigious with large typically sombre and cold Scottish stone houses from the 19th century. Such houses were very cheap compared with comparable ones in the cities. The class system in town was long established and unquestioned with the workers living in the centre of the town and in the ugly council housing estate about half a mile outside the centre. There was, of course, no mixing except through employment of the latter who were generally condescended to by the middle class. A not uncommon view of the locals was that the upper classes were not very bright and, among a few, very few, of the tradesmen, could be taken advantage of. One of these large houses, with stables and servants' quarters, was at the southern entrance to the town. All tradesmen, like my father, had to wear slippers when working inside. One of the painters in the town decided to skimp on a job of painting inside the house. The estimate specified two undercoats and one final topcoat. They skipped one of the undercoats. When the work was finished the owner, a very rich shoe heiress, took a sharp knife and scraped a small portion of the paint to count the number of coats. Her behaviour not to trust the tradesmen was - irrationally considering what they had done - considered outrageous by the painters. It all had to be redone.

The 'upper' class areas included, on their periphery, the shop owners in the town but again with little social mixing. The people in these upper class areas seemed to us children to be complete foreigners. My friend George Mundell's parents were on the edge of one of these areas since his father ran one of the grocer's shops in town. They came from a better class but had come down in the world. An uncle had been the Vice Chancellor of Glasgow University while another had been a well-known concert pianist. I was the first real friend George had had. He was a bit of a loner. His parents never ever showed the slightest condescension to me and always exuded kindness. I was always warmly welcomed into their house.

The Mundells had the first piano I had ever touched so I decided I must learn how to play. I started after the end of the war when we could just afford a very bad old second hand piano. I had a few lessons from a very small old spinster lady who had clearly come down in the world. After a few of these boring lessons in which I played and learned a few scales I asked her when I would be able to start playing Chopin, an idol from the movie that I had recently seen and which was the motivation to learn to play. I had never heard any classical music up to then and was quite overwhelmed. *"Many many years"* she said, so I quit the lessons and tried for several months to play Chopin practicing literally several hours each day. I learned by heart many of Chopin's works and played them with much enjoyment albeit with scant skill and sophistication. Although I failed to be the great pianist I envisaged, as a result of these months practicing I became facile enough to regularly improvise boogie later with a student friend when I was an undergraduate at the University of St. Andrews.

III

Dumfries Academy 1946-1949 and University of St. Andrews in Bygone Days 1949-1955

Practically everybody, certainly all the working class children, in the state school, Moffat Academy, left school at age 14, or 15 depending on their birthday when they started school. To get any further schooling you had to go to Dumfries Academy in Dumfries, the county town 20 miles south of Moffat. This involved boarding at one of the school's hostels: there was one for boys, called *Park House*, and one for girls, called *The Moat*. These two hostels, each with about 20 places, were sufficient for all the pupils from the small towns around the whole county of Dumfriesshire which is an indication of how very few went on to the "Academy" for any higher school education. It never occurred to my parents, nor the school in Moffat, that working class pupils should go on for any further education. I had clearly been a worry for my parents for a very long time since with polio I could not become a plumber like my brothers nor go into some other manual trade. Since I had been the top boy in the final exams in the school in 1945-6, I was the *Dux Boy* (Latin: *dux* – leader), so I was probably considered reasonably intelligent compared with my peers. There was always also a *Dux Girl* to ensure sexual equality although it was never ever thought of as such then. Coming top boy was a complete surprise to me. My eldest sister Jane was very bright at school. I later learned that the teachers in the school all thought she would clearly be the *Dux Girl*. Unfortunately her final year coincided with that of the headmaster's daughter who was awarded it instead. The headmaster was rightly called *Domine*. In a later age Jane would probably have gone on to higher education which would also have been the case for my brother John but without government grants it would have been impossible. Their intelligence and commitment was certainly put to impressive use in their concern and activity in the town as was described briefly in Chapter 1.

I later learned that my family's best hope for me was to try and get a job as a junior clerk in one of the local banks, of which there were three in the town at the time. They thought I might in time become a teller, the highest achievement my family could think of, not that they had anything to do with a bank or anything as sophisticated as a bank account.

I heard about the possibility of going on to Dumfries Academy but this required money which my parents certainly did not have. Fortunately in 1945-6 the concept of universal higher education (and socialised medicine) had literally just been introduced so I applied for, and got, a scholarship from the county to go on to Dumfries Academy, which I did in the autumn of 1946. I duly became a member of class 4B: class 4A was for those who were deemed better at English. The scholarship paid for the school hostel accommodation and all meals at the hostel.

Dumfries Academy: Senior final year (6th form) 1949 class. JDM is 3rd from the right in the second row from the back. All those with small white badges are the school Prefects (I was one) whose role was effectively to seat people at concerts.

Although there was another senior school in Dumfries, the "Academy" at that time was considered the elite academic one to which it was respectable for the middle classes to send their children. There was a uniform but it was not obligatory, but jackets and the school tie were encouraged for the boys. The uniforms tended to be worn by the children of the middle class. The girls generally wore a uniform, the standard shapeless black school smock designed to hide every possible female curve and suppress "indecent" thoughts in the boys. There were no overt class distinctions although the hostel boys were considered different, a touch rough and socially near the bottom, but among whom there was a camaraderie. The boys' hostel, an imposing 19th century stone mansion with quite a large garden, was about a mile from the school. It was regimentally, but not unkindly, run by the Warden, who was the senior history teacher, Mr. Russell, familiarly referred as Chubby, and his slightly severe, highly organised wife. They genuinely felt responsible for the boys and did what they could to try and civilise us. Food was plentiful and typical school fare with each day having its own unchangeable menu, with evening meals presaged with the usual grace: *"For what we are about to receive may the Lord make us truly thankful"*. Tuesday, for example, was always referred to as "Stewsday".

I had my first lesson in the inappropriateness of my dialect the first week when the Warden told me that it's not *"ma faither"* but *"my father"*.

He tried to instil in us a feeling of how important it was to speak properly which was an uphill battle since the boys all came from outlying rural communities where a strong dialect was the norm. After dinner we spent several hours doing homework in the prefect-supervised homework classroom in the house. I was surprised that so many of the boys did nothing during these sessions. Needless to say a significant number of them did not pass the

JDM in the Prefects' study, Park House Hostel, Dumfries Academy

final Higher Leaving Certificate examinations, which then were of a very high standard, but which have long since been watered down. In my final year at school I was a prefect and also one of the four prefects in the hostel for whom there was a separate study room which made an enormous difference.

We slept in small dormitories the largest of which had 12 boys with the others 4. The dorms were upstairs and we could only go upstairs when going to bed at exactly 9.30pm. You went to sleep with the background talking and snoring. The wildest, and most fun, dorm mate, on one occasion somehow managed to get himself drunk on hard cider, throwing the small bottles on the floor when he had drained them. Inevitably the Warden appeared, furiously shouting at him and kicking the bottles out of his way. Our dorm mate simply rolled around on his bed giggling. The rest of us were petrified. Needless to say the next morning he was duly punished with the *tawse*, the major but very rare punishment in Dumfries Academy.

Talk of sex was typical of that age group but with no evidence of any homosexual activity whatsoever, not that any of us had probably ever heard the word. One of the boys, a particularly odd one ended up befriending one of the hostel maids, a strange woman in her thirties; they would stand outside in the back grounds holding hands. We all assumed it couldn't be anything other than harmless given the characters involved and the limited facilities. She left not long afterwards whether by choice or she was fired we never knew.

Behind the hostel was a large shed, the hostel recreation room, regularly used and which housed a table tennis table. It was where we could all let off steam. I became quite good at table tennis and on one of the few occasions when the Warden came to see what was going on and, to be friendly, asked to play. I got much kudos for a while since I beat him something like 21-1 which if not politic we all greatly enjoyed. The Warden also believed in self-defence and provided the recreation room with huge boxing gloves with which some of the boys occasionally battered each other with total lack of skill and with never an injury, not even a bloody nose. Even then I thought boxing barbaric and totally incomprehensible.

There were, of course, the usual sports in the school. The only one I was involved in was the rowing club. The school had some four seated racing skiffs as well as several single ones in a building on the River Nith upriver from the school. I ended up as a cox for the fours since I could not quite get my polio leg sufficiently out of the way with the moving seats. There was a harmless right of passage for new members of the club which everybody came to watch. The new member had to get into a single skiff from the wooden deck on the water: he was told he would get the oars when he was ready. Such boats are incredibly unstable without the oars. More than half of the new members ended tipping the boat over while desperately trying to keep from falling into the river. When I was inaugurated I managed not to fall in but it was certainly touch and go.

III. Dumfries Academy 1946-1949 and University of St. Andrews in Bygone Days 1949-1955

Every Sunday we had to attend morning church service in a depressing looking Presbyterian church. We had to be suitably dressed with jacket and tie, which was fairly usual attire anyway. The church, which was literally across the road from the hostel, had a small, stout and sad looking minister whose sermons, at least to us, were boring and interminably long although they only lasted the standard 20 minutes. Since it was always exactly 20 minutes, perhaps he was as impatient as we were to get it over with. But then it would have been difficult to interest such a group of boys whose attendance was compulsory and interests could hardly be further from contemplating his Calvinist God. We also had to attend his bible class every Sunday afternoon where he tried hard to get us interested but to no avail. We were his only customers which must have been rather discouraging.

The education in the school was generally very good and, unlike the Moffat school, corporal punishment was extremely rare. Senior schools in Scotland had pupils of 15 and up. Interestingly during my time in the Academy there were usually around twice as many girls as boys in all the classes. At that time all teachers in senior schools in Scotland had to have an honours university degree in their subject and were, at least when young, generally interested in it. With the very small number of students who went on to university and the very much fewer number of universities in the country than now it meant that the academic level of the teachers was very high if not always matched by their teaching ability. During the first year you were divided in the subject classes as to whether you were going to take a "Higher" or a "Lower" in a subject, the decision being based on your first year exam results. The final year of the *Higher* course was roughly the equivalent of a first year, university course in the subject in respectable universities in the USA.

Many of the teachers had descriptive nicknames. Miss Margaret Williams, who taught "Lower" French, a language that was rarely heard spoken, was known as Dolly. I think she was probably in her forties, unmarried but still hoping. She dressed rather flashily which we were assured was very fashionable for the time with wild red lipstick that was often smudged. The Head of French, Mr. Hendry, was suave, superior and often gave the impression of being rather bored, although he was clearly not so, particularly when he talked about France when he tried to get us genuinely interested in France and its culture. He clearly loved the language and despaired of our accents on the rare occasions when we had to read something. He is on the right in a gown in the school photograph above. Such a class photo would be rare now: there is not a single overweight pupil. In fact I cannot remember any in the whole school. In my final year there were almost three times as many girls as compared with boys but only three of my final year class went on to university.

Our Latin teacher, Mr. Smith, was known as Horsey Smith a nickname which his face suggested. Mr. Smith was a demanding teacher and very good at getting you to learn, although enjoyment of the language was never thought of. He also had an unfortunate predilection for boys. He would walk up and down the lines between the rows of wide desks deciding which boy he would sit down beside. When he got up from his desk there was always a wave of shuffling by all the boys to make sure there was no obvious room on their desk bench to try and discourage his sitting down with them. Undeterred he would stand beside your desk and indicate with a flip of his hand for you to move over. He then sat down beside you and made it clear he wanted to hold your hand, continuing to teach the whole time. It never occurred to any of us to report his behaviour to anyone, and certainly not the remote irreproachable headmaster to whom I never spoke in my three years at the school. Some years after I left the school Mr. Smith's behaviour must have got worse since he eventually spent a few years in prison for paedophilia. His success in getting students through the Higher Latin examination was perhaps due in part from his use of knuckles banging on your head, and quite hard too. He hit your head with each word, for example: "*After hope, promise, swear, threaten and pretend you take the future subjunctive.*" or from Virgil's *Aeneid II* "*Quidquid id est timeo Danaos et dona ferentes*" (Whatever it is, I fear the Greeks even bearing gifts). More than 60 years later at a reunion dinner for my Oxford college, Corpus Christi, in New York the after dinner speaker, the oldest graduate there and a classicist asked the group, many of whom had studied classics, if any could now remember the Virgil quote expecting no one to remember. It came out as if I had learned it the day before. The other classics teacher, another spinster, Miss Margaret Howden, and the one who generally taught Greek, was a throwback to World War I. She was probably in her mid to late fifties. She wore long flowing flamboyant clothes, long necklaces down to her waste festooned with jewellery and some enormous keys. She was as rotund as she was tall. She was completely other worldly and adored Greek literature. Her translations were always poetic which she extolled with a faraway look in her eyes. We all thought she was as mad as a hatter but we greatly appreciated her elegant turn of phrase and imagery: we all felt very fondly towards her.

The head of the science department, Mr. Gall, was a humourless, tall, thin, dyspeptic man who taught physics with a complete lack of interest and with a seemingly firm belief he was wasting his time on philistines. He seemed suspicious of anyone showing an interest in the subject or with the unexciting experiments we had to perform and write up in minute detail. In contrast, the chemistry teacher, Dr. Laird, a man of genuine warmth and kindness, tried to enthuse the class with how fascinating chemistry was. He had given up a career in industry to become a teacher so as to be able to spend his spare time salmon fishing. He designed clever experiments, blowing elaborate glass parts for his experimental setup to demonstrate the theory he was teaching. He was the only teacher in my schooldays who was as close as one came to being a friend of the pupils; everybody liked him. After school sometimes he would patiently teach me how to blow glass to help with his clever and imaginative class experiments and generally talk about the world of science. When I went up to university I chose to read chemistry in part because of him. I quickly abandoned the subject, however, at the end of my first year.

The Senior Leaving Certificate (the *'Highers'*) was a formidable series of examinations which you took after two years in the senior school, generally at age 17. To get the Senior Leaving Certificate at that time you had to pass in at least 4 subjects, not counting arithmetic. So, it was a delicate choice as to whether or not you took a *Higher* or a *Lower* in a subject. Of the four subjects there had to be at least two Highers of which Higher English was obligatory, with each of the several papers having in bold large lettering at the bottom: "N.B. *Write legibly and neatly, leave a space of half an inch between the lines. Marks will be deducted for writing that is difficult to read.*" The maximum number of Highers you could take was five. I worried, lost confidence and decided to do Lower French which I knew I would easily pass and Higher Latin in which I was far from confident. I found the sciences and mathematics relatively easy. English consisted of rigid grammar and a truly in depth study of literature. Large sections of Shakespeare's plays, Chaucer's *Canterbury Tales*, and work of the major 19th century poets had to be committed to memory since answers had to be backed up with accurate apposite quotes. One question, for example, was "Illustrate from any *one* of *The Canterbury Tales* or from *The Prologue* Chaucer's sly humour." Chaucer was a major part of the

English curriculum whose humour and writing I particularly enjoyed. With the rampant hormones of that age the boys pored over the salacious parts of "*The Miller's Tale*": it was, of course, not one we studied in class. We all became fluent in Chaucer's Middle English. I was astonished when first going to Harvard years later to discover that there were translations of his work into modern English: no student I met had ever bothered to study it in the original. So many of the sly asides showed Chaucer's personal view of the church of the time. A lovely example is in the *Nun's Priest's tale* about the pride and arrogance of the magnificent rooster, *Chauntecleer*, who eventually went off, against the practical advice of his favourite and beautiful wife, *Pertelote*, with the clever devious fox, *Reynard* and was eaten. Chaucer adds towards the end: "*and on a friday fil al this meschaunce.*" (and on a Friday fell all this misfortune.) There are little digs at the church and its customs throughout the *Canterbury Tales*.

If you were planning to go on to university, which I had hoped to be able to do after my first year at Dumfries Academy, you spent a third post-certificate year in the school getting advanced qualifications in the subjects you were going to study. It was only possible for me to consider university then since liveable (only just) government grants had only recently become available to anybody who got accepted by a university. In this third year I did physics, chemistry and mathematics, which I had never found very difficult but, with the chemistry and mathematics, the more interesting. We were also supposed to prepare ourselves for the scholarship examinations in the university you chose to try and increase the chance of getting accepted. It was very competitive to get into a university particularly because there were so many demobbed military who naturally were given some preference. Winning a scholarship was a guarantee of acceptance. The teaching for these exams however, was totally inadequate in the Academy. I decided to try to go to the then small University of St. Andrews, which is on the sea, north east of Edinburgh and in a beautiful cliff location.

Since very few people in Britain went to university around 1949, less than 4% with very very few from the working class, particularly in rural areas. Then you had to be interviewed by the Dumfries County Director of Education, the major person associated with schools in each county. He was a man of great arrogance, pomposity and weight. He clearly thought it was inappropriate for me to think of going to university at all and was quite appalled when I said I wanted to go to the University of St. Andrews to which he replied "*If you insist on trying to go to university, you have to apply to your local university (Glasgow University). St. Andrews is not for people like you.*" In other words I was not of the right social class. It had never occurred to me that universities were so classified. I learned later that the University of St. Andrews was indeed a favourite choice for the "right" social class, particularly for students from English Public (in Britain that means "Private") schools, who had not been able to get into the universities of Oxford or Cambridge. I decided that I still wanted to try to go to St. Andrews so I duly took the scholarship examination. I couldn't even understand most of the questions far less answer them. Fortunately I was accepted on the basis of my Higher Leaving Certificate and the university interview.

The head of mathematics in the school, Mr. Ross, was a man who gave the impression he had been destined for greater things, but was nevertheless an excellent teacher. During my last term at school he decided to go round the class giving his *ex cathedra* judgement as to whether or not each pupil in his advanced mathematics class could do a university degree in mathematics. When he got to me he said "*Murray! No, no you'd never make it in mathematics.*" It was because of this that I decided I'd better do something else and so I chose chemistry as my intended major when I went up to university in October 1949.

University of St. Andrews 1949-1955

I stayed in private lodgings, known as a "bunk", rather than in a university dormitory: these were much more expensive and unaffordable with the state grant. I had a variety of lodgings. At the beginning of the year you trooped round those that were advertised. One, in a house on the road running along the top of the cliffs had the most spectacular view of the sea and the ancient 12th century ruined castle, which sits on a promontory overlooking the sea. The house was only a few minutes walk from the university. The only problem was that the landlady, who seemed to have stepped directly out of the 19th century, wanted to have two students who would have to share the same bed. I doubt if she ever got any takers. The regular landladies, or "bunkwives" as they were called, often took a genuine personal interest in each of us. During, and for the weeks of intense study before, my final examinations, my bunkwife for that year insisted I drink a raw egg each day, assuring me it would help to give me strength and keep me healthy. Where you stayed clearly got into the university archives since on returning nearly forty years later to be awarded

81

an honorary doctorate degree I was surprised to be reminded of where I had lived as an undergraduate.

In the first three years I stayed, with three of my friends, in a regular "bunk" terraced house about two minutes walk to the university. The house was run by a kind woman who was genuinely concerned about us all. I was fortunate to get the single room on the top of the house. In those days, after the war, there was still rationing and particularly rigid coal rationing: coal fires were the only means of heating the house, as was the case in all bunkhouses. The students' room for studying was the only one heated other than the kitchen. I preferred to be on my own, in my room, when studying and since there was no heat whatsoever in the room I wore lots of clothes and a pair of gloves. I wound elastic bands around my forefingers so I could turn pages without taking off the gloves. There were five students in the house two of whom had been in the army. There were quite a lot of older students who had been in the war and who were allowed to get a degree in one year less than the normal students. I became friends with one of them. He played the piano and on the old piano in the house he taught me how to play boogie. I became reasonably proficient and inventive: it was much easier than playing Chopin. It was a great relaxation. My friend married a local St. Andrews town girl and became a schoolteacher in a small town north of St. Andrews.

One post-doctoral German student who stayed in the same lodgings for a term was a gentle man who had gone to university in Germany during the war. His description of some of the customs was a revelation to us and increased my understanding of how the war, including World War I, with Germany had so much support in the country by the educated. He told us there were several undergraduate clubs whose members had an enthusiasm for physical combat the most prestigious being short sword duels resulting from trivial things, mostly contrived to initiate a challenge. The duellists stood close to each other and tried to slash each other's face. It was not sophisticated fencing. As soon as any bleeding occurred the duel stopped. It was very prestigious if you had a duelling scar on your face. This student told us that he had been challenged several times each year but had refused all of them: he was dubbed a coward. A visiting professor in classics, whom I got to know, confirmed the barbaric practice. He strongly did not want to return to Germany, but not just for that reason since Germany was still in such a mess.

III. Dumfries Academy 1946-1949 and University of St. Andrews in Bygone Days 1949-1955

There were several university dormitories for the boys and several for the girls around the town, usually in large very nice park-like surroundings. The entertainment of girls, however innocent, in the men's dormitories constituted a serious offence which could result, depending on the circumstances, in expulsion from the university.

Dormitories, at the time, of course, were rigidly segregated. The warden of one of the women's dormitories, a spinster, was a lecturer (a tenured position in the university) in inorganic chemistry. When the yearly dormitory ball took place she insisted that all the mattresses in the girls' rooms be removed and placed in the halls. The university was sufficiently small that we all knew what was going on. Although unwanted pregnancies were unheard of during all my time at university, there were several suicides each year, almost all by war veterans who had returned or came up to university after the war.

JDM in front of St. Salvator's College, 1959, with the scarf of the University of St. Andrews.

I found the intellectual and social world of the university a revelation, stimulating in a way I had never known before and immensely exciting. I felt liberated from the rural obscurity and conservatism in which I had grown up but, until then, had not realised. The old town of St. Andrews, where the ancient part of the university is, is dramatically and beautifully situated close to the cliffs with a romantic ruined mediaeval cathedral and cliff top castle replete with a bottle dungeon. St. Andrews is the oldest university in Scotland, founded in 1411, and is the third oldest in the English speaking world. At the time it was a small, mainly residential, university of around 1,500 students compared to about 9,000 now. Even now students still regularly wear the long traditional red gown although the red is now somewhat more garish. Students in each year had a special, universally used, name: all first year students, for example, were *Bejants* (from the

83

French *bec jaune* meaning yellow beak). It never occurred to us that it was a masculine word and should only apply to men. But then probably every student had taken French at school and was aware of the irrationality of the gender of many French nouns. Other names were used for each university year. Apparently when it was suggested a few years ago that the word *Bejantine* be used for female students it was the death knell of the old words which are now seldom used I gather. First year students are now all *Freshmen* although, no doubt, some have tried to use "*Freshwomen*" for female students which would have a rather different connotation.

The university attracted foreign students and numerous English students, many of whom, as I mentioned, had failed to get in to Oxford or Cambridge Universities. Importantly, for these students, St. Andrews was, and particularly now, considered socially acceptable which no doubt introduced a modicum of social gradation among the students but of which I was unaware. It was my first introduction to girls who had been educated at residential private girls schools in England. My first, short-lived, girlfriend described how in the term before leaving school the final year students were lectured to several times on the evils and untrustworthiness of men. We saw each other from time to time over the next four years. It was clear, and very sad, that she had never got over the twisted views with which she had been indoctrinated at school.

The teaching at university was generally reasonable except for chemistry and much of physics, where many of the faculty had either been medically unfit or too old to be in the army during the war. The physicists, particularly, mainly taught an outmoded curriculum with lectures they had clearly given unchanged for years. In the Scottish system you had to take several subjects in the first year eventually reducing the number to your speciality if you went on to a fourth year to get an honours degree. Classes in the first two years were uniformly large, of the order of a 100 or more, in huge tiered lecture theatres. In the final honours year the numbers went down to around 20. Contact with the faculty was practically zero, except for those who took the laboratory classes but even then it was minimal. Problem classes in the various subjects were supervised by the brighter senior students in the field and for which you were paid handsomely, 7 shillings and sixpence for 50 minutes which is equivalent to around UK£25 or US$35 now. I was able to do one every week for my last two years as an undergraduate: it made a huge difference to my student life.

III. Dumfries Academy 1946-1949 and University of St. Andrews in Bygone Days 1949-1955

Chemistry, my supposed major, was quite old fashioned and unexciting except for one occasion. One of the older lecturers in inorganic chemistry, the woman warden of the student residence mentioned before, was a rigid disciplinarian who never smiled: she was a formidable woman we were all scared of. She had been giving the same lectures, I'm sure, for at least the previous 20 years and always carried out the same class experiments in the huge chemistry lecture room, which was like a replica of a Roman amphitheatre and always filled. In one lecture the whole elaborate glass apparatus on the long table on the dais blew up throwing pieces of glass as far back as the top row of the large tiered lecture hall. Amazingly nobody was hurt, not even a minor cut. It got thundering applause which, in St. Andrews, traditionally involves thumping your feet on the floor. On one occasion someone in the third row from the top laid a marble on the step and it slowly rolled down towards the front bouncing on each step until it reached the bottom. After the first bounce the lecturer stopped talking, did not turn round but continued facing the blackboard. When the marble reached the bottom she said *"Will the student on the left of the third row from the top please see me after class"*: she'd been counting the bounces. We were all very impressed.

There were several dramatic, often bizarre, lecturers and professors. A particularly colourful one was Douglas Young, a popular lecturer in classics who always wore a kilt and was an ardent Scottish Nationalist. He was well over 6ft tall and towered over all the students. He was the head of the Scottish Nationalist Party during the war when the Party opposed conscription since it was only imposed by the British government, not a Scottish one. Because of his refusal to enlist he was imprisoned. During his time in prison he translated Aristophanes into Lallans, the dialect of south Scotland I spoke as a child in Moffat. He eventually emigrated to North America.

At that time, and until many years later, there was only one professor in each department, the other faculty being tenured lecturers or one of the very very few Readers (a higher level of lecturer who had been promoted for their research activity). The chemistry professor, Professor Reid, had also given the same lectures in organic chemistry for years. One of his regular demonstrations, of which he was particularly pleased, to illustrate symmetry in carbon molecules consisted of having a teapot in front of a small mirror and saying *"Now, if we could move behind the mirror like Alice in Wonderland"* at which point he'd lift the mirror and low and behold there was another identical teapot. We all knew about it and the year I took his class we had removed his second teapot. Since he never looked, he was astonished at the laughter and much foot stamping. He was furious and stormed out as he said he expected the teapot back immediately. He must have done some impressive research at one time since he was a Fellow of the Royal Society recognised as one of the most prestigious world academic societies not just in Britain and the Commonwealth.

The final nail in the chemistry coffin came from my laboratory partner when we were trying to determine the chemicals in a given compound. The laboratory, which seemed to be a museum piece from the 19th century, exuded long ingrained smells. Much of chemical analysis at that time relied on the colour which appears after various chemical manipulations. We were practically always wrong since it turned out my laboratory partner, and a friend, was colour blind and didn't know it. I discovered it one afternoon when he said shaking the test tube: "Look at this orange". It was actually red. I told him to stop fooling around because it was getting late and we had to finish the lab, but he insisted. It was only then we discovered he was colour blind. Astonishingly he had absolutely no idea that he was. We both decided, not because of that incident, to change our major in our second year to physics, or "natural philosophy", the old traditional name as it was called.

By the end of the second year I found the physics taught, and quite a few of the lecturers, equally out of touch. We had lectures on how to read and understand pre-war instruments that seemed to us had probably been fashionable in the beginning of the century. Although I continued for another year, which meant I had passed the equivalent requirements for a Bachelor's degree in *Natural Philosophy*, as it was then called, and also got the class medal in it, I decided that it was mathematics I really enjoyed and wanted to study. So, in my third year, I switched my major yet again. It was not without some lingering uncomfortableness remembering the school mathematics teacher's judgment as to my supposed lack of required ability even though I had also got the class medal in mathematics and the equivalent of a (three year) Bachelor's degree in Mathematics by the end of my second year. Because of the schoolteacher's view of me, and the lack of real interest in physics, I decided to do an extra subject, astronomy, about which I remember little except for the uninteresting syllabus and the lecturer, who was the professor. What I do remember about the course was that the lecturer, Professor Findlay Freundlich, recently promoted to the professorship, was a tall gentle man with poor lecturing ability who looked like a caricature of the mad professor with long, wild, totally white hair down the back of his neck. His early speciality was the Theory of Relativity. He told us that he had at one time worked with, and knew well, Albert Einstein when they were both in Switzerland. He kept telling us at regular intervals how Einstein had got the theory of relativity wrong but that Einstein didn't understand his reasoning and would not accept it. He never explained why although we asked several times after lectures. I decided, easily and quickly, that astronomy was also out as a possible major.

University of St. Andrews Tullis Medal in Mathematics, 1951

Because of the final school year of advanced mathematics I was enrolled in the second year course in my first year at university and in my second year (1950-51) was then taking the third year Junior Honours courses in which I won the Tullis medal. It has the university crest, based on the early 15th century one, on one side with my name, date and prize engraved in the middle on the other. These courses were sufficient to qualify you for a degree by the end of your third year, which many students did so that they could formally graduate with a university degree in only three years. When I decided finally to do an honours degree in mathematics I thought that perhaps having won the major prizes in mathematics, where I was a year ahead, and also the medal in physics in my third year, I could probably do it. The mathematics teaching was also very much better. I finally graduated with the top First Class honours in Mathematics and was awarded the Miller Prize, which is for the top graduating student in the whole Faculty of Science. I only learned about the prize, while sitting in the hall at graduation, from my neighbour since she had seen it written in the graduating lists which I had not yet looked at. I was very surprised. All the University of St. Andrews medals are by far the most dramatic looking I've received. The mathematics teacher in Dumfries Academy had unfortunately retired before I could return and have my small revenge - a typical ingrained Scottish Calvinist attitude I'm afraid.

Mathematics was generally taught very well and most of it fairly up to date. Some of the courses though were distinctly 19th century oriented but interesting nevertheless. The Regius Professor of Mathematics in my first year, Professor H.W. Turnbull, was a distinguished mathematician, a Fellow of the Royal Society, and deeply religious. He started his lectures, which were always a complete shambles, with a prayer and got away with it since he was a truly gentle and kind man: he retired at the end of my first year. He was succeeded in the professorship by Professor Edward Copson who could not have been more different. He had been a student in the University of Oxford and seemed never quite to have got over the fact that he had not got an Oxford college Fellowship and faculty position there. He was also never elected to the Royal Society which was much more discouraging. Even as students we saw how unsettled and anxious he was each year when the Royal Society Fellowship elections were announced. In contrast to Turnbull his lectures were paradigms of perfection and clarity. He appeared at five past the hour and started writing on the blackboard immediately, only rarely looking at the class. He finished his lecture at exactly five to the hour and immediately left. Students never asked questions in those days; it was simply not done. Copson firmly believed that if you were good enough to get a First Class Honours in St. Andrews you should then try to go to the University of Oxford and take another undergraduate degree but only if you were of the right social class.

The university regularly had students who came for a year from several North American universities, the women's *Sweet Briar College* in Virginia, for example was one. Exchange students were a great asset in broadening our view, and theirs, of the world. Because of the small number of students I got to know most of these visiting students. For one of these, a divinity student, it was life saving. It was the year when most people in the country were to be tested for tuberculosis with all the students in universities being tested in a large van which travelled around the country. He discovered that he had the disease quite seriously. He spent a year in a sanatorium, fortunately recovered and came back to the university. During my third year a visiting student from *Sweet Briar College* was quite the most beautiful and elegant girl many of us had ever met and we all buzzed around trying to date her but to no avail. She and I became genuine friends, however, and remained in touch after she went back to the US. Later in 1957 when I was at Harvard University and driving round America I saw her again in Virginia where I was warmly welcomed and entertained in southern style by her family.

The other regular and quite old social occasion, custom rather, in St. Andrews is after the Sunday service in the ancient university chapel, which is in St. Salvator's College the main part of the old university, there was the traditional pier walk – not that I ever went to chapel other than for music concerts. The walk, a little over a mile, was from the college chapel along the cliffs past the old castle and cathedral wall down the steep path to the long mediaeval pier at the harbour below. Most students, all gowned of course (as in the photos below), joined in the walk. The pier has two parts, a wide path along which there is a higher wall with a much narrower uneven path on top as in the photos. At the end of the pier the students returned, with the men walking back along the occasionally somewhat dangerous top walk and the women back the way we had all come. Surprisingly during my whole time at St. Andrews there was only one accident when one of the students, still a touch drunk from Saturday revelling, fell off the pier and just broke his leg: he fortunately landed on one of the very few sandy patches between the huge rocks and stones.

University of St. Andrews Sunday Pier walk, 1939. Photo is reproduced courtesy of the University of St Andrews Library IDs: GMC-18-50.1.

With the long, at least knee length, gowns and a strong wind it was sometimes rather scary but *de rigeur* for the male students to take the upper path back even in stormy weather as in the photograph below. Now any student who wants to, walks along the top. The long line of students can be seen, in the photograph above, all the way up and beyond the cathedral. Since the photo below from 1949, my first year at university, I am somewhere in it!

University of St. Andrews Sunday Pier walk, 1949, in a storm. Photo is reproduced courtesy of the University of St Andrews Library IDs:GMC-20-2-1.

University of St. Andrews pier and cathedral. Watercolour by A. Sutherland, 1926. Reproduced courtesy of a friend, William Zachary.

The major, and the largest, social occasion of a student's time, was the election of the Rector of the university by the resident students: it happens once every three years. The Rector could be anybody. He is formally the chairman of the University Council but was never expected to attend, far less preside. During my time the students elected Lord Burghley, who had won an Olympic gold medal for the hurdles in the Munich games of 1928. He was an open and friendly man who, even though only in his 40s, was already having great difficulty walking, in part as a consequence of his excessive sporting activities in his youth, and had to use two crutch walking sticks. The inaugural celebrations lasted several days and were the occasion for parties, a formal ball, midnight parades by red-gowned students marching around town and to the old pier with lighted torches. The university has had a very diverse group of people elected Rector such as Rudyard Kipling, Andrew Carnegie and J.M. Barrie to mention only a few. The comedian star John Cleese was elected in 1970 and was one of the most successful rectors and active in student life and the University Court of which he was officially the chairman. He was genuinely concerned with student rights. He brought new meaning the Rectorship. He was honoured by being elected a Regent of the Colleges of St. Salvator and St. Leonard.

As students moved into their next year in the university they could wear their gowns lower and lower on their shoulders as in the photo of JDM lighting another student's torch.

Rector's Pier Walk. JDM is in the middle, holding a torch in his left hand, beside his long term girlfriend Bridget Monkhouse on his right, 1949.

JDM lighting a student's torch.

All students belonged to the Students' Union clubs, one for women and another larger one for the men. They were housed in two buildings adjacent to the ancient St. Salvator's quadrangle. They were the social centres of the university, particularly the men's one where there were weekly dances, summer balls, a cafeteria (open to all students), table tennis, billiards, snooker and so on. Snooker was frowned upon by the purists as being not as subtle as billiards: I agreed.

The weekly dance, and regular ceilidh (only Scottish country dances) were in the men's Students' Union where we all went to meet girls, eyeing each other from opposite sides of the hall. It was all quite formal. One of the dreariest of the male students, would regularly appear at the door and while looking at the women across the hall would announce: "There's nothing much here tonight". He was one of the ugliest students we knew and was, unkindly, known as the Brontosaurus.

Gaudies in St. Andrews when I was a student were evening (male) get-togethers to sing – and generally drink, though surprisingly with hardly anyone ever getting drunk. They were held in the Students' Union. Often a student who had composed a bawdy song would sing it. This often involved the naming, or referring to, a lecturer who was particularly serious or formal. The funniest I remember was of a senior, rather severe, mathematics lecturer. These songs were traditionally funny. The gaudy was always started with everybody singing (in Latin of course) the first verse of the *Gaudeamus*, namely:

Gaudeamus igitur	(Let us rejoice therefore
Juvenes dum sumus	While we are young
Post jucundam juventutem	After a pleasant youth
Post molestam senectutem	After a troublesome old age
Nos habebit humus	The ground will have us)

Every student knew it by heart. I still do even though I've never sung it since. Gaudies in other universities are often very different. A Gaudy in the University of Oxford, for example, is generally a formal college dinner held once a year, although it depends on which college, or a specific graduation year anniversary dinner.

I became captain of the university teams of both table tennis and billiards but could never quite take them very seriously: they were just enjoyable to play. The teams travelled to other universities for intervarsity matches and locally to play other non-university clubs. On our trips to the Universities of Aberdeen and Edinburgh we always won easily and to Glasgow University where we were always soundly beaten. The captain of the Glasgow team was a Scottish international table tennis player with impressive talent. The Glasgow billiard captain spent most of his time playing the game and was really like a professional: he ended up getting a 3rd class honours in geology. Table tennis was becoming more and more accepted as an international sport and the university finally decided that it was time to recognise it as such. A *"Blue"* at university is awarded to those who represent the university in major interuniversity sports. Since the powers that decided these matters couldn't quite bring themselves to call table tennis a true sport they decided that it should have a *"Half-Blue"*. This, however, meant, that if it was awarded, you could have an elegant

University of St.Andrews
first *Blue* in Table Tennis

dark blue blazer with silver embroidery on the pocket listing the year and sport. So, I was awarded the first *Blue* in Table Tennis in the University. It was rather a fancy blazer with its silver threaded badge. Billiards, of course, was not a sport and had its misspent youth image.

Being somewhat slightly less fast moving around when playing table tennis I unconsciously had developed certain skills which clearly helped. Of course being left-handed also helped to confuse the opponent although actually not much. Along with the usual skills such as spinning the ball vertically and horizontally but with differing emphases I developed a technique for serving. I looked, for example, at one side of the table, which always implies that it is where you will serve, but without looking I served the ball to the other. Years later when I played my first game of tennis with a friend and colleague in the University of Michigan, who said he would teach me how to play tennis I found my old table tennis habits came to the fore with spinning the ball when returning it rather than just hitting it. My friend was mortified when he kept losing the games in the sport he was supposed to be teaching me.

I was elected Treasurer of the Students Union and as such visited other universities as one of the official St. Andrews Students' representatives. The best of these was always to the Glasgow University's Student Union for their annual ball with formal dinner beforehand and parties afterwards throughout the night. At that time the old pre-war trams which rattled along their sometimes half dirt filled rails on the streets were still very much in use and ran late into the night. Returning from the ball several of us were on such a tram, empty except for a drunk man, hardly able to keep upright in his seat, and another drunk, somewhat dishevelled middle aged woman at the front of the tram who was trying, without success, to stand up and sing. The man, with much chivalry, pulled himself up, with difficulty, and looking at us said: "Wul' ye haud the lady up while the lady sings?" (wul' – will, haud – hold) which we duly did and she sang drunkenly after which she slumped back into her seat and promptly fell asleep as did the man.

Golf was always enjoyable and often fun. My close friend Tom Robertson, who was also studying mathematics, was a superb golfer with a handicap of 2. He had grown up in the town of St. Andrews. He started me playing golf. His advice, against all the accepted norms of golf lessons, was to "Never mind this slow easy swing, just hit it as hard as you can." It turned out to be good advice since, although I was left-handed, such clubs were very expensive and never available second hand, so I learned to play right-handedly. Even with all his coaching I never made it with less than a 9 handicap. As students we had the choice of all the three golf courses in St. Andrews for the ludicrously low cost, even then, of £1 for a whole year. Now it is close to £100 for just one round on the famous *Old Course*. We regularly played the *Old Course* but which, with a choice of two others, was not considered particularly special. With all the students with whom I played, golf was never taken very seriously but was treated as something friendly and enjoyable. In all my years (6 of them) at St. Andrews I never experienced a single contentious round. In the spring when most visitors came to play we would often play a foursome with them. We behaved differently depending on what they were like, such as being desperate to get as low a score as possible on such a famous golf course, or simply wanting to enjoy playing on such a beautiful course on the sea. Such matches were always friendly but sometimes with a little teasing gamesmanship on our part. The visiting players were always men and with enormous golf bags with as many clubs as at least two or three of us put together and, of course, they always had a caddy. One gamesmanship ploy, if they were a touch pompous or condescending, was after everybody had played off, to go and pick up one of their tees to which the player would say, "I think that's my tee." The reply was "I was playing a blue tee, I think it's mine." The discussion would occasionally go through another few iterations the climax of which the student would say: "I don't mind, I've a lot of tees, you have it." This always resulted in an embarrassing "No, no I must have been mistaken". It was rather off-putting for the serious players. For such players, we also occasionally purposely did not mark down scores for a few holes and then say: "We'd better put down the scores" and started with one of the visitors. "You had 4 at the fifth, a 5 at the sixth, a 5 at the seventh, and a 4 at the eighth" knowing full well he had a 4 at the sixth hole. He'd reply; "No, no, it was 4 at the sixth". Whoever was doing the scoring would turn to his partner and ask "Do you remember?" to which the reply would be "I thought it was a 5" and so a brief discussion would arise with the scorer saying, "Oh well, it's only a game I'll put down a 4 for you". By about the 9th hole the visitors were generally completely relaxed, having realised we were teasing, and became much more friendly and concentrated on just enjoying the game. Everybody took the gamesmanship in good spirits after it was clear it was not at all serious. We always kept the correct score on their card for them to remember how they played on the famous *Old Course*.

The most enjoyable golfing visitor whom none of us could possibly have beaten was Bob Hope. He came to play the *Old Course* and had a large crowd of admiring students trailing behind him and with whom he joked the whole time while never being put off his very professional game. He had a great finish on the last hole, the 18th, with a final incredible putt of about 30 feet for a birdie of 3 - that is one under par, the accepted number for the hole which for the 18th is a 4. He raised his head in mock arrogance and casually cast his club on the ground for the caddy to pick up and walked off to much laughter and applause. He went round the whole course impressively in just over par.

Another well remembered golf experience was one year when the *Open Golf Tournament* was played on the *Old Course* in St. Andrews when, as usual, crowds, with many students, followed the major players. One player, a rather dour Scot, lost his temper with the crowd, perhaps not unreasonably. He had landed in a sand bunker beside the green of one of the holes and we all gathered round to watch. After he muffed the first shot with lots of flying sand but with the ball remaining in place, the students gave him mild applause and at the second muff even louder applause. He took 3 shots to get it out.

New golf balls were expensive for many students and we would buy them second hand from the men who spent hours every day looking for lost golf balls in the rough. One man, who had trained his dog to find balls, was particularly well patronised since he had better balls without cuts and they were not expensive. We only discovered later that his dog had been so well trained it ran onto the course fairways and simply picked up any ball that came near it. It caused a huge scandal in the town. I played little after university but my friend Tom Robertson ended up emigrating to the US where he got a position teaching mathematics and golf in Occidental College in Los Angeles.

My last game of golf was in Ann Arbor, Michigan some years later. It was both memorable and hilarious. My partner, a friend Tony Blackburn from my first University of Oxford time (as described in Chapter 6) had borrowed his aunt's clubs. By the ninth hole he had broken the heads off four clubs and I was nine up. By then he was down to borrowing some of my clubs and we finished the 18 holes with essentially one bag of clubs. The breaking of clubs was not a repetitive loss of temper. It turned out that his aunt's clubs were early metal-shafted ones which had rusted inside and even the inertia of a golf ball was sufficient to knock the head off. The whole game was like a slapstick movie.

One of the benefits of the small size of the University of St. Andrews at the time and the easy social life was that one had friends from a wide academic spectrum, such as medical students, scientists, philosophers, musicians, classicists and so on. With our friends' enthusiasm for their subject major we would often go to lectures in their field. In one philosophy lecture the course lecturer, Professor Wright, was absent and he had given his notes to a young lecturer who had been told that under no circumstance should he deviate from his notes. The lecture degenerated into comedy after the lecturer, who was reading the notes word for word, purposely I am sure, said: "*Here I thump the table.*" Some of us also took specimen adult intelligence tests developed by one of the graduate students in education whose thesis was on the design of such tests to help give him some practical feedback. In the one I took I achieved an impressive IQ score of 75 which I think is about the level at which you are almost mentally impaired. Our friend decided his test needed some revision!

Student pranks were not very numerous and harmless. One imaginative one, but which became widely known, involved the police and some road workers. In the middle of the old town, close to the old part of the university, there are three parallel streets, the middle of which was cobbled with almost no traffic whatsoever at the east end. There, two young workmen had started to dig a hole to repair a sewage pipe. Some students told them that there was a student dressed as a policeman coming to order them to stop digging and fill in the hole. The students then went to a young policeman further down the street and said there were some students digging a hole in the street. After much shouting and threatening, both sides realised what had happened because of the large group of students standing around cheering them on.

On one occasion we put our science to good use in a very different situation which was associated with the lobster pots of some biology graduate student friends. In the university there is the university marine station, the Getty Marine Laboratory, which was built along the shore south of the old harbour. Some of the students occasionally put out lobster pots, duly flagged, along with many others set by fishermen from the town. We found that our pots for some time were regularly empty and realised that the locals were stealing the lobsters since we didn't usually get out to ours as early or as regularly. It was impossible to catch the thieves in the act so we decided to stop them in another way. One of the chemistry students came up with the clever idea of tying, upside down, an open glass tube, like a long test tube, onto the lobster pot in such a way that air was trapped in it. At the top of this air-filled tube he attached a small piece of sodium. Pure sodium when it comes in total contact with water has a violent reaction and effectively explodes if in a confine space. The idea was that as the fishermen stealing the lobsters reached down to pull up the pot it would tip on its side thereby letting water flow into the tube and the violent sodium-water reaction in such a small space resulted in a small explosion shattering the glass before the pot came out of the water. Although it would have been absolutely prohibited and no doubt merit some disciplinary action had the university, or even the police, known, it proved immensely effective in stopping the theft of the lobsters within a week.

There was, in the university when I was an undergraduate, an exclusive all male club, the *Kate Kennedy Club*, which had a maximum membership of 60. Surprisingly it stayed all male until 2012 when, under pressure from the women students with the strong support of Catherine Middleton, Duchess of Cambridge, when she was an undergraduate in St. Andrews, it finally admitted women. In my day, all applicants were individually interviewed and heckled by the current members and, depending on how you performed, or rather survived, this determined whether or not you were elected. The club's primary purpose was to organise, each year in April, a long charity procession, known as the *Kate Kennedy Procession*, through the old town's three main parallel streets to celebrate the history of the university, the town and Scotland. It usually attracted, even in my time, around 10,000 onlookers who lined the streets. The population of St. Andrews at the time was around 10,000. The procession has a long history dating from the 15th century and was possibly a rite of spring but it was banned in the 19th century by the university and only resurrected in the 1920's. It took hours to pass and the whole centre of the town was closed during it. The lead figure, someone always tall and necessarily very fit, was dressed as St. Andrew, the patron saint of Scotland. He carried, in front of him, a huge cross as large as himself. Carrying it upright in front of him for hours was martyrdom in itself. The procession was incredibly long and when it had passed up and down through the three main streets in the old town it reached St. Mary's College with its beautiful 16th century buildings, which houses the Divinity School with traditional doves which nested in the stone tower. Everybody in the parade had a relaxing break and snack in St. Mary's before starting the procession back to the old part of the university by a somewhat shorter route. The procession included martyrs who had been burned at the stake in front of the university church, figures from the reformation, John Knox of course, various members of the upper class who had participated in the wars with England and so on. Kate Kennedy, a male student dressed up as a girl, represented the supposed niece, (or possibly illegitimate daughter) of Bishop Kennedy who was Bishop of the cathedral in the 15th century. However, less romantically, it is perhaps the old 1460 bell which has Katherine inscribed on it and is in the college tower at the entrance to St. Salvator's College. In the procession, "*She*" was pulled on an elegant horse drawn coach.

As a senior officer of the club I could choose whom I wanted to represent. Each of the two times I was in the procession I chose one of the mounted characters, of which there were only about five in total, at the time. All the characters, of course, wore the clothes of the time. One year I represented someone called James Crichton of Elliock, a renowned 16th century figure who went up to the university when he was 10, graduated when he was 14 and then went to France where eventually he joined the army. He got bored and left after a couple of years. He was fluent in numerous languages and was noted as a formidable undefeated debater in a variety of subjects. He visited several universities including Padua where he was called a charlatan so he challenged the whole university to a debate. He won the debate and as a result became famous throughout Europe and was known as the Admirable Crichton. About a year later, when he was 23, he was murdered by a bunch of drunks. The other character I played was William Murray, the Marquis of Tullibardine, also a student at the university, who became the Chancellor of the university. He fled to France but came back with the Jacobite Prince Charles Stuart, known as the Young Pretender (and in Scotland as Bonnie Prince Charlie) in 1745. He was glorified in our history classes at school in Moffat and his defeat and capture at the Battle of Culloden was attributed in part to the perfidy of the English. Culloden finished Prince Charles' attempt to return to the Scottish crown. He managed to escape back to France and was viewed as a romantic figure for the rest of his life. The Jacobites had a more tolerant attitude to the Roman Catholics than the rigid Scottish Calvinists at the time and even now. Tullibardine was eventually executed in the Tower of London. He had a magnificent costume (as in the photo) as did all the aristocratic characters.

Since most of the students, like myself, who played these mounted characters had never been on a horse before we had to take a series of horse riding lessons at the riding school in the town. The teacher was a young and extremely attractive woman in her early twenties. This, of course, was an added attraction for those who would ride horses. Before the first lesson three of the group tried to get the teacher to go on a date; none of them succeeded. The first lesson lasted just over and hour. The

Kate Kennedy procession with JDM as the Admirable James Crichton of Elliock,1953.

JDM as the Marquis of Tullibardine, 1954.

teacher told us nothing about posting and took us all trotting at just the right pace which had us bouncing up and down continually on the saddle.

We all staggered exhausted and sore at the end of the lesson thus extinguishing all amorous interests, which was clearly the purpose. We found out she already had a steady boyfriend. Subsequent lessons were completely professional and enjoyable as we rode along the shore and cliffs: we learned enough to be able to ride the extremely docile horses we used in the parade. Like those walking I found it relaxing to get off the horse for the break in St. Mary's since, although the horses were docile, I didn't know what might excite them, naturally or unnaturally, with so many students in the crowds.

There were the usual student clubs of which the St. Andrews University Christian Union (SAUCU) was one, not a particularly large one. It was generally not held in the highest esteem since it often exuded, to many of us, an air of sanctimonious self-righteousness. Actually, quite a lot of students practiced some religion or other and the college chapel was generally filled each Sunday as were the two Anglican churches in the town, one low and one high. I had a friend, who was studying divinity, and was a member of SAUCU who convinced me to take part in a SAUCA debate on *Science and the Christian Man*: politically correct titles were very much further down the road. Practically all the members were in fact men. I agreed to be the speaker, the only one in fact, for the science side and I marshalled my arguments with numerous quotes. It was clear that it was me against all the members. I felt that I completely demolished the opposition arguments. At the vote after the debate I got about 3 votes out of around 50 or so, which was actually more than I expected although I naively thought there might be some objectivity since we all supposedly subscribed to objective scholarship.

The only other time I gave a talk to a religious group was many years later when I was on the faculty of the University of Oxford. It was to *Opus Dei* which to most of us is a secretive society and a throwback to the middle ages. I was curious since it had a large beautiful old stone house on the River Isis, the name of the river Thames as it flows through Oxford. My talk, on how animals get their coat patterns, certainly had nothing to do with religion. It was a pre-prandial talk for members and potential members of the society. It could not have been more different to the SAUCU evening. The dinner was excellent as was the wine and conversation. Some of the members, or perhaps they were aspiring members, tried to be open to questions about their society. It was totally different to what I had expected. I learned later that such talks were to try and attract new members and so I declined the second invitation to, in effect, help their recruitment. All of the people were men and, since I think most of them actually lived in the house, some of them may have been *Numeraries* of *Opus Dei*: Numeraries practice corporal mortification which can vary in severity from sleeping on the floor to wearing a small chain shirt with inward pointing spikes called a cilice.

From my second undergraduate year on I had my first serious girlfriend, Bridget Monkhouse, a biology student. (There is a small photo of her above in the Rector's Pier Walk.) She was a lively, very nice and fun English girl who had gone to an exclusive well-known girls' public (that is private) school, *Cheltenham Ladies College*, and spoke with a natural upper class accent. It was a sufficiently serious relationship that, after we graduated in our 4th year, I was "summoned" to meet her parents who lived in an upper middle class neighbourhood in Blackheath in London. Her father was a scientist with a doctorate from before the war. Both her parents clearly felt that I was totally socially unacceptable. I was, however, invited to tea to meet them and spent an agonizing hour making small talk and being not very subtly quizzed. Everything was set out on an elegant coffee table in front of a large, light, expensively covered couch on which I sat at one end with Bridget at the other. About twenty minutes into the visit, interrogation rather, I somehow managed to spill my full cup of tea all over the couch. "Please don't worry, it can be easily cleaned." I was told. After another half hour the awkward visit ended. I made a lasting impression and never saw them again even though Bridget and I continued to go out together for the next three years when we were both graduate students but with slight perceptive cooling in part because of her parents' opposition. They were right about us but for the wrong reasons.

Bridget suggested, after the disastrous visit, that I should take elocution lessons to get rid of my Scottish accent. I was astonished and thought it was a ludicrous idea. I certainly didn't. She also suggested that I should try and use cutlery right handedly rather than left which apparently was also considered as a trait from a lower class. That one surprised me but I started doing it to please her and am now reasonably ambidextrous, at least with cutlery. The summer, after my Ph.D. graduation, I left for America and it was clear our relationship was at an end. Bridget eventually married a chemistry graduate student, of the right social class, from my own year at university and spent the rest of her life in a small university town in North Wales. None of us, who knew them both, could understand how she could have married him, since we all thought he was rather odd and someone who never made much of a mark on the academic scene in the university. Bridget visited Sheila (my wife) and I in Oxford many years later and I was so pleased to see that she seemed to be, and have been, quite happy with her life. She sadly died in her early sixties.

Accents played a critical social role at the time. All radio announcers had to have socially correct accents unlike the converse now. I learned of one splendid example after finishing the research for my PhD a year early and I was allowed to go off and take a lectureship until the requisite three years were up and I could graduate. I spent the year as a lecturer in King's College in Newcastle (a college of Durham University at the time) and lived in one of the university's student residences as a resident lecturer. A temporary university lecturer in classics became one of my close friends there. He came from New Zealand and had been an undergraduate at Cambridge University. The first year in Cambridge he was never invited out socially. He decided, correctly, that it was because of his strong New Zealand accent. During the summer after his first year he took elocution lessons and by the start of the next academic year spoke like an upper class Englishman. From his second year on he was regularly invited out to upper class social occasions, weekend visits to country houses and so on. It was thought that he had only just come to the university.

To supplement my university grants I had various jobs in the summer months. I was the ticket clerk in the small local railway station in Moffat which consisted of only three other people: two porters and a man who kept track of the various freight carriages which brought goods to the town and the small passenger train which ran between Moffat and Beattock, the mainline station two miles away. One of the porters, Wullie Smith who was near retirement spoke an almost pure local *Lallans* dialect and had a laconic wry sense of humour. There was a huge waiting room in the station which was never used except for a one-penny coin operated toilet, at one end. It was a favorite stopping off place for the very few tour buses which parked in the adjoining station parking lot, which was generally completely empty. On one occasion we heard muffled shouts and much banging coming from the waiting room which we ignored for a while thinking it was some children trying to goad us into a chase. Eventually Wullie went to examine and found that two woman had somehow locked themselves in the toilet and couldn't get out. They were frantic since they

III. Dumfries Academy 1946-1949 and University of
St. Andrews in Bygone Days 1949-1955

thought their bus might leave without them. Never one to move quickly Wullie finally got the key and let them out. In gratitude they gave him half a crown, that is two shillings and sixpence, a significant sum at the time, the equivalent now of around £10-15 (roughly $15-30). As he looked at them rushing off he turned to me and laconically commented *"That wis a guy deer shite."* (That was a very expensive shit.)

On another occasion, a young, 15 year old, applicant for a porter's job that had just become vacant came to talk to us. He asked us if there was any heavy lifting. Wullie answered; *"Naw, naw, laddie, thir's nae heavy liftin', we gir it on tae yur back."* (No, no lad, there's no heavy lifting, we get it onto your back.)

Part of my railway job involved going to Beattock station in the afternoon. There I had to write out, by hand, tickets for people going to other than a few major regular city destinations. The stationmaster there, a man who felt the position gave him pontifical authority over all the workmen, lectured me on my writing and said: *"It's clear you'll never make anything of yourself."*

The Scots have a delightful, and often idiosyncratic, humour but the dour pessimistic Calvinist side is also common. Once, standing with my father at the top of the *"Close"* to our house one of his acquaintances stopped to talk, a talk that was punctuated with quite long pauses. After the usual *"Whit fettle, Peter?"* (How are you, Peter?) there was such a pause and he then mused; *"Och aye, Peter, the nichts are creepin' in"* (Och aye - Oh yes; nichts - nights). This was just in the middle of July!

In the summer of my final undergraduate year at the University of St. Andrews I thought of possibly working on aircraft design since I had studied fluid dynamics as one course and was going to do my doctoral thesis in the subject. I managed to get a summer position in the design section of *Fairey Aviation*, a company situated in Hayes in Middlesex just a little west of London. It had been a very successful company particularly during the war. I cannot remember ever having been more regularly bored. I was given the most banal things to do but, importantly, it let me see how at least one aircraft industry operated and why this particular one eventually went out of business and was merged with another company. In the research group there was only one man who was innovative and bright. The people who worked in the theoretical design group were unimaginative, bored, and not in the least interested in what they were doing. I was given irrelevant calculations to perform that any high school student could do equally well and who would have been equally bored. Although it was clearly not representative of research jobs in the industry it did a great service to me since it stopped me forever considering a career in that world. The attraction of the place, however, was that I could easily go up to London and then on to Blackheath, south of the River Thames, to see my girlfriend, Bridget Monkhouse. We would meet but I was never invited to her home again. Late at night I would return to Hayes by train.

To get from south of the river in London to catch the train back to Hayes I had to walk through one of the, then pedestrian, tunnels under the River Thames called the *Blackwall Tunnel*. At that time of night, it was a favorite haunt of prostitutes. Regularly one of them would try and see if I was interested and when it was clear I wasn't they would sometimes walk through the tunnel with me to try the other side of the river, and talked about their life as a prostitute. It was such a totally unknown world to me. Several of them were working class housewives in their late twenties who worked the nightshift to try and make some extra money. They spoke of their clients, whom they scorned, the occasional violence, the wish for children, their dreams (sadly unrealistic) and always the future when they could stop having to be prostitutes. The trade, however, had, with some of them, been a family trade.

My last encounter with this twilight world was some years later when visiting my close friend from my Harvard days, Mark Gretton, who became a classics lecturer in University College London. Before he got married he lived in a brothel in one of the alleys in the area known as *Seven Dials* in the centre of London since a room there was incredibly cheap. The Madam felt he would give the house a modicum of normality and respectability. He rented a large, airy and light room because the brothel Madam could say it was just a boarding house. I met the Madam on only one occasion when she asked: "*Would you like to see one of the girls, Dearie?*" When I said it was Mark I had come to see I was directed upstairs. The prostitutes paid orders of magnitude more for their rooms. None of them lived there: they came in from the suburbs for the day or night shift. The prostitutes would regularly go to Mark's room for a break, a cup of coffee and sympathy. Mark, an extremely gentle and kind man, sadly died some years later from suffocation trying to put out a grass fire that was getting out of control in a field close to his family's home and estate in the Suffolk countryside.

I regularly met people in these summer jobs who took it upon themselves to lecture me on what they felt was my "wasted" life. At the end of my third year at university in 1952 I worked in an isolated petrol filling station about four miles from Moffat on the main Carlisle-Glasgow road. It was a very old fashioned place, with a restaurant. The petrol had to be pumped by hand pushing a long lever back and forward with the needle registering the gallons in quarters. The price of a gallon was around 3 shillings two pennies and three farthings 3/2 ¾ : it was during the short period of time when a farthing, a minute copper coin, a quarter of a penny, was irrationally reintroduced by the government. Decimal coinage was only introduced in 1971. One rather self righteous man had his car filled up which took something like 7¾ gallons for which he wanted to know the cost immediately[1]. I gave him a rough estimate and said I'd look it up in the office. When I came back I was given a lecture on how my mind was going fallow and that I should take a remedial correspondence course in reading and arithmetic. He even went to the trouble of writing out an address and gave me a tip of a shilling to help pay for it. I waved him off thanking him for his advice thinking I should have asked him what he made the price of 7¾ gallons. Another customer, a lively French tourist said that I should supplement my meager income by shooting rabbits in the forest opposite the filling station and sell them to customers.

My last undergraduate year at university was not unlike the previous ones except for the final fourth year examinations which, if you passed, you graduated with a, 1st, 2nd or 3rd class honours. At that time, and even now, which class of honours you got is of paramount importance particularly in the academic world. Its importance stays with you for the rest of your life. My close student friend (and golf teacher) surprisingly got a 2nd and so was not allowed to continue to do a research degree which is why he emigrated to the US. He could have easily done a Ph.D. degree but the departmental professor, Professor Copson, imposed the rule that a 1st class was obligatory.

So, I was accepted as a graduate student and duly started research in the autumn of 1953 under the supervision of one of the lecturers, Dr. Andrew R. Mitchell. Getting a 1st Class Honours meant that I was

---

[1] The arithmetic problem first required multiplying 3 farthings by 7¾ then dividing by four to get the number of pennies and farthings. This number had to be added to 7¾ times 2 pennies which had to be divided by 12 to get shillings. This sum then had to be added to 7¾ times 3 shillings and the result divided by 20 to get the pounds. The final answer is then given in terms of pounds, shillings, pence and farthings.

awarded a graduate Carnegie Scholarship for three years at the then enormous sum of £300 a year, almost twice what I got as an undergraduate: life was suddenly very easy. In present currency it is around two thirds of a typical tradesman's yearly salary. I moved to lodgings in a small longitudinally terraced tenement building, literally across the street from the university, which unlike all previous ones, consisted of two rooms. Amazingly, in 1953 it still had gas lighting, which was why it was so cheap, and an open fire for heat. The landlady was very anti-English. When my English girlfriend, Bridget, came to the door, the landlady, actually a very kind woman, would knock on my door and say: "*It's her again.*" If she had still been alive in 2014 she would certainly have voted for the referendum on Scottish independence. There was quite a strong independence movement during my time at university. I knew some members of the university who felt so strongly about it they would not travel through England to go to the continent but go, by ship in those days, from Scotland via Holland, Belgium and so on.

Many years later at a dinner for me after giving a lecture at the University of Dundee I asked what the guests, all permanent lecturers and one a professor in the university, thought of this new ridiculous Scottish nationalism upsurge. I was answered with stony looks and the English wife of one of them said, almost poking me with her finger, "*You people down there don't understand*". By then I was on the faculty in Oxford, which itself often gave rise to some silent resentment, and I clearly had lost any Scottish credentials I had in spite of my still rather strong accent. With the independence of the Scottish Parliament the Nationalists, mainly centred in the Glasgow and Dundee areas, passed a resolution to hold a referendum on Scottish independence in 2014 which was soundly defeated, mainly with the votes from the south and the north of Scotland. It is being brought up again, however, with the landslide election victory in 2015 by the Scottish Nationalist Party and the Brexit decision in 2016. In the snap election in 2017, however, it lost a large number of its seats but is still pushing it. As one person in southern Scotland said: "*Maybe we should just secede and join England!*" Certainly, if the new referendum for independence is successful Scotland will be governed for the foreseeable future, by the rabid left wing socialist nationalists mainly from the cities in Scotland particularly Glasgow.

It was perhaps appropriate to have old gas lighting in my lodgings. With my curiosity for old tools and customs I thought I'd try shaving with an old antique straight edge razor I had somehow acquired. I had seen them used regularly when, as a child, I had gone to the barbers' shop in Moffat. So, I started to shave with such a razor, stropping it every day. It turned out to be very easy and not at all dangerous. I only tried it for a month since the stropping was rather tedious. As a child growing up we had all heard of these razors which were always known as cut-throat razors possibly because they were used in gang fights in Glasgow before the war. The two major gangs supported the opposing major football teams in Glasgow, the Celtic and the Rangers. The Celtic supporters were mainly Irish, all Catholics, while the Ranger supporters were all Scottish and Protestants. They wrapped the razors with cloth or leather leaving only about half an inch of blade at the end with which they tried to slash people they were fighting. Although not lethal they were certainly very scarring. To us children, and everybody in Moffat, it was totally incomprehensible. Perhaps, like the student duelling in Germany, such scars brought prestige in their gang society.

The number of students in the university who went on to do postgraduate doctoral degrees was incredibly small: I was the only one in the mathematics department. Overall the number of research students was so very much smaller than is the case now, and almost never any from the working class students who only relatively recently, after the war, had been able to go to university at all. My thesis supervisor, Dr. A. Ron Mitchell, an applied mathematician, was, justifiably, the most popular and most liked of the mathematics faculty. He was very much a local Scot who grew up in Dundee and did not want to live anywhere else: he never actually lived in St. Andrews all the years on the faculty there. At one time he had also been a professional soccer player for the team, Brechin City, and known as "Elbows Mitchell". He was an excellent lecturer, funny, even his terrible puns, very open and approachable: he was a first rate research supervisor. He specialised in numerical analysis a subject I did not find very appealing but he also taught fluid dynamics, the hot area in applied mathematics at the time, and it was in that area that I started to do research. The research problem was associated with something called a pitot tube which was a small tube attached to the back of the wings of aeroplanes which measured their speed by quantifying the air flow over the wing. At the time the government's Air Ministry had published a list of the top ten research problems it had: the sixth of which was to explain pitot tube fluid dynamics, which was the one I solved. By the time I started graduate work the intellectual lustre and novelty of my early years at the university had started to feel a little *déja vu* and I felt there must be a more exciting intellectual world out there. Although as a student I had travelled around Western Europe with university friends I very much wanted to go to the USA and so I set about trying to do so as soon as I could. I was fortunate that my research went well. I finished enough research in eighteen months, had the thesis written up by the end of my second year and submitted for a Ph.D. in 1955. However, I could not graduate before the minimum three-year period so, with the encouragement of my supervisor, I petitioned the university to go off and get a job for a year until I could graduate. It was approved and I got a position as a temporary lecturer in mathematics at King's College, Newcastle. I was the replacement for the applied mathematics Professor Albert Green who was in the USA on sabbatical leave at Brown University. The thought of "Green" at "Brown" greatly amused my supervisor. So, I left St. Andrews in the summer of 1955 with great fondness and gratitude to the university.

King's College, Newcastle, at that time a college of the University of Durham, could not have been more different. Among other things it was very much a city university. On the few occasions I visited Durham, the official seat of the university, people in the university there regularly talked about the Durham colleges, comparing them with King's College whereas at King's College hardly anyone ever mentioned Durham. There was a strong feeling that King's was the centre of the university where exciting research was going on. The mathematics department was a friendly place and people were very welcoming, helpful and encouraging. However, it was a singularly uneventful year during which I wrote up some articles for publication based on my thesis, a process I found rather tedious, but then writing up articles after the research is finished often tends to be like that. Anyway, I certainly had no second thoughts about remaining when I was offered a permanent lectureship position at the end of the academic year and instead off I went to Harvard University and America in the summer of 1956.

I used the few trips to Durham as an excuse to visit the magnificent and beautiful mediaeval cathedral built around the end of the 11th and beginning of the 12th century which is dramatically and majestically situated on the cliff top above a bend in the river together with the monastery and castle. It is one of the mediaeval architectural splendours of England and fed my developing enthusiasm for mediaeval history, particularly the High and Late Middle Ages (roughly c1000-1500) and its architecture. Unfortunately many of the sculptures had been vandalised such as the mediaeval figures having had their noses broken off. On one visit I was berated by one of the custodians who, on hearing my Scottish accent, shouted: *"It's all your fault, you barbarians. It's no wonder we built Hadrian's Wall"*. When I tried to defend the Scots suggesting that perhaps it was during Oliver Cromwell's time and his people could have done it but he would have none of it; *"Don't you try and deny it. You Scots are all the same."* Certainly whoever did it were barbarians from later artistic and moral perspectives. In fact it could well have been the Scots since the cathedral was used as a prisoner-of-war camp in 1650 after the disastrous Battle of Dunbar during the Civil War. The Scots were in a superb position in all senses while Oliver Cromwell's army was in a precarious position. The Scots had the clear advantage and Cromwell had anticipated defeat. Among the Scots, however, there was a group of interfering religious fanatics, Covenanters in fact, who insisted that the army could not fight on the Sabbath. Cromwell, who had none of these religious scruples about the Sabbath, used the day to set up defences. The ministers of the church felt that they had God on their side and took command of the army and directed the battle: it was a disaster for the Scots, thereby changing the whole course of British history.

IV

America – a New World and Harvard University 1956-1959

During the year 1955-6 that I taught in King's College (University of Durham) in Newcastle I wrote to Professor Sydney Goldstein, who had recently joined the faculty at Harvard, to see if he had any post-doctoral positions for which I could apply. He was English and a major figure in applied mathematics, specifically fluid mechanics, the field of my Ph.D. thesis. He had been elected to the Royal Society in his mid-30's. He had written the two major books in the field in 1938, the only other book he wrote was in 1960 and with which I was very much involved although not as a co-author. His books were still highly respected although beginning to be considered rather old fashioned and somewhat out of touch. After having built up a major department of Applied Mathematics in Manchester University and not being offered the Professorship in Cambridge University, which he rightly felt he should have had, he went to Israel in 1951 to join the Technion, the Israel Institute of Technology, in Haifa as Vice-President and professor of mathematics. Both he, and his wife Rosa particularly, had Zionist leanings. It did not work out and after a few years he was appointed to a professorship at Harvard in 1955 at age 52. I was the first student or post doctoral who had written to ask to work with him since he had gone there and I was accepted by return mail which greatly surprised me but which I came to understand after I got there in the autumn of 1956.

My deciding to go to America was devastating for my mother. To her it was as remote as the moon. I had to promise that I would not stay there forever and that I would be back after a year or two. She never did reconcile herself to my going there and worried about it constantly.

The actual trip to the USA was a magnificent luxurious holiday. I got passage on the SS *Queen Mary* and found a group of similar students who were on their way to universities around the country. It was a five-day ball. We were all travelling 3rd class of course, but even so the meals were better and more interesting than I had ever tasted. Wine, which I knew little about, at lunch and dinner was simply accepted as part of the scene along with the ritual putting our watches back an hour each day. There was a constant round of entertainment and dancing every night, a table tennis tournament, which I won, various other games and a gymnasium. We all thought this was the life but, surprisingly, by the end of 5 days we were all ready for the end of the voyage. New York was such a different world in which we had to fend for ourselves on the meagre amount of money that was all a few of us had. Several of us stayed in a downtown very seedy hotel and ate the appalling food in the local greasy spoons, drinking lots of water to fill ourselves up. A kind American on the ship, who lived in New York, had temporally adopted the group of us to tell us about America, said: "*When in New York you have to come to Coney Island with me since anything you'll see in America will never be worse.*" So, two days later in New York he took us all to Coney Island: he was right.

Harvard Life

I felt I had really arrived in America when I got to Cambridge, Massachusetts and moved into one of the university student residences, Leverett House, at Harvard University. I had written to several student residences, called Houses, asking about possible accommodation and Leverett House accepted me and where, unexpectedly, I lived completely free. In my second year, when I was appointed a Gordon Mackay Lecturer in the university I was appointed the Tutor in Mathematics in Leverett House and was the Tutor until I returned to England in 1959.

Finally I was now in the land of opportunity, unexpected possibilities, casual sex, corrupt policemen and an openness to new and exciting ideas which I had never experienced before: I was quite euphoric. Even some of the language, or rather phraseology was foreign, such as in the cheap café where I occasionally ate when I first arrived until term started. I asked for bacon and a fried egg to which the owner replied "Sunny side up?" I wasn't sure whether or not he was breaking into song or talking about the weather. I replied: "Yes it is a lovely day". With a slight mild impatience he said: "*Yeah, Buddy, but do you want it easy over or sunny side up?*"

I wandered all over the university and the whole neighbourhood absorbing the atmosphere. America seemed just as foreign as any European country except that English was the language. I browsed in the bookshops, regularly saw a very fat policeman move slowly along Mt. Auburn Street writing out parking tickets and regularly checking his notebook to see if it was a car that should not get ticketed, the owner of which had bribed him. I learned later that it only cost a 12-pack carton of cigarettes or equivalent each month. Later, when driving an American businessman friend's car, a classic Thunderbird, because he didn't like driving, I pulled down the sun shield and out fell a large wad of parking tickets. When I expressed amazement he said: "*I forgot about them. Leave them out - I must get them fixed*" which meant negotiation with the local police.

A personal experience with the police, a Boston one, came about a year later when I had parked the old car - a Studebaker, I had bought - in Boston near the State House to look around the area. Coming to pick it up to go back to Cambridge it was being moved on to the back of a police van because it was illegally parked. I rushed up to the policeman whom I thought was probably of Irish descent, put on the best Irish accent I could, and apologised profusely. He was not a recent immigrant but clearly Irish, which I had hoped, and immediately ordered the van people to get my car off the truck. He asked me when I had come to America.

I felt that coming to America would be the most important thing in my life and how right I was. People in Scotland could not understand why I didn't go to Canada since that was where most Scottish people went: it had never occurred to me. I settled into Leverett House which at that time was the least popular undergraduate House but as a consequence of the random student assignment system in Harvard at the time it meant that there was a wide variety of students from very different groups, layers of society and countries. I was given a very comfortable suite of rooms and tutorials were rare, random and totally undemanding. One's role in fact was basically to be there to eat and mix with the students. Not being much older than the students I made friends, several of whom have been life long.

There were a number of families in the general area of Cambridge and neighbouring boroughs who had signed up with Harvard to invite foreign visitors to help them understand, and experience, what family life was like in the US. During the first year in Cambridge I was kindly invited to Thanksgiving by a family in Newton, a town close to Cambridge. It was my first introduction to what a middle class family was like and gave me an insight into some of the surprising views the less educated, or rather less travelled, had about foreign countries. The family could not have been kinder. It was the first time I heard the use of evasive words to cloak sad or difficult topics. The father, for example, travelled in caskets. Caskets to me were boxes for keeping things in like jewellery, tools and so on. When I asked what kind of caskets he sold he looked around, embarrassingly, and whispered: *"coffins"*. It was also the first time I ever heard children call their father by his first name. Their view of Europe was also surprising. I was asked what it felt like to put on a switch and see electric lights come on. I was asked where I learned English although to be fair, with what was still my strong Scottish accent that was not unreasonable. It was an interesting eye-opening introduction to American family life albeit not a typical one.

The second family invitation came, via a lecturer in mathematics in the University of St. Andrews. This family very much belonged to the upper class and was part of the old *Proper Bostonians* whose ancestors had come to America in the 17th century. They lived in a beautiful old colonial stone house just outside of Concord. They were extremely hospitable and kind. During the afternoon I was driven around various historical sites. One was to the bridge in Concord where the first shot in the American Revolutionary War was supposed to have been fired. The husband delicately kept referring to George Washington and his army as the "rebels". I was kindly invited back to visit them several times.

There was a very active social life in Leverett House, with many invited evening speakers, such as Tom Lehrer entertaining us with his first songs, Malcolm X, Jack and Ted Kennedy, and many others. Women students were allowed to come to the lectures, concerts and as lunch or dinner guests, but only allowed in the student rooms in the Harvard Houses on Saturday and they had to be out by midnight. As a faculty tutor I was exempt from this rule and since many of my friends were students they would occasionally bring their girlfriends to my room for me to take them out if it was after 12 o'clock. The public streets around the Harvard Houses were regularly patrolled by the university police among whom I had a reputation for wild living with so many different girlfriends coming out of the House with me at all hours of the night.

The Kennedys' visit to Leverett House in 1959 was just with a very small group of students and some tutors from the House, about a dozen in all. Jack Kennedy was still a Senator for Massachusetts but was already laying the groundwork to run for the presidency. He was socially easy, assured, asked questions of people and gave the impression of being genuinely interested in you and your answers to his questions. He was the apotheosis of the consummate politician but much nicer. Ted Kennedy could not have been more different, gauche and uninterested in everything and everybody. He struck us all as a bit of a boor and certainly not very bright. Later when we heard he was to run for the Senate it sparked a host of very funny jokes and exaggerated imitations of his behaviour. As a joke, after this social occasion, some of the students in the House suggested trying to raise money for the Edward Kennedy Scholarship in Spanish: this was the exam subject in which he was caught cheating and expelled. His appalling behaviour at Chappaquiddick was unsurprising. His subsequent career in the Senate astonished those who had met him at that time. We surmised, or rather felt, it must have been the case that his advisors had been very well chosen and by somebody other than himself.

One of the most impressive visitors who gave a lecture was, without question, Malcolm X. He gave an evening talk to a packed hall about what it was like to be black in the USA and why he had become a human rights black activist and a Muslim. He was certainly the major figure in the *Nation of Islam* in America. Even then he was concerned about his safety, from various groups, and particularly from some in the *Nation of Islam*. When he arrived, and during the lecture, he was surrounded by several tall, menacing bodyguards who never looked at him but at the audience and the doors. Tragically he was assassinated in 1965. A few, very few, of the students at question time, who felt they were so much smarter than this "uneducated black", tried to put him down. Malcolm X calmly demolished them with logic and articulacy that made the students look like pompous smart aleck fools. I knew two of them and they were. His visit changed how many of us felt about his activism and black discrimination.

Another well-known figure at the time was C.P. Snow whose book *The Masters*, about the election of the head of a Cambridge University college, had been a great success. Snow actually stayed in Leverett House for a few days and regularly mixed with everybody in the dining hall. His second major and controversial book *The Two Cultures* was soon to be published. The students, fellow tutors and myself, found Snow to be one of the most boring and pompous visitors and speakers any of us heard at our time in Harvard. If you were unfortunate enough to be seated at the same table in the hall for lunch or dinner you were subjected to a lecture on how uneducated you were if, for example, you did not know the 2nd Law of Thermodynamics. After the first couple of days of his visit you could see students purposely avoiding his table. After his visit there were student jokes about how they had decided to become writers since if Snow could do it successfully anybody could.

Francis Huxley, the son of Julian Huxley, lived in Leverett House for part of my first year. He gave a fascinating lecture on his recent anthropological research on an isolated tribe of Brazilian Indians, the *Urubus*, with whom he had recently lived for more than a year. His fascinating book, *Affable Savages*, describes his time with them and their complex system of myths, customs and beliefs. Missionaries had at one time made it into their area when cannibalism was still practiced. When Francis had enquired about the first man in the world, he was told he had come out of the ground from under a stone: the resurrection story had left a mark. Francis and I became friends and later, on a trip I made round the States and Mexico in 1957 I stayed with him for a week in Santa Fe where he was studying a tribe of American reservation Indians. During the week we went to some of the Indian reservations closed to the public. He also took me to one of the dramatic hilltop Reservations which had not been excavated but had the traditional ladders to climb to the plateau as in the photo below. Francis is a superb conversationalist with an imaginative and inquisitive mind. He also has an irreverent and delightful sense of humour. When I got back to Harvard he sent me a present of an authentic Indian drum, made by some of the Indians he was involved with. It was packed ostentatiously in a large box emblazoned with its previous contents, boxes of sanitary pads, which raised eyebrows in the Leverett House Lodge.

The *English Speaking Union* on Beacon Hill in Boston held regular evening social gatherings to promote and celebrate all things English, such as language, culture, art and, naturally, the royalty. It was a world from a different era, with occasional throwbacks to the old upper class English society. Many of them were very interesting, while several seemed to still inhabit the stiff social world of the 19th and early 20th century. They always dressed elegantly. People gathered in a large room under a huge painting of the recently crowned Queen Elizabeth II. The English Speaking Union liked to have English speaking foreign students and visitors from Harvard who were, of course, automatically considered socially acceptable. I was regularly invited to these social evenings. One met an interesting, eclectic, and sometimes eccentric, group of people such as members of old Bostonian and New England families, writers, artists, the occasional religious proselytizer and gatecrasher who managed to get in for a free drink. There was no formal invitation check at the door so gatecrashers were not uncommon. The evenings were always interesting and enjoyable. I once brought a close friend from outside the university, Lenny

Sugarman, who was a successful businessman in paper products. He had a very funny sense of humour (he used to write one-act comedy plays when at Yale) and an extremely quick repartee. At this party we were asked by one of the religious proselytizer gatecrashers: *"Do you know Jesus?"* to which Lenny replied: *"What's his second name?"*

University Faculty and students all ate together in the student Houses. There were mainly small tables with four places but which could be easily put together for larger groups. The large table beside the entrance to the dining hall was almost solely used by the athletes, particularly the football players. Their table was referred to as the "trough". At meals, if you were waiting for someone to join you, you propped a chair up against the table. It was also a way of preventing someone you didn't want to sit with you. While there, James Watson, of twisted helix Nobel Prize fame, was also a faculty member in the House and the least popular one. He was self-centred, often condescending and certainly all the students I knew, considered him a tedious bore. Often a student would rush in and whisper to friends: "Watson's coming." and you would see a travelling wave of chairs being lifted up against the tables around the hall. Jim Watson had already done the work for which Francis Crick and he got the Nobel Prize. He and I coincidently had dated the same girl, myself after Jim Watson. She went out with him just once and said that she didn't want to go out with him again, to which he replied *"You'll be sorry when I win the Nobel Prize."* This was in 1957. When she repeated this conversation to me I thought it was hilarious and ludicrous. It was clear that he realised how incredibly important their work was. Francis Crick, whom I first met at one of his parties, when he was visiting Harvard, was quite the opposite. He was easy, amusing, unpompous and who clearly enjoyed the social company of the young girls at the parties.

In 1956 Adlai Stevenson's grandson John Fell Stevenson was an undergraduate in Leverett House and a bunch of us, agreed to help him canvass for Adlai Stevenson's election run for the Presidency against Dwight Eisenhower even though we knew it was a lost cause. It was not that we were very political, or even Democrats, rather it was just to help John Stevenson. The election was a replay of the 1952 election when Eisenhower won by a huge margin. When the results were clear about a dozen of us decided to go to the Eisenhower celebration party since it was clearly going to be much more fun. One of the local radio station reporters came and started to interview people at the party. By pure chance the first 5 people who were interviewed came from our group who all said what a disaster and so on the election had been. Of course we overdid it to embarrass the interviewer, who kept saying "*Ah yes, as you say....*" mopping his embarrassed brow and quickly moving on. Not surprisingly the broadcast recording cut us all out.

Leverett House was an interesting social mix with friendships crossing social barriers. Some of the close friends I made there, and whom I saw from then on, in particular Bill de Spoelberch, a Belgian/American with an American mother and a Belgian aristocratic father who accidentally got killed before the war: he had been a test pilot. Bill is second from the left in the photo below (and in a photo in Chapter 11 in Taiwan with his wife, Choupette, my wife, Sheila and our two children). Karim Khan, always referred to then as K - is the present Aga Khan, and was part of the lively group. In his rooms once he performed on his bongo drums for me; he was very impressive. He was totally unlike his father who married the film star Rita Hayworth. K never drank alcohol. Bill eventually ran the *Aga Khan Foundation* and is still very much involved as a Director. In the photo below at the graduation in 1958 David Lange, on the left, the brother of the actress Hope Lange, became a film director and scriptwriter. David Sheppard, whom I never ever saw as serious, is the last on the right, on my left, in the photo. K did not graduate this year since he had been made the Aga Khan instead of his father and had to take the year off: he graduated in 1959. David and Lenore, who was a student at Wellesley College, got married that year. David often made outrageous and very funny comments when we were all together. One more serious one was to Sheila and I after he and Lenore's first son was born with a deformed leg: it was a consequence of thalidomide Lenore had taken when pregnant. David said he fleetingly wondered if he should suffocate him to save him from a terrible life with such a deformed and weak leg. He added that he immediately gave up the ludicrous thought remembering me with an even worse deformed leg. Unfortunately he and Lenore got divorced. David, who was English, moved back to England and where we met often. He emigrated to New Zealand and became a very successful financial economist. He sadly had a major car accident, which effectively made him a cripple for the remaining time in his life.

After two years I felt that I had to make a trip back to Britain which I did in the summer of 1958. Much of that summer was spent on a trip by car to Jugoslavia, the spelling still in use rather than Yuogoslavia, with my friend, Bill de Spoelberch. Before leaving we spent two weeks staying in one of Bill's extended family's chateaux in Belgium. Almost every day there was a social gathering of young people in one or another of the chateaux or large houses in the country. It was where the young aristocracy got together whether for tennis, swimming, dinner, or simply to meet each other. I was always warmly welcomed in the group.

From the left: David Lange, Bill de Spoelberch, JDM, David Sheppard in Leverett House at the Harvard graduation, 1958.

David and Lenore Sheppard at their wedding in 1958.

After the time in Belgium Bill and I took off for our trip to Jugoslavia. It was sufficiently close to the war and the communist cold war that there

118

was a lot of military around. Out of curiosity we went to one huge open-air coliseum type theatre to watch a film which turned out to be a war movie. Tito arrived just before it started. I was very nervous and didn't want to talk in case the soldiers around us thought we were possibly German. The roads in Yugoslavia along the coast in those days were in a dreadful state but it was spectacularly beautiful. Detours could be incredibly long; one was around 70 miles. The photo below (to which Bill added "Bill de Spoelberch and unidentified man on the right) was on one such detour. The photo below is of the old mediaeval bridge and buildings in Mostar, then not a very large town. All the time we were on the bridge there was not another tourist. It, and many of the ancient buildings, were destroyed in the war of the early 1990s. It is now crowded with tourists and Mostar has grown to more than 100,000.

Mediaeval bridge at *Mostar* in Jugoslavia, 1958 (now in Bosnia Herzegovia).

The students in Leverett House were a diverse group. The president of the students Common Room one year, was a very popular, dynamic, lively and bright African American student, who was seriously deficient in one important ability, namely he could not swim and had never wanted to try. When at dinner one night he told me this I could not understand why it was so important until he told me that to graduate all students had to be able to swim the length of the university swimming pool. He eventually did but only when a group of friends swam closely beside him for support and even under him as he struggled to make it. Those under the water

Bill de Spoelberch (left) and JDM on the Jugoslavia coast, 1958.

would exchange places as he moved down the pool. He finally made it and, of course, graduated. Another student, an extremely funny and lively one, kept dropping out of the university but had been reinstated several times: his father was extremely rich, in the arms business, and an inducement for Harvard to keep taking him back. He would describe with amusing detail the social gatherings at his home when, as he said, he would often be pressed into playing the piano, *"The Mother Sonata"* as he called it. I'm not sure if he ever graduated.

Meals in the House, which you collected cafeteria style on a tray, were often the scene of heated discussions about an astonishing spectrum of subjects. On one occasion I naively made the case that Mormonism was based on the most ludicrous premise and that Joseph Smith was just a charismatic imaginative showman who had tried various professions before. As the debate developed another Leverett House tutor, Ivan Vallier, a sociologist, who was doing a Ph.D., started in on me and completely demolished all my half-blown ideas. We became close friends and saw each other regularly and long after when we were both married and had children. He said "If you're going to talk about Mormonism you must at least read the *Book of Mormon* so that you've got some backing for your prejudices", which, in fact, he shared. Although long lapsed he had been brought up in the *Reorganised Church of the Latter Day Saints*, the Mormon branch that broke away from the mainstream and, among other things, did not practice polygamy. So, I read the *Book of Mormon*, a bizarre book which confirmed my prejudices. Many years later, when visiting the University of Utah in Salt Lake City, Sheila and I read the excellent book by Professor Fawn Brodie, "*No Man Knows My History*" on the life of Joseph Smith. It was actually in the city public library but it was kept under the counter: you had to ask for it. I still find it incomprehensible how Mormonism has been and still is so hugely successful. But then the origins of most religions are just as ludicrous to me: they're only older.

Social life, meeting girls and especially having sex was almost a full time activity for many of the students. One Leverett House student, during my third year at Harvard, came seeking advice on how to approach the parents of a girl he had been dating and was getting serious about. He had recently slept with her and she had gone home with the condom sticking to her skirt which her furious parents pointed out. I couldn't think of any useful advice. His affair did not last.

There were frequent parties around the university. There was also an almost ritualized code of behaviour, about dating such as not asking a girl out on Friday for Saturday night since it would generally get a refusal because it implied she didn't have a date for that Saturday. During my first year my first regular girlfriend, Virginia Hoyt, was a tall and beautiful redhead, an artist, who was at the Art School in Boston. She introduced me into the struggling life, and it was certainly struggling, of young artists, one of whom was George Dergalis who is relatively well known among the painting fraternity in the US. As they studied and painted seriously, they scraped a living by drawing such things as wallets for advertising companies, with their brief to make them look elegant and thin whereas they were poorly made, thick and ugly. A true representation would have been totally unacceptable and make it unsalable. In the summer, many

121

went off to the coastal tourist towns north of Boston, such as Marblehead, to sell their touristy paintings, small pottery dishes and artists' materials at inflated prices. They had nothing but scorn, albeit tinged with some envy, for the most successful of these roadside art stallholders. He specialized in selling paintbrushes with the hairs cut in special ways. There was, for example, an ivy leaf brush, a surf brush and many others. He would demonstrate, with a single deft stroke, how such a brush produced spray on top of a wave, the foliage of a pine tree and so on. Summer earnings were the only way they could continue to practice their serious art during the rest of the year. They lived in the poorer parts of Boston, a world away from Harvard. The six-month liaison with Virginia did not survive my long summer absence in 1957 but we remained good friends.

Trans–USA and Mexico Trip and the Summer School in Boulder, Colorado 1957

In the summer of 1957 with a close friend, Egil Törnqvist, a Swede from the University of Uppsala, who was visiting Harvard for a post-doctoral year, we decided to drive across America and then on to Mexico returning to Cambridge via the southern and eastern states. Egil became the Professor of Scandinavian Language and Literature at the University of Amsterdam specializing in Swedish playwrights and authors. He tried to teach me Swedish without success: all I really learned was the tonality and to say "Yes" like a native. The photo below is of Egil and his wife Rita Verschur at their wedding we went to in Amsterdam. It was a very lively occasion at which we were plied with too much excellent wine and superb food but which made the rather rough late night boat crossing back to England much easier. They stayed with us for a few days in Oxford with their three lively children around 1980 but they sadly got divorced not long afterwards. Their middle child, Marit, and our daughter Sarah, became warm enthusiastic friends and Marit stayed on for a while after the family went back to Amsterdam. Marit is an internationally renowned writer, illustrator of children's books and artist as is her mother, Rita.

Driving across America in those days with so much less traffic, showed us how immense and diverse the country is. The plains though seemed endless with similar rural scenery for hours and hours. We stayed in whatever we could find and thus met many of the locals. What a world apart it was from the intellectually sophisticated world of Harvard and Boston. On one occasion we slept in the barn of a farmer who, the following morning, invited us to breakfast. He bemoaned his isolation where television, radio news and newspapers were all totally local. His ignorance of the world outside of approximately 50 miles was astonishing: he was acutely aware of his ignorance and isolation.

During this trip I spent a month at a summer school in Applied Mathematics in Boulder, Colorado as Professor Sydney Goldstein's assistant. Egil went on farther west and south: we would meet up again in Mexico City after the summer school. One of the summer school participants, a truly remarkably single minded girl had decided that she was going to find a husband during the month. She made the most obvious play for one of the post-doctoral students attending the school. Her affairs were a running soap opera. When he did not work out she moved on to another. By the third failure we all watched with fascination to see who would be her next attempt: I was number six. She was even tougher and more single minded than I had ever imagined. She was a dreadful woman. When I was clearly not going to work out either she quickly moved on. We heard later in the year that she had got married and it was to one of the summer school participants, a man who had never participated in the various trips into the mountains or came to any of the parties that we had. We wondered if it would work out but seriously doubted it. She was, appropriately, a graduate of Hunter College, actually a respected public college associated with the City University of New York: the college name, however, very much described her.

The summer school had a variety of senior visitors during the month. One, Richard Feynman, the Nobel Prizewinner from the California Institute of Technology (Caltec), was one of the liveliest, not only for his lectures but also for his enthusiastic playing of the bongo drums at social gatherings of the participants. Some years later, when visiting Caltec for a few months, I occasionally had lunch with him and other colleagues. His curiosity was insatiable and his insight after only a brief description of what I had been working on for months was incredibly impressive. He was never ever condescending. I went to one seminar in a very pure area of mathematics (I had mistaken the date or would never have gone) and Feynman was also there, sitting in the front row. After about 5 minutes, Feynman asked a question that showed his ignorance of what the rather arrogant lecturer was talking about. The lecturer, who clearly did not recognise Feynman, condescendingly and dismissively answered him. This happened about every ten minutes with it beginning to dawn on the lecturer that this person was not some, not very bright, member of the audience. By half way through the lecture it was clear that Feynman had clearly grasped the whole concept of the talk and moved beyond the lecturer who realised it, with embarrassment, but to the enjoyment of the audience.

After the summer school in Boulder finished I drove down towards Mexico to meet up again with my friend, Egil Törnqvist. My car, an old Studebaker, was long past its prime and appropriately nicknamed Smokey. In one very small isolated town, through which the railway ran down the middle, the car broke down late afternoon on a Friday so I had to stay in the only, rather seedy, hotel. On registering I was asked if I'd be wanting a girl that night: I declined. The very small town and hotel were depressing and situated in a vast flat, bare, countryside. I thought it would be a very dreary weekend until the garage opened on Monday. I thought that if there was any intellectual life in the town it would be in the church so I decided, insincerely, to go to the church on the Saturday morning. The minister turned out to be about my own age and truly welcoming. He invited me to move to the manse and in the end it proved an enjoyable weekend. Being a non-believer was clearly not at all important. The minister felt very isolated but he genuinely and sincerely wanted to help people, a daunting task in that place.

Francis Huxley and JDM in traditional cowboy leather trousers, Santa Fe, 1957.

Egil Tõrnqvist and Rita Verschur at their wedding in Amsterdam 1960.

I finally got to the Mexican border at El Paso after a week with Francis Huxley in Santa Fe. He worked in in a reservation we visited: it was closed to the public. I then flew to Mexico City and Egil and I started our several weeks of travel in Mexico. Mexico City was safe and unpolluted in those days. It was just the wild drivers jumping red lights you had to look out for. The Mexican people exuded a warmth and welcome that, on a recent visit in 2012 to a meeting of the Mexican National Academy in the National University in Mexico City showed, has clearly not changed even if crime and pollution have. We did the usual sites in Mexico City including going to our first (and certainly last) barbaric bullfight in a totally packed huge stadium.

Most of the ancient sites we visited were isolated ruins and totally empty of tourists so unlike now. From Mexico City we had to take a train to go to *Tiotihuahcán*, which was a mile walk from the small station. The main inhabitants of the area were sheep. A Mexican, who lived in Mexico City had a country house there, caught up with us and kindly invited us to lunch. His house had the most magnificent view of the volcano *Popocatépetl*. He had a very impressive collection of ancient Mayan sculpture and artefacts. He paid the local people a pittance for anything they found and brought to him. The house from his large window overlooked a small collection of incredibly poor houses with dirt floors and several with crudely thatched roofs which were only about 20 yards from his property as in the photos below. Looking over them to the volcano he remarked how very poor he had found Italy. It was clear that he no longer saw the poverty and hovels with dirt floors literally in his back yard.

JDM on an ancient New Mexico Indian reservation, 1957.

Rug market in Taxco, Mexico, 1957.

We went by bus to various towns farther south, particularly the dramatic hillside town of Taxco, then a relatively small town with very steep very narrow cobbled streets with no cars, only donkeys, dogs and people. Our stop coincided with a rug market with the rugs pretty much all the same but there were also several people selling very tasteful blanket type rugs they had woven. I bought two that we still have and appreciate except for a sense of genuine guilt at the ridiculously low price asked and which I paid $2 and $5.

Mexican peasant house, *Tiotihuahcán* 1957.

Mexican peasant house, Mitlá 1957:

It was in Taxco that Egil and I experienced our first earthquake. We had found a room in a cheap boarding house with the window level with the outside street. During the night I was shaken out of my bed onto the floor. I thought it had been a truck driving wildly down the narrow steep road outside so I climbed back into bed. It was only the following morning we saw lots of damaged buildings and were told it had been quite a serious earthquake.

On the way south to Oaxaca, then a rather sleepy town, the bus was filled with people, sheep, chickens, dogs and a goat. We were the only non-Mexicans. There was, on the way, the most enormous tree I've ever seen: the diameter was about the length of the bus. It was quite famous in the area. The locals on the bus insisted the driver stop so that we could all get out to see the tree and for us to take photos. We were also kindly plied with food. The whole bus exuded the genuine warmth we had, by then, come to expect in Mexico.

The ancient sites around Oaxaca, such as *Monte Albán* and *Mitlá* were totally empty as in the photos below. We had a feeling of what it must have looked like when they were abandoned. The largest group of anything we saw when we were there were sheep both during the day and evening.

Monte Albán, near Oaxaca, Mexico 1957.

Monte Albán, near Oaxaca, Mexico 1957.

Monte Albán, near Oaxaca, Mexico, 1957.

Unfortunately I had to leave Mexico before Egil to get back to Harvard for a meeting so I flew back to El Peso, picked up my car, and drove up the east of the US briefly visiting some of the historic sites. I did visit a friend from St. Andrews University days who had spent a year from her university, *Sweet Briar College* in Virginia, but came from the south. Her family was very hospitable and I was entertained in southern style in her father's exclusive Country Club. She told me on the way to her home that under no circumstance should I mention segregation or even mention black people. Segregation was still pervasive: it was very difficult for me to understand – separate toilets (usually outside), separate eating areas in road cafes, separate entrances and so on.

America never ceased to surprise and delight me. In England there was still the rather restricted social behaviour, the constrictions of outmoded codes of behaviour, the discouragement of doing something too far from the norm. Such overt pursuing by a woman, as in Boulder, would have been considered unseemly to say the least. I got my first and only marriage proposal from an attractive woman I had met on a flight to San Francisco to give a lecture at Stanford and with whom I had dinner and had spent a couple of days being shown round San Francisco. It came in a letter she wrote which was beautifully and elegantly written but which did not make it uncomfortable to decline. The trip back from San Francisco was a dramatic one with one of the plane's engines catching fire and cut out. Irrationally it did not worry me and I reassured the young woman passenger sitting beside me there was nothing to worry about. The plane had only 2 engines. The pilot came on to say they were going to land at the nearest airport and that it was not a serious problem!

Back in Harvard, there were numerous dances and parties at one of which the most important event in my life occurred although I did not recognise it as such at the time. Two of my Leverett House student friends knew a girl from their hometown Marblehead, north of Boston, who was a student at Brandeis University in Waltham but, with some student friends, shared an apartment in Cambridge because it was much more lively and interesting than living in Brandeis about 20 minutes away. I went along with them to a party at their apartment. It was a very crowded, noisy, friendly affair with cheap Gallo wine. At it I met Sheila (Campbell), a first generation American who seemed and looked unbelievably young (and still does for her age): we briefly chatted together with some others and Sheila, who was not used to wine drank a bit too much and went off and fell asleep on her bed in her room.

Some months later I got a phone call from her, in which she said: "*This is Sheila.*" I had no idea who she was but after a little small talk, during which I was trying hard to remember, I did. She had decided she wanted to do a year abroad and had arranged to go to the London School of Economics (LSE) for her third year. I was the only British person she knew and she was looking for some information. So, we chatted about London and that was that. A few weeks later while walking in Harvard Square with a close English classicist friend, Mark Gretton - one of the gentlest people I've known - who also lived in Leverett House that year, I saw Sheila coming towards us carrying some books. Since there was no way not to stop and say hello I said to Mark, *"I'm afraid I'll have to stop and talk to this girl. I feel a bit guilty about her. Let's ask her to have some coffee with us."*. It was the start of our lifelong relationship; Sheila and I got married in London the following October 1959 and, as I say in the dedication of my main books written years later *"... and lived happily ever after"* now close to 60 years. I still have an occasional nightmarish thought that we might never have met again: it was such an incredibly unlikely chance meeting. From then on Sheila often had dinner with me in Leverett House and she studied in my room. I was sometimes teased by Leverett House colleagues, and student friends, about how incredibly young Sheila looked. One evening the first time Sheila and I both had dinner with Karim Khan, in Leverett House, the next day K accused me of baby-snatching, a view several of my other friends also had, although they all, not surprisingly, thought Sheila was marvelous, incredibly nice, warm, bright, lively and fun.

Sheila, Essex, Connecticut, 1956. Sheila on a short camping trip we took to Dartmouth, New Hampshire, 1958.

131

Harvard Academia

When I started working with Professor Sydney Goldstein he suggested two rather classical fluid mechanics research problems which seemed to me simply modifications of what had been studied mathematically before. I thought the problems were already rather out of date. He then suggested a quite different problem which arose in chemical engineering, namely ion exchange processes, his son, a chemical engineer, had worked on. This was a technique in which ions could be exchanged as the constituents flowed down a glass tube: it had significant and diverse industrial applications. It seemed interesting and an excellent opportunity to broaden my research experience outside of fluid mechanics. It was the start of my deciding to work on non-traditional problems which I have done for practically my entire career ever since. It became clear, although no one ever actually said it, that Goldstein was no longer the applied mathematics giant he had been, but rather a scientist living on his past reputation. It was rather sad. When I got there he had no graduate students or any post-doctoral students. He had, I believe, only one, during his whole time, about 14 years, at Harvard until he retired. My wanting to work with him somehow gave him respectability, not because of any distinction on my part, only that I had written wanting to work with him. Harvard, I feel, made a mistake in appointing him and he made a mistake in going there since his very active research life was in the past.

I certainly thrived on the intellectual freedom of American academia. I could do research on anything that interested me. Applying for research grant money was also very much less complex and without some of the ludicrous rules and regulations now imposed by Congress (and equally so in the UK and Europe) often for incomprehensible reasons. It is one of the most time consuming, often irrational, and irritating aspects of current academia. Many years later, in the 1990s, when I did research on marital interaction and divorce prediction my psychology collaborator wanted us to extend the work to study homosexual couples. It turned out that any grant application which had the word gay or lesbian in it had to be automatically rejected by the government research grant giving agency.

As a Gordon Mackay lecturer my lecturing requirement was certainly not arduous, essentially one course per semester, and most of the students were very bright and enthusiastic. Applied Mathematics, the group I was in, was taught in the Engineering side of the university not in the mathematics department which was essentially pure mathematics with the

JDM lecturing on the old chalkboards at Harvard, 1957.

usual scant connection to the real world. One student, an immigrant from Yugoslavia, who also lived in Leverett House, was quite clever but less than committed. He was bright enough to be on the Dean's list which requires a certain minimum high grade average. When he got a C in one exam I had set, I told him that he might be taken off the Dean's List. He said he wasn't in the least worried and said: *"I'll just take another arts class, sociology or something, and easily get an A with half the work."* I don't know if it was half the work but he took such a course, got an A and remained on the Dean's List. Even then the sciences were considered much more challenging intellectually.

Sydney Goldstein, and particularly his formidable, but not unkind, wife Rosa, tried to preserve the aura and prestige of a traditional European professor where, in that academic scene, the Professor was the pinnacle of academic achievement: it was a highly prestigious and much sought after position, certainly much less so now with the title of professor often having a different academic implication. Rosa was the archetypal European professor's wife and when invited to their house for dinner or whatever, she had a clear classification in her mind about how to treat and address the guests. Older Europeans were addressed by title, a few colleagues of similar standing to Sydney, by their first name and junior people like me by their surname. She expected Sydney be accorded the respect due to his position. It was only many years later I finally called him Sydney and then it was only after our young children, Mark and Sarah, called him that. The photo of Sydney, with his almost permanent pipe in his hand, is in the garden of our home in Oxford. I had invited him to spend a month in the University of Oxford in the early 1970s shortly after I had moved there.

Professor Sydney Goldstein FRS in our Oxford home, 1971.

Rosa felt that Sydney had never got the recognition he deserved. She told me several times that he was going to get a Knighthood (KBE) but didn't because they went off to Israel. When, very much later, I retired a few years early from Oxford in 1992 to go back to the US to the University of Washington I was told by several Oxford colleagues *"But you won't get your Knighthood now"* which often goes to Fellows of the Royal Society and academics who have directed or started a successful Research Centre in Oxford or other major universities and have an international reputation in their field.

By the end of my first three years at Harvard it was interesting to see how the supposed universal worldwide search for the best person for a position at Harvard was hardly the case. In my department, the king maker was Professor George Carrier, one of the cleverest applied mathematicians I have ever known and whose approach to modelling unusual physical problems has had a lasting influence on me. He only became an applied mathematician when his ambition to become a baseball player was dashed after he contracted tuberculosis. While in hospital he got interested in engineering and science, which he studied at university when he recovered. When it came to people and scientists, however, George's judgment was sometimes seriously flawed and resulted in several major mistakes in permanent appointments he was involved in making: the department is still generally not considered in the very top league. I became a formal faculty lecturer in the university in 1957 and when I was planning on returning to England, as I had promised, in 1959 George offered me a tenure track Assistant Professorship a position which had not been advertised. Harvard belongs to the very small group of major universities. UCLA (University of California Los Angeles) was another, whose offer, albeit much later, of a faculty position I turned down. I thought that my time in America had probably finished forever. Many years later our son, Mark, became an undergraduate at Harvard, and after graduating, settled in New York.

With considerable sadness at leaving I sailed back to England in the late summer of 1959 to be met by my beloved Sheila in Southampton. In the summer of that year, before I went back to England, Sheila, whom I only met in late 1958 as described above, had gone on to a Quaker Work Camp in Yugoslavia to work on building the road to Greece, literally by hand. She actually worked with a pick and shovel. The international *"brigada"* had people from all over Europe and North Africa. They worked every weekday on the roads. Muslims in the group would not go on the weekend holiday treks if there were any Jews on them, a religious prejudice surprising to the Americans: they followed ten minutes behind. On her way back Sheila went for a few days to Vienna to the International Youth Festival, effectively a Russian communist propaganda affair, since an old school friend, Sam Bowles, was singing in the Yale-Russian concerts in the Russian section.

After unloading my car, a Barracuda, we drove off to start our life in England. Sheila immediately saw one side of me that she didn't know. We got into a phone booth for me to call my parents in Moffat and she couldn't understand a word I was saying. I felt that I had to revert to the local Scottish dialect completely or I might have sounded phony and affected to my parents - not that I've lost my accent even now (even if I think so). Interestingly, now the meaning of some of the Lallans words have quite changed but then I haven't spoken Lallans for many many years now.

A work group in their *International Brigada* uniforms.
Jugoslavia, 1959: Sheila is the last on the right.

Sheila in Vienna, 1959.

V

Ted Hughes and Sylvia Plath 1958-1998

During my second year at Harvard in 1958 I met Ted Hughes, the poet, with whom there was an immediate warm mutual rapport, and also with his wife, Sylvia Plath. They had got secretly married in 1956 in London and had come back to the US in 1957. In 1958 they moved to Boston and rented a small apartment on Beacon Hill: the photo below of Ted and Sylvia was taken in their apartment. The one of Sylvia is when she's looking at their recently born son, Nicholas, in 1962.

Ted and I met purely by chance, outside the university environment, while sliding down Boston Common in the snow. Ted, I remember, was wearing a tie, like we all did in those days, but still looked a touch disheveled: he towered over me. He resembled a benevolent shaggy giant. He invited me back to Sylvia and his apartment for tea: it was the apartment in the photo. My wife Sheila, whom I had not yet met, and I became and remained close friends with Ted and Sylvia, for the rest of their lives. After our first meeting I regularly visited them on Beacon Hill.

Sylvia Plath 1962

Sylvia, also working on her poetry, had not yet written *The Bell Jar*, which, among other things, is an account of her early depression, fascination with suicide and other sad things. Ted was working hard to find his poetic voice and, although totally committed, he seriously worried about the future and whether or not he could make a living as a poet. A lack of money was a problem for them but much relieved with the Guggenheim Fellowship Ted was awarded in 1959. Even with my ignorance of that difficult literary world I never ever doubted that he would become a major figure in the world of letters. I strongly encouraged him, repeatedly pointing out the success of his first book, *Hawk in the Rain*, which had been greeted with such acclaim as well as beautiful and invocative poems he had written but not yet published but had read to me. By the early 1960s Ted was already a major figure in the literary world. We still have an engraving of one of his major early poems, *Pike*, which he gave me. Along with the poem there is an incredibly evil and sinister looking pike, etched by the American artist Robert Bermelin and printed by the American sculptor Leonard Baskin's Gehenna Press. *Pike* is also the first poem that Ted read to me and which drew shivers down my spine: as he read it he became the evil pike.

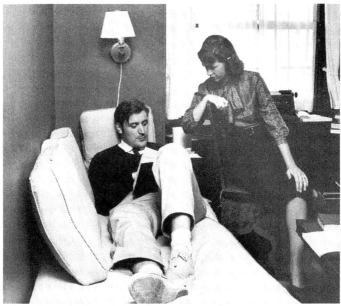

Ted Hughes and Sylvia Plath in their Beacon Hill, Boston apartment, c1958. Reproduced with permission: *Mortimer Rare Book Room, Smith College* © *Black Star*.

I sometimes found Sylvia a touch hyper which could, of course, have been related to her mental depression. She always warmly and very affectionately greeted me. She never ever mentioned Ted's poems nor talked about hers although they did together Ted told me. When talking to Sylvia about her writing once I asked if she would read one of her poems since she was working hard on her book *The Colossus* which came out in 1960 when they were living in London. She said she felt that poems were to be read rather than heard and gave me some to read. When Sylvia was preparing a meal (cooking was certainly not her forte) Ted and I would often go off together walking on Boston Common a short distance from their small apartment. Although I could never quite articulate it I felt on a few, very few, occasions a tension between Ted and Sylvia that left Ted unusually reserved and quiet with Sylvia trying too hard to be light and lively talking to me. I am sure it had a discouraging effect on Ted's writing and on Sylvia's. On these walks we talked of everything from family background and its effect on how we developed, to experiences with teaching, the academic world, English politics, what a belief in a God meant, the supernatural, Buddhism, what motivated his writing and countless others. Ted firmly believed that there was in our brains some innate and subconscious ability that surpassed upbringing and intelligence. We had very different views on many topics, usually associated with such things as extrasensory perception or, to me, irrational beliefs in similar things. Surprisingly Ted always believed in the occult. In all the years I, and later Sheila, knew Ted we never felt other than a very relaxing warmth when we were together.

When we lived in London from 1959-61 Sheila and I regularly had dinner with them at their Primrose Hill apartment or at ours in Muswell Hill. We moved to Oxford in 1961 just after their daughter Frieda was born. We sadly never saw Sylvia again but knew, of course, that Ted had left her and the children for Assia Wevill. Sylvia, who had tried to commit suicide several times, tragically succeeded in 1963 by putting her head in the gas oven but making sure the door to the children's room was sealed off. I was not as close to Sylvia, although she was always very warmly welcoming and enthusiastic about whatever I was doing or whatever we were talking about. She had left Ted shortly after they moved to Court Green in North Devon which Ted had bought around 1961 and where their son Nicholas, their second child, was born in 1962.

For a very short time, just after their time at Cambridge University, Ted had managed to get a temporary teaching job in a school and was given a class of backward 14-year old children to try and teach them basic arithmetic. He described his frustration and how he decided to try to extract reflex answers from them. He described his new idea, namely shouting out: "What's 5 times 3?" and to his astonishment back came the correct answer, shouted back enthusiastically by the whole class; it was a game. For the rest of the lesson it indeed seemed to him that there was a subconscious knowledge that just had to be brought out. He felt he had discovered a new way to teach children of low or backward intelligence and described how excited he was. The subsequent lesson, however, was a disaster and shattered his briefly held optimism: the class had resorted to its previous state with answers totally wild and unrelated. We did wonder, however, why it worked even once.

Ted did not have a very high opinion of universities, or rather the way literature was taught. He only came once to have dinner with me in Leverett House in Harvard although he would come to my rooms and we would regularly walk along the Charles River the other side of the road from Leverett House. He was genuinely curious about everything such as what research I was doing to try and understand how I thought. It was reciprocal since I wanted to know how he developed ideas and inspiration for his poems, how much honing he did and so on. In many ways we were at opposite ends of the intellectual methodology with Ted trying to get to the depths of the feelings of whatever he was writing about, whether it was a fish, a person, mysticism or whatever, while I felt that whatever I did in my work had to be clear, logical, direct, and verifiable which is very much less romantic, of course. On occasions he would read a poem to me, as he did with *Pike*, to get my reaction. What always affected me almost as much as the poem was his total immersion in whatever he was reading. He was a magnificent actor with a lovely resonant Yorkshire accent. He acted out the parts as he read, conjuring up vivid scenes: it always totally absorbed me.

At dinner one evening, just after we bought our first old mediaeval stone house, *Totleigh Barton*, in North Devon in England in 1968, and before he married Carol Orchard in 1970, Ted recounted, from memory, what he had written for an Australian radio station, about an historical walk across Australia by two explorers. He had Sheila and I living through the hunger, the slurping of boots in the mud and their staggering with thirst: they died before reaching the west coast. Ted was such a superb storyteller. He had come to dinner with a woman, hardly a soul mate but whom we found, pleasant, who did not seem very bright but then she did not get a lot of chance to talk. The only attraction we could think of was sex but in fact it was a more serious relationship. However, we never saw her again and shortly afterwards he married Carol Orchard whom Ted had been amorously seeing at the same time. We saw much more of Carol with Ted and Sylvia's children, Frieda and Nicholas, since after selling *Totleigh Barton* for the initial *Arvon Foundation* Centre, we found we missed rural Devon and so bought another mediaeval thatched house, *Sletchcott* - another major renovation project I talk about in Chapter 13 - in the country outside the tiny village of Kings Nympton a few miles from where Ted and Carol lived, in Court Green in North Tawton.

Ted had a gentleness and deep concern for his friends and his family. His vilification, totally incomprehensible and mean-spirited to everyone who knew him, by part of the press and extreme women's movements in the USA and in England can only be described as vindictive, sensational, self-seeking or at best totally ridiculous. Threats to kill him if he ever stepped foot again in America truly worried Ted. He only went back once many years later in the 1980s. He worried desperately when Frieda, his and Sylvia's daughter, went off with a local market gardener in Devon, not because of his social standing, which would not have occurred to Ted although he had little respect for the idle unintelligent rich, but at the narrowness of the world she was choosing. At dinner one evening, we all commiserated on how little influence we could often have on some of our children's obviously wrong decisions and, in the case of Frieda and this liaison, we were convinced it could never last, which it didn't. He felt for the hurt that she had in store. Frieda married him in 1979 and was divorced by 1982. The Frieda we met a few times in Court Green and at our house, Sletchcott in the country in North Devon, was then strong minded, lively and bright with a thirst for independence. Ted and Sylvia's son Nicholas was also a lively enthusiastic little boy who clearly loved nature as was clear whenever we visited Court Green. He became an ecologist on the faculty of the University of Alaska but sadly committed suicide in 2009. Our children Mark and Sarah, although they liked Frieda and Nicky, they were very critical of Nicky because they said he constantly cheated at Monopoly which they sometimes all played when he came with Ted and Carol to our house, Sletchcott.

Ted and I shared a love of almost everything old which had some human connection from the simplest to the sophisticated. Each of us had a barn full of old oak beams, wooden fire lintels and so on that we would get at farm auctions or from demolished barns in Devon and which we firmly believed would sometime be useful. Ted used some in his house in North Tawton in North Devon as we did too in renovating the old houses we bought in Woodeaton near Oxford, Totleigh Barton and later, Sletchcott, in Devon. We still have a massive ancient oak fire lintel, which I made into a coffee table, that Ted and I lusted after when we saw it at one of the farm estate auctions we had gone to together: there is a photo of it in Chapter 13. When Ted and Carol visited us in Oxford one time we showed them an old 19th century man's black bear fur coat we had found in New York's *Antique Furs* on 8th Avenue: the coat came down to my ankles. Ted donned it and said he felt like a seedy seaside resort actor. In the photo he certainly looks the part. Sheila had one as well which Carol tried on and is wearing it in the photo.

Ted Hughes and his wife Carol, in our antique 19th century black bear coats, at our home in Oxford in the mid-1980s.

In spite of his talent for lively readings Ted shied away from the thought of giving a lecture; readings were different he insisted. After we went back to Oxford in 1969 on my being appointed to a Fellowship in Corpus Christi College and a faculty position in the university, I tried during a couple of election times to get him to let me put his name up for the Oxford Professorship of Poetry but he would never agree, because, as he kept telling me, he was worried about lecturing. I tried to argue that it required only a modicum of acting, as all good lecturers realize, and practice, and that he would be the best professor of poetry all of us would have ever known.

Unfortunately, all my arguments were to no avail. It was a great pity since he was such an obvious choice as a major poet in the English speaking world. But then I, as well as many many others, feel he was the major 20th century English speaking poet. His poems, written when he was the Poet Laureate, are so much more beautiful than all the other Laureates' poems I have read.

Ted believed in the occult and subconscious in a way I could never understand. He had studied archaeology and anthropology at Cambridge which helped to nourish such a belief. He was, for example, firmly convinced that the wife of a friend in Devon who had belonged to a white witches' coven in Italy some time before and that it still had a permanent hold over her. As a scientist I argued for real evidence. He would describe the effect of some mystical experience which I would argue was all in his mind. Although he agreed it was in his mind he felt there was much much more, something physical. At dinners in his home, Court Green, he would be at one end of the conversation spectrum with his friend Leonard Baskin, the well known American sculptor and artist in the middle, and me at the other extreme of what I always thought was obvious rationality. Ted, in fact, believed in astrological predictions for example, about which we could never agree. He described how, at one dinner, an ionizing machine on the table had made everybody very lively and brought it out to show me. I couldn't convince him that it was the equivalent of snake oil. But then Ted never ever needed any artificial aid to be lively at dinner.

We saw Ted every time we went down from Oxford to our house, initially Totleigh Barton and later, much more often, at our house Sletchcott, in Devon as described in Chapter 13. Ted became a great favorite of our children Mark and Sarah, and he would often tell stories and make up rhymes. He wrote some doggerel for Sarah in the frontispiece in his recent book, *Meet My Folks* which he brought for us, when he and Carol came to dinner one evening. He regularly brought us a copy when a new book was published. In this case it was for Sarah's (Sarah Corinne Jo) 7th birthday:

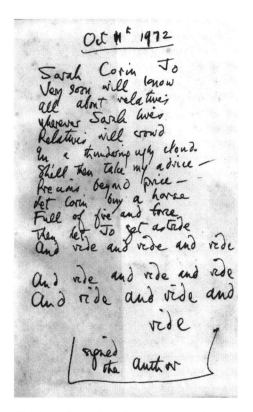

Sarah Corin Jo
Very soon will know
All about relatives
Wherever Sarah lives
Relatives will crowd
In a thundering ugly cloud
She'll then take my advice
Precious beyond price –
Let Corin buy a horse
Full of fire and force
Then let Jo get astride
And ride and ride and ride
And ride and ride and ride
And ride and ride and ride

signed
      the author

Ted loved words, of course, and rhyming in unusual combinations when he added one in the front of a new book for us, like the one in his 1979 book *Moortown*.

For   Sheila   Sarah
                and
          Mark   Jim

Some Devonian bucolics
And sundry frolics
Spiced with gripes and colics

                love
                from
                Ted
          May 1980

There are some other unpublished handwritten poems, some very funny, always along with a greeting to us all when a new book came out and he came to dinner or when we were at his house, Court Green. The one from his 1981 book *Under The North Star* is:

For Sarah and Mark
and Sheila and Jim
  with much love
    from Ted and Carol

Where
Is the Polar Bear?
Couldn't this book afford
One word for the caribou
horde?
I repine
For the offensive
porcupine
And heave a
Sigh for the desirable
beaver
All these pages haven't got a
Single mention of a sea-
otter.
And seeing no
Laureatising of the King
Salmon I fling
This book on the gas-
ring.

In the family greeting in the front of his *Remains of Elmet* (1980) Ted had added a Scottish border proverb I had never heard:

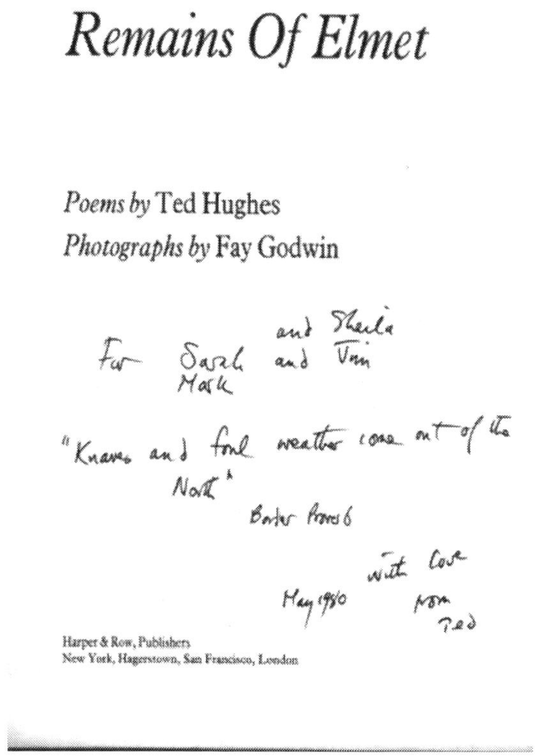

Remains Of Elmet

Poems by Ted Hughes
Photographs by Fay Godwin

For Sarah and Sheila
Mark and Jim

"Knaves and foul
weather come out of
the North"

Border Proverb

May 1980 with love
from
Ted

Harper & Row, Publishers
New York, Hagerstown, San Francisco, London

This book by Ted has drawings by Leonard Baskin who did all the illustrations. Ted and Leonard had been friends and collaborators in various projects for many years. Leonard became a friend of ours also after we first met him at dinner at Ted and Carol's Court Green in the 1970s. Leonard had an old stone house, *Lurley Manor*, not far away in Tiverton: he had bought it at Ted's suggestion.

Leonard played a significant role in the career of our son, Mark. Leonard, and his wife, Lisa, kindly invited him to spend a week with his family in their home in *Little Deer Island* in Maine when Mark was at Harvard majoring in English. With Mark's long time love of art Leonard convinced him to change to Art History, which he did, and which later helped him move into the art world. After graduating from Harvard Mark worked six years at Sotheby's New York and then started a gallery of his own for 19th and 20th century paintings in New York: *Mark Murray Fine*

146

Paintings (markmurray.com) now well known internationally. He celebrated the gallery's 25th year anniversary in 2017.

Another poem in the copy of the *Remains of Elmet* Ted wrote inside the book under the poem on page 60:

"I see a hill beyond a hill beyond a hill"
Cries the hen-bird with imperious eyes,
To her bottlenecked brood.
"I see a day beyond a day beyond a day beyond a day"
Cries the cock.
 Too late, heads high and wings low,
 They curve in from heaven.
 With a crash they pitch through stained glass
 And drop onto a cold altar
 Two hundred miles away.

Very sadly we never saw Ted, or Carol, again after 1988 since it was when we restarted our itinerant life again, back and forth across the Atlantic a year at a time. We moved back, permanently, to America in 1992.

VI

Return to British Academia and My Introduction to the University of Oxford 1959-1963

In the last few months at Harvard in 1959 I applied for tenured university lectureships in England, specifically in London since Sheila was going to be at the *London School of Economics* for her third year. It was very difficult for a couple to rent an apartment in those days if you were not married so we simply got married in October 1959. I had recently been at a wedding of a friend from Harvard. She was marrying an Englishman and since her father was not alive she asked me to give her (the bride) away. Listening to the church service I felt I could not, in all conscience, say "yes" to all the religious questions so Sheila and I decided to get married in a registry office close to where my sister, Annie, and her husband lived in Barking in East London and with whom we had been staying. The Registrar was clearly an alcoholic, mumbled all he had to say in a few minutes, and unsteadily passed the relevant papers to us to sign. We were now officially married with a marriage certificate so we soon found an apartment in north London close to Hampstead Heath within easy commuting to University College London where I had been appointed to a lectureship. I recently was told the address and phone number of our apartment more than 50 years ago in an odd way. I had written to the Mortimer Room archivist in Smith College, the women's college in Northampton, Massachusetts to find out who owned a photo of Sylvia Plath and Ted Hughes which I wanted to use in this memoir. The helpful archivist wrote to say she had found, out of curiosity, our old London address and phone number in Sylvia's address book in the college's Sylvia Plath archives.

In 1959 after Sheila met me at the boat in Southampton we went up to Moffat so that Sheila could meet my family and them her. My mother was particularly keen to do so and, not surprisingly, they felt an immediate warmth for each other which not only never waned but became ever deeper with the years. It was the first time Sheila had ever been in Scotland so she felt she had to visit her mother and father's extended families in Inverness and Glasgow. The last time my family were all together was in 1963 when the photo below was taken and which so accurately reflects the atmosphere of our family.

Murray family: Moffat, 1963. From left to right JDM, brother Peter, my mother Sarah Jane, my father Peter, my eldest sister Jane, my elder brother John with my sisters sitting, Annie (left) and Marion (right).

Sheila had spent her whole life up to then in America and is a native born American but with pure Scottish blood. Her Scottish parents had emigrated, independently, to America in the early 1920s. Sheila could easily pass, but only visually, as a northern Scot with her light fair complexion and freckles. Her visit to Inverness was a revelation to her. Those members of her mother's large family who had stayed in Scotland were living in a totally different (earlier) era to the two sisters who had emigrated to America in the early 1920s.

Since it was our first time together in Moffat we walked everywhere in the country where I had spent my childhood. The most spectacular walk was to an isolated loch, called *Loch Skene*, where I used to go poaching with my father as a young boy as I described in Chapter 2. It is about 10 miles northeast of Moffat, along, at that time, a narrow, seldom travelled, country road as in the photo below. It was typical of the countryside around Moffat. To get to *Loch Skene* you had to climb a narrow steep hillside footpath, about 1,000 feet high, past a small but dramatic cliff waterfall known as the *Grey Mare's Tail* which is about 250 feet high. The trail starts on the left of the photo below but crosses over to the right towards the top beside the bottom of the "*Tail*" waterfall.

As was typical of the country around Moffat there were many wild goats; there still are. A short walk from the top of the trail you come to the dramatic, beautiful, treeless craggy mountainous country with the loch

Trail up to the *Grey Mare's Tail* and to *Loch Skene* over the top of the hill, 1930s.

Sheila at *Loch Skene*, near Moffat, Scotland, 1959.

way down below you, as in the photo with Sheila lying on the shore. There are incredibly distant open views, totally empty of any sign of civilisation, and, in those days, never ever another person. It is one of the most beautiful, dramatic places I know in Scotland. It is probably no longer the same since the National Trust bought the area and publicised its beauty although the climb is no doubt still a deterrent. Loch Skene is also very near a now well-known fossil area called *Dobb's Lin* literally just up the road from the Grey Mare's Tail.

Moffat Water Valley on the road to the *Grey Mare's Tail*, 1959

Moffat Water Valley near the path up to *Loch Skene* on the left, 1959.

I had applied for advertised permanent lectureships in mathematics at universities in London namely King's College London (KCL) and University College London (UCL), two of the three major ones in London. I was offered the position in both. Although I had never been to either the decision as to which I accepted was not difficult. The official letter from King's College said that since I had spent the last three years in America they could offer me only two increments in the starting salary of a lecturer. The letter from University College said that since I had spent the last three years in America they could offer me five yearly increments in the starting salary. I enjoyed University College. My close friend Mark Gretton, had also been successful in getting a lectureship, in Greek, at University College. My teaching responsibilities were not arduous but the classes were large and initially more daunting and nervous making than at Harvard: my main first year class had around 150 students. I worried, unduly, about possible discipline problems which I learned were not that unusual. I never had any. There had never been any in my classes at Harvard.

University College has a long very wide hall, the South Cloister, in the main building of the university. At one end of it sits the skeleton of Jeremy Bentham in a splendid wooden box, case rather, dressed in his clothes of the time, the early to middle of the 19th century. The head is made of wax. Bentham was the spiritual founder of University College London which, as a consequence, meant it was not at all religiously oriented like King's College London had been.

I had complete freedom at University College and the chairman of the department, the Professor of Applied Mathematics (the other professor was in Pure Mathematics) told me that I was only required to come in to the university on the days I lectured, usually just two or three days a week. He also said we could live wherever we wanted even commuting from as far away as Oxford or Cambridge. He only came in around three days a week. It was a very friendly department and still had the custom of calling colleagues only by their surnames. At Harvard, particularly close friends, often just used surnames of course. However, we yearned for the countryside and so, after less than a year, we moved out to the country about 20 miles south of Cambridge and started our lifetime disease of buying old historic houses and spending endless time and energy personally renovating them.

This house, in the old village of Hempstead about 40 miles northeast of the university, was our first house and which we were able to afford through a bizarre but fortunate coincidence. We had found a wreck of an ancient thatched house not far away and were in the process of buying it when we had a ridiculous offer from a rich homosexual lawyer who lived on the very upmarket edge of Regents Park in London. He desperately wanted to buy it as a second house since he had a woman cleaner in the nearest village who did not object to his sexual tastes. We finally agreed and got twice what we had signed a contract to pay for the house: this tax-free profit was comparable to my yearly salary. So, we used it to buy an even more expensive larger house in Hempstead but which needed very much less renovation. The house was, at that time essentially in the country, with open views and just across the small country road from the

Sheila and JDM in the garden of their house *The Old Cottage*, Hempstead, Essex, 1962.

late mediaeval 14th century village church. Now it is close to London's *Stansted International Airport* which did not exist, nor was even thought of, at the time. As was customary in those days, the church was never closed: you could go into any part of it any time of day or night. In the crypt there were old 15th century, and later, lead coffins all over the floor, some randomly piled on top of each other. As we looked at some of the names, one of them was of William Harvey who discovered and described the circulation of the blood in the early 17th century. It took decades before his discovery was accepted but it was taught in all the medical schools before he died. This house, which unimaginatively had been named *The*

Old Cottage, was the start of our house buying and selling which has lasted all our life: we have, ridiculously, bought and sold fourteen each time thinking it would be our house at least for the rest of my career. Most of the academics I have known have remained in the university where they first got tenure and have lived in the first house they bought or, if divorced, another one in the same town.

One of the pleasures of University College was regularly seeing our close friend Mark Gretton. Lunch in the university dining room, unfortunately, tended to be departmentally, or rather subject, segregated but, as a friend of a classicist I was welcomed at their table as well as that of the scientists. Mark, a sincere but totally unself-righteous Roman Catholic, had seriously debated whether or not to go into the church on returning to England. On my trip across America in 1957 I got one postcard from him which started, "*Hail Murray, Full of Grace*". Towards the end of our first year in London Mark decided to get married to Corinne Lambert his long time girlfriend. The catholic priest who conducted the marriage, in a church near Mark's lovely family estate property in the Suffolk countryside, was singularly unpleasant and sour since he strongly disapproved of Mark - any Catholic - marrying a non-Catholic. I don't know what he had hoped to achieve by his behaviour.

We saw a lot of Mark and Corinne in London and met many of their friends, one was Tom Courtenay (now Sir Thomas Courtenay) the actor who was just finishing his time at RADA (Royal Academy of Dramatic Art). At one party, he said how very worried he was that he might not find a job. It was clear to us all at the final evening of graduate plays at RADA that he need not have the slightest worry. He became well known as an actor, only a few years later, in the 1960s. Mark tragically died many years later by suffocation when trying to put out a fire in a field of hay on their country property. It was such a sadness for so many people. As a measure of the respect University College London had for him there is now a Mark Gretton Prize in Greek. While in London we also saw a lot of my, by then our, close friend from Harvard days, Bill de Spoelberch, who was doing graduate research in the London School of Economics, who, in spite of all my nagging, decided not to complete a Ph.D. As it turned out he was right.

While living in London we met up with another friend from Harvard, Rupert Wilkinson, who had been an undergraduate and lived in Leverett House when I was there. He had invited us to his parents' home in Newbury, not far from Oxford, and had also invited friends of theirs they thought we might like, Bill and Paddy Hardy who lived, at the time, in the same village. Bill and Paddy became lifelong close friends.

Bill, a physics engineering university lecturer, had a love of old machines. He even had an old early 20th century steamroller he kept on their property and which he used to run various machines. Bill also loved old cars and had a magnificent large 1920s Bentley sports car which he maintained himself. Perhaps his favourite though was a First World War biplane which he kept on the then well known area called the *South Downs* but even better known from what is now one of the classic novels of the time, namely *Watership Down*. When he first took me up in it I could

Bill and Paddy Hardy, Kingsclere, England, 1963.

understand his enthusiasm, even if it could never be mine even though it was exciting and so different to flying now. I certainly felt much more comfortable knowing that Bill maintained the aeroplane himself. As we came in to land one time I shouted through the communicating flexible pipe that we were coming in on the upward slope of the field. Bill said he always did that since it made gravity on his side. Bill was always immensely practical except for his irrational (to me) love of riding his old motorbike.

Paddy raised and trained racehorses and had been an enthusiastic rider and member of hunts ever since she was a child. She had been thrown many times. When on our way back to America in 1963 we stayed with them. Their two daughters, Georgeana and Julia were just a few years older than Mark, our only child at the time. Bill and Paddy loved the country and a few years later managed to buy and move to a magnificent old early 19th century manor house and farm, *Totterton Hall*, near a small village in North Shropshire where they indulged in their love of the country, horses and farm animals. We visited and stayed with them regularly when we were in England. Paddy who always thought the best of people was often taken advantage of by people in the racing world. Georgeana inherited Paddy's love of horses and became the leader of various hunts. Sadly Bill developed Parkinson's which to begin with he refused to take seriously and only agreed to sell his old 1920s Bentley when he couldn't walk anymore.

At the beginning of my second year at University College we decided that we did not want to stay in London with my academic career in University College London even with its deserved high international reputation. It was also clear that Sheila would not go back to Brandeis to finish her degree. So, I started to look for other positions outside of London one of which came up at Hertford College in the University of Oxford which is generally referred to as just Oxford. I knew nothing about Oxford, other than its high international prestige. I had never, in fact, ever been there but I applied for the tenured Fellowship in Mathematics and gave the names of the required two referees, one my colleague from Harvard, Professor Sydney Goldstein, because he was English, a Fellow of the Royal Society and knew some of my work very well and the other, the mathematics professor from the University of St. Andrews, Professor Edward Copson, who was an Oxford graduate. I later learned he had been a colleague of Dr. Ferrar, the recently elected Principal (that is the President) of Hertford College, when they were both students in mathematics in Edinburgh University.

Appointments were decided by the Governing Body of the College which consisted of the permanent Fellows of which, at that time, there were only about 12 and these included two Fellows whose Fellowship was associated with the specific professorship they held in the university. Although the latter voted they took little part in the selection. The previous tutorial Fellow in Mathematics, Dr. Ferrar, was a fairly typical Fellow at the time. His election to the head of the college was for his last two years before retiring. He had been committed to the college and college teaching practically his whole career and had been the, not very imaginative, Bursar during the war. But, like many of the permanent college fellowship faculty in Oxford he had done some research but after he became the Mathematics Fellow and tutor, college teaching effectively took up all his time. He did, however, publish some highly respected undergraduate mathematics textbooks.

156

VI. Return to British Academia and My Introduction to the University of Oxford 1959-1963

I got the position in Hertford somewhat unusually, and, I found out later, in large measure for the wrong reasons. The recommendation letter from Professor Copson said I had got the top First Class Honours in Mathematics and the medal for the top graduate in the Faculty of Science but he added at the end of the letter: "*all things being equal you should take an Oxford man.*" Dr. Ferrar had a similar view. One of the more vocal and influential Fellows in the college was Dr. Neil Tanner, the Fellow in Physics. He became a very positive and strong advocate for me when he read the letter from Goldstein. He said, at dinner in Hall one evening after my election, that he was totally convinced I was the best candidate since anybody who got such a positive letter from Goldstein must be very clever. Somewhat surprised I asked him how he knew Goldstein. He replied: "*Everybody knows Goldstein because of his superb book*". The only problem was that it was a different Goldstein, one who had indeed written a well-known book, *Classical Mechanics*. I never ever met him and he certainly did not know me! So, we sold our Hempstead house and moved into a 5th floor walk-up apartment in London, Highgate, close to Hampstead Heath, until we could move to Oxford.

A few minutes walk from the apartment building is the old *Highgate Cemetery* which, at the time, was one of the most romantic and beautiful cemeteries with lots of old stone statues and collapsing headstones, set in a wildly overgrown garden filled with wild flowers. The many times we went there we were always the only people in it. It is now kept locked. The other side of the very small very quiet lane was the new Highgate cemetery, where Karl Marx is buried. His headstone was regularly adorned with flowers from his admirers, which certainly did not include us: with my working class upbringing I had no illusions about communism.

Chester (Chet) Bowles who lived in Essex, Connecticut had been the Governor of Connecticut, a Democratic Congressman, a colleague of President John F. Kennedy as Under Secretary of State and twice the US Ambassador to India. He had known and been kind to Sheila ever since she was a small child growing up there. He recognised how very clever, lively and very different she was to the other friends of his children who went to the local school. He had long hoped that when they grew up his son, Sam, and Sheila would get married. They were good friends and Sheila and I have seen Sam and each of his two wives several times in our academic travels.

Chet strongly supported Sheila's decision to go to Brandeis University knowing she was very interested in Southeast Asian Studies and knew one very good professor there. Another key consideration was that the scholarship from Brandeis was much bigger than the one offered to her by Brown University. So, I am forever grateful since otherwise we would never have met. When we got married, in London, in 1959 Chet's wife, Steb, had given him a very nice silver sugar and creamer to give to us as a

Chet and Steb Bowles, *Hayden's Point*, Essex CT, 1977.

Chet and Steb Bowles, *Hayden's Point*, Essex CT, 1978.

wedding present when he saw us in London and which we still have. As Under Secretary for State in 1961 he was officially visiting the UK and got in touch with Sheila before arriving and, in spite of his incredibly busy high level government meetings, he wanted to see her and meet her husband (to look me over) so he invited us out to dinner one evening. It was not a difficult evening. Chet was a kind and genuinely considerate warm man. Talking about politics, however, I was surprised how unrealistic I thought he was while he thought, and later told his very nice wife, Steb, that I was a bit of a real politic, not something with which he sympathised. He was, however, an excellent Ambassador to India during his eight years in the position. Every year, until Chet died, we would get a hand written card at Christmas with a recent photo of him and Steb. Each time we were back in Essex we would visit, and be warmly welcomed, by them in their large property dramatically situated on Hayden's Point on the Connecticut River. They were clearly so very pleased to see that Sheila and I were so happy.

Chet sincerely wanted to help less fortunate people and certainly practiced what he believed in. He stipulated that when his estate was sold the proceeds were to be given to charity with the bulk of the land made into a public park. This was done when his wife, Steb died, which happened a few years after him.

Hertford College and University of Oxford 1961-3

In Oxford at the time the old custom was still in place which stipulated that the only other university degrees which were officially recognized by the University of Oxford were those from Cambridge University and Trinity College, Dublin. My degrees from the University of St. Andrews were not recognized as degrees. To be formally appointed I had to be given, or rather required to buy, an Oxford MA degree. It cost £16 (about $30 then), which was about 1% of a starting university lecturer's yearly salary at that time. Talking to the Principal, Dr. Ferrar, I jokingly asked if he could do it any cheaper. He was not amused and tartly said: "*You can claim it off your income tax.*" This requirement has long since not been required of new faculty from other universities.

Hertford College is in the centre of Oxford and one of the three university colleges and libraries which make up the beautiful 18th century Radcliffe (Library) Square together with the 14th century University Church of St. Mary. It is across the small road from the 17th century Bodleian Library. The college had been part of an old residential group of buildings from the 14th century when it was called Hart Hall, but never became a full college and went into decline. However Hart Hall had its share of famous students, such as William Tyndale, John Donne, Jonathan Swift and Thomas Hobbes, of whom there is a splendid painting in the college which gives an indication of how he viewed the world: the black and white photo here is one I took of his head when I was a Fellow: it hung in the Senior Common Room. Hart Hall was finally created a college, Hertford College, in 1874. Most of the buildings, however, are 19th century.

I started my Oxford career in the autumn of 1961. The teaching requirements, which I should have known about, were quite a shock. I was responsible for teaching the complete mathematics syllabus and all the mathematicians in the college, around 15 at the time. My teaching

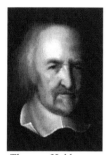

Thomas Hobbes
1588-1679

responsibility was to give individual tutorials every week to each of the students who would appear with their homework and be prepared to answer questions on the work I had set. In the humanities students wrote a weekly essay. Students then had to wear their student academic gown to tutorials. The Oxford undergraduate gown is a short black one. The formality of tutorials helped, and made them one of the most important parts of their academic studies. I often had as many as 16 one-to-one hour-long tutorials a week and never less than 12. There are however, only three 8-week terms in the Oxford academic year so the vacations were available to do research and travel or whatever. Hertford was not considered part of the high academic or social scene in Oxford. Evelyn Waugh, was a student there but, as a social climber, he always felt he should have been at Christ Church, one of the major socially elite colleges at the time. Waugh finally left without a degree. My room in College was in the main quadrangle and one subsequent claim to "fame" was that it was used in the BBC 1981 television series of Evelyn Waugh's *Brideshead Revisited* which were memories of Charles Ryder's friendship with the upper class Sebastion Flyte who, in one episode leaned out of the window of my former room to throw up in the garden bordering the building.

The university played a relatively small role for college Fellows at that time. After a year I was automatically officially appointed a lecturer in the university, called a Common University Fund Lecturer, which was not as prestigious as a university lecturer. As such I was required to give one 16-hour university course each year in the mathematics department. Students did not have to attend lectures and many did not since they had college tutorials which covered the same topics even if not at the same time. Several of the faculty were appalling lecturers which I suspect was perhaps sometimes intentional since if no one turned up for the lectures, or only for the first few and then stopped attending, the lecturer had satisfied the university's statutory lecturing requirement. Students were not required to attend lectures and certainly for the first two years many did not. It was not unlike what the college system was like in earlier centuries where students were taught only by Fellows in their college. With the more specialised areas in the third year, however, having to attend lectures was essential. At the time, most degrees, particularly the science ones, took only three years whereas now it is four.

Hertford College at the time was generally at the bottom of what is called the *Norrington Table* which compares all the undergraduate colleges on the basis of their final Honours examination results. There were just over thirty colleges at the time. The score for a college is calculated by giving a score of 5 for a student getting a First Class Honours degree, 3 for a Second Class Honours 2:1 degree, 2 for a Second Class 2:2 degree, 1 for a Third Class Honours degree and 0 for a pass, and an unclassified Honours degree, called an *Aegrotat*. The percentage rank is then calculated by dividing the number by the total possible score the college could have got which is the number of honours degrees times 5. Oxford had a 4th class honours degree before the second class was divided into 2.1 (Upper second class) and 2.2 (Lower second class) a system which was introduced in 1986 long after my time at Hertford.

It was, and still is, incredibly competitive to get into the University of Oxford. Students applied to specific colleges (the colleges were not mixed at the time) and everybody had to take the series of extremely difficult entrance examinations in their subject. The Fellow in the subject in the college had the final say as to who was accepted. Hertford was very much in the lowest group of the colleges and did not attract the brightest students but most of them were still clever on an absolute scale. There were schools around the country which intensively prepared their pupils for the Oxford Entrance Examinations. Now the system is different with the standard countrywide examinations, called A-levels (Advanced Levels), playing a major role. Up to the late 1960s the majority of students accepted came from these long established Oxbridge (the name for Oxford and Cambridge universities) oriented schools.

All possible students for the college were interviewed. To try and determine a little more about their innate intelligence as distinct from excellent teaching and impressive exam results I asked simple, but unusual, questions which might help to distinguish the brighter applicants. For example, I would start with an easy question, such as: If you have ten balls forming a triangle pointing upwards with 4 on the bottom row, then 3 then 2 then 1, what is the smallest number of ball moves you need to make the triangle point down? The answer is 3. If they answered that correctly I then moved on to something like: Is it possible to have a constant diameter two (and three) dimensional figure that is not a circle? If the answer (the correct one) is yes, they were asked how to construct it. The UK 50 pence piece is a two dimensional example of a seven sided constant diameter shape. Another question was: How many ways can you divide a square into equal and similar areas? (The answer is infinite.) If the applicant got all of these correct I went on to more subtle questions which also had nothing to with their school mathematics syllabus.

Since entrance examinations were of such a very high standard they strongly favoured the better schools, many of them private fee paying schools (called *Public Schools* in Britain). The finances of the individual colleges also played a role since the richer colleges could offer scholarships. Hertford was one of the poorest colleges. Applicants had to list the college of their first choice and a few others in order. Hertford was very very rarely a first choice of the brightest applicants and it was often never listed at all. In the second year of my time in college I was appointed (with no option as to whether or not to accept) Tutor for Admissions. This was essentially an administrative position and which had no effect on my required tutorial duties other than taking even more of my time from research.

My first impressions of the college were not very positive. I thought many of the attitudes and practices were incredibly outdated and accounted for much of its low academic standing in the university. A small, very small in fact, group of Fellows, all relatively new Fellows, namely David Bentley the law Fellow, Richard Malpas, the philosophy Fellow, Dr. Neil Tanner the physics Fellow, and myself, the mathematics Fellow, started to think how we could drastically change the system of entry and the attitude of the other Fellows in the college – not a very easy task. We felt strongly that the college must try to do something radical about raising the academic standard of the applicants.

We came up with the idea that the college should cease to take part in the standard admission procedures which required all applicants to take the very difficult entrance examinations. Instead we thought that we should interview potential students and make decisions on that basis and not even always make acceptance conditional on the level of their passes in the final school Advanced Level Certificates of Education. This was a very revolutionary idea and raised a lot of opposition, not only in Hertford, but in other colleges and in the university departments. I was subjected to considerable pressure from colleagues in the mathematics and science departments, but certainly not all. A strong supporter was Dr. John Lewis, the Fellow in mathematics in Brasenose College and a friend, who joined me in trying to push Brasenose to join the new system and was with me defending it in the Mathematics Department. During the 1962-3 academic year I visited several schools to talk to headmasters and students about the new procedure. Although I resigned from the college in 1963 to return to the US, with the colleges' independence Hertford could start the new process which it did in 1965. It was so successful that, by the late 1960s Hertford College had risen to the top of the Norrington Table with the top number of First and Second Class Honours of any college. The university threatened to disassociate Hertford from the admission process but Hertford did not back down and the Hertford admission process quickly became universal in the university. The effect of this revolutionary new approach was that students from a very much wider class of schools who normally would never ever have thought of applying to Oxford did so and on the basis of interviews, were offered places in the college. The admission process we developed in Hertford certainly changed the social strata of the university. The typical student during my time in Hertford was still mainly from the upper and wealthy middle class. The new system we introduced was recently (2016) celebrated in Hertford with a portrait display, in the Hall, of the first cohort of such students.

Many years later, in 1987, at which time I had been a Fellow of Corpus Christi College for many years, I had another involvement in the college. Hertford was in the process of appointing a new Principal (that is the president of the college). I encouraged a friend, Professor Christopher Zeeman, an internationally renowned mathematician, to apply which he did. Some of the older Fellows, who had been in the college when I was a Fellow and when the Principal then was a mathematician and certainly not a great one, were reluctant to consider Zeeman. My old friend and colleague in college, Richard Malpas, who was one of the small "revolutionary" group in 1962, asked me if I would come and talk to him about Zeeman. I convinced him that I thought he would be an excellent choice and somebody who would bring new ideas to the college. Christopher Zeeman was elected Principal in 1988 and certainly did bring new ideas and approaches to some of the college's practices such as student recruitment and acceptances.

Hertford College life was essentially what it had been before the war and long before. There were several unmarried Fellows who lived in college in their own suite of rooms. Fellows dined in Hall along with the students but importantly at a table, known as *High Table*, which is about 6 inches above the students' tables but the food is orders of magnitude different. In the colleges it was, and still is in the older colleges, very much haute cuisine with excellent wine. Free meals are still one of the Fellows' perks. For some Fellows the College was the centre of their life both social and academic.

There is a chapel in each of the traditional colleges but in Hertford none of the Fellows in my time went to church. When I was there the college appointed a new chaplain, an enthusiastic but somewhat naïve young man. He tried very hard, without success, to get at least some of the Fellows to attend a Sunday service. At the time there was a named yearly sermon, officially for the conversion of the Jews. The new chaplain asked my close personal friend Dr. Peter Ganz, who had recently been appointed a Fellow, to give it. Peter was a non-religious Jew who had fled Germany just before the war. He politely declined! Peter Ganz and many other German Jews had ended up in concentration camps at the beginning of the war: they had left Germany in the late 1930s. The British government quickly realised the incredible waste of intelligence of these people so they were released and immediately recruited into British intelligence. Later Peter Ganz was appointed to the new Professorship of Mediaeval German which meant he had to change to the college the professorship was assigned to, in this case to St. Edmund Hall. In spite of the appalling Nazi persecution Peter decided to go back to a senior academic position in Germany when he retired from Oxford a couple of years early and was appointed an Honorary Professor in the University of Göttingen. When I asked him how he could do that he said it was really because of the mediaeval manuscripts but he agreed it was not the only reason. Sheila and I regularly saw Peter and his wife Rosemary and their family socially, being particularly close family friends. Dinners with them were always very lively evenings. Peter and I did not agree politically: Peter was a principled, if not a deeply felt, socialist, perhaps reflecting his well to do upbringing while my lack of appreciation was no doubt due to my working class one.

Old Upper Farm, Woodeaton - our first major house renovation

As when I was at University College London we irrationally again bought an old period house in a very small village, called Woodeaton, six miles from the centre of Oxford. There were less than 10 houses in total in the whole village area, with several complete ruins as in the photo below. The old stone house, *Old Upper Farm*, was built in the early 1600s. It had to be completely renovated. It was our first major renovation project which taught us how much more work there would always be than we had anticipated, particularly with our, then, lack of experience. It is now a Grade II listed historic building. The previous owner had moved from one room to the next as it became a ramshackle with rotten windows, dilapidated plumbing, holes in the floors, leaking roof and so on.

Village Green, Woodeaton, Oxford with *Old Upper Farm* on the left, 1961.

At the beginning of the war the huge manor house in the village, literally across the small road, was made the centre of the government's

Potato Board. Two of the young women who came to work there married the very much older owners of Lower Farm and Upper Farm: it was one of them who had lived in Upper Farm before we bought it. We learned she had a proclivity for young men who if they came to the door were invited in with "*Come on in, Dearie*". She had quite a reputation. We learned about her from the ambulance driver who drove Sheila back from the hospital after she gave birth to our son Mark. We had planned on Mark being born at home in Woodeaton but there was some minor complication so Sheila had to go off to the hospital where she had a bed

Holy Rood Church, Woodeaton (Taunt & Co. 987, early 20th century. Reproduced with kind permission of OldUKPhotos. http//t.co/gawpy19e.

in one of the corridors since the hospital was full. That same year we had a visit from a man who told us he had been the husband of the woman who had lived in the house. He must have been at least 25 years younger than she was. He told us she had recently died of cancer and he was looking at the parts of the *Old Upper Farm* which he had inherited. When we said we were very sorry to hear about his wife he said: "*Oh, yes, yes. I wonder, since you recently bought this house, what do you think I could get for the field up the road and whether I could get planning permission which would make it worth a large amount of money?*"

When Sheila became pregnant with our son Mark that first year in Oxford we could not however, stop working on the house. Sheila would always be in dark blue workman's overalls, up a ladder, cement pointing the old stone walls for example, and having to stand sideways because of her large pregnant belly. She became an expert stonemason, rebuilding among other things, the two large old chimneys in the 'before' photo above of the house and her renovation in the 'after' photo below. The stone tiling on the roof also had to be replaced but for that we hired a bunch of pleasant young roofers albeit a touch dishonest; they only nailed the stone tiles when we were looking. One of them, when he learned that Sheila was an American, asked *"What kind of clubs are these paternity societies over there?"* We tried not to laugh.

Old Upper Farm before renovation with Sheila at the gate, 1961.

The whole village was incredibly friendly and warmly welcoming to us: we were by far the youngest couple in the village. The village itself was essentially a throwback to the beginning of the 20th century but in very much worse state and many fewer inhabitants. An old Clydesdale horse was regularly grazed on the small village green on which there is the stone shaft of a 13th century Rood (a cross) as in the photos of the village above. The traffic through the village was minute. Some of the locals regularly brought us vegetables from their gardens. There was a very kind German ex-prisoner of war who had decided to stay in the area after the war. Every week he came by to see if we needed any help which we certainly sometimes did. The *Manor Farm* in the village was run by two brothers one of whom, a very gentle kind man, was interested in art and poetry but had little chance to indulge. He had been a walking friend of Robert Graves for the few years when Graves had lived in Islip, a much larger, but still very small, village just under two miles from Woodeaton.

There was, at that time, still the fairly rigid social stratification although not among the local villagers who numbered in total only around 15. The vicar from the neighbouring village, Islip, drove slowly past one day to see what was happening to *Old Upper Farm*. Sheila, who was wearing her workman's overalls and up the ladder pointing the walls standing sideways because of her pregnant belly, shouted good morning as did I, also in workman's overalls. The vicar did not reply while looking disdainfully at us, these working class people, who deigned to speak to him before he had addressed them first.

When our son Mark was born we had him christened, to please my mother, in the very small, beautiful 11th-12th century *Holy Rood Church* in Woodeaton village. The church fortunately has kept most of its original and unusual features, such as the large 14th century wall painting, albeit certainly not a major work of art, of St. Christopher carrying the Christ child across a small stream. The pews have lovely wooden carvings at the aisle, unfortunately mostly riddled now with woodworm. The 17th century bells can still be rung. Since there had not been a vicar in Woodeaton for many years the christening, of course, required the presence of a vicar, who in this case was the Islip vicar who covered several parishes. By then he had discovered I was an Oxford faculty member (an Oxford Don as they are referred to) and his grovelling was at the other end of the greetings spectrum from the previous encounter.

Since we loved the open countryside and the old house, and felt so at home and welcome in the village, we gave our son the name of the village, Woodeaton, as his middle name. The christening of our son, Mark Woodeaton Murray, was a whole village occasion along with other friends from Oxford. The small church was filled, which was very very rare. The Islip church choir came to sing. The singing gave rise to uncontrolled laughter. The choir was up in the very small minstrels' gallery at the back of the church. Because there were so very few services ever held in the church it was completely empty of any people most of the time so there were many bats which permanently inhabited it. They were greatly disturbed by the unusual noise. They flew back and forth up and down the aisle and as they approached the choir loft the choristers all ducked which gave rise to wild voice variations from the Doppler effect. The gentle farmer from Manor Farm had painted a lovely watercolour of the church door which he presented to us to celebrate Mark's christening and which Mark still has: a photo of it is below.

The Argyle family who lived in the large former church manse, felt responsible for the church and, essentially, the welfare of the village: they became family friends. Ina Argyle, originally from Holland, kindly organized the christening and, at the reception in their house afterwards, on behalf of the village, presented Sheila with a small silver mason's trowel in the photo below. They had commissioned a silversmith to make it in recognition of Sheila's masonry skills, originality and total lack of inhibition in doing such unusual manual work, much to the kind amusement and admiration of the village.

Watercolour of the South Chancel Door, *Holy Rood Church*, Woodeaton, Oxford: gift to Mark at his christening, 1962.

Small silver trowel (4 ½ ins. long) a villagers' gift to Sheila at Mark's christening, 1962.

The renovations seemed endless. There was, for example, only one dilapidated toilet bathroom. The first winter was rather primitive, essentially camping, since it was unusually extremely cold with lots of snow and low temperatures as a result of which the pipes to the bathroom froze and the kitchen pipes burst so we had no running water for about a week. Neighbours kindly brought us water.

In part because the old walls were far from straight we removed the plaster to expose the old stones which we then had to point. We developed our own pointing technique, and did it very much more efficiently, and certainly aesthetically better, than the mason who very occasionally we had hired to help with a few heavier things. For some reason no workers, however, wanted to lay concrete floors so we had to do that ourselves. This required taking up the rotten wooden floors, mixing the concrete by hand and wheeling endless barrows of it into the house where we laid three floors. We were rather concerned about the cracks near the bottom of the road wall outside the sitting room and hall so when laying the floor we put in several strong metal girders as in the renovated house photograph below to contain the wall.

Old Upper Farm front after renovation with the chimneys Sheila built, 1963.

The east wing of the house was in an even worse state than the front Wing: it had been used as a barn although in former times it was part of the house. We enclosed the old barn entrance using old oak beams from the wrecked houses in the old village photo above - the one with the horse in the village green. In former times this part of the house was more like a barn which accounts for the old beam above the entrance. Unfortunately all the lintels above the windows and doors had been painted white. It would have been an impossible job to get them back to the original wood which is why we repainted them white.

Old Upper Farm: east wing terrace with the old well, 1963.

Sheila, posing jokingly, with Mark in his old antique pram at the entrance to Old Upper Farm, Woodeaton, Oxford 1963.

While we slaved on the renovations our baby son, Mark, was, helpfully, very happy just sitting and lying in his old pre-war pram with enormous wheels gazing at the birds and the sky.

Mark with his grandparents Sarah Jane and Peter Murray during a visit to Moffat, Scotland in 1963.

Hertford College and Research 1961–3

Each Oxford University College has what is called a *Visitor*. The Visitor is the last refuge of appeal in any unresolvable controversial problem Fellows have in, or with, the college. The Visitor is generally someone of distinction in the outside world, such as in the church or politics, and is practically never ever called upon to resolve a problem. It is essentially an honorary position. Hertford College's Visitor was the Conservative Prime Minister Harold Macmillan. The Visitor came to a special Visitor's Dinner in college once a year. For part of the evening, at that dinner, I was seated beside him. He was not in very good health and resigned shortly afterwards which perhaps in part accounted for his sitting somewhat slumped and dourly in his chair, although I thought it was because he was there only as a duty. The evening was clearly not an occasion he much cared for. I tried very hard to try and get him to talk about life as a politician and his dramatic and varied life but without any success whatsoever. I decided to try another approach. I remembered that he had done "*Greats*" as a student in Oxford and had been an undergraduate at Balliol College one of the top academic colleges for a very long time. *Greats* is the name for the classics degree which lasted 4 years, one more year than the honours degrees in other subjects at the time. It is also called

Lit. Hum, short for *Literae Humaniores*, which is the study of Latin, ancient Greek, ancient Roman and Greek history and philosophy. As a last attempt to try and get him to talk I said: *"Don't you think that Greats is a totally impractical degree for anybody to study who wants go out into the real world?"* He turned to look, scowl rather, at me, and slowly shuffled himself on his chair to be able to look at this academic philistine. He then started a fascinating and highly articulate defence of the degree and criticism of my expressed and, in his view, ignorant uneducated view of the field and the outside world. He totally demolished any mild argument I tried to put up (to try and keep him talking). It was a fascinating monologue which lasted the rest of the time we sat together at dinner. At the end, before we went off, as was customary, to have dessert and port in another room in college, he asked me what my subject was and when I said mathematics, he just said *"Humph"*.

What with all the tutorial teaching and endless house renovations, of which the latter was certainly not Oxford's fault, my research suffered enormously. Not completely, however, since one of the major benefits and pleasures of Oxford High Table socialising is that you meet some interesting and dynamic visitors. Although it was not considered proper to discuss anything serious, like research interests, at High Table I ignored this and always wanted to know what the visitors worked on, their views on research and so on. As an applied mathematician I have always been interested in the application of mathematics and mathematical modelling in a wide variety of fields in the real world and several of my major research projects arose from such High Table conversations.

Although I did not find time to do much research on the area until after returning to Harvard in 1963, an experimental chemical engineer who was a guest at High Table told me about a phenomenon called fluidization. It was my most absorbing research during my time at Hertford and for some time after. I developed the basic theory of fluidization which I published in several articles in 1965. This is an interesting phenomenon widely known to chemical engineers. It is easy to describe. For example, if you have a container full of sand and you blow air up through the sand from the bottom, at a certain, not very large, volume flow rate the sand suddenly rises up slightly and starts to act like a fluid. The reason it does so is that the air causes a drag on each particle of sand which then tries to move with the air. The overall effect is that all the sand particles become effectively separate from each other and give the impression of a fluid. Quick sands are like this with water instead of air.

The process is still widely used industrially in diverse applications. For example a container full of peas subjected to hot air from the bottom separates the peas and cooks them much more efficiently since each pea is surrounded by hot air as it flows up through the peas. Another unusual example is related to a particular small grey fly, about 5mm long, which frequents shorelines. They put their mouth on the wet sand, bounce their body up and down about 5 times per second, which sucks up the water thereby fluidizing the sand and as a result the insect's food comes floating up to the top where the fly eats it.

There was at the time no acceptable theory to explain the fluidization process and the theory and explanation I produced became the standard theory. When visiting Kyoto University in Japan many years later in 1975 to give some lectures in the applications of mathematics to biology and medicine one of the chemical engineering faculty in the audience who was curious about the new field started to talk to me about the Murray theory. I had no idea what he was talking about until he explained it was the theory of fluidization I had worked on more than ten years before. He wondered if I was the 'famous' Murray! Names attached to theories generally do not last long so I doubt if it is still used even in Japan. I have not worked in any fludization theory or its application since the 1960s.

An extremely worrying and unusual consequence of this fluidization research arose a few years after I published it when I was on the faculty of New York University in the late 1960s. A friend and colleague, Ed Spiegel, a Professor of Astronomy at Columbia University, showed me photos of a moonscape which had large circular flat areas with a wall-like ridge around the perimeter. I said that it looked like what happened when a bubble of air in a fluidized bed broke through the surface and the fluidization had been stopped. This air bubble formation happens when more air is used than needed to fluidize the particle material. I had explained this particular phenomenon in one of the fluidization research articles I had published. We thought that the fluidizing gas could perhaps have come from meteors hitting the surface of the moon with enormous velocity and momentum and, as they penetrated the moon's surface, they generated enough heat to produce a sufficiently large amount of hot gas to fluidize the material above it but only for a very short time. Ed and I published a research paper "*Fluidization on the Moon?*" in 1969. Ed, a very practical, and world-renowned scientist, thought we should do some experiments to help to confirm our theory. We decided to use a large plastic square box about three feet square with about two feet of dry cement as the particles we would fluidize. This we did and to our delight when the bubbles broke through the surface and the air immediately turned off to mimic the effect of a meteor they gave rise to what looked very like those circular flat areas with ridges round the edge such as observed on the moon: it was very exciting.

What made the study and the experiments unusual, however, was that about a month after we had both moved on to other research, Ed developed serious problems with his eyes which were extremely red, painful and inflamed. The doctors he consulted did not know what had caused it and for several months he was told that he might actually be going blind, a horrifying thought. We were all extremely worried about it. It was after several tests that a new specialist Ed had gone to consult asked him if he'd been near a lot of dust before the problem had developed. Ed remembered that when we were doing the experiments he had sometimes leaned over the edge of the fluidized cement and asked me to increase or decrease the airflow to see the effect on the number of bubbles and on the surface patterns. It turned out that it was the cement "dust" which was the cause of the problem. Within a few weeks of basic eye drop treatment the whole problem was cleared up to the immense relief of us all.

Although I found the atmosphere and intellectual life in Hertford College very congenial and the students bright, and necessarily hard working, I felt that I did not want to spend my career in Hertford in primarily a teaching career role with so little time for research. So, much to the displeasure of the college Principal, Dr. Ferrar, I decided to resign with effect from the end of the following academic year, in 1963: such a thing was extremely rare since, when appointed to such a Fellowship it was traditionally essentially for the rest of your academic life. Formally I had been appointed for *"21 years in the first instance"*. Faculty were never fired except for *"blatant and persistent immorality"*. Some years later after we had returned to Oxford on my election to a Fellowship at Corpus Christi College, at dinner one night I asked the University Registrar, an Honorary Fellow of Corpus, Sir Douglas Veale, what "blatant and persistent immorality" was and he jokingly said: "being caught more than once soliciting dogs for sex on the High in the middle of the day". (The "High" is the traditional name for the High Street in the middle of the town on which there are several colleges.) Since essentially no faculty member was ever fired I also asked him if anybody had ever been fired. He said: *"Yes, of course! There was a case - before the war."* That time he was serious. He told me that it was a chemistry faculty lecturer who said that he had discovered and developed a new method for refining sugar. He demonstrated it by inserting the raw sugar into the apparatus he had built and when it finally came out the other end it was pure refined sugar. The only problem was that the refined sugar had been bought in a grocery store and inserted into the apparatus.

My resigning was considered highly unusual, and certainly irrational, since the general view of people in the university, universities rather, was that no one would seriously contemplate resigning when they had a lifetime faculty appointment in such a prestigious university. I formally gave notice of resigning from the summer of 1963 and started to look for another possible academic position to start in the autumn of 1963 but not in Britain. I thought seriously about applying for an advertised named professorship in the University of Melbourne. That thought was quickly squashed by the three people I wrote to see if they would write letters of recommendation, if they were asked to by the University of Melbourne. To my astonishment two of them immediately wrote back simply saying "*Absolutely not.*" When I replied wondering why, they both replied saying, in effect, that Melbourne was the back of beyond and they couldn't possibly help me go there. At the time, they thought Melbourne was an academic backwater and I would be burying myself. Coincidently two years later, when I was a professor at the University of Michigan, we met the man, an Englishman from King's College, Newcastle, whom I knew, who had been appointed to the Melbourne professorship. He confirmed my friends' views: he was trying very hard to get a position to return to England's academia, which he eventually managed. For many years now, of course, the situation could not be more different: the University of Melbourne is a major world-class university. The third person I had contacted, was Professor George Carrier at Harvard University, who also knew about my fluidization work. He immediately replied inviting me to come as a senior research visitor to Harvard for a year and take time deciding what to do. He added that, unfortunately, the position I had been offered four years earlier had been filled. So, Sheila and I, with our very small and much loved son, Mark Woodeaton Murray, sailed off to America again, in the late summer of 1963, this time on the *USS United States*.

VII

Peripatetic Odyssey from Oxford to Oxford via America and Paris 1963-1970

The voyage back to New York on the SS *United States* was nothing like as luxurious as the one I had on the *Queen Elizabeth* a few years before in 1956. Not only that, the weather was wildly stormy the whole 5 day trip. Sheila and I were seasick practically the whole time while Mark was totally unaffected. We sat miserably on deck chairs with a rope tied to my chair and the other end to a walker. Mark, who still could not walk easily without a walker, happily wandered around the deck for hours.

Back in Cambridge we quickly found a small apartment a few minutes walk from Harvard and I was again invited to be a faculty member of Leverett House but now being married I was less involved in the House life. My research really took off with so much of the time no longer spent renovating houses. The autumn in Harvard in 1963 was a spectacularly beautiful one and we quickly fitted back into the social life of the university and the Cambridge atmosphere. Since the position that I had been offered 4 years before had been filled I had to start looking for another position almost right away. I had two offers and decided to accept a tenured Associate Professorship at the University of Michigan in Ann Arbor. It was, however, in Engineering Mechanics since I had a colleague there, Professor Chia-Shun Yih, an internationally renowned fluid dynamicist, who, with his family, became our closest friends in Ann Arbor and lifelong friends. It was also the department where, in effect, genuine applied mathematics research was done.

We rented a house for a few months and started to look for one to buy as much in the country as possible. We found one, in the country, near a small town called Chelsea but, fortunately, this time we decided it was stupid, particularly with our already peripatetic academic life. Ann Arbor in those days was a very much smaller town than it is now. We soon decided it would be much more sensible to look for a house within walking distance of the university and we managed to buy a house about half a mile across a park from the university and my department there:

houses in this area were generally not on the market more than a few hours. When we were looking for such a house we went to the town's newspaper office on a Friday, around noon when the weekly paper came out. I waited in the phone booth while Sheila got the newspaper which had the advertisements for houses for sale. We immediately scanned them and during our second week found one advertised which was on Granger Avenue the road along the park. I phoned and offered the asking price without seeing it and we immediately went there to sign a contract. When we sold the house three years later it was sold, for the asking price, similarly within an hour of the advertisement coming out. There were several backup buyers who were surprised we wouldn't accept their higher offer because we had not yet signed the formal contract. There was no need, of course, to have a real estate agent with their outrageous commissions as compared to those charged in Europe.

Mark, aged 3, in our Ann Arbor house and on his train on which he became astonishingly skilled, 1965.

It was our first experience of the accepted lack of privacy in the US with the house's small garden that was open to the neighbours' gardens. We decided to build a fence between us but before we did we asked the neighbours who, without exception, were delighted to have at least some privacy. Mark, who was almost four at the time had friends along the street and they played together totally unsupervised: it never occurred to any of us to worry about their being on their own in the park or road.

Mark's closest friend was Suzi, the lively fun daughter of a dentist neighbour across the street: a photo of them is below.

Mark, with his ginger-haired close friend Suzi on Granger Avenue, Ann Arbor, 1965.

Sheila in our Ann Arbor home garden, 1965.

How Chia-Shun Yih and I first became friends was a consequence of the generally accepted practice in academia at the time of giving common American names to academic Chinese visitors and immigrants following the defeat of Chiang Kai-shek by the Communists in 1949. Chia-Shun was a brilliant researcher and lecturer. In 1948 he had been awarded one of the few Chinese scholarships to pursue research abroad; he chose the USA. Chia-Shun was assigned the ghastly name of "Gus". When I was at Harvard in the late 1950s I was invited to give lectures at various places across the country, all set up by Professor George Carrier. He had arranged, through Chia-Shun, for me to give a lecture in the University of Michigan. On meeting "Gus", who could not have been more welcoming, there was an immediate warmth and rapport. I asked him what his real name was and he said that no one ever used it. I insisted he tell me and from then on I called him Chia-Shun and used it whenever I talked of Ann Arbor or of him in academia. When I heard anyone call him Gus I asked why they didn't call him by his proper name, which was very easy to say and so much nicer and friendly. Within a surprisingly short time the academic world always referred to him as Chia-Shun Yih. When I joined his department in 1963 I never heard anyone refer to him by other than his proper name. It became something of a crusade for me with Chinese colleagues. Although it no doubt would have happened anyway, since now, with some exceptions, Chinese academics are almost all called by

179

their proper names, even if not the Chinese way of last name first nor with the correct pronunciation.

JDM in our garden in
Ann Arbor, 1966.

Chia-Shun Yih and Mark planting a tree in
Chia-Shun and Shirley's large garden, 1967.

Shirley and Chia-Shun Yih, Sheila and JDM, Ann Arbor, 1967.

Chia-Shun was an immensely cultured and kind man. He and Mark had a particularly warm relationship as is clear in the photo above. When we stayed with Chia-Shun and his warm hospitable and very nice family (his wife, Shirley, came from Maine) he would occasionally talk of his life in China and the culture before 1949 – even singing in traditional Chinese style on one dinner occasion. He came from the upper administrative strata and so it was well known when he decided not to return to China after the defeat of the Nationalists and Chiang-Kei-shek's flight to Taiwan. He had been married in China but when he did not return his wife divorced him. After President Nixon's visit to China, it was then possible for some of the distinguished Chinese academics in the USA to return to China for visits: Chia-Shun was one of the first. In the local newspaper, where he grew up, there was a photo of him with Chou En-lai. With the fame and importance of Chou En-lai and the culture at the time, Chia-Shun's former brother-in-law wanted Chia-Shun to remarry his ex-wife!

It unfortunately became clear towards the end of my second year that accepting a position at the University of Michigan had been a mistake since, although I was an applied mathematician, I was not allowed to teach anything that had mathematics in the title or syllabus or even in the general applied mathematical area since I was officially in Engineering Mechanics: applied mathematics was officially in the Mathematics Department. At the time the faculty in that area in the Mathematics Department was mainly second rate and the courses taught certainly not at the forefront of the field. I would not have been particularly happy in that department either. Although at the end of the first year I was promoted to a full professorship in Engineering Mechanics it was becoming clear to us that we would not stay and I would have to seek yet another position. The year, however, was important in my moving even further from the field of my recent research and from the subject of my thesis, fluid dynamics.

It seemed to me that the future of innovative and real applied mathematics should be practical, in interdisciplinary science, and in a major innovative way, specifically biology and medicine. Much has changed in the Mathematics Department since then. A former doctoral student of mine, Trachette Jackson, who did a Ph.D. on modelling certain aspects of cancer, has been a full professor in the mathematics department for some years now. Much later in the early 1990s when I retired early from Oxford to spend some time in American academia again, I was chastised by one of the Michigan mathematics faculty for not getting in contact with him since the mathematics department would have been delighted to have had me join their department.

Although the research I did with Sydney Goldstein in the late 1950's was related to biochemistry it was the development of the new mathematical techniques which was the prime object. The first real biological problem I worked on while at the University of Michigan was how oxygen got into pea nodules, a problem suggested by one of the senior professors in botany who contacted me thinking I was a graduate student: he offered me $2 and hour! It turned out to be a somewhat easy mathematical modelling problem but it was the first genuinely biological one which solved the biological question which had been posed. A more challenging problem came from a faculty member in Anatomy, namely how specific back injuries occurred with pilot ejection seats, why they were so dangerous and what should be done to prevent them. Along with a younger colleague friend, an Assistant Professor in my department, Y. King Liu, we showed how the mechanics of the process and the spinal structure would generally result in very severe non-vertical back stresses which cause the injury. Our anatomy colleague said he would carry out experiments to check our predictions. I wondered who on earth would participate in them. He told me how. His experiments involved strapping unclaimed cadavers (from the mortuary in Detroit) to an elevator chair with strain gauges on their backs to measure the changing strain during sudden stops of the dropping elevator thus mimicking the pilot ejection process. Both King Liu and I passed up the chance to watch the experiments. This work was a major turning point in King Liu's career. Although he certainly should have, he did not get tenure at the University of Michigan and moved to Tulane University where he became an expert on whiplash problems and a regular witness in court cases.

There was a laboratory in the Mechanical Engineering Department in the University of Michigan and also a photographic dark room which was practically never used. It initiated my interest in serious photography, black and white of course. I spent many weekends developing film and playing with development techniques: I found it immensely satisfying and relaxing. Since we went back to Britain every summer I took many photos of the countryside around Moffat, a particularly photogenic place and of my family. I had a large format camera with old-fashioned 4x5 inch negative plates. The photo below of our son Mark when he was about three to four years old captures his life-long gentleness and warmth. The top right one of Sheila in New York is one of the "artistic" ones which captures her beauty and gentleness.

Photography was not enough to keep all of my interests in doing things with my hands so we started designing and making furniture. We began with an 8-foot long table of American black walnut. We got the wood from a sawmill a few miles from Ann Arbor. The owner, a man of around 70 had six fingers, distributed between his two hands. We saw why when he cut some wood for us on an ancient, incredibly dangerous, saw run by an old tractor and a ludicrously long (around 15 feet or so) old pulley with not the slightest safety feature anywhere. His hands were regularly only a few inches from the saw blade.

Mark, Ann Arbor, c1967.

Sheila, Ann Arbor, c1966.

JDM, Ann Arbor, c1967.

Sheila, Ann Arbor, 1966.

We had the idea of cutting a wide beautifully grained black walnut board into two along its length and inserting another wide flat edged black walnut one in between so that the finished top looked like a slice from an enormous hardwood walnut tree a yard in diameter with the natural irregular sides of the tree. The table almost seemed to have a personality. There is a photo of a similar type coffee table in Chapter 13. I thought we were somewhat ahead with a new original style but I learned about 50 years later that a similar idea had also been developed by a fashionable furniture maker, George Nagashima, in Pennsylvania. When we were back in England some years later we made other "antique" pieces from ancient 16th and 17th century oak which came from demolished buildings in Oxfordshire and Devon. The large dining room table shown in Chapter 13 is an example: it is Elizabethan in style. Our first such table was one we made from a slice of a large oak tree which we saw at a coffin maker's sawmill after Sheila met me at the Southampton dock on first returning from America in 1959. We left it in Old Upper Farm, the early 17th century house we renovated in Woodeaton village near Oxford.

In 1966, the year after our very lively and fun daughter, Sarah Corinne Jo, was born, I again started to look for other possible faculty positions, specifically in the US, but only in mathematics departments. In 1967 a position was advertised at New York University which seemed a good place to be, not only for its reputation, but because it was easy then to fly back and forth to England. Also, during that year I applied for, and was awarded, a Guggenheim Memorial Fellowship which, during the year, allowed me to go anywhere in the world I wanted to, do whatever research I wanted to do or start and, highly unusually, without any report whatsoever being required after the end of the Fellowship. Not surprisingly there is always a vast number of applications. Guggenheim Fellowships are awarded in a wide spectrum of areas, such as in the Fine Arts, Religion, the Sciences, Film and so on. In my case tenure of the fellowship, as well as benefiting my research enormously, changed our whole future life in a way we never envisaged and for which we have been ever grateful.

I was invited to New York University for an interview for the position, a professorship in mathematics. On arriving in New York the evening before I was worried I might not sleep and be fresh for the interview so I took what was a new experience for me, namely a sleeping pill provided by our doctor in Ann Arbor. I then thought that it was probably not enough so I took two. They worked far too well, so that in the interview the next day I could barely focus and have little idea of what I answered to the questions. After lunch, however, I was, compos mentis again and I was offered the position in the mathematics department. So, I gave notice to leave the University of Michigan as from the end of the 1967 academic year much to the regret of my friend Chia-Shun Yih, but he was very understanding of my reasons.

Sarah, New York, 1968.   JDM, New York, 1968.

My parents were pleased we were moving closer even if it was only to New York. Unfortunately with all the moving around we missed their 50th wedding anniversary in Moffat: there is a photo below. They had been so happily married to each other and were, by then, living with no financial worries and enjoying their grandchildren who lived so close to them. The photo of them below was on a visit to one of the old ruined cathedrals, typically destroyed by the Calvinists, in the Scottish lowlands.

During my time in Hertford College, Oxford, I had become a friend of another applied mathematician in Oxford, Dr. Alan Tayler. He knew of my disappointment with the University of Michigan and in late 1966 wrote to ask if I would like to be put up as the second choice for the *Distinguished Visiting Fellowship* in his college, St. Catherine's College, a new Oxford college officially founded in 1956. The candidates suggested for this prestigious Fellowship were all very well known international figures in the world. Alan argued that the chances of any of them accepting was low so the college would then have to seriously consider the second rung of candidates: that is exactly what happened. I was awarded it and in the late summer of 1967 we went back to spend the first term of the Oxford University academic year, Michaelmas Term, in St. Catherine's College, Oxford.

The college is a dramatic modern architectural masterpiece situated in a huge meadow. It was designed by the Danish architect, Arne Jacobsen, who was a controversial choice at the time. Jacobsen played a role in the design of everything including the furniture in Hall and even the cutlery. The very modern soupspoons, however, were designed only for right-handed people, which for me as a left-hander, posed a slight problem. Although fairly ambidextrous, drinking from an unbalanced spoon full of soup pointing the wrong way round was a little tricky. The head butler at High Table who noticed it afterwards always kindly had another spoon brought to me wherever I was seated.

JDM's parents' 50th wedding anniversary, Moffat, Scotland, 1967.

Catz, as it is known in Oxford, was a very lively college with lots of visitors. Unlike most other colleges at the time there were occasional social gatherings of the Fellows and the graduate students, who had their own Middle Common Room. The graduate students were a lively diverse group. During the time there one of them I met was Benazir Bhutto, the newly elected President of the Oxford Student Union, a position for which she had very professionally lobbied. She was already a tough, rather cold, unlikeable, very bright, self centred and highly focused politician.

That time in Oxford was a pleasure as well as being extremely productive from a research point of view. I visited a lot of other universities, giving talks. We all had a particularly enjoyable time except poor Mark who started school that autumn but desperately didn't want to leave us: it was his first school.

I had no teaching nor any formal responsibilities in the college. I was just part of the academic social life. High Table dining was particularly lively with Allan Bullock (later Lord Bullock) a very dynamic man primarily responsible for the official acceptance and founding of the College. He had written the fascinating book on Hitler: A *Study in Tyranny* which we had read. He thrived on College politics and found Governing Body a constant stimulating challenge. I could never understand that but he defended it enthusiastically to Sheila at dinner one evening at the house we were renting. I was clearly missing something. The unexpected implanted seed of that time in Oxford was that I wanted to return to Oxford permanently, but only if the right position came up in an ancient college, acceptable to me, and with high academic standing.

Sarah and Mark , Oxford 1968 a photo which captures   Mark, Paris, 1968
their warmth.

Guggenheim Fellowship in France and Italy

Although it had not been my first choice from a research point of view, I had arranged to spend the rest of the academic year from January 1968 in Paris, at the highly respected Pasteur Institute where I had been in touch with two biologists whom I thought might be interested in interdisciplinary collaboration. We had found a romantically situated large expensive apartment, certainly in need of major electrical renovation as we discovered, overlooking the *Place Maubert* alongside the *Boulevard St.*

187

Germain. Although the Pasteur Institute had many internationally distinguished scientists I unfortunately had chosen two of the second-raters and after a few visits decided it could never be interesting, challenging and productive so I simply carried out research in our apartment.

Initially, when setting up the Guggenheim Fellowship collaboration, I had written to the distinguished American biologist, Professor Jeffries Wyman, formerly a professor at Harvard University for 23 years, a Member of the American National Academy of Science but then living in Rome and a professor on the faculty of the University of Rome. Jeffries had been the first scientific adviser to the US Embassy in Paris. He loved living in Europe so much that he decided to stay and resigned from Harvard.

Jeffries was a brilliant scientist whose work I knew and which overlapped with my current interest in something called facilitated diffusion. It is related, among other things, to why we do not get muscle cramps more often, why the sea snake doesn't get the bends and in many more biophysical phenomena. Basically, in the case of muscles, it explains how oxygen gets into the muscles since only diffusion is not enough. For some reason my original letter to him had never arrived, not unusual in Italy at the time. When I wrote again after the Pasteur Institute disappointment I got an enthusiastic reply and an immediate invitation to go to Rome which I did on several occasions that spring.

Jeffries Wyman was a truly distinguished, internationally highly respected biologist who had closely collaborated in France with Dr. Monod, a Nobel Prize Winner. He had accepted a permanent professorship in Rome where he remained for 25 years. While there, he was elected to the Italian Academy of Science, the *Accademia Nazionale dei Lincei*. Although not a theoretician, Jeffries was very interested in mathematical modelling and enthusiastic in starting a major collaboration together, which we did and wrote a research article together. It became one of the general areas I worked in for a few years. We kept in touch and I saw him each time I was in Rome and later in Paris after he had retired.

Sheila and I became family friends of Jeffries, and particularly Sheila with his incredibly warm, lively, kind and fascinating Russian wife, Olga whom he had met when living in Paris. Olga was a Romanov princess whose family fled to Paris in 1917. She had been officially engaged to a Lithuanian prince when she was 5 years old! Jeffries, who came from a highly respected old New England family, was immensely rich and, surprisingly, unbelievably mean with anything associated with money, even research grants. When I was staying with them in their apartment in the *Piazza Farnese* in Rome, Jeffries asked, before dinner the first night, if I'd like some sherry. He then proceeded to pour out the smallest glass of sherry I'd ever seen. Olga, clearly used to this, immediately took the bottle from him and we all had a decent sherry. It was clearly a problem Jeffries had. When they came to visit us in Oxford for a week a few years later, Jeffries went to stay with an old academic colleague who was the President of St. John's College while Olga stayed with us. It turned out that she had to look for clothes in second hand shops in Paris because Jeffries did not want to spend money on new clothes. Sheila made her a dress when she was staying with us.

Olga's description of the Russian community in Paris was fascinating. She described how many of the men, who fled with them when the revolution started in 1917, thought they would eventually return to their former status and positions in Russia while it was the women who were the realists. At dinner one evening in Rome, when I was visiting and staying with Olga and Jeffries, a cousin of the leader of the Italian Socialist Party was going to be there. Olga proudly wore the piece of jewellery she still had from her family, a magnificent royal Romanov broach and she was clearly ready to defend her views against the socialists, as well she could. Politics, however, did not come up. Soon after Olga died Jeffries, who was then in his late 80's moved into the apartment of Olga's sister in Paris who felt obligated to look after him which she did with great kindness until he died in 1995 at the age of 94. Sheila and I visited him there the year before he died. It was so sad. His mind had deteriorated. He could no longer hold a conversation and was totally absorbed in looking at his lower leg with a flashlight since he thought he saw cells flying into the air from an open sore which was clearly gangrenous. He could not walk and had to be carried everywhere in the apartment by a male nurse. It was incredibly hard on Olga's very kind sister.

Our life in Paris in 1968 was an interesting and immensely enjoyable one, to begin with anyway. We thought Mark and Sarah should go to a French school and I duly went off to talk to the appropriate authority together with the required birth certificates, smallpox vaccination certificates and so on. It was my first experience with the incredible, and arrogant, bureaucracy of France, something about which all our later French friends also complained. Everything was acceptable except for the smallpox vaccination certificate even though it was written in English and in French. The problem which made Mark and Sarah unacceptable for a state school, was that their certificates were written in English first rather than French! It was the only time in our many years in France that I showed a controlled loss of patience but it achieved nothing. French bureaucrats, the "*fonctionnaires*" are all-powerful and, of course, from their point of view, never wrong. So, we looked around the *Place Maubert* area and enrolled Mark and Sarah in a small school run very strictly by nuns: it was just a very short walk from the *Place Maubert* with a small playground in the shadow of *Notre Dame* cathedral which was literally just across the Seine from the school. They kindly accepted Sarah, even though she was not yet three, because she was already toilet trained. Sarah started to speak French like a native. Hearing her shout in French "*Attend Mark*" (Wait Mark) was an odd sensation for us. Each day when school ended the parents had to be waiting outside the large wooden double doors, essentially a gate. You could look through a very small window to see if the children were waiting. They had to sit demurely on either side of the hall until their parents came. Most days we would see Sarah running all over the place, the only child, with the severe first year teacher shouting to her to sit down. Mark was always sitting as he should. They both loved the school. Mark learned to write, French of course, in the required elegant script the pupils had to do each day; it's a skill - the writing - he has never lost but sadly now no longer practices.

Mark and Sarah were always very close with a genuine warmth and concern for each other and, when children, Mark was incredibly protective. This is clear in photos of them together as children, here and in Chapter 13 when they would go walks and Mark would always hold her hand if in the city. Even as a young baby Sarah's face would light up whenever she saw Mark. By the time they were teenagers they had developed very different interests and impressive talents but the warmth between them has never waned.

During the children's time in school we went all over Paris and got to know it incredibly well, walking and riding in the large standing open back area of the buses which were prevalent at the time. Most of the walking trips were with Mark and Sarah. A favourite place was the park at the bottom of the *Ile de la Cité*, only a few minutes walk from our apartment in the *Place Maubert*. The *Ile*, which always had a spectrum of Paris life from the man relaxing with a bottle of beer, to hugging and kissing couples oblivious to the rest of the world, models being photographed and so on as in the photo below. In one of the photos below the man who had been sitting on the bank drinking is drunkenly lying asleep just in front of the posing model. From this part of the *Ile de la Cité* you have a dramatic view of the impressive buildings on the banks of the Seine with the magnificent dome of the *Institut de France* which houses the five awesome French Academies. It never remotely occurred to me that many years later I would be elected and inaugurated as a Foreign Member of the French Academy under that huge dome and heralded in by the long trumpets of the elaborately dressed trumpeters in the presence of the spectacularly traditionally dressed Academicians in their gold encrusted suits.

We had a partial view of *Notre Dame* from one of the rooms in our apartment. Every night it was dramatically illuminated although the most dramatic view was a few minutes walk from our apartment to the path along the Seine as in the photo which I had to wait until our return to New York before I could develop and print because it was black and white film. *Notre Dame*, which was started in the high Middle Ages around 1160 was a favourite place for us all. Then one could wander practically everywhere in the cathedral so we sometimes climbed up to get dramatic views of the whole of Paris at our feet and a slight mediaeval frisson of fear of the gargoyles which are so dramatic and all quite different. The meticulousness of the sculptor is so impressive. Even the back is carved with realism, a feature totally unseen by the people below.

We would have stayed in Paris with much pleasure for the rest of my time on the Guggenheim Fellowship, since my research was also going very well, had it not been for the 1968 student protests – the "*manifestations*". A large number of police, those that controlled protests as opposed to the gendarmes, regularly arrived in their sinister looking small black buses which they parked in the *Place Maubert* and on the small narrow street *rue des Carmes* below our apartment. It gave us an insight into how the government, or possibly only the police, view protests. Many of the police wore quite short black capes which hung amazingly straight until we realized that there were weights, probably lead, around the bottom. Many of them also wore knuckledusters. We saw quite a few of these protests from our windows. The vast number of protesters, mainly students, marched along the *Boulevard St. Germain*, which leads into the *Place Maubert*, always loudly chanting "*Vietcong vaincra*" (Vietcong will overcome) which they eventually did of course. The police, often standing together in the small street leading in to the *Place Maubert*, were clearly going to suddenly confront the protesters: it was all very scary. It was the tear gas, however, which drifted up into our apartment, which was the final factor in our deciding we had to leave. About a month later, after we had left, the protests got very much worse and more violent. So much so that we heard some years later from a French research collaborator and

Paris: *Isle de la Cité*, 1968.

Mark and Sarah with the fashion model being photographed with the beer drinker, on the left, having fallen asleep in front of her feet, 1968.

family friend in Grenoble, Professor Jacques Demongeot, who at the time was doing national service in Germany, that his father wanted him to somehow come back to France since he seriously believed, as did many, that there was going to be another French Revolution. Unlike in Britain, it is traditional for students in France to be politically active with protest marches.

Notre Dame gargoyles overlooking Paris, 1968.

Notre Dame cathedral from the bank of the Seine, 1968.

Mediaeval sculpture

It was when we lived in Ann Arbor that our enthusiasm and appreciation of mediaeval art and sculpture got a major boost during a visit, and subsequent ones, to the Detroit Museum of Art which has a splendid collection of mediaeval art. Later, the Cloisters Museum in New

York enthused us more as did the fascinating public lecture series, "*Civilisation*", given in New York, when we lived there, by the art historian Professor Sir Kenneth Clark. However, it was during our time in Paris that our infatuation with old houses, mediaeval churches and cathedrals, small castles, mediaeval sculpture and so on could be easily and seriously indulged. We had, of course, from the old period house point of view, our exposure with our early 17th century house in the village of Woodeaton near Oxford but a significant contribution was a French television programme on the huge number of period properties in France which were in danger of collapsing, being destroyed or demolished thereby losing a huge part of French history. We bought the book, published from the programme, "*Chefs d'Oevres en Péril*" (Major Works in Danger) which listed a vast number of threatened buildings, mainly very old ones. We thought that we could keep a foot in Europe if we found one of these we could buy and renovate. So, we started a regular monthly few days pilgrimage to various parts of the country looking at many of these old buildings and touring many of the ancient towns and religious sites. Some, alas, would never be restored. One magnificently situated building south of the *Massif Central* was an old, large stone former mansion, dramatically situated on top of a hill with it's own windmill on the next hill. As we got closer we saw that the roof was a makeshift one and the door was half open. It was all very romantic. As we opened the door wide we saw in front of us the most magnificent very wide, approximately 3 metre in width, very elegant spiral stone staircase. It was the highlight, the only one unfortunately. The staircase ended about 5 metres up and that was all there was inside the whole house. It was essentially a large open space but with a magnificent staircase. The properties we ended up looking at were, without exception, certainly "*en peril*" but either impossible to renovate or ugly or total ruins. We decided that it was impractical so, on the trips for the next three months, we simply toured the mediaeval sites and developed our genuine love of France, and which we indulged, as we had wished. Many years later we bought an ancient 14th century house, formerly a fortified manor house, with other mediaeval buildings on the property in the Dordogne which we renovated and had for 15 years as described in Chapter 13.

VII. *Peripatetic Odyssey from Oxford to Oxford via America and Paris 1963-1970*

Mont St. Michel, France, 1968

Mont St. Michel, France, 1968.

A typical empty staircase in *Mont St. Michel*, France 1968.

Prior to the more violent protests in 1968 in Paris, and elsewhere in France, we had made several trips around France to see many, mainly untouched, mediaeval villages, isolated churches and major cathedrals which at that time were always open. I indulged my enthusiasm for photography while Sheila, Mark and Sarah wandered all over them, and, what is impossible now, we had most of them totally to ourselves. It was in the early spring of 1968, a time when the number of tourists was minute. We were enthralled at many of the major mediaeval sites and cathedrals, particularly *Autun, Chartres, Conques, Mont St. Michel, Vézelay, Tournus, Issoire, St. Nectaire* and many others. The dramatic cathedral of *Mont St. Michel*, as in the photos above, even in April was empty. It is situated at the end of a promontory which was cut off when the tide came in. We stayed in the small hillside town below the cathedral. Now the number of tourists each year is more than two million.

On one trip we went southeast stopping at *Autun*, to see the 12th century Cathedral of *St. Lazare* with its beautiful imaginative Romanesque sculptures which rank with the most original, very human, superb mediaeval sculptures of any cathedral or church, even *Chartres*, that we have ever seen. Uniquely the sculptor is known. On the west façade is written in Latin: *"Gislebertus hoc fecit"* (Gislebertus did this). One example, now in the museum, but originally on the lintel of the north door shows a guilty sensual Eve furtively taking the apple while another is of the very human waking of the three sleeping Magi by an angel. Gislebertus carved the sculptures around 1120-1140. Fortunately you could take photos everywhere then, including the museum.

Autun: Musée Rolin. Cathedral of St. *Lazare:* Temptation of Eve taking the apple.

Autun: Musée Rolin. Cathedral of St. *Lazare:* Waking of the three Magi.

Chartres, of course, was a must and again it was practically empty. The sculptures are so expressive with different human sentiments depending on the angle you look at them, sometimes arrogant, sometimes kind. Two of them are in the photos below. The last time we went to Chartres in the winter in 2008 it was very different. Getting there was a challenge because of the incredibly complicated system of one-way streets. We asked a local resident how to get up to the cathedral who said the one way roads were irritatingly constantly being changed and she wasn't sure if she was up to date but told us what she thought.

Chartres Cathedral sculptures, Chartres 1968.

It was in the High and Late mediaeval periods which saw the increasing influence of the church and ever increasing corruption. There was also a profound religious change in people's attitude towards Christianity. The former awe and fear of the severe judgmental Christ was replaced with a more emotional dynamism. This is clearly seen in the changing ecclesiastic architecture from the solid Romanesque to the soaring Gothic cathedrals such as *Notre Dame*, or the very much less known Abbey church of *Sainte Foy* in *Conques* which was started in the late 11th century but with clear Romanesque influence. The small isolated mediaeval hillside village of Conques, in the Aveyron in the southwest, is dramatically situated in the mountains with narrow streets and, at the time, no traffic was allowed. It was on one of the pilgrimage routes to *Santiago de Compostela*. It has some dramatic sculptures and a magnificent interior. A church had actually been built on the site much earlier and known as *Sainte Foye* specifically to house the saint's relics which had been stolen by a monk to put in the church. The old church was demolished so as to build the present much larger abbey church as in the photo. There are many others on the various routes to *Santiago de Compostela*.

Cathedral of St. Foy, Conques, France. 1968   *Black Madonna*, Rocamadour, France.

In this period there are more sculptures of Christ suffering on the cross for mankind's sins. However, the Virgin Mary came more and more into the picture since it was believed that if she was convinced and sympathetic to a sinner she petitioned Christ for forgiveness. *Notre Dame* in Paris is dedicated to the Virgin Mary. There are hundreds of shrines to Mary all over Europe credited with miracles.

In the small isolated hillside town of *Rocamadour* in the *Lot* in Southwest France there is a beautiful 12th century Black Madonna in the church of *Notre Dame*. There are a huge number of Black Madonnas in France. There is a legend from this period that the Devil complained to God that Mary was taking away many of his strong candidates for Hell.

We drove further south and had a surprising personal insight into how uneducated mediaeval people must have viewed some of these magnificent sculptures with religious messages. A major attraction in *Beaune*, the wine capital of Burgundy, is the *Hôtel-Dieu de Beaune*, a huge 15th century alms house and hospital built for the poor which housed, among other things, the enormous dramatic *Le Dernier Jugement* (The Last

199

Judgement) by Rogier van der Weyden with its central panel showing the weighing of the souls. Our 3 year old daughter, Sarah, casually stopped in front of it and was suddenly transfixed. The visual effect must have been similar to those 15th century people who first saw it – horror, fascination and fear. We literally had to drag her away. She was completely absorbed by the imagery, how on one side the figures were happy while on the other they were terrified. Who were these people she wondered?

We left Paris in the spring of 1968 when the student protests were becoming ever more violent, as were the police. Cobblestones were hurled at the police who responded with tear gas and physical attacks. It was certainly time to leave the *Place Maubert* which was very much in the centre of the student protests and violence so we went back to England, specifically Devon since we had decided that we would like to keep a foot in England and be able to spend summers there away from New York. We started to look for an old house and quickly found a remarkable, many centuries old one, a ruin rather, called *Totleigh Barton*, together with an ancient old barn, ruined pigsties and the toilet an old outhouse, in one of the beautiful and most rural parts of North Devon near a small market hill town, called *Hatherleigh*. I describe in Chapter 13 our unusual life there, spanning several years, the foundation of the *Arvon Foundation* (the immensely successful charity foundation which runs residential courses to promote creative writing mentioned in Chapter 5) and the close and fascinating friends we made which lasted for the rest of their lives.

New York 1968-70

The apartment you could have in the university housing owned by New York University was determined by a lottery although your academic position played a part: I was a full professor which helped. Even so, we were also very lucky to get a large three-bedroom apartment on the 29th floor of one of the new 30 story apartment blocks a few minutes walk from Washington Square and the Courant Institute of Mathematical Sciences where I had an office. In the middle of the three apartment buildings area is a huge impressive Picasso sculpture. The apartment faced west and got the most magnificent sunsets, filtered through the pollution from the oil refineries in New Jersey. The highway past them was known as Cancer Alley.

Life in New York was certainly not dull but not the easiest with young children. New York was not as safe in the late 1960s as it is now. Mark went to school, PS41 (Public School 41), a few blocks up Manhattan. As

Sheila and Sarah walked him there they regularly passed numerous down and outs sleeping on the benches in Washington Square who, when awake, always spoke to Sarah who was at their own head height. Being a very sociable little girl, she always wanted to stop and talk. Sarah was used to the down and outs and drunks from the Bowery, which was close by and very much the depressing downmarket area it had been for years. The down and outs occasionally came into the children's sand pit close to the buildings and on one occasion one offered some of the children a drink of methylated spirit, a common drink of the poorer alcoholics at the time. Parents had to keep a very sharp eye on the children.

PS41 was certainly not a great school. In case we stayed in New York, we had put an application in to the United Nations School which had bilingual teaching in English and French. After being interviewed Mark was accepted but after we met the headmaster, an arrogant, not very bright man, we decided not to accept the place. From our point of view, and Mark's, there was, fortunately, a teachers' strike in the public schools which lasted quite a long time. A few of the teachers, who lived in or near the university buildings decided to run an informal school which was excellent and untrammelled by the ludicrous inhibiting Teachers' Union rules. Mark fortunately never needed to go back to PS41.

Mark and Sarah in our New York apartment, 1968.

New York was a different world to anything we had known. It was very tough and you had to be careful where you walked, especially in the evening. There was an unwritten rule when my colleagues and I were leaving the Courant Institute of Mathematical Sciences, close to Washington Square, to walk back to our apartments. If there were only three of us, we took the longer better-lit way, while if there were more we could go the shortest route. Much of that part of New York was undeveloped and still full of warehouses. Across the street from my room in the Institute on Mercer Street there was a rather grubby building. As soon as the lights went out in the building numerous rats immediately appeared everywhere running along the windowsills and the tables inside that you could see.

Sarah adjusted to the kindergarten certainly much better than Mark at PS41. She came home one day and said: "Richard hit me." Full of sympathy we asked whether it was sore and what did she do. She casually said: "I hit him right back". Sarah would have survived in New York.

Occasionally we had a baby sitter for the children when we went to the theatre, or evening lectures, such as the splendid series, *Civilisation*, by Kenneth Clark. One of the babysitters we had was a 15 year old boy, the son of one of the university faculty. We asked him once: "Do you ever go out to the country?" to which he replied, "Yea, I went once. It's boring, there's nothing to do."

Living in an apartment was a new experience for us and we all missed having space. The apartment had two bathrooms so I decided to use one as a dark room and a small workshop since I had decided to start teaching myself jewellery making, specifically silversmithing which did not require other than a very small table and a few tools. Examples of some of the jewellery, which I still indulge in making for the family, are illustrated in Chapter 13. Both of these pastimes were a relaxing break from research when in New York.

My research progressed in various directions, the major one was, as I mentioned, in what is called facilitated diffusion and was related to the work I did on the Guggenheim Fellowship in Paris with Jeffries Wyman. A phenomenon, which was not understood at the time, was how enough oxygen got through human tissue to muscles and whether it could possibly be enhanced through the combination of the oxygen and haemoglobin in the blood. I also collaborated with an experimentalist, Dr. Jonathan Wittenberg, of the Albert Einstein School of Medicine who had been a research collaborator of Jeffries Wyman. He set up and carried out clever experiments to quantify the process for which I had developed a mathematical model and had made experimental predictions. It turned out to be an interesting and novel mathematical analysis and research problem which on returning to Oxford I continued to work on for a short time. The process is intuitively quite simple. As confirmed experimentally by Jonathan, if you have tissue which contains haemoglobin and on one side of which there is a high concentration of oxygen the oxygen diffuses through the tissue but at the same time it combines with the haemoglobin the combination of which also diffuses thereby contributing, to the overall passage of the oxygen through the tissue. There was an amusing, somewhat embarrassing event associated with this work later when I was back on the faculty in Oxford. I had published a research paper on it in the *Proceedings of the Royal Society*. Prestigiously I was invited to give a lecture on it at the Royal Society in the large lecture hall, a lecture I prepared with great care. It was the era when you produced full-page transparencies which were then projected onto a large screen. I was duly introduced by the President and I nervously put my first transparency on the projector which, on switching it on, emitted a loud bang, a flash of light and everything went blank. It turned out that there was no other projector in the Society. The President then said I could use a blackboard, the only movable blackboard, which was duly carried in. It was the smallest I had ever seen, at most 3 feet by 3 feet. The chalk consisted of scraps since no one used chalk for lectures with projectors around. I started to write and quickly filled the board so I looked around for the duster: there wasn't one. The President, gentlemanly, offered me his handkerchief! The lecture was certainly not the greatest success. Many years later, as a Fellow of the Royal Society, I was awarded the *Royal Society Bakerian Prize Lecture* 2009, the Society's premier physical sciences medal and public lecture, but then with all the sophisticated equipment of the 21st century. I recalled, at tea before it, my first Royal Society lecture experience. The Vice President, who introduced me, told the audience the story. Not that this lecture was without problems too. The filming did not take in both my speaking and the lecture slides on the screen so, much of the time, I had my back to the large audience pointing at something that could not be seen in the film of the lecture. Also the recording is only of my voice with no recording of the audience's reaction of which there was considerable. The online video has since been modified, however, so that at least the relevant slides are seen at the same time as I speak.

Back in New York, having to give lectures a few days a week in the Bronx campus was tedious and discouraging. Public transport took ages and was very inconvenient and, at that time, the area was not very safe. I had clearly underestimated the downside of the position. I ended up driving and became the de facto chauffeur for colleagues who also lectured there. There was also the feeling in the Bronx campus that one was a second-class faculty member even though we all had offices in the downtown department in the Courant Institute. The students in the Bronx campus were also not as bright. By the end of the year it became clear that we would not stay in New York under such conditions even with the possible move to the downtown campus which I was offered when I said I was leaving. Eventually some years after I had left New York the Bronx campus was sold.

While there I had my second experience of a student trying to get me to change their exam grade. The student, a tall, elegant, beautiful girl came to see me. She started a sad story but first shut the door of my office, which made me uncomfortable, so I got up and opened it. She recommended her sob story and after a while said she would prefer to talk to me more in private and got up and shut the door again. So, once more I reopened it saying the room got a bit stuffy. She clearly decided that she was wasting her time so off she went to talk to one of the other professors who told me she had similarly tried closing his office door. Except for that occasion I usually never kept my office door open when talking to a student. The first request I had to change a grade was when one of the brightest students in my class when teaching at Harvard had, surprisingly, got a C in the mid-term examination. With his ability that was odd. I had noticed he had a bad cold during the exam but he also looked somewhat detached and unsettled. He came to see me about possibly raising his grade to a B since otherwise he would be removed from the Dean's list. He then told me why he was in such a state. He was a Chinese immigrant and had a serious American girlfriend whom he wanted to marry. Her parents were totally against it. He also said that she was pregnant. Based on his record, obvious ability and stressful problems I decided to do it; it is the only time I have ever changed a grade. I would not have done it though in the final examination. I don't know how he sorted out the personal problems but the following year he was back again to his straight A status.

There were many student protests and unrest around the world, although not so in Britain, in the late 1960s because of the outrageous

VII. Peripatetic Odyssey from Oxford to Oxford via America and Paris 1963-1970

Vietnam War directed by the incompetent Washington politicians. There was even a bomb placed in the university computer centre at New York University near Washington Square but it was fortunately defused. Although I found my colleagues excellent and we had friends in the university, the unsatisfactory job conditions and, more importantly because we had decided that we would prefer to have our children Mark and Sarah educated in England, at the beginning of the second year yet again I started the process of looking for possible positions in England. Up to then our academic life had been much too peripatetic. This time, however, we were only interested if it was a position in the University of Oxford and only if it was attached to one of the better, from my point of view, colleges, which meant one of the old, rich and academically major ones. Such appointments were rare. Fortunately, however, such a position came up. It was the tenured Fellowship in Mathematics at Corpus Christi College, the smallest college in the University of Oxford: it was founded in the beginning of the 16th century. It is architecturally beautiful, academically in the top tier and quite wealthy. I applied for the Fellowship and was invited to fly over for an interview. The committee had only one mathematician on it, a pure mathematician whose field was so far removed from mine that he could not ask a single question related to my research. However, there were those on the committee who did, albeit from different fields, so my answers had to be for the non-specialist which, being an applied mathematician, I preferred. Immediately after the interview, as I was leaving, walking towards the college entrance, one of the committee caught up with me to tell me that I was offered the Fellowship. I was delighted, accepted immediately with pleasure, and I was formally appointed the Fellow in Mathematics as from December 1969.

Finally I had arrived at a place I really liked and would stay until I formally retired from the university 23 years later albeit with different University positions and types of college Fellowship on the way as I moved up the academic ladder. I am now an Honorary Fellow of the college and Emeritus Professor of the university. It did not, however, stop our travelling and visiting many universities around the world when on leave or sabbatical. So, we moved back to Oxford in January of 1970 and I restarted life as an Oxford Don in Corpus Christi College which, except for the students with their horses in the 19th century print below, still looks exactly as it did centuries earlier. Apparently one of my referees had mentioned that I was also a mediaevalist manqué so the retiring President, who felt he could make all such decisions as to who got which room, offered me the magnificent 16th century President's room, the one with the window that juts out just above the entrance and where the horse is standing in the etching reproduction below. The other large window in the room looks out into the old quadrangle. I accepted it immediately, of course, before any of the other Fellows could protest.

Entrance to *Corpus Christi College*, Oxford, from an early 19th century coloured etching.

VIII

Oxford and Corpus Christi College 1969–

The University of Oxford is like no other university I have known in the world. There is a significant number of universities where I have had formal appointments, a much larger number where I have had visiting professorships and a huge number which I have visited to give invited lectures. A major reason is the unique Oxford college system and its age, of course: it celebrated its 500 year anniversary in 2017

The richer and older, traditionally self-governing, Oxford colleges, such as Corpus Christi College, have houses which tenured Fellows can live in, often, even after they retire. It was one of the perks of being a Fellow of these colleges. One such house, which had just become vacant on the retirement of the Bursar, was a large property in Boars Hill, a very upmarket area of Oxford, with lovely views out over the open countryside. It was essentially in the country but only about 3.5 miles from college. The college paid all taxes on the house and for any repairs or renovations which were required, such as central heating, plumbing, decorating and so on. So, in the summer of 1970, our first year back in Oxford, we moved into the college house, called *Pinsgrove*, so called because of the enormous

Pinsgrove: our Oxford home, 1970-1990.

Back of our Oxford home, Pinsgrove.

Pinsgrove: early evening view west across part of the property to the open country.

old pin oaks around the property and in the woods. The house, with its old neglected tennis court and tennis shed, had been built in the 1920s in a totally private 3 acres about half of which was a beautiful bluebell wood.

We enjoyed living there for the next 20 years although we bought it from the college in 1976.

Mark and Sarah loved being back in England, not that they complained about living in New York but they were not city people, at least not yet for Mark. In the photos below Sarah is wearing the trousers and Mark the shirt which were just two of the many fun clothes Sheila made for them as children. Sarah's silver necklace was the first piece of jewellery I made for her. Earrings were the more common pieces but she had, not yet, pierced ears.

Mark and Sarah started private schools in Oxford: private schools then were not coeducational. They are uniformly expensive which, on my academic salary, launched years of austerity for us. The school Mark went to is a small one, called a prep school, which is connected to New College, and called New College School. It was founded the same year as the college, in 1379, to educate the choristers in the New College Chapel which also dates from the 14th century. Prep schools prepare pupils for education at upper schools from the age of 12 on. It was an excellent school which Mark greatly enjoyed. The first week there he was asked what musical instrument he had chosen to learn to play. All pupils had to

Mark and Sarah in our home in Oxford, c1975.

take music lessons. Since we tended to travel a lot we suggested it should be one that was easy to carry with us, so he, we I suppose, chose the oboe. It was clear very soon that it was a superb choice for him: he loved playing and practiced for hours. The pupils were encouraged to study and take the national music examinations, of which there were eight at the time, run by the Examination Board (ABRSM) of the Royal Schools of Music in the UK, still called Great Britain at the time. Mark impressively passed all eight by the time he was 12 before moving on to the upper (grammar) school, another private boys one, Abingdon School, a few miles further out of Oxford but closer to our home. The headmaster was actually a student friend from my undergraduate university days. These music exams were required if one wanted to be a music teacher. To qualify as a music teacher you had to have passed these eight examinations and only one more which was not of musical ability but how to teach and required a knowledge of teaching practice as opposed to musical talent. Mark, at 12, was certainly not ready to think about what he would choose as a profession.

Sarah, Oxford, 1971

Sarah's school time was quite different. Since we had not yet moved into *Pinsgrove* she started at the closest local state school to the temporary house we were in, also owned by the college, until moving into Pinsgrove but she was not long at this school. It was not only not very good academically, but also because she started to acquire the ugly local Oxford accent, so we moved her to a very competitive academic private school in Oxford called *Grey Coats*. This one also did not last long because we went to a parent's evening and were incredibly unimpressed with the teachers and their attitudes. The third one was very good and she stayed there and enjoyed it until having to move to another private upper school at age 12. She moved once more after passing the first national examinations called "O-Levels" to yet another private upper school in Abingdon-on-Thames. With both Mark and Sarah going to school in the same small town the daily commute was so much easier. Sarah, who chose the flute to study, never developed the same enthusiasm. Her talents were much wilder, original and highly imaginative as I describe in Chapter 13.

Just as when I was the Mathematics Fellow in Hertford College in 1961-3 I still believed in the traditional formality regarding tutorials. The undergraduates had to wear their short black academic student gown and must have done all homework that I required of them from one week to the next. I still felt it was part of the tradition that inevitably would die out, as it has, but which my students would look back on with romantic nostalgia. I recently heard from some of my former students from the early 1970s that it is the case. The more important reason was that if it was a formal occasion I felt the students would work harder and need to have a very good excuse if they had not done the work required or have had special dispensation from me. Two of my very clever and very nice students in the 1970s, Ian MacLean, and Edward Troup reminded me of this recently when they came down from London to Oxford to attend a public lecture I gave in Oxford in 2014. They both got First Class Honours and have had very impressive and successful careers. Ian was a major rower in the college races held in Trinity Term (the third term of the year) and he reminded me that more than forty years before I had given him special dispensation to delay some of the set work until the summer. Such dispensation from me was exceedingly rare. Edward was recently awarded a Knighthood and is now Sir Edward Troup.

A very clever, very down to earth and fun student was Andrew Fowler, who also, very easily, got a First Class Honours. He is now a Professor of Applied Mathematics in Oxford and has been a true friend from his student days more than forty years ago. He is the groundbreaking world figure in applying mathematical modelling to glaciology, geophysics and other fields. His book *Mathematical Geoscience* is justifiably the major text in the field. Andrew kindly, and warmly, dedicated the book to Sheila and I, and, very unusually in any dedication, included a photo he took of us together at our house in Litchfield, Connecticut in 2010 when he visited us: it is the last photo in the epilogue of this memoir. Andrew succeeded me as a Fellow in Mathematics in Corpus Christi College. He is also the Stokes Professor in the University of Limerick where he kindly organized an international conference to celebrate my 80th birthday.

As undergraduates there was no question of them using my first name. I felt, and it was frequently confirmed, that such formality would make the students work harder. They never ever missed their tutorials. I was fortunate in having excellent students which of course was in major part a consequence of Corpus being one of the top academic colleges, small, ancient and particularly beautiful. Bright students, of course, also stimulate each other. An excuse for not doing what was set had to be cast in stone. I suppose, somewhat dictatorially, I felt such intellectual discipline and responsibility was essential for a successful career in whatever profession they chose after university. One of my college Fellow colleagues, from an extremely wealthy family, and politically extremely left – a Maoist in fact – took the opposite approach and his students used his first name from the very beginning. He regularly had problems some of which he had to bring up at formal Tutorial Committee meetings. I continued to give tutorials, although reduced to 6 a week in 1972, until 1983 when I became the Director of the *Centre for Mathematical Biology*, the first in the world, based in the Mathematical Institute.

Another aspect of the academic freedom in Oxford until well into the 1980s was that there was neither any check, nor formal reporting, as to whether or not you did any research. It was generally known in the department who did research. Oxford's world-class research reputation was a consequence of a relatively small percentage of the total faculty. I knew many Fellows who published essentially nothing their whole career. There were some faculty members I did not see in the Mathematical Institute from one year to the next. They spent practically all of their time in their college, sometimes being a bursar, a dean, admissions tutor or some other administrative position in the college as well as being a mathematics tutor. No one could force a Fellow to take such a position in Corpus: it was moral pressure or a desire to have such a position.

When the full time Bursar Fellow in Corpus, a retired Rear Admiral, was asked to resign in 1975, I agreed to be the Estates Bursar for a year until a replacement was appointed. It was certainly not a trivial job. During the year the position as Bursar, formally a Fellow of the College, was nationally advertised. I had been on the Estates Committee for some years so I knew what was involved. As Estates Bursar I still had to do all my other college and university duties. It was an interesting, albeit an incredibly full year since Corpus had, and still has, a number of large estates, mainly large farms, around England. I had to deal with the many problems which arose primarily because of the estates. Once a year the Estates Committee went on an official "*Progress*" to one or other of the parts of the country where there were a sufficient number of farms to visit. We were treated royally wherever we went and had to drink some of the sherry and wine and eat something of the lavish spreads provided, irrespective of the time of day we arrived. It was exhausting but gave me an impression of what it must have been like as a mediaeval lord and landowner, which in a sense the college was. It is important for Fellows to do such progresses since much of the college's income comes from the estates, and only recently from the sale of one of them, an extremely rare occurrence.

After my election to the Fellowship, as when at Hertford College, I was appointed by the university to a Common University Fund (CUF) lectureship. This was normal and automatic for Fellows elected by a college although the colleges by then generally required the approval of the university department. These were associated with tenured tutorial college Fellowships and they were for 5, officially probationary, years in the first instance at which time there was a formal, but in effect, irrelevant review, for reappointment until required retirement at 65 at the time, although now retirement is university specific.

As a new Fellow, and recently appointed CUF lecturer, I was asked to serve on the Mathematics Department's Appointments Committee which, among its roles was to make recommendations as to whether or not such probationary CUF lecturers should be reappointed. Having spent a considerable number of years in American universities I was naïve in thinking that such reappointments would now be considered seriously and similar to promotion requirements in major American universities I knew. How wrong I was. With one case which was brought up for a formal decision I naively said "Well this one won't take us any time." to which the chairman, clearly surprised, asked "What do you mean?" I said "She's published nothing in 4 years; she's clearly out." There was a hushed silence after which the chairman said: "We can't do that." When I was adamant and said I could not vote for reappointment, he very reluctantly suggested a compromise, namely that she would be put on probation for another two years, to which he added: "Her College will be absolutely furious." It was clear that before the two years were up I would be off the committee and her reappointment would be unanimously confirmed, as it was. The CUF system no longer exists but probation is still part of the system.

A major part of the problem was that all the undergraduate colleges were single sex as were all the Fellows in the undergraduate colleges. In mathematics the choice of Fellows for the women's colleges was, at the time, severely limited with only a few applicants compared to the large number of applicants for positions in men's colleges. The women's colleges were also noted for the excessive number of tutorials required of a Fellow, so, with many not as distinguished academically as in the men's colleges and with the excessive tutorial load, research was not their first priority and certainly not a requirement. At the time, in some women's colleges, such as Somerville College, arguably the major women's academic college, Fellows with a Ph.D., including those who were active in research, were not allowed to be called Dr. only Miss. This included a female friend, Dr. Hilary Ockendon, the wife of a colleague and friend, who would have had absolutely no difficulty, whatsoever, getting a Fellowship in any college. Fortunately this sex requirement has all changed.

Corpus Christi College and College life 1969-
I was, and still am, delighted to have been, since 1969, a Fellow of Corpus Christi College, known as CCC, or simply Corpus. It was the smallest of the Oxford colleges, one of the most academically distinguished and was generally at, or near, the top of the Norrington Table which each year orders colleges academically according to student results in the final examinations as described in Chapter 6. There was a move to get rid of the official Norrington Table since some colleges felt it was not good for the less good academic ones but it was not successful.

Corpus Christi College quad in the winter of 2009. Photo is reproduced, with the kind permission of Patrick Meyer Higgins, a Corpus alumnus.

Corpus was founded in 1517 by the wealthy and formidable Bishop Richard Fox, Bishop of Winchester: there is a photo of the college portrait of him below. He was greatly admired by Erasmus for his founding of the college with its original intellectual, more humanistic and less religious focus. Erasmus actually visited the college and in a letter in 1519 described the library as trilingual because of its books in Latin, Greek and Hebrew

Corpus Christi College back garden (*University Almanac, 1867*) with the Fellows Building on the right and cathedral in Christ Church College next door. The garden overlooks the large open Christ Church meadow and is bounded by the mediaeval city wall.

which are actually still in the 16th century college library. He described the library as one of the "chief beauties of England". Fox (sometimes spelt Foxe) had originally thought of founding a monastery but a real-politic and friend, Hugh Oldham, Bishop of Exeter, advised him against it anticipating the dissolution and thievery of the monasteries by the thuggish Henry VIII. Fox gave a large number of mediaeval manuscripts and books to the college and established it as the major classics college in Oxford, a reputation it still has. One of Fox's founding statutes required such humanist members to *"root out barbarity from our garden"*. Fox was immensely influential in the court of Henry VIII but was usurped by the ruthless Thomas Wolsey who succeeded him as Bishop of Winchester. One Fellow in the early days of the college and who lived in Corpus in the 1520s was the Spanish humanist Juan Luis Vives who was the tutor to Mary I of England. He was an early believer in educating women.

215

As well as a splendid internationally recognised mediaeval manuscript and book collection the college has the most impressive collection of renaissance silver plate. Fortunately the college somehow managed to avoid having to give it to Charles I during the civil war in the 17th century: practically all the other colleges gave their collection of plate to help the king financially. The magnificent Corpus crozier is now on loan to the Ashmolean Museum in Oxford but during my time it was kept in the college and brought out once a year by the *Keeper of the Plate*. I later

Bishop Richard Fox (c1448-1528)   Dr.John Reynolds (1549-1607)
Founder of Corpus Christi College.   President 1598-1607.
(Reproduced with permission of Corpus Christi College, Oxford)

became Keeper of the Plate but I only did it for one year. One responsibility for the Keeper was, once a year, to arrange a public showing of the major mediaeval pieces in Hall and once a year the Keeper had to check that all the antique pieces were still in the college. The latter was a tedious job since it included, as well as the superb antiques, the huge amount of silver cutlery, silver beer tankards, usually gifts from alumni, and so on which are still in regular use in Hall: it took a very long day.

One year the college Governing Body decided that we should have the college silver valued and had experts from Sotheby's Auction house in London come down for the day during which all the major college silver pieces were put out in Hall. They were invited to stay to dinner and I was seated beside one of the senior men. I asked him: "So what value did you put on the crozier?" to which he replied "Five million pounds". I said: "What!" and he replied "Well ten million." It is indeed priceless.

As the only mathematics Fellow I had complete control of how I taught the students and importantly which student applicants to accept. I gave the usual 12 tutorials a week and arranged for other tutorials in subjects I did not teach. It was gruelling teaching which somehow I had managed to put out of my mind from my Hertford College days. It was tutorials rather than lectures which were still the main basis of Oxford teaching at the time. Even then many students hardly ever went to lectures in their first two years. I also had to give the required 16 lectures each year, namely one course. It was the tutorial teaching requirement which was again proving a detriment to my research but, fortunately, because of my research and publication record, I was promoted to a Readership in Mathematics in 1972. A Readership in Oxford meant your primary responsibility was research and to the university rather than the college. However, I could remain the mathematics Fellow but now I only had to give 6 tutorials a week which I continued to do until 1983 when I was appointed the founding Director of the new interdisciplinary *Centre for Mathematical Biology* at which stage I was appointed a Professorial Fellow with no college teaching. I was appointed to a personal professorship, Professor of Mathematical Biology, in 1985 after being elected a Fellow of the Royal Society: Professors could not be tutorial Fellows in the colleges nor could they give college tutorials. The current system is now different with tutorial Fellows being able to apply for the title of professor but not the formal position. They still have to give their tutorials and their main responsibility is still to the college. Readerships now no longer exist.

The university was even more unforgiving about a student's responsibility than I was. In the final examinations if you did not turn up for one of the examinations (in the many required) you failed the degree. Even in the case of serious illness there was no way to retake the examinations until they were given a year later and then only with university dispensation. One of my students, a very good mathematician but otherwise surprisingly uneducated, which was not unusual with the early specialisation in school, sadly developed mental problems in the last term of his final year. About 2 weeks before the final examinations, called *Schools*, he was admitted to the local mental health hospital, the Warneford, which I thought would last only a few days. Unfortunately it was much more serious. Around 9 am on the first day of *Schools* I was contacted and told he had not appeared. I rushed off to the mental hospital and, irrationally, felt it was a lack of will power on his part, so I literally ordered him to get up out of bed and put on his "*subfusc*". This is the required academic attire when students take formal examinations in Oxford. For men it is a dark suit, dark socks, black shoes, white shirt and white bow tie and the black undergraduate academic gown. For women it is a white blouse, black tie, black skirt or trousers, black stockings or tights, black shoes and the undergraduate academic gown. (The dress requirements now are still the same.) I drove him to the large examination building, known as the *Examination Schools*, where he took the exam. I did this twice a day for each of the five days of examinations and after each, returned him to the hospital. It was extremely sad since his mental state had a major effect on his performance. He should have easily got a 1st Class Honours. His performance, however, was highly erratic but it showed the examiners that he had real innate ability so instead of failing he was awarded what is called an *Aegrotat* degree (one without any class attached to it) which allows a candidate to have formally passed the examinations and could graduate with a BA degree but whose performance was clearly affected by illness or some other acceptable problem. The following year, having somewhat recovered I thought, as did the hospital, he did a Master's research degree with me but at the end of the year he tragically committed suicide by jumping off the roof of a building. When his parents came to the college to see me for his funeral I said how very very sorry I was and what a tragic loss he was, they said, offhandedly and seemingly unconcerned: "*Well, it was God's Will.*"

One of the dynamic and fun students I taught in Corpus was Orlando Gough. Orlando led an incredibly full and varied student life in Oxford, being involved in a host of diverse activities. I told him he would really have to cut down on some of these activities if he wanted to get a *First* (class honours). He was a truly talented mathematician. He totally ignored my advice and in the final examinations still got a First Class Honours. In his final year he lived in an apartment in a house in one of the very much less upmarket roads in Oxford and one evening invited Sheila and I to dinner with some of his friends for 7pm. Dinner finally arrived on the table around 9pm. He had cooked it all himself and it was absolutely superb, innovative and certainly haute cuisine with excellent wine. After graduating he had a variety of bizarre jobs and is now a well-known composer of opera (recently with one performed at Glyndebourne), ballet, modern dance and others. Orlando is a man of great warmth, and impressive diverse talents who was right not to go into academia. He was one of the students in one of the brightest group I ever had, in the early 1970s, when a remarkable five of my seven final year students all got First Class Honours.

In the mid-1970s there was a move to make the traditional men's colleges coeducational. The Governing Body, which consisted of only permanent Fellows of the college (24 at the time as compared with about double that number now), was responsible for making such a decision. Like other colleges Corpus Christi's Governing Body discussed this coeducational change. As with some other colleges, although for different reasons, we managed to defeat the proposal. The group of Fellows, of which I was one, strongly opposed it because, if women were to be admitted, there was to be a quota on the number accepted. I felt, strongly, with justification from my experience in the US, that such a system would result in the women being considered second-class students. If defeated we knew the proposal would come up again the following year but, crucially, that women would have to compete on an equal basis with the men, namely intellectual ability and academic excellence. This time it passed easily, although there were still a few Luddite opposing voices to allowing women in at all. As mentioned, Fellows were the major decision makers as to which applicants would be accepted in their field. The following year I accepted the first woman student in mathematics. What helped to influenced me, positively a little - although it perhaps shouldn't have - was the letter from the headmistress of her all-girls private school which said *"Jane is a good mathematician - for a girl."* I felt for the pupils who had spent several years in such an atmosphere. She was, if not outstanding, a reasonable, hard working, student who got a respectable 2nd class honours degree. The all-women's colleges were very much later in going coeducational with St. Hilda's College only doing so in 2008.

The class of degree a student got, although still important, was immensely more important then. The class, 1st, 2nd or 3rd, and still a 4th in early 1970s, was in effect etched on the student for life. The 4th class was later abolished with the 2nd class divided into an upper (2.1) and lower (2.2) class. There are thus still four "classes": class 4 was considered very down market academically with the general view it was a student who had led a very full social life. When I was on the bursarial committee in Corpus for the appointment of the new college bursar, one senior member of the committee said of one very good candidate I thought would be an excellent choice: *"But he got a 3rd."* even though it was more than 30 years before and he had had a very successful career in the financial world. Even so, he was not appointed.

My college colleagues in other subjects were generally excellent academically and several became personal and family friends. With the college noted as an intellectual college, particularly for classics and philosophy: there were considerably more Fellows in these general areas than in the sciences.

Corpus Christi College entrance, late 19th or early 20th century, with the 16th century permanent Sundial with the pelican on top pecking its breast to feed its young. My room, with the large window, was the one directly above the entrance to the college. When I became a Fellow in 1969 the Quad was unpaved like this, but without the sundial fence.

Belonging to an ancient and architecturally beautiful academic establishment was a source of pleasure to me. My room was the most historic in the college along with the beautiful library with its unique collection of illuminated mediaeval manuscripts. My room, like the library, was unspoiled with its old original oak panelling, old fireplace, stained glass windows and elaborately plastered ceiling as in the photos.

My room was the one over the entrance to the college with four carved arched windows as in the print at the end of Chapter 7: each window had a stain glass panel. The window at the other end of my room in the second of the photos below overlooks the ancient quadrangle with the 16th century perpetual sundial (it is cylindrical and certainly not trivial to use it correctly) with a symbolic carving of a pelican pecking its breast to feed its young on the top. My room also had a splendid view of the cathedral in Christ Church College from that window.

JDM in his room in Corpus Christi College which he had from 1969 to 1986: the window faces outside the college – the large one in the etching in the last chapter.

My room was the living room of the President's suite in the 16th century and of considerable historical importance. Dr. John Reynolds (Rainolds) was a student, Fellow and eventually President. He was the scholar who suggested to King James 1 (formerly James VI of Scotland) that he should sanction a new translation of the bible which was written in the elegant and beautiful language of the 16th century and is the King James Version of the Bible. Reynolds was the principal figure in the two Oxford translation panels but unfortunately died in 1607 just before it was finished and published in 1611. The Reynolds portrait above is in the college as is that of the founder Bishop Fox.

The college grounds, buildings and quadrangles were as they were centuries ago. The enclosed small back chapel quad has been filmed in various television series because, with appropriate lighting, it can look quite sinister. The Fellows' garden is bordered by part of the old city mediaeval wall along which you can walk and overlook the vast Christ Church meadow which Oxford city wanted to put a road through to relieve traffic: fortunately it was a proposal soundly defeated. During my time in Corpus the Fellows garden was almost exactly as it is in the 19th century almanac photo above. From the old city wall in the Fellows' garden you have a lovely clear view of the romantic tree and garden supposedly where Lewis Carroll wrote *Alice's Adventures in Wonderland* published in 1865. Lewis Carroll was Charles Dodgson, a very retiring mathematics lecturer in Christ Church College. He greatly disliked the fame and public recognition and in a letter to a friend in 1891 wrote: "*I almost wish I had never written any books at all.*"

JDM's room and its dramatic ceiling in Corpus Christi College. The window, with stain glass crests, overlooks the college quadrangle and the Pelican.

There is a door from the chapel quad into a small garden quad where college student outdoor plays were usually preformed. At such performances you could never be sure they would go as planned. On one occasion, in Shakespeare's *Romeo and Juliet*, during one of the romantic scenes a student opened the door from the chapel quad and released one of the college's several wild cats: it was petrified and ran wildly up and down behind the actors. The audience burst into laughter much to the astonishment of poor Romeo and Juliet. The most dramatic part of all the student plays we saw in Oxford was when we went to see *Midsummer Night's Dream* in Worcester College which has a very has a very large garden with a lake. In one scene Ariel runs off the stage and, in this

JDM in front of the elaborate fireplace in his room with the carved Corpus crest.   JDM in the library at his home, c1986.

16th century Corpus Christ College library.   JDM in the Corpus library, c 1979.

performance, literally ran across the surface of the lake. It was very dramatic and astonishing. The students had very imaginatively placed concrete slabs in the lake which were only just covered by the water but which could be clearly seen so as to run on them.

Fellows, particularly of the older wealthier colleges, have an immensely privileged academic and social life. High Table, with its haute cuisine dinners every evening for the Fellows and any guests they have. Any tenured Fellow in Corpus who retires in any Fellowship position has such High Table privileges for the rest of their life. Since traditional tutorial times are from 5-7pm, dinner afterwards is a relaxing time with superb wine. You gather, academically gowned of course, in the *Senior Common Room* to have sherry or whatever, before dinner, meet the guests and generally socialise. You then parade into Hall where the students are already waiting, standing until after grace. Students also have to wear their gowns. The Fellows are all seated at High Table on the raised floor a few inches above the long student tables. Grace, in Latin of course, is given by the President or, if not present, the senior Fellow, the short versions of which are, *Benedictus benedicat* or, the slightly longer one, *Benedictus benedicat Jesum Christum domine nostrum* (Blessed is He and may He bless (this food) through Jesus Christ our Lord) became ingrained in your brain. There is an even much longer one but if said it was always by one of the classics Fellows. Dinner is terminated by *Benedicto benedicatur* after which the Fellows all troop out. The food at the students' "low" table is totally different and typical university student fare. Most colleges, certainly the wealthier ones such as Corpus, have an excellent large wine cellar with a Keeper of the Wine Cellar, an official position I held for 5 years. The Keeper's responsibility was to maintain the cellar wine, port, sherry and Madeira and so on at the right level of taste and sophistication. This necessitated going to the several wine tastings held in one college or another during the academic year.

These tastings for Keepers of the Wine Cellars, and a committee if there was one, which there wasn't in Corpus, were followed by an elaborate superb lunch with the most up market wines provided by the wine merchants hosting the tasting. I had a difficult time with the immature red wines since to me they all generally tasted awful. I once asked a few of the other Keepers how they could tell if it was going to be good when mature. It was clearly an embarrassing question since it was generally greeted with obtuse obfuscation. I then asked the wine merchant who dealt with the vineyards to which he answered: "I know the vineyard and they tell me if it's going to be a good year or not and for this specific wine I can now tell it will be very good." There were quite a lot of wines you had to taste and I quickly got used to the swilling of it around my mouth and then spitting it into the boxes around the table which were filled with sawdust specifically for that purpose.

JDM at a typical College garden party, c1975.

JDM before a formal College dinner, c1991.

Wine and the quality of High Table dinners have no doubt always played an important part in college life. The chef is known as the *Manciple* and is highly respected. When the *Manciple* retires the appointment of a new one is quite an important affair. During my time this happened and a short list was drawn up from the numerous applicants around the country. The first choice, from the recommendation letters, was someone in York. Since I was going to give a lecture at the University of York it was suggested I go, incognito, to the restaurant and taste the food. I did and found it second rate which started the appointment process all over again. It is difficult in an interview to determine whether or not somebody will be a first rate chef so it is crucial to get first hand experience of their talents. We fortunately appointed an excellent one who stayed until his retirement. For the first few years after I joined Corpus in 1970, the dinner menus were still all written in French. The dinner wine, of course, was always French.

Outside of the 8 week term time you were essentially free to do whatever you wanted. Many academics, of course, did research but this was certainly not at all obligatory. As mentioned, in the early 1970s, the majority did little or no research whatsoever. Some of us, of course, travelled to other universities, all over the world. Unlike now, some of the older Fellows in Oxford when I joined Corpus did not have doctorate degrees, only "brilliant" 1st Class Honours degrees. The academic excellence of Oxford had long been due to the extremely clever students and a significant number of the faculty. It was listed first in the world in the 2016-2017 rankings. On one occasion when visiting a university in the US to give a lecture one of the local faculty in mathematics said how impressive the Oxford department and its world class research were. I asked him which faculty members he had heard of who contributed to the high standing. After thinking a little, he named about ten members of the faculty and did not initially believe me when I said there were nearly 90 tenured faculty in the department.

The privileges of a Fellow were numerous (and most have survived in the ancient colleges particularly) such as free rooms to live in if unmarried, or needed them, a free house if you were married, your college servant, known as your Scout, who served and cleaned up after parties, and so on. He lit the coal fire in my room in the winter for several years until an electric fire was put in. My scout was a kind, not very bright, well-liked, rather overweight short man called Godfrey. He also felt responsible for the wild cats which frequented the college grounds. The scratches he regularly got when feeding them often became infected. He was also one of the servants in Hall at meals but not at High Table: they had to be more sophisticated and be aware of how to treat guests and Fellows appropriately but not obsequiously. They also tried to keep an eye on who was perhaps drinking too much and restrict how much wine they put in their glasses although they never quite managed that with one of the more difficult and disruptive Fellows, Trevor Aston, a mediaevalist historian of distinction who had regular attacks of depression, mental problems and increasing bouts of drinking too much.

Trevor Aston was impressive intellectually and I always found him interesting to talk with although I cannot remember ever seeing him smile. We shared an enthusiasm for almost everything mediaeval. Trevor was also the main repository of knowledge about the college plate and was the official Keeper of the Plate for many years and thus always in charge at the annual showing in Hall: he was somewhat proprietorial. He was rather put out at one showing when something was pointed out that he had never noticed before. I had brought our young daughter Sarah who was about 7 years old. She was fascinated by all the engravings on the silver, particularly on the magnificent 15th century crozier. She found, roughly at her head level, to Trevor's and everybody else's astonishment, a small caricature face about an inch high halfway down the shaft.

Had Trevor Aston not had such mental and alcohol problems I believe he could perhaps have been elected President. Sadly he got progressively worse. I was one of the very few Fellows who managed to get on with him. We both felt strongly, for example, about preserving the old buildings on the college estates which were scattered around England and had been in the college possession for centuries. We were the de facto committee on the preservation of old buildings, such as 17th century stone barns and so on, in tenant farms and also for the college buildings. The tenant farmers on these estates often wanted to demolish an old stone building and replace it with a modern one to which we were always opposed. Our recommendations were almost always voted down by the Governing Body. I could never understand, and still cannot, why most of my Fellow colleagues did not feel strongly about the preservation of such ancient buildings.

As Trevor Aston's drinking and irrational manic behaviour deteriorated he would come to dinner but speak to no one other than to me if I was sitting beside him. His drinking put a considerable damper on High Table dining where he would sit morosely facing down. He also gave the President, Sir Kenneth Dover, a particularly hard time with numerous letters and other direct personal methods of complaint. He tried to commit suicide several times but Kenneth never quite believed he really wanted to succeed. Kenneth Dover was one of the major international ancient Greek scholars. He was President of the *British Academy* from 1978-81which included the time when Sir Anthony Blunt's spying for Russia came to light. Kenneth personally thought Blunt should be expelled from the Academy but, for political, or rather academic, reasons, reluctantly felt he should not. It was in part because of the unpleasantness and difficulties of dealing with Aston that Kenneth decided to retire early in 1986 and return to St. Andrews where he was appointed Chancellor of the university: he had formerly been the Professor of Greek. Being head of a college was to me the worst faculty position to have in a college. The problems even now are endless. During my time in Oxford some Fellows in two colleges, Keble College and St. Edmund Hall wanted me to allow my name to be put on their short list for the head of their college. Needless to say I politely declined both.

Trevor Aston became progressively more difficult and erratic. Walking into college one morning in October 1985 I was greeted in the quad by a beaming and obviously delighted Kenneth Dover who, when he saw me, came up rubbing his hands and said "He managed it." I asked "Who managed what?" to which he answered: "Trevor finally managed to kill himself." Astonishingly, on reading Kenneth's incredibly frank and honest memoir, *Marginal Comment*, which he published in 1992, he describes some of the serious concerns and problems for the college with Trevor Aston and says: "*But it was clear to me by now that Trevor and the college must somehow be separated. My problem was one which I feel compelled to define with brutal candour: how to kill him without getting into trouble.*"

Committees, of course, play a crucial part of the college's running. One committee decided on student applications for financial support for whatever project the undergraduate wanted to do during vacation, whether it be to spend time in France to learn French or go to India to investigate ideas they had about relevant historical connections, join a group of ecologists gathering data on wild animals or whatever. The projects were incredibly diverse, many interesting and highly novel. The only time I remember the committee not giving a grant was an application from an undergraduate student from Pakistan, who was always dressed in elegant traditional clothes, who was having temporary difficulty paying for the stabling and feeding of his racehorses.

There was in most colleges a fairly common custom that you did not talk shop when dining in Hall, a custom, as I mentioned I regularly ignored since I found guests often very interesting. In fact, quite a number of the interdisciplinary research problems I have worked on arose from dinner conversations with visiting guests, or as a dinner guest at other colleges and also with some of the other Fellows in Corpus specifically in medicine. Until the college became co-educational women academics were accepted as dinner guests of course but other than women academics there was only one evening a term when they could be invited: it was called Ladies Night. During my first term in college in 1970 the then senior ancient history Fellow, a kind man, a very good tutor but not a greatly distinguished academic, took my arm at sherry before dinner one evening as we walked to Hall and said "*Jim, I see you're bringing a guest to Ladies Night on Sunday. I just wanted to say that you must be careful to keep the conversation at an appropriate intellectual level so as not to embarrass the ladies.*"

He was serious. Apparently I was already getting a reputation for asking guests about what they did academically, were enthusiastic about and so on, rather than keeping the conversation at a general, often uninteresting, level.

The variety of guests I met at dinners, not only in Corpus, made for a lively, interesting and intellectually stimulating time. At a formal black tie dinner in Merton College one evening in 1972 I was seated beside J.R.R. Tolkien, a Fellow of Merton and an extremely friendly warm person. It was a touch frustrating, however, in that I was very curious to hear how he had originally developed his ideas for *The Hobbitt, Lord of the Rings* and so on while he, on the other hand, was very curious about how, as a mathematician, I did research, found problems, had original ideas and so on to apply in the real world, something he did not think existed with mathematicians, which, of course, is generally the case. Unfortunately he got his way. We got on so well that he insisted I sit beside him at dessert as well. Elaborate desserts are always served with port and Madeira in another room at these regular formal dinners so that guests could have the opportunity to meet with some other people. It was generally not done to sit with your dinner neighbour. It is how I also got to know Sir Isaiah Berlin who was another lively dinner guest several times in Corpus in the late 1980s and early 1990s. He had been a student at Corpus and was an Honorary Fellow when I met him. He had a lovely and lively sense of humour and always gave the impression that you were one of the most interesting people he had met. There were many others, such as W.H. Auden, a rather self centred and somewhat distant man, Sir Thomas Bromley, the former ambassador to Ethiopia, a gentle, immensely kind, man who, with his wife, Allison, became close family friends. Tom Bromley talked about his time in Addis Ababa and his experience and relationship with Haile Selassie and his daughters. The daughters felt everybody should be at their beck and call wherever they were. When they visited Oxford after Tom had long retired, and the coup in Ethiopia by the Left in 1974 had taken place, they expected his whole attention and commitment to them. The enormous intellectual benefits which can accrue from having such regular social dinners is one of the intellectual pleasures as well as an important avenue for cross discipline research, and much more. Such regular academic dining is lacking in practically all universities in the world that I know. In many, of course, there are occasional such get-togethers but nothing like the regular Oxford High

Table system with its superb cuisine, vintage wine and often fascinating guests.

From a research point of view I started to work almost exclusively in interdisciplinary science, which I did from the early 1960s, primarily on the application of mathematical modelling in biology, medicine, epidemiology, ecology, psychology and so on. I was often asked, by the more curious dinner guests, what I was working on. On one occasion, when the guest sitting beside me asked, it was when I was doing research on the spatial spread and control of rabies, and in particular how it would spread, and how it could be controlled, in England if by chance it got introduced from the continent. Animals are not vaccinated against rabies in England so it would be extremely serious with the large fox population, particularly in the cities and towns, and the huge number of domestic dogs. Foxes were major carriers of the disease in Europe. I had developed a model which showed how the disease would spread and what containment strategies would work. By way of example I assumed it was introduced around the port of Southampton. The guest, Patricia Morrison, a fascinating *Financial Times* reporter, who wrote articles, rather than as a reporter of news, said she had recently been in Maastricht in the Netherlands in preparation for an article, and had gone into the cathedral to meet one of the permanent clergymen. He had talked to her about rabies in the middle ages, the role of the church and how the 7th century Bishop Hubert (later Saint Hubert) was an animal lover with the reputation that he could cure rabies. There is a large metal ring in the cathedral to which a person was tied if they had been bitten by what was possibly a rabid animal. Part of the treatment procedure for such a victim was called *"la taille"* (the thread) whereby a small incision was made in the forehead, a small piece of thread was inserted and the wound then closed up. After about 10 days if the victim did not develop rabies it meant that God (or St. Hubert) had interceded on their behalf. If they developed rabies then, of course, they died and went to hell. The thread supposedly came from the cloak of the church's patron saint.

After this dinner I researched the history of the cathedral. Apparently in the early middle ages the cathedral was having a hard time financially and needed a new patron saint. One story is that when the young nobleman Hubert died they decided to make him a Saint, took his cloak as a symbol of his religious power and it was from this cloak that the *"la taille"* process started. Patricia, on leaving the church, asked the minister if *la taille* was still done to which he answered *"No, no, but if anybody wants to have it, of course, we still do it.*" It must have been an enormous cloak to still be able to supply a thread after more than a thousand years with the constant prevalence of rabies during that mediaeval time and until now.

With Corpus being the major classics and ancient history college in Oxford there was limited knowledge and not very much interest in the scientific world. My academic career, as is clear, was very peripatetic as described in Chapter 11. I spent a considerable amount of time visiting other universities, particularly after being promoted to a Readership as described briefly before and below. There were also the usual academic sabbaticals where you had a year off (with salary) every seventh year although I had many other extended periods abroad on unpaid (by Oxford University) leave. At dinner in college one evening one of my distinguished classics colleagues, also a family friend, said, "I hear you're off visiting again. Where is it this time?" I said it was *Caltec* (California Institute of Technology) in Pasadena, California. He asked: "What's Caltec?" I said it was arguably the most high powered prestigious scientific academic institute in the world with the highest percentage of Nobel Prize winners of any academic institution to which he said: "Oh, really." as he took another drink of his wine. Classicists, although certainly not alone, can be surprisingly isolated.

The title of Reader in British universities and some parts of the Commonwealth, such as Australia and New Zealand, is an academic appointment for international recognition of original research and scholarship rather than a senior position based on length of tenure. In the US it similar to a Research Professorship. In Oxford the number of professorships was very small and essentially limited in number by the university. My Readership appointment made an enormous difference to the time I could spend on research. I was fortunate, however, to still keep my splendid college room which I had until I was appointed to a professorship, the Professor of Mathematical Biology, in 1986. As a university professor you could not be a tutorial fellow but you could still have a college room but this was at the college President's discretion.

The successor to Sir Kenneth Dover, Professor Keith Thomas, was appointed that year. He would not have been my first choice but I had no influence since I was unfortunately on leave in the USA the year he was elected and so could not vote: you had to be present at the Governing Body to vote. Keith Thomas said I must now share my room. This was totally ridiculous, of course, from a research supervision and research point of view so, with considerable sadness, I gave it up. Keith was the same President who, when some years later, I said I was retiring five years earlier than required, (the retirement age for professors was 67, two more than non-professors), to go to the University of Washington to start up mathematical biology in the Applied Mathematics Department he lectured me at dinner at High Table one evening saying that it was my duty to stay in Oxford and continue to be Director of the Centre for Mathematical Biology. He was a touch dictatorial. Unlike most of the Fellows he also disliked the original, imaginative, and unique natural college garden which was introduced and developed by the newly appointed lively, imaginative and original gardener David Leakie but fortunately in this he did not have his way. The college quadrangle, for example, was more like it is in most early 19th century etchings; that is with no plants whatsoever. Under David Leakie it is as in the more recent photos above of the quadrangle with lots of plants and flowers.

In the college at that time, it was customary for professors automatically to be appointed an Honorary Fellow[1] when they retired. When I retired in 1992 the Professor of Latin retired at the same time: he was immediately elected an Honorary Fellow[1] but in the President's view I was clearly some kind of deserter and was not elected. In the first term immediately after Keith Thomas retired in 2001 I was appointed to an Honorary Fellowship although by that time the system of automatic election of professors had been suspended in favour of other criteria, including international academic standing in your field, success in your world outside of academia, political party leaders, heads of government departments who had been at Corpus and so on. Thomas was not particularly popular in the college, with several Fellows regretting their initial support. He retired some years earlier than he was required to. In spite of my college experience with him, however, I have enjoyed reading his books on mediaeval history.

I felt strongly, and still do, about historical aspects of my college and, as I mentioned before, was for several years on the college Estates Committee. Many of the college's properties are farms with old buildings from the late 16th and 17th centuries on. On one occasion, in spite of what I thought a very strong case, I lost the vote not to allow an old stone barn

---

[1] In the early 1970s I went, as the representative of Corpus Christi, Oxford to the annual gaudy dinner in Corpus Christi College, Cambridge and was seated at High Table beside an alumnus who had just been appointed an Honorary Fellow. When I congratulated him he gruffly replied: "*High bloody time.*"

to be demolished. After it was demolished I was able to salvage some of the old oak timber from the barn which I used to make various pieces of "antique" furniture as described in Chapter 13. The furniture pieces are hardly antique but the wood certainly is.

As I said above, Corpus Christi College was founded by Bishop Fox in 1517. He had been Lord Privy Seal of England for more than 25 years and had a strong sense of the importance of preserving important documents, specifically in muniment cupboards. He actually gave specific rules as to how the records should and must be kept. The walls of the room above my one in the college tower were lined with early 16th century oak muniment cupboards. Fox required that various records should also be kept in large, very strong, wooden, generally oak, coffer chests. While I was on leave in America one year the college decided to "renovate" the room with the muniment cupboards, which were removed and were to be thrown out along with some of the old 16th century coffers. Antique banks of chests of small drawers, in which the old documents relating to the college properties around the country were also to be thrown out or burned. When I heard of it I was absolutely appalled and felt it sacrilegious, totally irrational and unbelievably irresponsible. By the time I got back to college, the head maintenance man, George Beckley, who shared my respect for traditional and historical aspects of the college, showed me some of the pieces, like the muniment cupboard doors, and small chests of card size drawers, which he had not yet thrown out, or rather he had not the heart to do so. He was delighted for me to have them rather than throw them out since he knew of my concern and interest in such things, mediaeval. He knew that they would be preserved. A few, very few, of the other Fellows in the college also took some pieces rather than have them destroyed. Some of what I took were the old 16-17th century muniment cupboard doors. I used several of them to make various bits of "17th century" furniture including an "antique" double door cupboard about high, 5 feet wide and 2 feet in depth which we still have and use. There is a photo of the "mediaeval" coffer I made in Chapter 13. We also still have two of the small drawer muniment cupboards which housed details of the college estates: some still have the original elegant copper plate ink-written details of what the drawer contained. Hopefully the college will want them returned someday. I returned to college before all of the large old coffers were thrown out. My protests were fortunately listened to with regard to some of the mediaeval coffers so several of these are still in the college. Nobody wanted them in their room except me. I had one in my college room for some years which has preserved it. It is behind my desk in the photo above of my room – the one with me at the desk.

In the 1970s the Oxford town health authorities decided to carry out inspections of the colleges' kitchens the purpose being to ensure they were up to required standards of hygiene. The two 16th century kitchen tables, which consisted of enormous single slabs of elm heartwood, were stupidly condemned because they had grain indentations and so were required to be removed. The smaller of them was taken by George Beckley, the college maintenance man, to use in the college workshop as a way of not destroying it. He told me of the large one, 9'x3' by 6" thick, and its massive oak base, which dates from the time of the college's foundation in 1517 and which was going to be taken off to the garbage: there is a photo of it in Chapter 13. Once again I could hardly believe it so I took it and it has been with us ever since. It is an enormous heartwood piece. The tree must have begun growing sometime in the first few centuries AD.

Other things in the kitchen which were deemed unacceptable, though hardly related to health issues, were early 16th century wrought iron beacon holders buried in the ancient stone walls behind the plaster: they were also going to be thrown out. Two of these I also still have and again hope that in time the college will realise the loss and also want them back to preserve as part of the history: they could easily be replaced where I remember they came from in the large college kitchen.

Generally I was rather surprised to see, over the years, how most of the Governing Body had so little concern for preserving ancient parts of the college and its historic possessions. When dining with friends and colleagues in their colleges I asked several if it was the same in their college; their discouraging answer was yes. One that I felt particularly strongly about and tried several times in the early 1970s to get changed, but without success, was regarding a small (about 12x9 inches), very beautiful, incredibly well preserved, piece of mediaeval tapestry depicting the deposition which was hung, literally, on a nail in the chapel. I said that it could, and almost certainly would, be stolen by someone just lifting it off the hook and walking off with it under a coat or jacket. No one agreed with me that it should not be in the chapel at all which was open 24 hours a day. To try and pacify me, which it certainly didn't, it was rehung with two screws, one at the top and another at the bottom of the frame, but in exactly the same place in chapel. Sadly, my prediction was borne out about a year later when it was indeed stolen and it has never been recovered. The large elegant 18th century antique wall clock in the old Senior Common Room was also stolen since its doors were never locked either.

Another example, which to my surprise did not arouse the college's concern the way I thought it would was associated with the college's rare mediaeval manuscripts, about 500 of them. The President. Keith Thomas, wanted to have them deposited, on loan, in the Bodleian Library. Although I agreed in principle, if not enthusiastically, I strongly opposed doing it as did quite a few other Fellows. The reason I was against it was that I had recently spent days, over a period of several months, looking up various old texts in the stacks of the Bodleian Library and was appalled at the condition of a large number of the old books, such as their spines and covers falling off due to the lack of any humidity control, others were piled on top of each other in the shelves, and so on. Normally people were not allowed into the stacks and I can see why. The humidity conditions were dreadful. When I mentioned this to one of the librarians in the Bodleian Science Library she completely agreed about not recommending that the college manuscripts be deposited in the Bodleian Library. Unfortunately it did not come to the Governing Body so the President had his way and the mediaeval manuscript collection was duly moved to the Bodleian Library. Because of the conditions, later realised after I retired, the collection was moved back to the college.

The college's 500th year anniversary was 2017. There was an appeal to commemorate it by building a new library specifically to house this unique manuscript collection. Among other things it has arguably the most important collection of early Hebrew manuscripts in the country. As mentioned, they were given to the college at its founding by Bishop Fox and others at that time, from their personal libraries since, unlike other colleges founded before it, Bishop Fox's vision for Corpus Christi College was a centre for, among other things, Latin, Greek and Hebrew which it certainly became, and currently is, for Latin and Greek.

Another desecration – the correct word I feel – was associated with the ancient 13-14th century building belonging to the college called Beam Hall after one of the 13th century chancellors of the university, Gilbert de Biham. It had a magnificent reception room with the walls lined with original mediaeval oak wood panelling. My mediaevalist colleague, Trevor Aston, and I persuaded the college to renovate all the woodwork to its original mediaeval state: it was done very professionally. When the new president, Keith Thomas, decided as President, he did not want to live in the college president's apartment, and that he would move to Beam Hall, not an unreasonable wish to live outside the college walls, so he moved. What shocked me was that he had the splendid linenfold wood panelled room walls painted a light colour. For a distinguished mediaeval historian, in particular, to do so was, to me, totally incomprehensible. With such college decisions (although many of them did not come to Governing Body) regarding ancient aspects of the college, including the lack of concern with the beautiful mediaeval tapestry of the deposition, I should not have been so surprised at such lack of appreciation. The future will hopefully be better since the college appointed a part time archivist a few years ago. One recent dramatic find by him was of a piece of old cloth in the attic of one of the college buildings. It turned out to be Bishop Fox's cloak from the early 16th century.

Notwithstanding some of the college's lack of concern about the number of things associated with the College's history about which I still feel strongly my warmest memories of my many years at the University of Oxford are those associated with Corpus Christi College. It is also where I met guests of the college several of whom became close friends. Our fond memories of Corpus are resurrected every time Sheila and I are back in Oxford with the welcoming and kind reception we get when staying in college, the pleasure of walking around Oxford, going into old colleges (now severely restricted because of the huge number of tourists but Fellows of other colleges are exempt) and spending time with long time Oxford friends.

It was at High Table in Corpus Christi one evening that I was seated beside the senior surgeon in the Oxford hospital, Malcolm Gough. Surgeons in Britain are not called Dr. always Mr. which is much more prestigious in hospitals. Without the social life in college we would never have met. He, and his wife Sheila, became close family friends whom we have seen regularly ever since but sadly miss them when we moved back to America. They had lived for a short time in the village of Woodeaton described in Chapter 6 but moved to a lovely house in the country a few miles north of Oxford where we often dined with them and stayed after retiring from the University. The photo below is of Malcolm (opening a bottle of champagne) and his wife Sheila in their lovely very large back garden one evening before we went in for dinner.

Malcolm carried out several surgical operations of the many, certainly more than my share, which I have had. He took out my appendix, for example, and fixed two carpal tunnel problems for me. Malcolm is a very down to earth very caring doctor who, like so many of the more senior medical world, despairs of what has happened to the National Health Service in Britain, the atmosphere in hospitals, and imposed egalitarian social behaviour of the doctors, nurses and staff which have had a detrimental effect on patient care. Malcolm was the 1991-2 President of the *Association of Surgeons of Great Britain and Ireland* the major society of surgeons. When he came on an official visit to the USA he and Sheila stayed with us a few days on Bainbridge Island. As the official *Association* guest at the American societies he had to wear the presidential necklace but it was a very good copy in case the original one, made of gold, somehow got stolen.

Dinners at the Goughs were always superb, always very lively, and where we met many fascinating other guests, Alex Pasternak, for example, the brother of Boris Pasternak. A particularly warm one, who became a family friend, was Lucy Faithfull who had led a fascinating life and was the prime mover in the protection of children from sexual abuse. She started a foundation for that purpose and which was renamed the *Lucy Faithfull Foundation* after she died. She was made Baroness, which she originally refused until persuaded by the Prime Minister Margaret Thatcher, and was in the House of Lords where she regularly did not follow the government whip if she did not agree or follow what was proposed: she was nicknamed "Baroness Faithless." She also became a family friend. I had lunch with her in the House of Lords on one occasion – pretty third-rate food, a bit like what you got in railway stations.

We visit Malcolm and Sheila every time we are back in Oxford, sadly nothing like often enough. In the middle of dinner one Saturday evening at the Gough's the Oxford Hospital telephoned with a patient emergency: Malcolm had to leave immediately. It was a problem with an obese patient who was being operated for an appendectomy by a young, not very experienced, surgeon. It turned out that he had started to open up the traditional part of the body to remove the appendix and had estimated where it should be based on the assumption that body organs were essentially distributed proportionally as in non-obese patients. He proceeded with the surgical incisions but because the body organ positions are not proportional to body size in obese patients he had missed the appendix and had literally gone through the body to the table.

Malcolm and Sheila Gough before dinner one evening at their home, c1978.

Some years later I collaborated on a research problem with some medical colleagues in the university on obese patients although on a very different problem. The research on obesity, which I did, was how to quantify the correct medication level, which had traditionally been based on body weight, for treating something called *hyperlactataemia*: too much is dangerous. I solved it using a simple mathematical model and it was confirmed with experimental and patient studies. The research article we wrote together proposed an accurate method for determining the correct medication level: it has been used clinically now for patients with liver disease for more than 25 years. With obesity, an increasing world wide epidemic, I have given lectures on the medication procedure to undergraduate premedical students in Princeton University for some years now. I sometimes briefly describe the above problem with the obese patient and her appendectomy to help highlight just one of the many major medical problems with the ever increasing number of obese patients.

One of the very warm family friends we have had and whom we met purely by chance in the late 1970s were Professor Vittorio Gabrieli and his wife, Mariuma when they were visiting Oxford. Vittorio was a professor of English in Rome. We convinced them, fortunately easily, to come back to

Oxford for a term. Vittorio was officially appointed a Visiting Fellow of Corpus Christi College and was such for many years. We saw them regularly out at our house where our son Mark and daughter Sarah loved to see them. Their kind daughter Carla spent some time with them when in Oxford. Vittorio and Mariuma exuded a warmth, sensitivity and gentleness so very rare as is clear in the photo below. We saw them in Rome when we were there as did Mark, most recently in 2013. Vittorio recently died, in his sleep, at the age of 100, in the summer of 2017.

I remember once telling Vittorio and Mariuma about our time in Paris in the late 1960s when there was a lot of violent student unrest - around Europe generally - about the Vietnam War. I described some of our experience of it in the last chapter. Vittorio told me about similar dangerously violent student protests in Rome. Although he strongly disapproved of the dreadful war he certainly did not support the students' violence. Some student protesters ludicrously accused Vittorio of fascism because he did not condone their violence. This was so ironic since Vittorio had actually been imprisoned for four months in the *Regina Coeli* (Queen Coeli) prison at the beginning of the second World War because of his protests against the thuggish Mussolini and his fascist mob. Student protests in Britain are extremely rare and never violent: they are like the one in 1971 in Oxford which I describe in Chapter 9.

Professor Vittorio Gabrieli and his wife Mariuma. The photo is reproduced with the kind permission of their daughter Carla.

Sheila's accident

An accident in 1981 resulted in by far the most terrible, horrendous, terrifying and worrying time of my life. Sheila, who has never been nervous about heights, used to clean the gutters in our house, *Pinsgrove*. Each time I always stood, nervously, at the bottom of the ladder. On this occasion, following an exhausting visit by Sheila's mother from the USA, Sheila said that she felt a little faint and would just put her head down on the roof for a minute. It was so vividly clear to me that she was starting to faint. I shouted that she mustn't do that and come down immediately. Tragically it was too late, she fainted and fell the 20 feet from the top of the ladder. Every single second and image of the whole affair and accident is indelibly etched in my mind. I desperately tried to break her fall but, of course, it had absolutely no effect and she fell unconscious on the stony ground at my feet, hitting the right side of her head and ribs on the ground. The ambulance took her to the hospital in Oxford where she was unconscious for two weeks in intensive care. Her survival was very much in the balance for about the first ten days. I was consumed with desperate hope that she would survive, the thought of the vast emptiness of life without her and the terrible tragic loss to us all. I was the only person who managed to get the slightest live signs and recognition when I sat speaking to her for hours in intensive care. Poor Sheila was unable to speak for another three weeks, and even then with great difficulty and only simply. She was also totally unable to walk or balance standing for a further four weeks. She only ate when I was there to feed her. In effect I was treated as the attending nurse. The hospital was pleased to leave the responsibility to me and certainly so was I. When she started to recover I felt my life had started again. Recovery, however, was very long. While still in hospital she did not know, for example, that she could not walk, and tried on several occasions to get up when I was not there and immediately collapsed. She also had double vision. Friends in the university were incredibly kind, particularly the very warm and sensitive Liuba Stirzaker, the wife of a mathematics colleague and friend, David Stirzaker, who came every day. After Sheila could eat easily, Liuba regularly brought her a fresh French croissant from the French bakery close to the hospital and which she knew Sheila had always enjoyed. Liuba, who came from Czechoslovakia, had become a doctor.

By the end of seven weeks in hospital Sheila was moved to a rehabilitation centre which was totally useless, almost reversing her slow improvement. By that time Sheila had recovered sufficiently that she felt responsible for other patients, even though she could not walk, so I insisted on bringing her home where we all were, including Mark and Sarah who were still living at home before going to college, and where she was surrounded by her adoring family. We all remember our incredible delight and excitement the first time Sheila was able to walk, very unsteadily, from one end of the kitchen to the other without a walker. Sheila continued to improve and certainly so very much more quickly than she would have in the rehabilitation centre. The lasting effect of this dreadful, and certainly preventable accident, is that she had to adjust to double vision, which she eventually did, and when you talk about it all she feels a certain numbness down her left side. The doctors in the hospital never even thought of any eyesight problems and it was only when visiting California Institute of Technology for a term two years later she also had her eyes tested and her vision was transformed although still with a depth perspective problem. We only discovered the depth perception problem a few years ago in a particularly thorough eye test.

When I think of this whole dreadful horrifying frightening affair, which I still do, it is to feel an unbelievable gratitude that I have been able to be with Sheila, the light of my life, ever since. Sheila, of course, can remember nothing of the accident. The accident would have been prevented had there been regular blood tests as is more common, certainly in the US. Had she had them it would have been clear that she had serious anaemia which caused her to faint.

It was not a good summer for our family. Our daughter Sarah when staying with our friends Bill and Paddy Hardy and their two daughters, who lived in a small village, called Highclere, about 30 miles south of our home near Oxford, had an accident on the bicycle she was riding. She ran into the front of a car and fortunately only sustained a serious bruise with broken flesh on her nose. She slid all the way up the bonnet of the car only stopping at the top of the windscreen. She was whisked off to the local hospital. When she got back home to Oxford our surgeon friend Malcolm Gough was appalled at the incompetent job the surgeon had done. If nothing was done she would have been scarred for life. He immediately took her off to the Oxford hospital and arranged for a surgeon friend of his to repair and sew it up very professionally. It is now practically impossible to see where the injury was unless you know where and look carefully.

My low opinion of the medical profession in general, its irresponsible lack of influence on the UK National Health Service, the fact that many did not, and still do not, believe in regular checks of any kind, the frequent incompetence and scientific ignorance of many of those advising the government, were all reinforced. Not that the government medical committees in the US are any better informed as I describe later when briefly describing some of my collaborative medical research in Chapter 14. My medical research collaborators, however, were uniformly very bright and felt strongly about how patients should be cared for, completely ignoring medically irresponsible government recommendations.

IX

University of Oxford, Centre for Mathematical Biology and the Changing World of Academia 1969-

We returned to Oxford in late December 1969. This was the beginning of what was to be my longest university stay. I took up my position as the Fellow in Mathematics in Corpus Christi College and I started lecturing again in 1970. I taught courses in applied mathematics but with the University of Oxford's rigid system by which students prior to coming up had to choose the subject to study, and stick with it; the courses were only for mathematicians. The classes were large, generally more than 100, in the first two years of the then three-year honours degree course. Students never asked questions of the lecturer unlike the custom in American universities; it was simply not done. For the first few years there were the old rolling green boards that you wrote on with chalk. I wore the traditional black academic faculty gown; it kept the chalk off my clothes. All Fellows of the older colleges had to wear gowns at dinner in college and still do. For that I had a different rather fancier one, an "every day" higher doctoral one with elegant frills which I left in the Senior Common Room cloakroom where we all left our gowns: astonishingly mine was actually stolen after I officially retired.

The Oxford University year consists of three 8-week terms, always referred to as Michaelmas, Hilary and Trinity so there was essentially half the year available for research or whatever you wanted to do. Most of the faculty were genuinely concerned with the education and intellectual stimulation of the students ~ not that all the faculty succeeded. When research reporting was introduced, initially it was voluntarily, so most of the faculty simply ignored it: many of the faculty never published anything anyway. The excuse for college Fellow tutors was often the time consuming requirements of their college which was not a totally unreasonable excuse in some cases.

Mathematics students in Oxford in their final year had to take at least two special subject courses. There were about 30 such courses on offer and even with the typical final year mathematics class of around 400 mathematics majors the number in each course was very small, often not even double figures. There was still the general feeling that the specialised courses should be geared towards those students who intended to make a career in academia which was not the case, of course, for the vast majority.

I had been doing research on the application of mathematical modelling in the biomedical sciences for some years by the time I went back to Oxford in 1969. So, with the rapidly expanding new field of mathematical biology in the early 1970s and its increasingly recognised importance I decided to offer the first course in mathematical biology. The primary aim was to show the students how useful, fascinating and helpful mathematics could be in the real world and to introduce the radical new concept of genuine interdisciplinary science in the biomedical sciences. Courses related to the physical sciences, of course, had been taught for many years. Students flocked to the mathematical biology course with typical class sizes each year of 90-100. This caused considerable angst, particularly among the pure mathematicians, and gave rise to remarks such as: "Of course the final exam questions in mathematical biology are so much easier." I do not feel it was necessarily my lectures, although I tried very hard to make them novel and interesting, but rather that students felt that the mathematics they had learned could have a real relevance in the outside world.

By the late 1970s it was clear to me that mathematical biology was a new academic field which would continue to grow exponentially. More and more researchers from around the world wanted to come to Oxford and be involved in the ever-increasing mathematics-biomedical interdisciplinary research going on. I thought that a *Centre for Mathematical Biology* would be a major boost to the field in Oxford, and internationally, so I started to work on how such a Centre could be funded and approved by the university. The UK Science Research Council was the obvious place to start if the university agreed. I was fortunate that, at the time, Professor Sir Richard Southwood was the Chairman of the Zoology Department and a friend with whom I discussed the possibility. With his influence in the higher administrative echelons of the University (he later became the Vice-Chancellor, that is the President, in 1989) it was clear it would be very helpful if I got his support which he immediately gave. After much discussion the university agreed to its foundation and the *Centre for Mathematical Biology* was formally founded in 1983, the first in the world and I was appointed Director, a position I held until retiring early from Oxford in 1992 to go back permanently to American academia.

IX. University of Oxford, Centre for Mathematical Biology and the Changing World of Academia 1969–

After the official founding I submitted a grant application to the *Science Research Council* for the Centre and the Council agreed to fund it. The money from the Research Council was certainly not large, even for that time, UK£55,400 in total for the first four years. Crucially, I was given total control of how to use the money unlike the current nitpicking, often ridiculous, inhibiting rules by grant giving bodies and the ever increasing interference by university administrators and department chairs.

Because of the unique aspect and academic atmosphere of the Centre and, of course, because it was in the University of Oxford, practically all the visitors were self-supported. Several actually gave money to the Centre for its use in whatever way I felt would be most beneficial. As a result there were numerous postdoctoral visitors, money for travel for graduate students and so on. The freedom to use the money in any way I wanted for the Centre and developing the field made an enormous difference to its success.

The Centre very quickly became immensely successful and acquired a large international reputation primarily because of the number of major world figures in the field who came to visit for varying periods from a week to a year and also the research which was carried out and published. There were more than 70 visitors during the initial grant period. It also attracted extremely bright research and postdoctoral students wanting to move into the field. It was a very exciting time and the many visitors whom I met at various meetings or their universities, years later, remembered their visits with nostalgia. The photos below are only a very small sample of the many visitors and post-doctorals. The photos give a clear indication of the warm friendly atmosphere in the Centre.

The university provided me with a private secretary, whom I required to be able to take shorthand dictation (a dying talent), and a building, the first and nicest of which was a large 18th century house belonging to the university in the middle of town across St. Giles from the Mathematical Institute and in the back garden of which the photos were all taken. The house was the Centre for the first few years.

The research output associated with the *Centre*, in the form of published research papers in major journals, was enormous - comparable to the number written by the whole of the rest of the mathematics faculty in the Mathematical Institute in the same period. Many of the internationally well-known senior visitors had been friends of many years.

There were also many group interdisciplinary meetings on problems brought by colleagues in other biological and medical departments in the university. There is a small selection of some of the visitors to the Centre in the 1980s with a selection of their academic positions below: many moved universities during their career.

Prof. Lee Segel
Weizmann Institute

Prof. Akira Okubo
NY Univ. Stony Brooke

Prof. Carla Wofsy
Univ. of New Mexico

Dr. Byron Goldstein
Los Alamos Nat. Lab.

Prof. Mark Ferguson
Univ. of Manchester

Prof. Art Winfree
Univ. of Arizona

Prof. Simon Levin
Princeton Univ.

Prof. Zack Powell
UC Berkeley

Prof. Hans Othmer
Univ. of Minnesota

IX. University of Oxford, Centre for Mathematical Biology and the Changing World of Academia 1969–

Prof. George Oster
UC Berkeley

Prof. Jacques Demongeot
Univ. of Grenoble

Prof. Enzo Capasso
Univ. of Milan

Prof. Mayan Mimura
Tokyo Univ.

Prof. James Sneyd
Univ. of Auckland

Prof. Mano Manoranjan
State Univ. of Washington

Prof. Paul Kulesa
Stowers Inst. (Medical)

Prof. Damiel Bentil
Univ. of Vermont

Prof. Mary Myerscough
Univ. of Sydney

Dr. Alan Perelson
Los Alamos Nat. Lab.

Prof. Mimi Koehl
UC Berkeley

Prof. Mark Lewis
Univ. of Alberta

Prof. Philip Maini   Prof. Jonathan Sherratt   Prof. Meghan Burke
Univ. of Oxford   Heriot-Watt Univ.   Kennesauw State Univ.

Towards the end of the first grant period of four years I had to submit a report to the mathematics committee of the government's *Science Research Council* the majority of which consisted of pure mathematicians many of whom had no idea, nor cared, what mathematical biology was all about. Coincidently I was on the Research Council during this time, so, as was the custom, I had to leave when my report on the Centre was discussed. Grants were given a grade based on the report, namely outstanding, average or below average. When I got back I was told that the Centre's activity, the more than 50 articles published, the more than 70 senior visitors, the high international reputation the *Centre of Mathematical biology* had acquired and so on, was graded "average"! The committee then briefly discussed a report for a similar grant period from a pure mathematician in the University of Manchester who had published two papers in three years. He was given an "outstanding". The ridiculous grading was the butt of jokes, some very funny, among colleagues, biomedical collaborators and visitors for quite a while. My grant renewal application for the Centre, however, was unanimously renewed.

Of course with any successful new institute in academia the politics become more and more intrusive. The Chairman of the Mathematical Institute on one occasion asked me to go and see him because he wanted to talk about finances. He wanted me to agree to contribute some of the money the Centre had been given by visitors to the Mathematical Institute to help support pure mathematicians and others who were unable to get research funds. I originally thought it was a joke. Not surprisingly the short answer was no.

Politics are, of course, certainly not new in academia; they are almost worse when the benefits of any gain are small. Around this time at dinner in college one evening I was sitting at High Table beside a visiting scientist who worked for the WHO (World Health Organisation) in Geneva. He was the major person specifically involved with certain programmes in rural Africa. I asked him: "*After you have the programme set up, the money assigned and agreed by the WHO, the scientists and doctors agreed on, what is the most important thing you have to do before starting the project?*" He replied: "*Hire somebody to guard my back.*"

Reasonably I had to do my share of sitting on various departmental committees. A non-obligatory responsibility, until many years later, was to be an Examiner, for a three year period, in the formal examinations, *Moderations* at the end of the first year, which were also class graded, and *Schools*, the final honours examinations on which the class of the degree awarded was determined. It was incredibly time consuming since there were only a few examiners who were responsible for all the examinations other than in the special subjects in the final year. One particularly arrogant, self-centred, mathematics Fellow in Magdalen College was appointed such an examiner but his questions were so ridiculously difficult he was relieved as an examiner, which, of course, was possibly his intention. Part of his university requirement was to give the normal one course of 16 lectures a year. His lectures were totally incomprehensible and so he was also relieved of his lecturing responsibility. At a formal faculty meeting I said that he had not given any lectures for some years and should be required to give his statutory number of 16 lectures. This put the Chairman of the Faculty in a difficult position, even though in principle he and others in the committee agreed, but he suggested we not do anything since it would cause all sorts of problems. I persisted and he reluctantly said he would approach the college to discuss it. Apparently this Fellow had similar difficulties with tutorials in college. Magdalen College finally, in effect, bailed the university out by releasing the Fellow from his tutorial duties by appointing him to a single non-renewable five year Research Fellowship on condition he resign his tutorial fellowship and leave the university. This is exactly what he did and he went off to India: no one I knew in Oxford ever heard of him again. Another positive thing was that it freed up a position in the college and the mathematics faculty to which a very good mathematician was appointed.

Social life in the university side of Oxford was relatively scant and spasmodic, except with family friends, since the academic social environment is almost totally based in the colleges. In the early 1970s not all the faculty had a college connection and several new graduate colleges were founded in part to accommodate them. The system in these is very different, with no formal High Table with its excellent cuisine and wine. Faculty and students eat together which of course has its good aspects.

On returning to Oxford in 1970 I thought that it would be the final university move. I should have known better but I was at least formally a faculty member for more than twenty years. As a tutorial fellow with so much teaching it was difficult to find the time for any graduate student supervision. My research, however, was such that after only two years, as mentioned before, I was appointed a University Reader in Mathematics when my tutorial responsibility was halved. I felt I could start serious doctoral research supervision and, until retiring early in 1992 to return to the US, I supervised the first 21 Oxford students, who obtained mathematics doctorates - called a D.Phil. in Oxford - in mathematical biology. I was immensely fortunate to have had a very bright and enthusiastic bunch of students. It is fairly standard in the UK for students to get their doctorates in three years, unlike the typical five in the US. One reason, which focuses the mind, of course, is that the government grant support for doctoral students was only for three years.

With all the moving back and forward to the US and the relative short periods in various universities, in all of which, except the University of Oxford and the University of Washington, I realised very quickly that I did not want to spend the rest of my academic career for a variety of reasons as I have described. A major consequence of this peripatetic academic life was that I initially did not feel I could take graduate students since it would be very disruptive for them if I changed universities during their doctoral research. I was wrong about this, and from the early 1980s, I simply took my graduate students and post-doctoral students with me. Without exception, they all found the new environments interesting, stimulating, enjoyable, educationally a mind expanding experience, and it had absolutely no deleterious effects on their research; in fact very much the opposite. The extra experience also helped in their obtaining permanent academic positions in whatever country they chose.

Almost all of my graduate students and post-doctoral students are now in senior academic positions around the world, several of them internationally renowned leaders in their specific field. To mention only a few, to give some idea of the diversity of the field, Philip Maini, is the Professor of Mathematical Biology, recently elected a Fellow of the Royal Society, has been the Director of the Centre for Mathematical Biology in Oxford since I retired early in 1992: it is now called the *Wolfson Centre for Mathematical Biology*, a consequence of financial donations. Dr. Paul

Kulesa is the Director of the *Imaging Laboratory* in the *Stowers Institute for Medical Research* and is internationally known for his innovative biological imaging. Professor David Lane, of the Henley Business School, University of Reading uses his mathematical systems dynamics expertise in genuine business applications. David and his partner of many years, Dr. Elke Husemann were awarded the Operational Society's President's medal for 2014. James Sneyd, a Fellow of the Royal Society of New Zealand, a professor of mathematics at the University of Auckland is the major world figure in mathematical physiology and in calcium dynamics: calcium is involved in practically all cell development. He had tenured positions in the USA at UCLA and the University of Michigan before returning to New Zealand. He is also well known for his extremely funny, irreverent and original humour. His book is co-authored with one of the senior visitors to the Centre during my time as Director, namely Professor Jim Keener from the University of Utah: their book is the key reference and classic in the field. Jonathan Sherratt, a professor of mathematics at Heriot-Watt University, was the second youngest person to be elected a Fellow of the Royal Society of Edinburgh, and is a renowned figure in ecological modelling.

Doing research, supervising students, collaborating with visitors, academic journal work, seeing people who wished to come and talk to the group about a possible collaborative project and so on was the immensely enjoyable side of my position. Dealing with all the increasing administrative chores was certainly not so but it was still not excessive. However, it was the trivial, irritating, time consuming and occasionally dishonest politics which finally made me decide to retire early in 1992 to return to US academia. My successor has even many more to deal with. This was five years before I would have had to retire as a professor, at age 67, which, at the time, was two more years than non-professors. Now all faculty in most British universities can stay until they are 67: universities in Britain now, however, impose their own rules. In the US there is no retirement age which certainly has its good and bad aspects.

When it became known that I was possibly going to leave Oxford several universities in the US were interested in having me join their faculty. I, Sheila and I rather, finally decided to move to the University of Washington in Seattle where I had visited for a year's sabbatical for the academic year 1988-9. The university wanted me to move permanently and set up a group in mathematical biology in the Applied Mathematics

Department. We really liked the university and the American Northwest. With my Oxford political experiences, before accepting I said I would require rather a lot of guarantees, such as a private secretary, never to have to do any departmental administration, leave for several months a year to be back in Europe, never to be required to be chair of the department and a few others all of which were agreed. Unlike many guarantees and promises by universities I have known, the University of Washington kept every single one of them to my surprise and the astonishment of my university colleagues. So, after a further year's leave of absence from Oxford in 1990-91 to make sure that Sheila and I would like it since it was clearly going to be my last permanent faculty university move, I retired formally from the University of Oxford and became officially Professor Emeritus of Mathematical Biology. All my Oxford graduate students and post-doctoral research students moved with me. The mathematical biology group became the largest and most dynamic research group in the department with numerous publications: it changed the dynamics of the department in Washington. It was one of the pleasantest permanent academic appointments I have had. It had one major drawback compared to Oxford, however, namely the lack of the interesting regular High Table college life which effectively exists nowhere in American academic life – a great pity and a great loss to academia.

One of the benefits and pleasures of being actively involved in research is that you get invited to travel widely to give lectures at conferences and universities around the world. A major meeting for the mathematical biology field was held in 1991 in the dramatic *Alpes D'Huez*, a ski resort in the French Alps close to Grenoble, where my long time friend and collaborator, Professor Jacques Demongeot was a professor of mathematics in the university and medical school. He is almost unique in that he has a medical degree as well as a doctorate in mathematics. He is a major world figure in the field and, unfortunately, a victim of some unpleasant academic politics described below. This meeting was the first major one in the applications of mathematics in medicine and biology. I had been invited to give the opening plenary lecture. The conference attracted several hundred participants and it was then that the *European Society for Mathematical and Theoretical Biology* (ESMTB) was officially founded. Even though I no longer lived in Europe I was elected the first President for the first three-year period 1991-4 which turned out not to be as time consuming as I anticipated. It is now the major European Society in the field, comparable to the US Society for Mathematical Biology.

IX. University of Oxford, Centre for Mathematical Biology and the Changing World of Academia 1969–

Politics, of course, are common in the university world, and have been for centuries. It is sometimes helpful and sometimes outrageous. Jacques Demongeot, whose photo is above, is the scientist who discovered and proposed the technique to reduce the common, very distressing, problem in Parkinson's disease, namely the uncontrollable shaking. He suggested implanting an electronic device in the brain, which stops the shaking, when activated by the patient by an external switch. It was an incredibly clever invention and immensely helpful. It is now in worldwide use. The system of patents in French universities is that the university, not the discoverer, has the patent but, of course, only if the university applies for it. The surgeon who performed the first implant, and sensed a Nobel Prize, with not atypical surgeon arrogance, said of Demongeot, when it was pointed out that Demongeot had discovered it: "He's only an engineer."

Another unfortunate example of academic vindictiveness is what happened to a French colleague, research collaborator and long time friend who, for his impressive body of research, had been an obvious choice for election to the French Academy for many years. He has never been elected because of the system of election and a case of academic vindictiveness. Each year the Academy has a specific number of places in chosen general areas, such as mathematics, biology and so on. There is also a specific age range which varies each year. My colleague, who has successfully proposed several colleagues for election, put up a former graduate student of his who was in the young age range of that specific year and he was elected. A candidate could effectively be blackballed by an academician in the candidate's field. Since then, every time my friend has been put up for election he has been opposed, successfully, by this former student.

A well-known major figure in the field who was also subjected to incredible vindictiveness was a colleague and friend of many years, Professor Arthur Winfree. He was one of the world figures in the field of physiology and mathematical biology and the author of a major work: *The Geometry of Biological Time*. Art also visited the Centre for Mathematical Biology for several months when it was first started. He obtained a Ph.D. from Princeton in 1970. In the early 1980's, when he was a professor at Purdue University, he decided that he would like to move to the west coast and applied to two major world-class universities there. I was one of his colleagues who wrote a letter of recommendation as did some others who knew his work well and whom I know also wrote exceptionally strong supporting letters. We all thought he would clearly be offered a faculty position since any university would have been delighted and honoured to have him. To our astonishment he never got any offers. Later we discovered from a colleague in the university that Winfree's supervisor in Princeton each time he had been asked had written a derogatory letter. When Art was told, it came as a complete surprise since he had thought he had had a good colleague relationship with him. Art accepted such behaviour without rancour and moved on.

Another astonishing affair was related to Art Winfree's research work on biological clocks and jet lag. He cleverly showed scientifically how to reset your biological clock to avoid jet lag. Depending on the hour difference you had to look at the sun for about 15-30 minutes, crucially at a specific time of the day after the flight. He had carried out a number of clever experiments on animals, and humans, which confirmed his hypothesis and calculations. Others, as well as myself, suggested that he take out a patent which gave the appropriate time to reset the body clock using a simple hand calculator. He told me that he had thought about it but when he investigated it he found that someone at Harvard had used his idea to carry out an experiment on one 50-year old woman and the university had filed a patent petition. Art told me the Harvard lawyers threatened to sue him if he pursued in his patent project. As was typical of Art Winfree, he showed neither anger nor rancour and simply moved on.

A particular outrageous example of incomprehensible politics that I know of was in the University of Paris. A colleague, and later a friend, had proposed me for what was called a *Chaire Européenne* (European Professorship) a professorial appointment which let me spend one month in the summer every year for three years from 1994-6, at one of the university campuses in Paris, the same university centre as my friend. He is a distinguished academic, somewhat purer mathematically oriented than I am, with a major world reputation for developing a completely new and highly original area of mathematics. Research support was somewhat similar to that in the other European countries and was usually for periods of several years, around 3 to 5. When the first renewal came up the university asked him to have sent three letters of support from internationally well-known non-French mathematicians. I was asked for one and another was a distinguished colleague in the University of Washington; he knew the third referee. I know that we all wrote exceptionally strong supporting letters. We all assumed renewal would be automatic. I only heard the sequel some months later when having dinner in Paris with my friend and he told me the grant had not been renewed. When I asked how that could possibly have happened he told me that someone in the university responsible for the renewal application dossier had, dishonestly, said that none of the foreign referees had written a letter of support. Shortly afterwards my friend resigned and spent most of his time at a university in Italy which he had visited regularly over the years and where he is highly respected.

French universities are often hotbeds of political intrigue. I had seen some of this from the time I spent in the Universities of Angers, Grenoble, Paris and others. Academics, at least to me, were more accepting of it than I would have expected. My friend, who did not have his grant renewed as described above, during one of my visits in 1995, wondered if I would consider moving to the University of Paris. In spite of the marvellous city, our love of France, many family and academic friends and colleagues in France, the fact that we had an ancient house and farm in the Dordogne, in the southwest of France, I used the excuse that I was too close to the European retirement age to move.

Encaenia

The major University of Oxford event of the year, called *Encaenia*, is held in 9th week, the week after the official end of Trinity Term, the third term, when most of the students not graduating had already gone down. Encaenia is the Oxford equivalent of Commencement in the USA and Graduation in other universities. A major difference, however, is that no students actually go on stage to graduate formally during the ceremony. That is only for those being awarded honorary degrees. At Encaenia a brief description of the major events in the university during the past year is also given - all in Latin. The ceremony is essentially unchanged since the mid-17th century when it was moved to the university's Sheldonian Theatre from St. Mary's church, across Radcliffe Square, where then it generally involved satirical, sometimes scandalous, speeches.

In the morning of Encaenia, there is the formal procession to the magnificent architecturally dramatic Sheldonian Theatre, designed by Sir Christopher Wren. The procession starts from one of the colleges with a strict order, led by the various university mace carriers, then the Chancellor of the University, Heads of the Oxford Colleges, some university dignitaries then the Doctors of the University. The latter are faculty who have a more advanced doctoral degree, such as a Doctor of Divinity, ranked the highest, with a Doctor of Science, which I have, ranked around fifth: a D.Phil., the Oxford equivalent of a Ph.D., is not considered prestigious enough to be in the procession. The Honorands come last. Everyone must be in strict formal academic dress with white bow tie. One year, Sir Alan Bullock, whom I knew well from my time as the Distinguished Visiting Fellow in St. Catherine's College in 1967 and who, for a few years, was the Vice-Chancellor (equivalent to the President in North American Universities) told me he was chastised for not being properly dressed: he had a rose in his lapel and was told to remove it. He was reprimanded with: "*People look to the VC for correct dress.*"

Prior to the formal procession there is a gathering in the college, where the procession will start, for those participating in Encaenia so as to partake of *Lord Crewe's Benefaction.* Lord Crewe (1633-1721), for a time the Bishop of Oxford, had left money for those taking part in the Encaenia procession to enjoy champagne and strawberries prior to the procession to the Sheldonian Theatre. I decided to go to the one in 1971 when Edward Heath, the Prime Minister at the time, was getting an honorary degree. The party, that year with glorious weather, was in the garden of Wadham College. It was very crowded with an abundance of excellent champagne and delicious strawberries. It was a very colourful group - many of the academic gowns are a wild red and gold. Because Edward Heath, the conservative Prime Minister, was getting an honorary degree there was going to be a demonstration against his getting the degree by some left wing students. Among those attending the benefaction there was only very mild interest with no one in the least concerned about the demonstration. The Chancellor, Sir Harold MacMillan, the former Conservative Prime Minister, in his elaborate gold encrusted gown with his train-bearer, joked in his quiet Oxford voice: "We'll have to watch at Broad Street where they have good crossfire."

So, off we trouped, through the large crowds of spectators, with the Honorands bringing up the rear. A short distance from the college there was spasmodic clapping which at times became a slow coordinated clap with shouts of "Heath out" amidst the clapping. Some of the demonstrators were clearly quite carried away with emotion while others had incredible looks of fury. They looked rather ugly in a pathetic sort of way. How much more effective a silent protest would have been. The police were out in in force and were incredibly patient while the blue-suited bowler hatted university police, traditionally referred to as the

"Bulldogs", were everywhere in the quadrangles. Heath's presence clearly worried a lot of people.

University of Oxford *Encaenia* procession, 1971. These are the formal Doctors of the university with their wild coloured gowns. (JDM is first on the left).

We slowly shambled through the beautiful 15th century Divinity School quadrangle and then on to the Sheldonian Theatre where everybody was waiting. We all sat round the Chancellor on the stage with those getting Honorary Degrees in the body of the theatre. My school five years of Latin was no longer up to understanding the ceremony but there was an English printed copy available.

Academies, Societies and publications

There is a large number of academic societies around the world which publish newsletters, journals, organize conferences, elect members and Fellows in various fields. The pre-eminent ones, those which really count, are the national Academies to which members are elected and which are often limited in number. Election to these bodies immediately changes the international and academic status of the Fellows and their university. The *Royal Society* (UK) and the *Académie française* (France) were founded in the mid-17th century with the *American National Academy of Sciences* in 1780.

The French Academy consists of five equally prestigious separate general subject academies, of which the *Academy of Sciences* is one. Together they constitute the *Institut de France*, which is housed in the magnificent domed building on the *rue de Conti*, on the river Seine in middle of Paris: there is a photo of it in Chapter 12. Since the numbers elected to these academies are limited this contributes to the international prestige of the Fellows. Each society also elects Foreign Members from around the world. The Royal Society, a scientific society, has around 1600 Fellows, while the French Academy of Sciences (*Académie des sciences*), for example, has approximately 150 French "*Académiciens*" and around 240 Foreign Members (*Associés étrangers*) so elections to these is even more prestigious. There are various subject committees which recommend candidates so, not unexpectedly, politics can play a role but surprisingly not as much as might be expected. Members' formal dress in the *Académie française* is the most dramatic with a gold encrusted dark thick cloth suit which in the summer is unbelievably hot.

Having research papers published in the "*Proceedings*" of the academies has always been prestigious but to a lesser extent in the French Academy because until relatively recently articles had to be written in French although not now. English has essentially been the sole language of science since roughly the end of the Second World War, before which German was still widely accepted. France did try to keep French going by requiring lectures given at conferences by French scientists, both in France and abroad, be given in French, which in practice was widely ignored, certainly at those conferences outside of France.

Until around the early 2000s, academic research, particularly in the sciences was primarily published in academic journals rather than in books. Most of these journals still carry on with more or less the same system although increasingly they are online. Articles are formally submitted to journal editors who send them out to specialists in the field to referee, anonymously. The number of journals has now grown unboundedly with the exponential rise in those solely published on the web. When I was at Harvard as a visitor in 1963 my post-doctoral supervisor for a year 1956-7 was Professor Sydney Goldstein FRS, who when retiring, told me he had published 67 research papers in his life (three of which I wrote and we were both listed as authors), a number of which he was clearly very proud: he felt it was an enormous number. By the time I formally retired from my last university professorship I had published close to 250, about half of which are singly authored. Now, a few of my own former graduate students, very good ones admittedly, but only three quarters way through their careers have almost published that number. The more active researchers will probably publish around a hundred more before retirement.

The number of publications also depends on the discipline, with chemists, for example, publishing many many more. A major difference now is that published articles frequently have a large number of authors whereas formerly most articles generally had only one or at most three authors. In medical journals now it is even worse. The prestigious *New England Journal of Medicine*, for example, now limits the number of "authors" who can be listed to a ludicrous 26 with, if there are more, all the others referred to as *et al.* The major author on a paper is now listed at the end or beginning with others listed according to how much they have been involved: how the order is determined is often controversial. In many of the research papers with which I have been involved the authors were generally listed alphabetically which was not such a bad idea if, as was the case with some of my publications, it was not possible to say who the major contributor was – something we simply did not think about. The whole publishing business is now completely out of hand with more and more journals online in which you can publish for a fee: this was rare up to about the mid-1990s. I still get several invitations almost every week, from web journals inviting me to submit a research article. Many of these online journals do not have the articles refereed. One scientist in the US a few years ago decided to highlight the problem by sending an article for consideration to around a hundred journals which charged a publishing fee if published. The article was complete rubbish which, as he said, a 14 year old would have immediately seen. Approximately 80% of these "academic" fee-charging journals accepted it for publication. Needless to say he never published it.

In the late 1980s and early 1990s there was an increasing number of conferences devoted solely to mathematical biology. These became larger and larger with the fast growing number of researchers in the field around the world. At the conference in 1991 at the ski resort Alpe d'Huez near Grenoble the European Society for Mathematical and Theoretical Biology (ESMTB) was founded, as mentioned above, it was attended by around 250, many out of curiosity rather than active researchers in the field. In 2005, when an ESMTB major conference was held in Dresden, the number of people attending had to be restricted to just over 900 because of space constraints. In spite of its exponential increase in numbers and interest, and its clear scientific, practical and applicable importance in the biological sciences, and increasingly in medicine, it is only barely recognised as a real field of mathematics which, as Professor Philip Maini FRS, my colleague and close friend in Oxford, jokingly remarked it was because it was not useless. Mathematics is widely considered to be only pure mathematics.

The hassles of dealing with the time consuming politics while running the Centre for Mathematical Biology were taking more and more time but it was mainly the progressively less time for research which finally convinced me in the late 1980s that I did not want to do it for the rest of my academic career. University politics, envious reactions to a group's success and so on have been, of course, a feature of academic life for centuries. Those I experienced in Oxford were actually quite few and not very serious with some simply ludicrous. Historically in my alma mater, the University of St. Andrews, it had, in earlier times, clearly been much worse. For example, in the late 17th century, the first Regius Professor of Mathematics, James Gregory had a very hard time. He was a real applied mathematician: he had invented the first reflecting telescope and had tried to set up the first observatory but was essentially thwarted by other faculty members in the university. According to the professor of mathematics in my first year at the University of St. Andrews, Professor H.W. Turnbull FRS, Gregory should be recognized as one of the discoverer's of calculus together with Newton and Leibnitz. Major figures were often accused, sometimes justifiably, of stealing from each other; Newton and Leibnitz feuded for years. Gregory was particularly worried about Newton, who was, from all accounts a pretty awful and vindictive man, and Professor Gregory, according to Professor Turnbull, withheld his innovative work on calculus until Newton published his. Newton only did so after Gregory had died. Gregory got so fed up with all the backbiting and so on in the University of St. Andrews he wrote to a friend in Paris explaining why he left St. Andrews:

"I was ashamed to answer, the affairs of the Observatory of St Andrews were in such a bad condition; the reason of which was, a prejudice the masters of the University did take at the mathematics, because some of their scholars, finding their courses and dictats opposed by what they had studied in the mathematics, did mock at their masters, and deride some of them publicly. After this, the servants of the colleges got orders not to wait on me at my observations: my salary was also

kept back from me; and scholars of most eminent rank were violently kept from me, contrary to their own and their parents' wills, the masters persuading them that their brains were not able to endure it. These, and many other discouragements, obliged me to accept a call here to the College of Edinburgh, where my salary is nearly double, and my encouragements otherwise much greater."

It is not like this now. A friend and colleague Mark Chaplain, who is a major internationally well known mathematical biologist, was recently appointed to the Regius Gregory Professorship of Mathematics. He told me the university could not be more welcoming and helpful.

Decline of University Academia

The university research norm, particularly in Europe, is now so different to what it was for most of my time in academia with incredibly detailed yearly reports, how much grant money you bring in to the university, what you did with it, what has been the influence of a lecture you gave two years ago at some other institution, how many people came to it, the incredibly time consuming business of writing grant applications the award of which is often bizarre, and so on. From the mid 1980s there were regular audits but with nothing like the requirements now. It was what sowed some of the seeds of my thinking of returning to America. The number of secretaries and administrators has grown enormously from around 8 or so in the 1970's when the faculty was around 90 to more than 40 now for a faculty of just over 100. There are numerous emails I get a week (around 25 or so), some of which are as important as what you have to do about unwashed coffee cups left on your desk; this was actually one email. Those I get from Oxford are in a class by themselves in their frequency and often irrelevance. Sadly, I would now not recommend a very bright student go into academia, a view quite widely held by academics now.

Another extremely negative event as regards UK academia and research in general is Brexit. Even before the negotiations have started some serious problems are already appearing with an increasing number of concerns. There is, for example, a significant percentage of foreign permanent faculty around the country. Also Euro grant giving bodies will probably no longer consider research applications from British universities.

Unlike most of my time in the University of Oxford there is now the ludicrously, ever expanding, number of bureaucrats as in most universities, which, among other things, has contributed to the greatly increased fees for students. Even so there are still major financial problems. Faculty in Oxford have recently (2016) been offered voluntary redundancy even to major world figures in their field. A friend said that at the end of the letter they received it was added that enforced redundancy would not happen just yet! This has happened in other universities too in Britain, in some of which there will be enforced redundancy. In some universities there is pressure for older faculty to retire early since they are paid more than younger faculty. Another factor contributing to the financial problems is that there is now sometimes no retirement age, as is the case in America, although not in Oxford. There is also an ever increasing number of silly, stupid rather, inhibiting rules of behaviour in universities which has had a contributing negative impact on the number of people wanting to have a career in academia. I hear from colleagues around the world who describe how it has had a major inhibiting effect on research as well and on the number of very bright students who simply do not want all the hassles to pursue a research degree. As mentioned, for most of my time in universities there was no university required report on whether or not you did research, published scientific articles or what you did in the very long vacations. Getting research support was encouraged of course. Now, if a graduate student wants to go to London, a meeting, or wherever, they have to get written permission from their supervisor and file it with the university. So much of a senior faculty's time is spent dealing with unbelievable bureaucratic regulations. They are now almost universal. At conferences I frequently hear people say that if they were starting out again they would not go into academia: certainly I would have very serious doubts. Administrators and governments have much to answer for.

The rules regarding research grants are also often unbelievable. One ludicrous example, but perhaps less unexpectedly in America, was associated with my research with a psychologist colleague in the University of Washington on marital interaction and divorce prediction which is described in Chapter 14 (and is surprisingly accurate). We decided to extend our study to gay couples and submitted a grant application to the appropriate government (US) agency in the late 1990s: it was rejected, essentially by return. It turned out that the government had directed that any grant which mentioned any of the words lesbian, homosexual or gay was to be denied immediately without being sent out to referees. In Oxford, in 2015, some grant applications to various charities, such as the *Wellcome Trust*, were not allowed in some departments because the overheads for the university or department were not considered large enough. This is particularly ironic since when I first approached the Wellcome Trust many years ago to try and get it to support mathematical biology I was asked to meet the committee in London and was grilled, very pleasantly and thoroughly, on this new area and why the Wellcome should support it. It has been a major supporter of interdisciplinary mathematics, biology and medicine research ever since. The Wellcome Trust is a charitable foundation, arguably the leading one, which supports research in the medical world in the broadest sense. For some years I sat on one of the committees which considered research applications. It has had an important and crucial impact on the field. Such a departmental or university rule regarding overheads will have, and already has, a significant negative effect on research.

University academia and respect for it has plummeted and not just in Britain. Until around the early 1970s the title of professor conferred an automatic respect both in and outside of universities. This was in part because there were so few professors, roughly two per academic department, in the then relatively small number of universities. With the explosion of the number of new universities the professorial standing started to diminish rather quickly. In the University of Oxford in the 1960s there were approximately 6-8 professors in the large mathematics department, with approximately 90 permanent faculty. When I first went to America in the late 1950s during my time at Harvard I travelled around the country giving lectures at various universities. I was surprised that practically none of the professors used the title professor but rather Dr. I quickly understood why with the power and influence the medical profession had. In Oxford now the title of professor can be given to anyone in the faculty who applies for it and has done some research, essentially unrelated to its level of excellence. As a result the American system of using Dr. as one's title is becoming more and more widespread particularly when used outside of academia. Interestingly the effect of this is that relations between students and university teachers have markedly changed affecting the whole academic atmosphere. It is a universal phenomenon I gather from colleagues around the world.

The exponential increase in administrators not to mention the increasing number of ludicrous rules and forms to be completed it is not surprising that university academia is becoming so much less attractive to the detriment of practical research in all branches of science, medicine and technology. In spite of this, however, vacancies in positions still attract a large number of applicants: there are simply so many more people seeking jobs. University education is also becoming less attractive to prospective students with the ever increasing fees to keep the university going as a business. Graduating students now often have enormous debts as a consequence. In a recent email in 2016 I was told of the mess the budget was in, in one English university to which the administrators' answer was to fire roughly 20% of the tenured faculty and close various departments.

I feel immensely privileged to have had an academic career with complete intellectual freedom and without the numerous current hassles. As Professor David Lane, one of my former graduate students, recently said, I had experienced the *"Glory Days of Academia"*.[1] All the academics I know agree with him. The article[1] referenced in the footnote, should be required reading for anyone contemplating an academic career as should the *New York Times* article in 2017 regarding online research publishing.[2] The latter article describes how a fictitious person, dr hab. Ana O. Szust (*oszust* means "fraudster" in Polish) submitted a fake article to a large number of open access journals (which charge a lot for publishing an article). Her degrees were also fake. The article was accepted by almost 50 of these "academic journals" and several listed her as Editor in Chief but with no responsibilities.

---

[1] Professor Marina Warner describes the current situation in a very timely, well documented, frank and factual article: Warner, Marina. Learning My Lesson *London Review of Books* 19th March 2015: Vol. 37, pp. 8-14.
[2] New York Times article by Gina Bari Kolata on "academic" journals:
A Scholarly Sting Operation Shines a Light on 'Predatory' Journals
https://www.nytimes.com/2017/03/22/science/open-access-journals.html

X

Return to America: University of Washington and Bainbridge Island 1988–2005

As I mentioned, various universities in the US were interested in having me join their faculty even before deciding to leave Oxford, so I narrowed it down to two possibilities, the University of California Los Angeles (UCLA) and the University of Washington (UW) in Seattle both of which Sheila and I visited for a few days. They are both excellent universities, the drawback of UCLA, however, was that it is in Los Angeles. We finally decided on the University of Washington since we felt the climate and living in the Seattle area was more to our taste. So, for the 1988-9 year I was appointed the first Robert F. Philip Professor in Applied Mathematics and Adjunct Professor of Zoology with the understanding that the year was to see if I would move to UW permanently. Although still responsible for the Centre for Mathematical Biology in Oxford it was incredibly relaxing, in part because of the very welcoming and friendly department atmosphere, enthusiastic students and my post-doctoral research students. Back in Oxford at the end of the year I wrote to UW with a few of the concerns I had about moving permanently: all of them were completely and immediately resolved. It was, however, a major decision but by the end of the academic year back in Oxford we decided to go back to UW for another year in 1990-1 on another unpaid leave of absence from Oxford to be absolutely sure. The University of Oxford said it would agree to the leave if I promised to return permanently to Oxford after it: I said that I could not agree to that condition so Oxford backed down. So, off we went again and this time it was clear that we would definitely leave Oxford and I would join the faculty in UW on a permanent basis. The conditions I required from UW, as I mentioned, which were immediately agreed to, were certainly not all typical of new appointees. A particularly important one was financial support for some of my Oxford graduate and post-doctoral students, who would move with me, until I obtained US funding which I did the first year after moving.

We returned to Oxford in 1991 and, not without some sadness but somewhat mitigated by the changed atmosphere in Corpus Christi College after Sir Kenneth Dover retired as President, I submitted my resignation, and from 1992 officially became Professor Emeritus of Mathematical Biology of the University of Oxford, and Sheila and I returned permanently to the US.

The University of Washington in Seattle is the major state university set in a large campus with practically all of the departments, including several interesting museums, within easy walking distance of my department. One of the major attractions of the university was that there was a separate, quite small, Applied Mathematics department with 12 faculty members at the time. The mathematics department, with around 70 faculty members, consisted essentially of pure mathematicians. An indication of different departmental academic standing was how much research grant money was obtained annually by each department. Even though the pure department was around six times the size of the applied department the external grant money was about the same which is an indication of the academic and research standing of the Applied Mathematics department as compared with the Pure Department. The atmosphere in the department, known as Amath, was very friendly with few departmental tensions other than from one, unproductive member, who felt mathematical biology had taken over, particularly during the several day survey of the department by a national external committee which was carried out a few years after I had moved permanently.

The atmosphere in the department, for practically all of the time I was there, was primarily due to the chairman who was appointed in 1993 after some unusual and astonishing administrative financial irregularities which resulted in a university audit of the department. Professor Ka-Kit Tung (KK), who became a personal friend as well as a very supportive colleague, was persuaded, pressured rather, by the department, to become the Chairman. He unselfishly held the position until 2007 which is so much longer than any other chairman I have known. No one in the department, including all the students and administrative staff wanted him to stop. He was unquestionably the most popular, the most committed to academic excellence and the most respected chair by any department I have ever been part of. He was a major figure in raising the prestige and standing of the Amath department to being first equal with Princeton Applied Mathematics in the national six-year assessment during his tenure in the early 2000s. Generally I have found that by far the best chairs are those who do it out of duty rather than wanting it for the power. KK is also a distinguished scientist and in 2014 published, in the prestigious journal *Science*, one of the important seminal articles[1] on climate warming which explains why there have been temperature plateaus.

My lecturing duties were minimal and were only for graduate students. The department is in effect a graduate department. With a permanent full time personal secretary, no departmental or university administration, and no tedious university and departmental politics to deal with, it was a particularly productive and enjoyable time for me and my research group. The first secretary I had, Jessica Bastian, was married to a graduate student who was finishing his doctoral dental degree and Jessica was only taking the secretarial position until he finished. Surprisingly Jessica learned shorthand which I required of my secretaries but in her case it wouldn't have mattered. Jessica was unquestionably the most lively, incredibly warm, indispensably helpful and enjoyable, bright secretary, assistant rather, I have had in my academic career. I think of her as a friend, not as a former secretary. During her time as my secretary she asked once if she could be away for a few days to go to Santa Fe where she

JDM the first Robert F. Philip Professor University of Washington, 1989.

Jessica Bastian on a few days fashion modelling leave, Santa Fe, 1994.

---

[1] Xianyao Chen and Ka-Kit Tung. Varying planetary heat sink led to global-warming slowdown and acceleration. *Science* 22 August 2014: Vol. 345 no. 6199 pp. 897-903 [DOI: 10.1126/science.1254937].

did some modelling for a fashionable shop there, called *Spirit of the Earth*. The photo above is one of Jessica as a model. Unfortunately her time as my secretary was much too short and she and her then husband (Dr.) Barkley Bastian went off to Hawaii where Jessica (Haskin) still lives.

When joining the university I was also appointed an Adjunct Professor in the Zoology department: I had several research collaborators in the department. Our research was primarily in ecology and epidemiology fields in which I had several graduate students in Applied Mathematics. I still believed in the UK, European in effect, university tradition and suggested several specific research topics to each doctoral student for them to choose which might interest them most. Before starting research each student had to pass a series of formal departmental examinations based on the required courses they had to take for the qualifying exam. All of my students passed these after one year and so were able to devote the next two years to research. I felt that the sooner they obtained their Ph.D. the better, and the sooner that they could start their own life, compared with practically all American graduate students where the norm is five years and sometimes more.

One student, Jane White, who was a mathematics undergraduate at Oxford, came to do a Ph.D. on the interesting problem of wolf pack interaction and their prey survival. It was almost, in an Oxford High Table way, that Jane, along with a post-doctoral student, and former graduate student of mine in Oxford, Mark Lewis, and I ended up working on the project. I had given a lecture at the University of Vancouver and at dinner afterwards one of the guests mentioned how very clever wolves were. I asked that if the wolves are so smart how did the wolf prey, such as deer and moose, survive to which no one had an answer. Returning to Seattle I started to think about it and we began studying wolf behaviour and found that territory formation was a major aspect of how wolves survive. Inter-pack conflict plays a major role. Wolves mark out their territory, and specifically the boundary area, with urination by the alpha pair, which is the major male and female in the pack. These territories are huge, around 125-300 square kilometres. Basically the wolves move out from their den daily, looking for food, but generally do not go beyond the pack territory boundary because of the possibility of inter-pack conflict which can often be fatal. We then thought that prey must be aware of the pack boundaries and restrict their movement to the regions between the packs since it is much less likely to be attacked by a wolf of either pack. Our quantitative applied mathematical research confirmed this hypothesis. My graduate student Jane went off for two weeks in upstate Minnesota to try and get some field data on wolf behaviour for our model. Unfortunately she never saw a single wolf but certainly smelled lots of pack territory urination boundaries! Jane has been a family friend since she was my graduate student: she is a faculty member in the University of Bath.

Some time later I was reading about intertribal warfare among North American Indians and the existence of buffer zones. The Chippewa and Sioux were traditional enemies over game in the buffer zones where, as with wolves, non-migratory game was abundant, mainly Virginia red deer. There were roughly 10 to15 deer per square mile. From around 1750-1850 in western Wisconsin and central Minnesota from the Chippewa River in the southeast to the Red River in the northwest, the, in effect, buffer zone was around 50 miles wide where intertribal conflict made trapping precarious and dangerous. There was almost constant warfare between the tribes. During truces between the tribes, which were rare until around 1820, game could be trapped in the buffer zone with deer regularly chased into it. With the increasing scarcity of prey, fighting would again break out between the two tribes.

In 1825 the French imposed a boundary treaty, the *Prairie du Chien* which lasted 13 years and increased hunting near the boundary region. Famine affecting the Chippewa and Sioux was reported around 1828 with a climax in 1831 and again in 1835-38. Complaints about boundary violation were common and wars broke out until the Indian reservation period of the 1850s. With the lengthy truces the prey was greatly reduced which resulted in starvation, resumption of hostilities and the restoration of the buffer zone which again increased the deer population and food. The effect of the constant warfare preserved the deer in the buffer zone and the survival of both the Chippewa and Sioux. Although it must have been terrible, the continued survival of the tribes justified their intertribal warfare.

Another of my students, Paul Kulesa, came from the University of Southern California where he had got a Master's degree, much of it in pure mathematics. When he came up for interview to see if I would accept him as a student he asked me what kind of theorems I proved. I thought he was joking and had perhaps heard of my views about the uselessness of pure mathematics and was teasing me. Paul, a pleasure to everyone, to have had in the group, worked on an unusual and interesting problem, namely how the complex, and, seemingly irrational, order of teeth appearance in the alligator embryo was achieved in development: it is certainly not obvious. Along with several of my post-doctoral students, including my friend, James Sneyd, we developed a mathematical model which predicted the order of the teeth based on the embryonic jaw growth. The results were confirmed by experiment, not done by Paul but by an experimental colleague of mine in Manchester University, Professor Mark Ferguson, a world authority on crocodilia. After Paul got his Ph.D. in Applied Mathematics he decided that he would like to get involved in experiments and spent some years in a prestigious post-doctoral position in Biology at the California Institute of Technology (Caltec) which launched his career as an experimentalist. He is now a highly respected major world figure in early embryonic imaging and is Director of Imaging and Professor of Anatomy and Cell Biology in the University of Kansas Medical Center. Paul has been a particular family friend ever since we worked together in the University of Washington.

The research my students, post-doctorals and I worked on has been incredibly varied. Three of them, Jonathan Sherratt, Gerhard Cruywagen and Julian Cook, for example, worked on different aspects of wound healing, among other topics, which greatly increased our understanding of the process and subsequent scar formation. Another, Trachette Jackson, worked on methods of drug control delivery. Gerhard, a Rhodes Scholar, who came from Stellenbosch University in South Africa had written to me in Oxford to ask if I would take him on as a graduate student. I am ashamed to say that I knew little about his university and, I suppose arrogantly, felt that it probably did not have the high standards of Oxford courses. I accepted him and when he arrived I suggested he should take some of the senior undergraduate applied mathematics courses to catch up. I felt rightly ashamed when it became clear he was much more mathematically educated than the students from Oxford. Gerhard, who is also extremely clever, wrote an excellent D.Phil. thesis (the Ph.D. in the university of Oxford) and accepted a faculty position in the University of Cape Town but decided not to stay in South African academia. I think he made the right decision. Post-apartheid prejudiced politics was becoming more and more a part of university life. Another Oxford D.Phil. student Mark Lewis, now the Canada Research Professor in Mathematical Biology and Fellow of the Royal Society of Canada, is a world figure on ecological invasions and spatial ecology with a major research group in the University of Alberta. When, a few years ago, I mentioned the incredible escalation in bureaucracy in universities he told me that he has a half time secretarial assistant whose only job is to fill in all the ever increasing number of administrative forms required by the government and university. Most of my former students and post-doctoral students are now in senior positions in academia around the world.

During my formal uninterrupted academic time in the University of Washington from 1992-2000 I had nine graduate students, several post-doctoral students and numerous senior visitors, such as Professor Jacques Demongeot from Grenoble and Professor Toshio Sekimura from Chubu University in Japan. The visitors came for anything from a few weeks to a year. I did not have to do any administration other than that associated with my group most of which my personal secretary did. I was therefore able to spend my time in the most enjoyable way in academia, namely lecturing, doing and supervising research which covered a large number of diverse areas and travelling wherever and whenever I wanted, to attend conferences and give invited lectures. Invited lectures, other than at conferences, were always particularly friendly occasions during which you were royally treated. Often the introductions were well researched and funny. At one public lecture, in Minneapolis at the University of Minnesota, a friend Professor Rutherford Aris - a particularly erudite and enjoyable colleague - introduced me and during it mentioned that his maiden aunt had been a teacher of young children. She had given them an essay to write on the pleasures of childhood. One young innocent girl ended her essay with: *"These are some of the pleasures of childhood, but they are as nothing in comparison with the pleasures of adultery"*.

All my time at the University of Washington I was fortunate in having a group of particularly nice, friendly and very bright graduate students whom I pushed to work hard enough so that they graduated in the traditional UK time of three years: none of them ever complained, at least to me anyway. They have all been genuine friends ever since. About half the post-doctoral students also came from Oxford and, without exception, enjoyed the chance to spend time in the US. Since I felt the students should broaden their experience I regularly got them involved in research projects other than that of their thesis. Some unusual ones were with psychology graduate students on problems they were doing research on, such as modelling date rape, violence in kindergarten and others, which, at first sight, looked impossible to model mathematically. It was, in effect, an informal course for graduate psychology students to educate them in the genuinely practical use of applied mathematics. A major one, on which I personally did a lot of research, is marital interaction and its surprisingly accurate divorce prediction: it is described in more detail in Chapter 14.

One of the more unusual projects arose from a phone call one day from a Washington State Policeman, Sgt. Rod Gullberg. He was in charge of the Washington State drug laboratory, particularly alcohol, and of the State Troopers on the roads checking for drivers over the limit. He wanted to come and talk to me about whether or not we could design a better alcohol breathalyser. I had, many years before, worked on particle deposition in the lung and more recently some research on alcohol metabolism in alcoholics, so I felt that it would be interesting to hear about the problem. He said he would drive over the following day. I mentioned that he would find it impossible to park but he said he didn't think it would be a problem. He arrived mid-morning in a huge police car and parked immediately in front of the university building where my department was situated, on the top floor. The building was part of the main university quadrangle with a large fountain pond in the middle where any car would be hauled away after about a couple of minutes at most and the driver fined. It was like having about 20 solid yellow lines in front of the building. He came in to the building, bristling with the usual police weapons, a baton, a gun and so on and asked where he could find me. As a crowd gathered around him he was told where I had my office, which was on the top floor, and so he started climbing up the stairs with a crowd following him perhaps thinking I must have some drug cartel as a side activity. They were jokingly very disappointed.

Rod started to describe the problem they had with the accuracy of the standard breathalysers. How it works is that the person takes a deep breath so that the air gets as far into the bottom of the lungs as possible. There, the small alveolar sacs, part of the lungs, are closest to the blood vessels and a measure of the alcohol concentration in the blood diffuses into them so the exhaled breath gives an indication of the alcohol level in the blood. The problem is that it underestimates the alcohol level in the blood. An added difficulty is that if a driver on the edge of a road is over the limit with the breathaliser they have to be taken to a police station and have a blood test taken to get an accurate measure of alcohol blood level. One problem with this is that there is a delay between the breathalyser measurement and when the blood test is taken which lowers the alcohol level in the blood. This can sometimes be sufficient to reduce the blood alcohol level below the legal limit.

I started to describe a possible way of modelling the process and how it related to breathalysers. When he asked what was involved I said that the model would involve something called a differential equation to which he replied, to my astonishment: *"Is that a partial or ordinary differential equation?"* It turned out Rod had a Masters degree in mathematics. It was the beginning of an interesting and very friendly enjoyable research collaboration along with another of Rod's laboratory colleagues, a post-doctoral of mine, Sharon Lubkin and my Oxford colleague Philip Maini who was visiting the department in UW for a few months. The result was that we showed it is not possible to design a better breathalyser and we jointly published a research paper in the journal *Alcohol and Alcoholism* in 1996. The final unexpected part of the collaboration was an invitation from Rod and his colleague to a party in their laboratory where alcohol was available but, if you drank any, you had to have a blood test before leaving. It was a way of getting more scientific data. When I asked Rod who most of the people were who came to the party, he said: "Lawyers". It was a dramatic party since it coincided with one of the earthquakes, albeit small, in the Seattle area.

Philip Maini and I had done some research together before on alcohol problems with medical colleagues in London. Then we modelled how quickly alcohol metabolized using a control group of volunteers who came to the laboratory and drank a specific amount of strong alcohol after which we took blood samples over time. Before the study I naively asked one of the colleagues in the laboratory: "Where can you get volunteers to come and drink a significant amount of whiskey at 10 o'clock in the morning?" After the laughter died down they said there would be a long queue of volunteers waiting outside the door.

In the late 1990s the financial problems in many universities resulted in them encouraging older faculty to consider retiring with certain, quite generous, financial incentives. With no official retiring age in the universities in the US some tenured faculty simply continued well past 70 with no intention of retiring in the near future and whose official responsibilities were minimal. There were many in the university who fortunately did not. There was one case of a professor, not a major figure academically, nor one who had published much, in the Mathematics Department, as opposed to the Applied Mathematics Department, who decided to take the option of retiring with a significant financial incentive. Since I was thinking of retiring in 2000 so we could spend more time in

France, I decided to go and talk to the Academic Vice-President responsible for the faculty. I said that I was thinking of retiring and mentioned the financial arrangements he had negotiated with the pure mathematics professor and I wondered if I could get the same generous terms. He immediately, and laughingly, said: "Absolutely not." When I asked why, he said: "You have to have a track record of doing nothing for years." I would have had to have had years in which I had not brought in any grant money, had no research students, published no research papers, was not invited all over the place to lecture, in effect to have been retired for years. It was clear, as he said, that he, and the department, did not want me to retire. I still decided, however, to do so. Being at the University of Washington in the Applied Mathematics department was a particularly incredibly nice and genuinely warm way to finish one's official time as a university academic.

My time as a professor at the University of Washington was extremely productive and one of the most enjoyable times I have spent in academia. With the incredibly generous conditions of my professorship Sheila and I were able to spend several months each year in France where I attended numerous conferences to give plenary lectures and separate invited lectures around Europe. It also let us indulge our long time love of France, enjoy our passion for its mediaeval architecture and history and see a lot of our many friends who lived there. A significant part of our time in the first few years in Europe from 1991 had been renovating the early mediaeval stone house and outbuildings in the middle of 50 hectares (c125 acres) in the Dordogne as described in Chapter 13. On retiring we spent the whole of the first year in our house in France: by then the renovations had been completed for several years.

Bainbridge Island, Washington State 1991-2005
When I decided to move permanently to the University of Washington in Seattle in the early1990s we started looking for a house in the city near the university but after some months we decided it was too removed from our ingrained housing and living tastes away from a city so we bought one on an island, Bainbridge Island, a 30 minute ferry ride to Seattle. It is the nicest, and the most upmarket, island commutable to the city. The house was on a cliff overlooking the wide estuary on the west side of the island but, like practically all the waterfront houses built on the island, it had only 100 feet of waterfront but was surprisingly private particularly after we built a fence which was welcomed by our neighbours. The house was

about 100 feet above the shore with a rather worrying looking, but actually safe, elevator down to the stone beach. We had the house totally changed. This time, however, we had a construction firm do the major, in effect, reconstruction which included a huge drawing room, a new deck so that we could sit out in total privacy with the most dramatic views of the water and sunsets over the Olympic Mountains in the distance across the estuary: a typical view is in the photo below. We drew the plans for the structural changes, making it surprisingly private, which greatly pleased us of course.

Our house on Olympus Beach on the west cliff on Bainbridge Island before renovation: among other things it was painted an ugly red.

Olympus Beach house after renovation, c1992.

275

South wing of our renovated Olympus Beach house, c1992.

View west from the large living room of our Olympus Beach home.

Western view to the Olympus Mountains from our Bainbridge home.

Western view from inside our Bainbridge Island house and cliff deck.

Sheila and JDM with our son Mark and our daughter Sara on our Bainbridge house deck.

Sheila on the deck, 1995.

Sheila, on the right, with our daughter Sarah and son Mark on the deck, c1998.

The commute to the university was hardly ever less than 2 hours each way. However, other than the actual half hour ferry crossing, it involved sitting in the car queue waiting for the ferry. The car I used for commuting was a large, reliable, old Cadillac which I set up, in effect, as an office, without internet and cell phone in those days, so I got a lot of work done. I also was allowed to arrange for all my university responsibilities in the university to be done in three days so I was able to work the other days, usually the other four days of the week, in my home study with its dramatic view over the water to the mountains. I was also fortunate to have had excellent personal secretaries which helped enormously, of course.

A friend in the Applied Mathematics (Amath) Department, Professor Jirair (Jerry) Kevorkian, grew up in Armenia: his family was driven out by the Turkish army and later, when living in Israel to where they had fled, they were driven out by the Israeli army, since his family were not Jews. The Israeli army came and put up machine guns in the street and all the non-Jews were given 30 minutes to leave their homes - for ever.

Jerry was an avid and superb sailor and convinced us that we would love sailing and should buy a yacht. We duly did, buying an elegant 33 foot Japanese Fuji sailboat which we renamed *Chauntecleer*. We sailed all around the Puget Sound and the San Yuan islands north of Seattle: they are extremely beautiful and romantic.

In spite of our friend Jerry Kevorkian's encouragement we did not find sailing that relaxing having to constantly concentrate on the wind, the sails, currents, docking when windy, and so on, so we sold it and bought a very comfortable upmarket 32 foot *Grand Banks* trawler which we also renamed *Chauntecleer* and which our friend Jerry called a stinkpot, his name for all non sailboats. We kept *Chauntecleer*, the second, for two years and once again travelled around the Puget sound, the San Yuan islands and the islands near Seattle. It was so much more relaxing than on a sailboat.

In many ways Bainbridge Island was beautiful with a particularly nice atmosphere but we subconsciously were missing the ancient buildings and sense of being more in our European culture and history. We decided that we would rather spend more time in the Dordogne. So, we sold the boat, and we were right. We did not quite realise what a hassle it had been since we felt so relieved from all sorts of responsibilities of which we had not been conscious.

Our Fuji sailboat, *Chauntecleer* c1996, Bainbridge Island harbour.

Our Fuji sailboat, *Chauntecleer*, with Sheila taking down the sails, c1996.

X. Return to America: University of Washington and Bainbridge Island 1988–2005

Our Grand Banks trawler, *Chauntecleer.* coming back into dock in Bainbridge Island with our granddaughter Mazowe beside JDM on the upper deck with Sheila, below, getting ready to cast the line, c1998.

During my time at the University of Washington, and when living on Bainbridge, Public Television (PBS) WQED Pittsburgh got in touch with me in 1998 to ask if they could make a film associated with my research, as a mathematician, on animal coat patterns. The film is *Life By The Numbers: Math Like You've Never Seen It Before*: the section, on my work lasts 20 minutes. Some of the filming was very inventive. The television team, five of them, came to Seattle and particularly wanted to do most of the filming on Bainbridge Island and duly came for four days and did an excellent job. One of the PBS team was a particularly nice, enthusiastic, helpful young woman who was in the training stage with WQED and was considered a bit of a dogsbody: she had recently got an MA degree. Part of the movie was filming me reading Rudyard Kipling's "*How the Leopard got its Spots*". The helper said to me that we should get Mr. Kipling's permission to include it in the movie and did I know how to get in touch with him. To spare her feelings I said: "It might be a little difficult but I am sure he won't mind." I stopped myself adding: "but I'll try" and instead said: "Just leave it to me." Rudyard Kipling (1865-1936) is known by almost all children in Britain but not, as I realised, in the US.

281

On Bainbridge there are some very large wooded parks and preserved land. The film team had clearly done their homework. The most original part of the movie had me walking through the dense woods partially hidden by the trees and branches and, as I continued to walk, the scene merged smoothly into a tiger walking through a dense, similarly coloured, jungle. It is the most dramatic, and, I thought, the most imaginative section of the movie. It is certainly the best of the various movies and clips that have been made on my work. In 2010 the Korean Public Television flew a team over to film and interview me in our home in the country in Litchfield (CT). It is much longer, less accurate scientifically but with some splendid animal filming in Africa.

We stayed on in Bainbridge Island a few years after I formally retired in 2001 but we decided to sell our house in 2005 to move to the east coast to be closer to New York where our son Mark lives and has an internationally well-known 19th and early 20th century fine paintings art gallery, *Mark Murray Fine Paintings*. It was also much easier and shorter to fly to France.

One can almost believe in Lamarckian evolution since our love for living in the country must have got into our active genes so, not surprisingly, we started to look at areas not far from New York and again

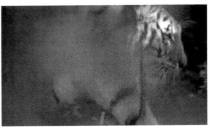

Public Broadcasting (PBS) movie extract: *Life By the Numbers* 1998.

bought a house in the country, this time in Litchfield in Connecticut with 8 acres and a large pond. It was a rather tedious and boring drive to New York and I missed a closer connection with academia so in 2010 we sold the Litchfield property and we moved once again. This time to Princeton where academic friends and the university welcomed me, appointing me *Senior Scholar*, and where I have given informal courses and until 2015 regularly gave some undergraduate lectures to biologists and premedical students. Living in town, albeit on a quiet road near the Battle Park where there was a major defeat of the British in the *War of Independence*, proved too much of an in-the-town feel so we sold it and once again - irrationally and, as our friends said, irresponsibly at our, or rather, my age - looked for a place once again in the country. Country, like we had in France and England, rarely exists on the mid-Atlantic east coast of America, certainly near university towns. Nevertheless we were fortunate in finding a property in Solebury in Pennsylvania in 2013 and where we now live and continually appreciate being back in the country. It is beautifully situated a few minutes walk from the Delaware River in the middle of 12 acres with not another house in sight yet easily commutable to Princeton. Although we had to do some renovations in all the houses we bought in America, with the exception of the major one on Bainbridge Island, the renovations, decorations mainly, were, for us, trivial. All the American houses, however, have had none of the romantic emotions we always had in our ancient European homes although our Olympus Beach one on Bainbridge, in spite of its cheek by jowl housing position, came closest because of its spectacular views and the ease of looking after it.

XI

World Travels and Sabbaticals

Every seventh year, as a tenured member of the faculty in Oxford, you could apply for a year's leave of absence with full salary to go wherever you wanted, to collaborate with colleagues in some other part of the world, write a book, think about what new research you might want to get involved in and so on. In fact it was a year to do whatever, and go wherever, you wanted and you were answerable to no one. I was amazed that so many of the faculty never ever took such sabbaticals. You could also apply for other leave, without salary, to visit and collaborate with colleagues around the world whose universities paid your salary and expenses. I was fortunate to have been able to take several of these. Such trips and visits were over and above the numerous ones to other countries and around Britain to give talks at conferences and to give research lectures. I used these leave privileges to travel, with our family, to various universities around the world with the side requirement that it should be an interesting new place to visit. Our children, Mark and Sarah, did not initially want to leave their schools for such long periods but in fact always found the trips exciting, fascinating and, in retrospect, an enormous international educational learning experience from which they have benefited all their lives. They look back on them as an immensely privileged time. Wherever we went we benefited from the kind hospitality and local knowledge of our hosts which gave us such a different view and insight into each place from that of typical tourists and visitors.

Conferences in the 1950s and 1960s for applied and pure mathematicians were orders of magnitude fewer than the typical one a week now somewhere in the world: they are often clearly commercially motivated. They were also nothing like as specialised and were certainly not expected to make any money, only cover expenses. The first I went to was when I was a first year graduate student. It was in 1954 and the first *International Congress of Mathematicians*: it was in Amsterdam and attracted about 2,500 participants. These Congresses have been held every four years since although they are now essentially just pure mathematics. The formal reception was in the *Rijcksmuseum* and was attended by several government ministers. I am, surprisingly, actually listed as a Member: the whole conference, all attendees etc., is now on the web. We were free to wander everywhere in the museum, carrying glasses of wine or whatever: there were none of the barriers typical now and you could go as close to a painting as you wanted. I still remember one senior faculty man from UC Berkeley who was drunkenly swaying with a large glass of whiskey, about a foot from the huge Rembrandt painting, *The Night Watch*. He was not the only drunk staggering around.

After returning to England in 1959 the first international conference I went to, with Sheila of course, was in Stresa, a very small town on Lake Maggiore in Northern Italy. We drove from London in our small old Morris Minor car, which was in a rather poor state, and only just made it over the Alps and whose windscreen wiper packed up with the first rain. We all stayed in hotels in the town. The major relaxation event for the participants was a trip on a large tourist boat on the lake for an afternoon. I remember little about the conference except for an amusing incident with a friend from my time at Harvard, Professor Bernie Budianski. As a young lecturer, and coming from Britain, we stayed in a one-star hotel while Bernie stayed in a 5-star one. Having lunch with him the second day he told us that his bed had bed bugs. When he complained, the hotel manager said: *"You must have brought them with you, Sir."*

Because my theory of fluidization, which I had developed, had become quite widely known by the mid-1960s I was invited to give talks at various conferences in the field of chemical engineering, not my normal venue for conferences. While at the University of Michigan I was invited to one in Naples. Since much of the meeting was in areas I knew nothing about there was considerably more time to be a tourist with visits to various sites of which the one to Pompeii was by far the most interesting. With practically no other tourists I got a different sense of the atmosphere of it than one now gets. I also liked to walk around the old part of Naples which was not a fashionable tourist area at the time but gave a very different view of the town than the tourist areas. One piece of gossip at the conference, which astonished us, was that one of the lecturers in the University of Naples had recently sued his department's professor for stealing some of his research and had won the case.

Turkey, India, Taiwan, Japan, Thailand, Nepal and Italy 1975
I had not yet been in Oxford for the required six years to apply for sabbatical so this 8-month trip to the Far East was a leave of absence, paid for by the host institutions. Because of our friend, Sir Thomas Bromley we

had originally thought it would be interesting to spend time in Ethiopia since he had been the British Ambassador to Ethiopia for some years and spoke about what a fascinating country and people they were. We quickly gave this up since a military coup against Haile Selassie had just taken place. We had then thought of going to Japan for the extracurricular art activities but our close friend from University of Michigan days, Professor Chia-Shun Yih, said we should go to Taiwan instead because the *National Museum* in Taipei housed the most magnificent collection of Chinese art taken, or stolen, depending on how you view it, by Chiang Kai-shek when he fled with his Kuomintang followers after their defeat by Mao Tse-tung. So, that is what we decided to do and I was appointed a Visiting Professor for six months at the National Tsing Hua University in Hsinchu in Taiwan. There is also a Tsing Hua University in Beijing, which is the original one and also called the National Tsing Hua University.

I had invitations to give lectures and visit various universities on the way to Taiwan in January 1975. After giving a lecture in Istanbul at Marmara University - President Erdogan is an alumnus - we spent a few days doing the usual tourist sights, which were almost totally empty of people at that time. The magnificent *Hagia-Sophia*, for example, was like a barn since some of it was still being renovated or rather re-renovated. The splendid enormous Ottoman Sultans' *Topkapi Palace* was equally empty of people. We could also go into most of the buildings and rooms many of which are now closed to tourists. The Sultan's harem was large and beautifully situated as was the quarters where a brother or son of the Sultan lived before their execution if it was politically expedient.

After Istanbul we flew to India for a month. Our first indication of the poverty among many Indians was on our drive from the international airport into Bombay. There were uncultivated fields lining the highway with many traditionally dressed, clearly very poor peasants, defecating in the fields. The first academic visit was to the Indian Institute of Technology (IIT) in Delhi. It is one of the top universities in India with a large campus. We were treated royally, given a huge luxurious apartment replete with servants and meals, unfortunately non-Indian rather bland ones, served whenever we required them as well as anything else we wanted or required. It was an experience of upper class Indian society.

During my time in St. Catherine's College in Oxford in 1967 I got to know one of the visitors who came from Delhi so we were invited to his home for dinner one day. He was extremely welcoming and hospitable. It gave us an idea of how the upper class lived. The servants, incredibly obsequious, were treated as if they didn't exist. It was interesting to see how differently our children, Mark, then 12, and Sarah, 9, reacted. Mark, a very sensitive and considerate little boy, simply accepted all the privileged attention as if it was normal while Sarah talked and made friends with the women servants. I gave several lectures in the university for a few days with the rest of the time free to be tourists.

We went to see the usual local Delhi sites, including Old Delhi with its bubbling activity, no cars, lots of beggars and terrible dilapidated looking housing. It was a totally different world to what we had in the university and experienced in the Delhi home and neighbourhood of our Oxford acquaintance.

Being January there were even fewer tourists. Of course we went to the usual tourist sites, such as the dramatic red sandstone *Qutb Minar*, begun by Qutbu'd-Din Aibak in the late 12th century to celebrate the defeat of the last Hindu kingdom and for the mu'azzin to call the Muslims to prayer. We all climbed the roughly 250 feet to the top of the minaret with its splendid dramatic views. We only met one couple, on their way down. We went on to the *Red Fort* which was even more dramatic in the late afternoon light.

The architectural gem is, of course, the Taj Mahal which was almost deserted and again in the dramatic late afternoon light when we visited it. After all the hype about the Taj Mahal we thought of not even bothering to go since it was possibly perhaps all overdone: what a mistake that would have been. We first saw the Taj Mahal from the Agra Fort where the great Mughal Emperor, Shah Jahan, who built the Taj Mahal in the mid-17th century, was confined by his son for the last eight years of his life and never again able to set foot in the Taj Mahal. It must have been sad but he could, however, still at least see the Taj Mahal from the Fort as in the photo below. The lively and amusing Agra Fort guide (we were his only clients) told lots of anecdotal stories including one that Shah Jahan was kept in the Fort because he was a bit of an alcoholic.

The town of Agra gave a very different view of life to the magnificent temples and forts. Many of the narrow streets, alleys in effect, were very dark but often surrounded by dramatically carved ancient stone buildings in pathetic states. The streets were incredibly crowded, bustling and noisy.

Fatehpur Sikri Temple, India, January 1975.

Taj Mahal from the Agra Fort, 1975.   Agra Fort, early evening, January 1975.

Agra, January 1975.

Agra street scene, January 1975.

I had been invited, after our visit to IIT, Delhi, to go and give some lectures at the Indian Institute of Technology (IIT) in Bangalore. It is also well known internationally. It is situated in spacious grounds with much of the town itself still as it was before the war but without as much poverty or slum areas as we found in Old Delhi. Surprisingly, we were initially told we had been assigned a single student room in the undergraduate residence which when I said that there must have been a mistake we were moved to the First Class Hotel which was the original arrangement. Perhaps, though, it was another example of the corruption that was prevalent in India or perhaps it was just administrative incompetence. The department was welcoming, although a touch disorganised, and rather arrogant because of its academic reputation. It felt it was unquestionably the premier university in India and a major one in the world. It was certainly the most disorganised that I visited in our whole trip, not just in India. The present city of Bangalore, one of the international centres of information technology, could hardly be more different now.

After Bangalore, we went down to the University in Madras where I had an invitation from a colleague from my time in New York. He was a distinguished applied mathematician who had decided to return to his native area in India and resume living and dressing in the traditional way. It was a totally different country (and atmosphere) to Bangalore. The faculty and most of the students wore traditional Indian attire unlike IIT Bangalore and IIT Delhi where everyone wore typical western clothes. Because we had young children the university put us up in our own separate guesthouse on the campus, with its numerous wild monkeys, and our own beetle nut-chewing red lipped personal cook. So, instead of the usual bland official guesthouse food we had genuine, albeit sometimes a touch too hot, Indian cuisine.

After finishing my lectures we took a trip south to *Mahabalipuram* in Tamil Nadu, on the Bay of Bengal, one of the most spectacular ancient sites we have seen and, like so much we saw in India, as usual practically empty of tourists. It helped to show us why India had been such a fascinating country for so long for so many British colonial ex-patriots.

One of the wall sculptures, in the photo below of a family with the father having his arm around his son and holding his wife's hand is one of the warmest human ones we saw in India. So many of the temple sculptures with human figures, albeit highly original and dramatic, are often of wild sex, obsequious or devout god worshipping or imaginative mythical animals. The local Mahabalipuram children were incredibly friendly, totally unbegging in spite of clearly being very poor. They were very curious about our children, particularly Sarah because of her blond hair.

Mahabalipuram: Temple sculptures, January 1975.

Mahabalipuram Temple: one of several such sculptures, 1975.

Local very friendly Mahabalipuram barefooted children, 1975.

While in Madras, we went to listen to and watch some genuine Indian theatre performances. We first went to a concert by the legendary sitar player Ravi Shankar (later Knighted by Queen Elizabeth), in a remote, large, basic hall, more like a barn, an hour away in the city outskirts which we got to in a rickety old bus. We sat on wooden benches in the mosquito ridden crowded hall for about an hour before he started to play to the packed audience. We were the only non-Indians. He had been on the stage almost an hour waiting to be inspired, and how inspired he was when he played. Everyone was entranced. The other major theatre occasion was on our way back from Taiwan when we spent a few more days in Delhi and its surrounding area. We went to a concert by a dance troop the main male star of which was, surprisingly, somewhat overweight and incredibly arrogant looking. We wondered how he could dance at all. When he did he held the audience in the palm of his hand with his unimaginable and, to us, totally unexpected elegance and grace.

Being tourists in India in those days was an unforgettable experience. The photos give an indication of what it was like before the tourist explosion. Even at the Taj Mahal, the Red Fort, Fatehpur Sikri and other famous sites we were practically the only tourists there, which by then we had come to expect. We feel privileged to have had such a clear vision of the unbelievable splendour of so much of historic India.

Taiwan 1975

Landing at the airport in Taipei we saw a young man smiling and waving vigorously. We ignored him thinking it was for someone else since we knew no one in Taiwan. He persisted and we realised it was indeed us he was waving at. It turned out to be the son of a retired Kuomintang General, a student friend of whom we had met in Oxford. He had a chauffeur driven car waiting to take us to a hotel for the night before going on to the university in Hsinchu. Surprisingly he gave us some bottles of water. We didn't know the tap water was considered unfit to drink. Some weeks later, his family, who were extremely kind, had a magnificent dinner, banquet rather, to welcome us to Taiwan. His very lively and warmly friendly sister generously gave us a present of an impressive Chinese scroll painting which she had painted. The family also arranged, some weeks later, for us to have a personal guided tour of the National Museum by the Deputy Director: it was fascinating and totally absorbing. What an incredible collection it is. Of course, we returned several times. We understood why the mainland Chinese are so resentful and feel so many of their principal art treasures had been stolen.

The National Tsing Hua University was established in Hsinchu after the Kuomintang fled China. Hsinchu, when we were there, was a small, traditional Taiwanese city about an hour by train from Taipei. It was certainly not a large metropolis in 1975. The university was on the edge of the town. Open sewers ran down the streets and the small children all had trousers which had the long back open seam so they could squat over the open sewers. Many of the people, particularly the agricultural workers on their wagons, people in the market and many children, still did not wear shoes.

Taipei friends with Sheila and our children Sarah and Mark in our faculty house on the National Tsing Hua University campus, 1975.

The university was an oasis of greenery. We walked everywhere but were surprised that we were the only people who ever walked in the lovely bamboo groves. We learned later that no one walked there because of the abundance of poisonous snakes, of which there is a large number in Taiwan. Some of the students, who clearly believed it, told me the snakes had been brought in by the Japanese during their occupation of the country during the war. Japan was certainly not popular among the local Taiwanese. The students were very friendly, particularly nice to us, very polite, mostly bright, very attentive in lectures and anxious to learn about the new applied mathematical field of mathematical biology. I think it was, of course, also in part because I spoke English. There was a clear division between the native Taiwanese students and the mainland Chinese students, whose parents had fled with Chiang Kai-shek. Occasionally we felt minor tension between them, considerably less than with some adults we met.

My university duties were far from onerous. I was required to give only one course on mathematical biology but without having to give an exam or grade the students in any way. The class was not large, around 20, so I got to know the students quite well, particularly since about ten of them also came to our house about once a week usually to play games, part of the time, with Mark and Sarah, which all helped their English. The students were extremely hard working and committed, with most of them wanting to spend time abroad.

University students at one of our regular Friday gatherings. JDM standing left, Sheila, Mark and Sarah (seated) are on left, 1975.

I wrote some articles which were published in the university, including one about Oxford about which people were very curious. My departmental colleagues were extremely hospitable to us all and we were often invited to dinners, including the occasional banquet specifically for us. I also gave lectures at various universities around the island. We all went on these visits to the other universities. It was, and no doubt still is, the case that if you agree to give a lecture, by the time you left you would have been asked if you would mind giving two or three more lectures. I didn't mind. During one of these lecturing trips we had a lovely visit from my close friend from Harvard days, Bill de Spoelberch and his wife Choupette. Bill and Choupette were then living in Jakarta for a while when he was with the Ford Foundation. They flew over to see us and to see a little of Taiwan. Sadly Choupette died of cancer in 1998. Choupette and our daughter Sarah had a particularly warm relationship.

Bill (3rd from left) and Choupette (last on the right) de Spoelberch with Sheila, and our children Mark and Sarah. Taiwan, 1975.

The university provided us with a three-bedroom house on the campus, and a very warm and sympathetic woman servant, who came each day to clean the house. Instead we had her do some of the cooking which she preferred to do: she was an excellent cook. We had bought her a Chinese cookbook so we could tell her what we'd like. The book had very clear coloured photos of the dishes since we had discovered she couldn't read. We learned from one of the students who occasionally translated for us that she had been able to read when at school but she had forgotten it all; not at all uncommon apparently. The house had basic furniture and numerous, very welcome, mosquito nets but nothing else. On moving in we discovered that all visitors had to buy dishes, cooking utensils and so on since the day a visitor left the university the house was stripped. Burglary was also a bit of problem, particularly for foreigners, since they had more to steal, so we had to hide such things as passports, camera and so on. The bottom of the garbage can seemed a good place. On one occasion I got my wallet pick-pocketed, very cleverly by a few men who jostled me, not roughly and with profuse apologies, when in a crowd in the large temple area in Hsinchu. I mentioned it to a colleague who said I must report it to the police, which I did not want to do but I agreed. The police, who were full of apologies for the thieves, asked all sorts of questions and wrote down the answers, but it was clear there was nothing they could do. We never, however, ever felt in the least unsafe physically.

Mark and Sara at the swimming pool

Mark and Sarah had home schooling in the morning each day: it was good for my Latin which Sarah was doing. The schooling must have been pretty intense since it only took the mornings of 4 days a week. In the afternoon they often went off swimming in the university pool.

Sheila, along with the wives of the three other visitors took Chinese cooking lessons each Friday evening from the former personal chef of the President of the National Tsing Hua University in Beijing before leaving in 1948 with Chiang Kai-shek. He also lived in a university house. His kitchen was unbelievably grubby but he produced superb Chinese meals first casually wiping dead flies and mosquitos off the kitchen counter before he started. He never ate anything himself but as we sat at the table eating the delicious Chinese food which he had just prepared, he joined us at the table but only sat drinking a huge glass of gin. Not just at his place but in our house we used chopsticks and we all became highly skilled at using them in the Chinese style. At one banquet, which the parents of one of the students kindly gave for us, we had to pick up small pigeon eggs (without their shells) floating in water, not an easy task, but being impressively adept we could do it easily. It was a friendly test since everybody stopped eating to smilingly watch us. I doubt if any of us could do it now.

We learned a lot about Chinese customs and attitudes to life. During our time there, in April 1975, the US decided to completely pull out of Vietnam after the North Vietnamese army took Saigon. The Americans left ignominiously with some Vietnamese desperately trying to get on to the helicopters as they took off. The arrogant, ignorant American politicians responsible for it have a lot to answer for the thousands of lives lost in the stupid war. At the same time, in April 1975, it was announced that Chiang Kai-shek had died. The newspapers were filled with photos and articles about him but with nothing about the American withdrawal from Vietnam. Some of the students said that he had probably been kept on ice until it was necessary to distract the population from some event which might have serious political consequences for the ruling Kuomintang in Taiwan. Perhaps they were right. This practicality was reinforced with a Chinese proverb one of the students told us: "*Whoever gives me milk, I'll call mother.*"

It was a fascinating time for us all. Mark, 12 at the time, would go off on his bicycle to the market on the edge of the campus each morning to buy Chinese *youtiao*, which are deep-fried bread sticks, for breakfast until one morning he witnessed a very serious accident of a bus hitting a farmer on a buffalo drawn cart. It was apparently quite common which is why so many of the farm workers wore crash helmets as they drove their carts, which were generally pulled by a water buffalo. People in the market were always very helpful and friendly to Mark. He at least learned to count in Chinese. After going to a Chinese opera in the temple in Hsinchu Sarah and Mark used to imitate the up and down Chinese opera singing by singing the numbers 1 to 10 in Chinese. It sounded very Chinese ~ at least to us. Sarah always had an impressive talent for mimicking accents.

Hsinchu in those days was sufficiently isolated that small groups of locals would follow us as we walked in the market or in the temple area. They were particularly fascinated with our daughter Sarah, as usual because of her blond hair. In buses they often tried to touch it to see if it was real. Getting on buses was always a hassle. Wherever we were in the queue we were always last to get on. Going by train was different. You had to buy tickets, and book seats, at the station the day before. Students were always sent to the station to get them for the faculty since there were always queues. On the journey you were traditionally offered tea with a variety of choices, but then we were able to always travel First Class.

There were only a very few foreign visitors to the university. The President of the university, who had emigrated to America, had recently returned to take up the position. At the formal lunch for the visitors he sat in the middle of the long rectangular table and boringly and condescendingly pontificated. This turned out to be a very positive thing since I was sitting at one end opposite a visitor from Japan, Professor Kenji Araki from Tokyo, who felt the same about the President. We started to talk together. It was the beginning of a lifelong family friendship with Kenji and his wife Kaneko who was there with their youngest child, Hiromi: the others stayed in Tokyo with their grandmother. Sheila and Kaneko developed a very warm friendship as they regularly wandered around the campus and downtown Hsinchu with the children for the remaining 5 months we were both there. We visited and spent some days with them in Japan and met Kenji's mother, who lived to be 98. Kenji and Kaneko later stayed with us in Oxford when Kenji had come to Britain for a conference. Our feelings, and views about Japan and the many Japanese we know who became friends, are uniformly warm.

Our friends Kenji and Kaneko Araki with their children, from the right Hiromi, Maki and Takashi, 1977.

With our enthusiasm for art, Sheila and I decided to take Chinese painting lessons which we did for about 4 months. The teacher came to our house for two hours in the evening twice a week and patiently tried to teach us. He did not speak a word of English. He was very gentle and encouraging. He taught us a lot about Chinese brush painting in a systematic way which meant we had to paint bamboo trunks, leaves, trees, birds and so on, over and over and over again. We used the traditional ink, which we made from grinding the solid black blocks in the traditional dishes, and used the traditional round hair paintbrushes. He was actually a very professional and talented reproduction painter but sadly his own paintings were without much taste particularly when he tried to paint European type watercolours which we knew rather a lot about. We practiced several hours each evening: we felt the results were incredibly unsophisticated and rather pathetic. When we left Taiwan we used the special, soft, Chinese painting paper sheets we had filled with our paintings as packing paper for the few pottery antiques we had bought in the town. Only a few years ago we came across a box full of them which, somehow, had not been put out in the rubbish. As we stretched some of them out I was very impressed with some of it! It was an unexpected surprise to see how one's critical artistic judgment of Chinese painting over the years had so deteriorated. I thought one looked quite reasonable even if not great art. It must have been one I thought not totally unreasonable since I had jokingly appended my formal seal at the bottom in traditional style before crunching it up to pack things.

When learning how to use a Chinese dictionary I also became particularly interested in Confucius and specifically the *Analects* (5th century BC) many of which I found so insightful and surprisingly relevant to our world. A well-known one is in the elegant script of it in the photo below. It was kindly given to me by one of the students whose talented sister had written it in classical style for him to give to me since I had mentioned my interest in Confucius. Reading down the right column first then the left it translates as: *Learning without thought is labour lost. Thought without learning is perilous.*

The bureaucracy in Taiwan and the university was certainly original, at least to us. We had, not unreasonably, to get a visa to enter the country. What was unusual was that you had to get a visa to be able to leave. To get paid, like everybody in the university, I had to go to the university's post office and produce my small, about ½" square, Chinese wood carved seal with my name, engraved in Chinese: it is shown in the small photo of the seals below. I had been given it by the university, which had it carved, based on how to pronounce my name in Chinese, surname first of course.

It was easier to use just a part of it so the seal is pronounced *mù*, the symbol on the right, then *yǎ gé* for the two on the left for James. Sheila had one made also but for her somehow, Murray became *mái lái*. We never did learn much Chinese other than how to look up Chinese-English dictionary and pronounce the words, including the tones. You have to

JDM Chinese practice paintings with his seal on his scroll painting on the right. 1975.

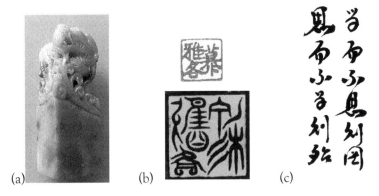

(a)   (b)   (c)

(a) Carved dragon marble Chinese seal. (b) JDM seal in classical Chinese characters engraved on the bottom of (a) with the Tsing Hua University JDM salary wood carved seal above. (c) Confucius analects in Chinese calligraphy.

count the strokes to form the symbol and to do that you have to know how to write them so as to get the right number: it is not just the number of separate looking lines. I soon became quite expert at looking up words in the dictionary. Since I liked the idea of seals I did some research in the library on what my name would have been in ancient times and had the marble one sculpted with a dragon on top: it is (a) in the photos of the seals above: it cost practically nothing to have sculpted.

I was paid very well by the university so we always travelled First Class by train to Taipei, and around the country, and stayed in the best hotels. There was no point in saving any money since you could not take it, nor its conversion into some internationally recognized currency, out of Taiwan when you left.

Taiwan is a spectacularly beautiful, mountainous island although sometimes scary because, at the time, a hillside road occasionally collapsed into one of the many narrow gorges, particularly in the Taroko gorge on the east side of the island in Hualien county. Most of the places outside of Taipei, which we visited, were, as we had come to expect, again empty of any tourists of any nationality. Photography was officially not allowed in any of the ports we visited, a not unreasonable paranoia with all the sabre rattling and threats from the mainland at the time. I ignored it in the harbour in Kaohsiung in the southwest in which most of the boats were still old early 20th century (probably earlier) ones the fishermen used as in the photo below.

The one week long trip we took was round the south of the island, including, briefly, Kaohsiung, and then by bus up through the spectacular Taroko gorge in the Hualien province to see the Xiangde temple and the beautiful dramatic mountain scenery. The road was indeed a little scary, being very narrow and it passed through occasional short very narrow tunnels on the side of the mountains. We could see why there had been occasional road collapses. It was unfortunately raining quite a lot of the time but it meant we were the only people staying in the hotel near the temple. Walking from the bus towards the hotel we passed a dramatic, practically hidden dragon sculpture shown in the photo below. During the walk there was another example of how dogs automatically reacted to Sarah. This dog ran quickly towards us and immediately rubbed itself against Sarah, totally ignoring us. It is bizarre, but animals seem to sense how she feels about them.

Sarah and her new dog friend at Xiangde Temple, Taiwan, 1975.

Hsinchu market, Taiwan 1975: live chicken sellers and basket weaver, 1975.

Kaohsiung Harbour, Taiwan, 1975.

Hsinchu Temple figure.   Taroko Gorge garden dragon.

Taroko Gorge, Taiwan, 1975.

Taroko Gorge Xiangde Temple, Taiwan.

Dragon temple roofs, Taiwan, 1975.

India and Nepal 1975

By the end of our stay in Taiwan we were ready to leave, so, at the airport we gave in all the Taiwanese currency we had left and took off, certainly with warm feelings towards our friends, hosts and students in Tsing Hua University. On our way back we had decided to stop in Thailand, specifically to see the Buddhist temple in Bangkok. It was certainly impressive and dramatic but with our taste for mediaeval European architecture we found it all a touch too bright and almost gaudy.

We were back in India for a week, this time only as tourists. There was considerable tenseness around since the Prime Minister Indira Ghandi had just issued a State of Emergency. It did not however really affect us but it certainly did the Indians, particularly the poor, as a consequence of the incredible brutality of the police, which was certainly sanctioned, or even initiated, by the government in their attempt, for example, to surgically enforce birth control to which so many were subjected.

Delhi in the summer was absolutely stifling and hotter than any country we have ever visited. The primary reason for going to India, however, was to go to Nepal for a week. Nepal, long before the civil war and the communist takeover, was relatively isolated. Kathmandu was nothing like the noisy crowded metropolis of today nor torn by political dissention and radicalism. Our first night in Kathmandu was somewhat dramatic. We found a small hotel and a room for all of us and, exhausted,

305

Bangkok: Buddhist monks and some sculptures in their temple, 1975.

we quickly went to sleep. Around midnight we woke up and were surprised that the colour of the room had changed from light to an irregular dark. The reason was that the ceiling was totally covered with cockroaches! We were so exhausted we almost immediately fell asleep again. When we woke up the following morning there was not a single cockroach in sight with the ceiling back to white.

Although Kathmandu was interesting, it was the early mediaeval royal temple towns of Patan and Bhaktapur which were particularly fascinating. The old part of Patan, the only part we visited, gave us a view of what life had been like for centuries. We were followed by friendly smiling small groups of children clearly fascinated by these foreigners, as usual particularly Sarah. The whole time we were in Patan and Bhaktapur we never saw another tourist. The towns are full of ancient dramatic Hindu and Buddhist sculptures – some quite obscene. With rare exceptions all the people we saw were barefooted. Most of the adults were not unfriendly, just uninterested. Walking down one rather dilapidated street we saw one woman sitting on the step in front of her house, removing lice from her daughter's head. It reminded me of the similar operation I regularly had during the war in Moffat shortly after the Glasgow evacuees were moved to the town. The houses on the narrow streets in the middle of the town were quite dilapidated with inhabitants sitting quietly talking outside. In the old part of the towns we did not see a single car or motorcycle. It was like moving back to a different century.

We flew back to London from Delhi with a week in Rome where we felt so much at home again in a familiar European culture. As the *Air Italia* plane landed in Rome the whole plane, practically all Italians, burst out clapping: we genuinely joined in. Mark and Sarah were delighted to be back in their familiar schools and culture. However, like all our itinerant academic life it had a lasting positive effect on their (and Sheila's and mine) attitude to life and we look back on it with gratitude for having had such a glimpse of such different worlds which no longer exist.

Bhaktapur, Nepal, 1975.

Patan, Nepal, 1975.

307

Temple goat, Bhaktapur, Nepal, 1975.

Temple sculptures, Patan, 1975.

Patan, Nepal. Musician family, 1975.

Bhaktapur temple sculpture, 1975.

Japan

During our time in the University of Michigan in the mid-1960s we had become friends with a very open, kind and warm Japanese visitor, Professor Hiroshi Hansawa, from Hokkaido University. He heard from our mutual friend Professor Chia-shun Yih that we were in Taiwan so he wrote inviting me to go to Japan and give a lecture in his university, also in Kyoto University, and to spend a few days so he could show me some of the sites and experience some of the traditional customs. Unfortunately Sheila, Mark and Sarah were not able to come with me.

I was warmly welcomed on landing in Tokyo, and looked after incredibly kindly during the few days in Tokyo by the very nice sister of our Japanese friend Kaneko Araki in Taiwan who had written to say I was flying in to Tokyo. She wanted her sister to give me a taste of as much of traditional Japanese culture as possible in a few days. This included touring the old city, eating in traditional superb restaurants, going to a *No* play and to a *Kabuki* one. The former was a bit too slow and ritualized for me – and for my host - but I greatly enjoyed the Kabuki with its lively story and marvellous costumes and actors' makeup. The genuine kindness, sympathy and understanding of Kaneko's sister, even though we could not

309

communicate verbally, was like I had never experienced before by someone I did not know.

After Tokyo I flew up to Hokkaido where, after my formal lecture which, flatteringly, attracted an audience of several hundred, Hiroshi had arranged some very interesting things for me to do and see. One included a personal tour of the main factory of *Japan Steel* the Director of which was an old school friend of his. The most fascinating part of the factory tour, to me, was the small traditional blacksmith smithy in which Samurai swords were made in the old traditional way ever since the factory had been built in 1918. The two smiths, dressed in traditional Samurai clothes, were clearly highly skilled with one holding the ingot on the anvil while the other hammered it with a large hammer. They clearly knew exactly when to forge the ingot again and to what temperature level. The male ancestors of my friend, Hiroshi, the gentlest of men, had all been Samurai. At the end of the war the family Samurai sword was taken, stolen rather, by one of the American soldiers.

Japan Steel put us up in a beautiful, very old, traditional Japanese Inn with magnificent rooms each of which included a very respectful personal, constantly bowing, servant in traditional Japanese clothes. Her duties included, for example, setting out traditional Japanese clothes for us after our bath in the large hotel pool, laying out the elegant bedclothes for us, waking us up in the morning and so on. It gave me an insight into the formal luxurious life of the privileged. Hiroshi's friend, the head of *Japan Steel*, also spent the evening and night in the inn.

Professor Hiroshi Hansawa and JDM in the old Japanese Inn, 1975.

Another tour was a personal one of the main hospital in Hokkaido by the senior surgeon who was quite famous in Japan since he had carried out the first heart transplant in Japan. He had spent time in the US and his English was like a native borne English speaker's. As we went round the hospital as soon as he was seen everybody immediately stopped what they were doing, including nurses attending patients, and moved to the side or to the edge of beds and bowed low as we went past. The surgeon was an incredibly easy, friendly person who had arranged a splendid Japanese dinner for me along with his recent very young new wife. At dinner I was presented with a certificate of my visit!

I also gave a lecture in the University of Kyoto, one of the major world class universities, and was taken around the beautiful old city and its fascinating temples. Kyoto was the main university for theoretical ecology in Japan. In the university I met a particularly lively, and clearly very clever, final year doctoral graduate student, Masayasu (Mayan) Mimura, with whom I felt an immediate rapport and who, with each of his two very nice and gentle wives, Toshiko (Tokon), and later Yoko, have been warm

Mayan and Toshiko Mimura with Sheila, Mark and Sarah, Oxford, 1976.

311

friends of all our family ever since. After we got back to Oxford, Mayan, with his first wife, Toshiko (called Tokon), came to spend a year as a post-doctoral researcher with me and we collaborated on several research projects. Our children spent a lot of time with Toshiko whom sadly Mayan later divorced because Toshiko could not have any children. In the photograph of them Sarah is hugging her favourite animal that Sheila had made for her that Christmas. It's a lemur called Leonardo. After returning to Japan Toshiko very kindly made and sent Sarah a kimono for Leonardo. Sarah still has Leonardo forty years later: he has aged somewhat.

Mayan became a senior professor in Hiroshima University where years later we visited him and his very kind and welcoming second wife, Yoko, and their two sons. With Mayan's increasing international recognition and research he moved to Tokyo University. Mayan is recognized as one of the major mathematical biologists in Japan and an international figure in the field. We have seen Mayan and Yoko (there's a photo below) many times since, the last when they came to participate in a special conference in the University of Limerick in 2012 which was kindly arranged in my honour and organised by our friend Professor Andrew Fowler, one of my students in Corpus Christi College, from 1971.

Toshio and Akemi Sekimura with their young family, at our home on Bainbridge Island c1993: Sheila is on the right, c1992.

XI. World Travels and Sabbaticals

The last time I was in Japan was with Sheila in 1992 when I was a *Fellow of the Japanese Society for the Promotion of Science*. We also had a particularly nice few days family visit staying with our friends Kenji and Kaneko Araki near Tokyo. The academic side involved visiting various universities giving lectures, one of which was at Chubu University. This was the start of a particularly interesting and successful research collaboration with Professor Toshio Sekimura and a warm family friendship ever since. We had a lovely and lively social few days organised by Akemi, his wife, and Toshio's elder sister, Akiko, who had arranged for us to experience some of the traditional Japanese ways such as a formal tea service just for us, to visiting a pottery and having us try to make a Japanese pot. We still have the pots Sheila and I made – hardly great artistic pieces. Their family spent a very nice family time with us when Toshio visited my research group in the University of Washington. Toshio, along with their eldest daughter, Mitsuyo, came to a conference in 2003 in my honour in the University of Dundee and gave us this elegant scroll (approximately a metre in height) the calligraphy of which Akemi, a *Master calligraphist*, had done for us. It is not easy to translate exactly but it is a four character Japanese idiom, *Ichi-go ichi-e* (一期一会 "one time, one meeting") which essentially recalls the unique once in a lifetime warm occasion we all had together. It reminds people to cherish it since so many such particular meetings can never be repeated.

Conferences – a small selection

Conferences play a major role in academic research. They are also generally very interesting, very social and well organised occasions although I gather now that this is not always the case. One unusual meeting, in 1982, not really a conference, was a *Dahlem Workshop* on *Evolution and Development*. It involved only fifty participants who were divided into four interdisciplinary groups who had related research interests. There were no lectures, only discussions on specific areas. A specific time was allowed for the discussion of a specific topic, usually starting with a short talk by one of the group. When the time was up rather deafening bells were rung. A few people in each group (I was one in my group) wrote a short article in an area of interest in their group with a final group-approved article written for the end of the workshop. The collection was published in a book, *Evolution and Development*, edited by Professor John Bonner, from Princeton, who edited it and had organised the workshop.

The expressions on people's faces in the photo below of the section I was in generally reflect their character at the meeting except for the unusually serious looking person Professor Pere Alberch, who was Spanish, standing slightly behind me on my left. Pere was a friend, an impressive highly original researcher and important experimental collaborator on a major research project I worked on for some years. Pere very much burned the candle at both ends and sadly died at age 43 in 1998. He had married an Argentinian woman but the marriage did not last long. He told me that at their wedding her father had taken him aside and told him that he should beat her every now and again. When Pere asked him why and for what reason, her father said: "You don't have to know but she will."

We all worked extremely hard except for one day when we could be tourists. Some went off to East Berlin to go to a museum, which turned out to be unexpectedly closed, the decision to do so having just been made that morning. It was a rather depressing day for them. Some of us went to sites in West Berlin. The *Pergamon Museum*, which I went to with a colleague, is superb. There is also a group of museums called the *Dahlem Museum Complex*.

The workshop was held in a very upmarket hotel in Berlin, or rather West Berlin, as it was at the time: it overlooked the well-kept ruined Kaiser Wilhelm Memorial Church which has not been rebuilt as a reminder of World War II which was close to the East Berlin wall. The self-service breakfasts were immensely elaborate and, surprisingly, with lots of wine and champagne available – not that any of us drank it. We did however, also have it available every evening before dinner, and it was excellent. Each evening we were all dined in a different first class restaurant.

Of the many conferences I have been involved in a particularly warm and friendly one was organised by Professor Willi Jäger in the University of Heidelberg in 1996. We had spent a month at the university many years before and had been close family friends with Willi and his wife Gabi ever since. Willi is one of the major applied mathematicians in Germany, chairman of the Applied Mathematics group in the university and a major international figure in the field. This conference was kindly arranged to celebrate my 65th birthday. Willi also organised a special, and superb, organ recital concert in one of the large ancient churches in Heidelberg. It is the only conference I have ever attended at which there has been such an enjoyable cultural event.

Dahlem workshop, West Berlin, 1982. JDM is third from the left in the back row beside his friend and collaborator Pere Alberch fourth from the left. In the front row Armand de Ricquelès is first on the left with Stephen Jay Gould the last on the right.

Professor Dr. Dr. Willi Jäger and JDM, Heidelberg, 1996.

The invited keynote speaker was the distinguished, internationally renowned, biologist, Professor Lewis Wolpert FRS, who had been a scientific editorial colleague for several decades. We had very different approaches to key aspects of biological development: Lewis' theory was very controversial. Lewis, a friend of many years, is also internationally known for several non-technical books about a wide variety of subjects. (There is a photo of him in Chapter 12 when he stayed with us in France for a few days.) He is also scientifically well known for his theory of biological development called *positional information*. It was very different to the theory that Professor George Oster and I had proposed and developed and with which Lewis did not agree. I describe it in Chapter 14. He thought of experiments which might disprove it. Although none of them did they actually resulted in some new biological insights which, of course, is the prime aim of research.

Dundee University conference in my honour, 2003. From left to right, standing: Philip Maini (University of Oxford), Jane White (University of Bath), Nick Britton (University of Bath), JDM, Jonathan Sherratt (Heriot-Watt University), Mark Lewis (University of Alberta), Kristin Swanson (Mayo Clinic Medical Research Center), Mary Myerscough (University of Sydney). Sitting: Rebecca Tyson (University of British Columbia), Meghan Burke (Kennesaw State University), Daphne Manoussaki (Technical University of Crete). They are just a few of my former graduate students.

At such major lectures there are usually lots of questions, sometimes critically questioning the theory: Wolpert's theory was rather controversial even though it had initiated a lot of enlightening research. When I said to

Lewis at the dinner after the talk, how very nice it was of him to come over from London to give the inaugural lecture in my honour, he jokingly said: "I couldn't pass up a chance of talking about *positional information* and you not being able to ask any critical questions." This was, actually, never my custom to do so after lectures.

Another conference, again in my honour, was held at the University of Dundee in 2003. It was kindly organised by a long time friend and colleague, Professor Mark Chaplain. He had written to several of my former doctoral students some of whom came from countries all over the world. The atmosphere and genuine friendship is captured in the photo above of some of them who were there when the photo was taken.

During many of our trips to spend time in our house in the Dordogne we went to various European countries and universities where I had been invited to give lectures. At one in Oxford in 1997 three friends, all former doctoral students, Gerhard Cruywagen, Paul Kulesa, who were also visiting, and Philip Maini, who succeeded me as the Director of the Centre for Mathematical Biology in the University of Oxford (see the photo) arranged a *"Three continent dinner"* for Sheila and I. Gerhard is the Chief Investment Officer in *Sanlan Investments*, a major public company in South Africa, and Paul, the Director of the Imaging Centre in the *Stowers Institute for Medical Research* in Kansas.

Drs. Gerhard Cruywagen (South Africa), Philip Maini (Europe)   Prof. Andrew Fowler
Paul Kulesa (America). Oxford, 1997.   University of Oxford

At the conference in the University of Limerick in Ireland, to celebrate my 83rd year in 2014, organised by a long time friend Professor Andrew Fowler, who is a professor in the University of Oxford and also in the University of Limerick. Andrew's field of research is in a totally different field, Mathematical Geophysics, an area in which he is the major world figure with his book the definitive text in the field. Colleagues and friends, many with their wives, again came from around the world including my Japanese post-doctoral of many years ago, Mayan Mimura. Professor Mayan Mimura, has been a close family friend for more than 40 years. Mayan brought his extremely gentle and kind wife, Yoko, whom we had known for many years. Mayan regularly very kindly comes to conferences if Sheila and I are going to be there: see the photo below.

Conference at the University of Limerick, 2014. Professor Masayasu (Mayan) Mimura and his wife, Yoko, with Sheila in between.

Although not a conference nor leave of absence as such, I spent, unfortunately without the family, a month as a Visiting Research Professor at the University of Florence in 1976. I had met one of the professors, Aldo Belleni Morante at a conference and we had become friends. It was he who invited me to visit the University. The visit gave me a somewhat different insight into Italian academic life, at least in Florence. While there I became friends with one of the very bright doctoral students, Vicenzo Capasso. He is now one of the distinguished internationally well known Italian professors. Both Enzo, as a post-doctoral student of mine, and Aldo subsequently visited the Mathematical Institute in Oxford for periods of a month or more and we saw them regularly over the years. The University of Florence seemed a bit of a shambles without any sense of a "campus". Also most of the department faculty left the university after lunch as a result of which I got to know Florence extremely well. Several of them surprisingly had jobs in two different universities: one faculty member had one in Florence and another in Bari.

I was surprised how often and how many of the major museums in Florence were closed, seemingly arbitrarily, for a few days at a time, supposedly for renovations. This was possibly the case with the unbelievably complex tortuous rules and regulations in Italy associated with any repair of historic buildings. The ancient churches and cathedrals, however, were always open, and in which quite lot of the interiors certainly were in need of repair and renovation. As a faculty visitor from the University of Oxford I was invited to dinner at Bernard Berenson's *Villa I Tatti* which he had left to Harvard. It was an enclave of Englishness - upper class Englishness - not unlike the English speaking Union in Boston but very much more selective as to who was invited.

America 1979-80

The year 1979-80 was my first real sabbatical, the first term of which was at the Massachusetts Institute of Technology (MIT) in Cambridge, at the invitation of Professor Harvey Greenspan, a friend and colleague, from when I first came to the US in 1956. The Applied Mathematics faculty, of which I was a Visiting Professor, was situated on one floor with Pure Mathematics on the one below. It was not a very productive research time since most of the research was still in the traditional applied mathematics areas like fluid dynamics in which I was really no longer interested. The interdepartmental and departmental tensions were surprising and made me very uncomfortable, which is why I spent more time away. I was invited to give quite a number of lectures at various universities in the US northeast including one as far north as Dalhousie University in Nova Scotia. I made a faux pas in Dalhousie at the dinner for me after my lecture when I was told about the referenda in 1948 when Nova Scotia was not yet part of Canada. One of the senior professors said there had been a possibility of joining the US at the time. When I unthinkingly said: "Well, you certainly messed that one up." There was a sudden hush and an immediate change of topic.

When at MIT, we had rented the house of a Harvard colleague in Lexington, just next door to Cambridge. He was on sabbatical. Mark and Sarah were able to attend the excellent local high school, The Latin teacher was so popular students had to sign up a year before if they wanted to be sure to be able to take his course. Because we were visitors, Sarah, who was doing Latin in her school in Oxford, was allowed to join the class and loved it. She learned an enormous amount of Latin, so much more than a year in Oxford. However, on returning to her school in Oxford she was not allowed to be in the class she would have been in because she had spent a year in an "inferior" school for Latin in the US! The effect of different school districts in the general Boston area was made very apparent in the real estate prices. Very close to where we lived in Lexington there was an almost identical house just a very short distance down the road. It was, however, in the neighbouring school district. As a result the house was roughly half the value of the one we were renting because of the school district it was in.

Since I was visiting various universities around the country we had decided to bring with us the American car, which we had shipped to England in 1970, so we could drive across the country to the West coast after MIT. It was a popular, and then a much sought after vintage car, called a Barracuda, Being winter in some of the remote incredibly flat country areas of the mid-west the roads seemed endless, were dead straight and all looked the same. It was also the scariest close serious accident we have ever had. The dual carriageway had a rather deep grass area between the roads. We hit a patch of black ice on the road and the car swerved wildly off the road, down into the small grass dip and up towards the other carriageway with cars and trucks tearing along in the opposite direction. I have no idea how I managed to turn the car slightly so it was going up the steepest part thereby slowing it down a little and I was fortunate to be able to turn it around, with the kind help of gravity. It then hurtled, skidded rather, back up onto the original carriageway which, fortunately, was empty of any traffic for the few seconds. We swirled around until we slid off the ice patch and I could gain control of the car again. Not surprisingly it shook us all up and we stopped at the next motorway hotel to recover. We felt it was an omen we had survived without any injury since the nearest small town we stayed in was called Oxford (Iowa)!

As we drove across the country I was surprised that the Mid-West seemed to have changed so little from what I had read about it in the 19th century. It was also just as boring as I remembered from the trip with my Harvard friend, Egil Tõrnqvist, way back in 1957, although the roads were better so you could get through the country much faster.

Our destination after leaving Cambridge in 1980 was to the University of Utah, in Salt Lake City where I was a Visiting Professor in Mathematics for a few months. During our time there we had some spectacular drives through many of the dramatic national parks. The mathematics department in the university was, and still is, an excellent one. Mormonism, which dominates the State of course, was practically never mentioned unless in some joke. In one of the biology laboratories where I often went to seminars, since I was very involved in interdisciplinary mathematical biology research, there was a poster with photos of the 12 Mormon apostles, all very old. There was a red line through some of them, those who had recently died, with word "Gone" irreverently written beside the photo.

We had visited the University of Utah several times over the years so we knew the area and city well. Mormonism certainly has an enormous influence and effect on daily life in Utah and the schools. Our children, Mark and Sarah, went to the local, very good, high school. There were no classes on Mormonism. Although only 16, Mark was so far ahead academically from his excellent Oxford schooling, admittedly a private school, that he graduated from the Salt Lake City school that summer. He had a very nice Mormon girlfriend, his first girlfriend, who initiated the relationship. She invited us all to the Easter service in her church. Being an excellent oboe player Mark and his girlfriend, who played the flute, gave a small recital at the service. Another part of the service was a description by a young woman who had done her missionary stint in South America and only recently returned. It was fascinating in that it gave us a personal insight into Mormon missionary life. She described, for example, how she went from house to house and, if allowed, gave the "spiel" (her word). I became somewhat re-interested, not religiously, in Mormonism and, while at Harvard, had read the Book of Mormon, written by Joseph Smith in his twenties and as described in Chapter 4. At the time an excellent book on Joseph Smith, the founder of Mormonism, had just come out. The book, written by a history professor at the University of California in Los Angeles (UCLA), Fawn Brody: she had had a Mormon upbringing. It is called "*No Man Knows My History*". In the Salt Lake City library one day I asked the librarian if the library had the book to which she replied "Yes, but we keep it under the counter here. You have to specifically ask for it."

Alcohol, of course, was very much frowned upon and any alcohol had to be purchased at one of the few Utah State wine stores. You could drink wine in some restaurants but you had to bring your own bottle. At the local wine shop where we bought our wine the teller clearly disapproved of all the customers. Once in front of me at the checkout was a very sad, down and out, man, clearly somewhat of an alcoholic. He had in his hand a very small bottle of whiskey, like a sample bottle. He slowly counted out the change he had involving dimes, nickels and cents. The teller was clearly delighted when she said: "You're 15 cents short, put the bottle back." I felt sorry for the poor man and gave him the 15 cents. The teller was furious and made it clear by her look that I should, and would, certainly go to hell.

The university was a world apart. The time was a very productive research one for me. I did some more, particularly enjoyable, and, to me, exciting research, on animal and snake coat patterns, described in Chapter 14, and on butterfly wing patterns. It was also a time we travelled around the state, as tourists, which has several incredibly spectacular and dramatic national parks. Driving and stopping briefly, in some of the more remote small towns, however, was occasionally slightly uncomfortable, it being obvious that we were strangers and viewed with a certain suspicion. The wife of one of the professors, a lapsed Mormon, did social work, particularly for wives in polygamous marriages. She estimated there were about 70,000 such marriages in Utah.

As in most universities there were public lectures by well known figures, such as Jonas Salk, of polio vaccine fame, and Kenneth Galbraith a major world economist and American liberal who had been involved in the administration of several US Presidents as well as having been Ambassador to India. The honoraria for lectures by famous people are generally enormous but certainly do not always result in interesting or well-prepared lectures. In the case of Salk, he talked about population growth: he had somehow found a classic article on population growth about a well-known 19th century equation for population growth associated with the 18-19th century (Thomas) Robert Malthus. Salk based much of his lecture on describing, and clearly believing, what were well known erroneous conclusions based on this model known as Malthusian growth, but of which he had clearly no idea. Galbraith's lecture was totally unprepared and also embarrassing. It was a completely rambling rather pathetic lecture. I hope family and friends will tell me well before I get to that stage in public lectures. It's ok up to now - I think.

Flying back to Salt Lake City one time after a short lecturing trip I was seated beside a very lively young girl, an undergraduate at Brigham Young University, the Mormon university in Provo, south of Salt Lake City. It is quite a good university but, from the long conversation we had together on the plane, Mormonism was involved in almost every aspect of student life. About 30 minutes before we landed she said she had to go and change her clothes since, as she said: "I'm wearing slacks and am being picked up to go on to the university". She came back very much more traditionally dressed and, importantly, wearing a skirt. She said it was obligatory for female students to wear skirts. When I asked what would happen if she didn't she said she'd be severely reprimanded and told to go immediately and change. When I then asked her what would happen if she did it again she replied: "You'd get expelled."

It was in the University of Utah that I became absorbed again in one of the more interesting, and enjoyable, research projects I have worked on, which I mentioned above and which I describe in a little, non-technical, detail in Chapter 14, namely animal coat patterns and how they might be formed, with a lecture title "*How the leopard gets its spots.*" I had started working on the area after reading Kipling's "*Just So Stories*" about how the leopard got its spots to our young daughter Sarah in 1969 when she was four. The mathematics required doing a considerable amount of computing, although now it would be considered very easy and not require much time at all. Computing, never my favourite part of mathematics, at that time involved spending hours at the huge university computer. So as to spend as little time as possible it helped if there were not many people on the computer. So, I got up around 6am every Sunday for a few weeks to go to the university and use the university computer which on Sundays, and particularly at that time, I usually had totally to myself for several hours. It confirmed my early distaste for computing but I finished it successfully. I managed to download practically all the subsequent necessary computing in my research onto my graduate students and post-doc collaborators. Only very recently I had to do some myself again, for the last time I hope, associated with invited articles and lectures during the Alan Turing Centennial Conference mania in 2012: there was literally a conference somewhere in the world about every two weeks.

After our time in Utah we drove to Los Angeles and to the California Institute of Technology (Caltech) in Pasadena. It is one of the most distinguished scientific universities in the world, where I had been invited to spend several months and where I had several long time colleagues and friends, one with whom I collaborated on a research project. We had visited it several times in the past but I was astonished one day during this visit when looking out of my office window to see mountains in the distance: it was the first time in my many visits, that the smog had not blocked them out. Although scientifically very productive for me we found we actually missed clouds in the sky and got rather tired of the unexciting interminable sunshine and cloudless skies. That must be something in our genes!

It was interesting to renew my acquaintance with Richard Feynman, the Nobel laureate, whom I had first met as a postdoctoral student many years before. His curiosity about everything and the speed and ease at which he grasped the complexities and started to ask penetrating questions over lunches still astonished me.

During our stay, as had become customary, I was invited to give lectures at various other institutions: I accepted those within easy driving distance of Los Angeles. We also had several trips out into the desert tourist areas many of which are spectacularly beautiful often with not a person in sight the whole day.

While at Caltec, one place I visited in Los Angeles to give a lecture was the University of Southern California (USC). I did not know beforehand that the university wanted to try and get me to join the faculty so I was even more royally treated. At the large, more formal, evening dinner I was seated beside a very young and new girlfriend of one of the distinguished faculty, Professor Richard Bellman, who, I was told, got through quite a considerable number of them. She was about half his age, not an academic and dressed in the height of fashion. The only problem was she wore a hat with a large wide rim which she kept on during the dinner and every time she turned to talk to me I would have to sway away to miss it as did the person on her other side. The university is not in the best part of Los Angeles but in any case I was not yet interested in leaving Oxford; that came much later. We had rented a house in Pasadena and had time to visit the various superb museums, such as the Norton and the Huntingdon, which are close by.

The lecture visits to universities in and around Los Angeles were immensely helpful when ten years later I began to think of possibly moving back to the US. One of them, the University of California Los Angeles (UCLA), as I mention later, offered me a professorship when we finally decided to go back to the US permanently in 1992. It is an outstanding university with world-class departments and in a pleasant campus but we finally balked at the thought of living in Los Angeles. As we walked around the campus to get a feel of the place we found the lovely, small, enclosed sculpture garden, surprisingly not always known to former UCLA students I have asked. One of the dramatic, if not our favourite, sculptures we found was by our friend Leonard Baskin, the well-known American artist and sculptor.

Some of the lectures I gave at various universities during 1979-80 were named lectures, which meant that they were more for a general audience rather than on specific research: as usual we were always royally treated. After Caltec, we spent a week, for example, in Iowa City, as the Ida Beam Visiting Professor at the University of Iowa. My friend and former colleague from the University of Michigan, Y. King Liu, was then a professor there. He also volunteered in the hospital as an acupuncturist to help patient pain control, usually those with terminal cancer. He had also used it in the hospital in New Orleans to relieve pain in terminally ill patients.

While at Caltec I had developed a painful back problem (from sitting too long at too low a desk) so King said he would give me acupuncture which he did every day for five days. Acupuncture, of course, involves inserting needles at various specific points in the body and, ideally, vibrating them constantly. Being a practical scientist he decided to connect all the needles to a 12-volt battery, with a transformer, which vibrated them all at the same time and with the same frequency. It was the electric vibration and current which was like mediaeval torture. However, it was very efficient and agonising, not the needle vibration but the electric current. Anyway it did not seem to have any affect but when we got back to Oxford a couple of weeks after Iowa the back pain had completely disappeared. When I wrote to tell King that it had disappeared, probably on its own, he wrote back saying everybody said that. With that experience and what we had learned while in Taiwan we are totally convinced of the benefits of acupuncture if done by an appropriately skilled practitioner. How it works is still very much a mystery. When King Liu was studying acupuncture in France he described how, on one occasion, two rabbits were connected via their blood supply and one was given acupuncture the effect of which was also felt in the connected rabbit. If acupuncture is effective because of "meridians" in the body they must somehow be activated, or at least partially so, through the blood.

The Department of Mathematics in the University of Iowa was fairly typical in that pure mathematics essentially decided on the rules. The department chair, a very hospitable one, asked me if I would consider joining the faculty which surprised me. An example of the dominance of pure as compared to applied mathematics was that all Ph.D. students had to take some graduate pure mathematics courses but not the other way round. I would never have dreamt of joining such a department.

After visiting Iowa University we then drove up to Canada to spend a month at the University of Vancouver. Our son Mark during that month had gone to Boston to get some experience of the business world working in a business started and run by a good friend, Tony Blackburn, from my time in Hertford College in the early 1960s. We all thought it would give Mark an idea of what it would be like in such a profession: it did not appeal to him and had a considerable influence after he graduated from Harvard some years later.

A feature of many invited university lectures, public as well as technical, are their association with a name of the person who gave the original money to finance it. I had been awarded many of these. At that time expenses and honoraria, which were certainly not large but at least they were given unlike practically all such lectures now, were simply sent to you with the absolute minimum of details required. That is except in Switzerland where in 1997 I gave a month's course of lectures in Lausanne. Since we drove from our house in the Dordogne in France I had to fill in the actual hour we left home and the hour we arrived in Lausanne with the same when we returned a month later. Now it is even worse in Britain. Recently in 2014 when I gave such a named lecture, the first Hooke Public Lecture in Oxford, I had to sign a legal statement for expenses (there was no honorarium of course): "I confirm that the claim is in respect of bona fide business expenses, incurred wholly, exclusively and necessarily on behalf of the University." When I said to a colleague how ludicrous it was getting he said it was possibly in part because of the recent scandal and spate of false expense claims by some Members of Parliament. The use of legal forms is more and more common in practically all universities with the increase in bureaucracy as I briefly described in Chapter 9.

From around 1975 on I gave an ever increasing number of invited lectures at various universities and conferences, primarily around Europe, the US and Canada. We also had extended visits to various universities associated with research collaboration with colleagues such as a month in Florence, Paris and Heidelberg. There were so many fewer conferences then.

Both Sheila and I remember such times with much pleasure and warmly recall and often see the many family friends in academia we have around the world.

XI. World Travels and Sabbaticals

America 1984-5

As a break from running the Centre for Mathematical Biology in Oxford and dealing with the time consuming minutiae I applied for another leave of absence for 1984-5 to get on with some of the research I was particularly enthused about. I had been invited to spend the first few months at Rensselaer Polytechnic Institute near Albany, NY but at the last minute, totally unrelated to me, it fell through due to a strong resurgence of long-term antagonism between the chairman of the department and the Dean. I was told it was just another example of academic politics and personality differences. Since I had already arranged to be away from Oxford for the year I accepted an invitation to spend a term at Southern Methodist University (SMU) in Dallas. It is a pleasant campus and we lived within easy walking distance of the university. I gave some lectures including a public one which was reported in Reuters. It was my introduction to how Reuters could be used. A report appeared in newspapers in various towns and cities with each newspaper reporter making additions or changes which the reporter thought would make it more interesting for the local readers. The most astonishing one, that I heard, was later in the year, when visiting the University of British Columbia in Vancouver, a colleague said he didn't know I was a *Born Again Christian*. When I asked where on earth he had heard that he said that it was in a newspaper report of my public lecture in Dallas which had been taken from Reuters. I should not have been surprised with the experiences I have had with newspaper reports, BBC interviews seeking advice about some programme and so on. In 2014 I was consulted about one on animal coat patterns because of the research I had done on this topic years before. What was going to be broadcast was simply scientifically wrong but the BBC editor said it was too late to change so it was broadcast!

Dallas itself seemed just a vast network of roads. The museums, however, particularly the one in Fort Worth, close to Dallas, are very impressive so we spent quite a lot of time in them. SMU felt very superior to some of the other Texas universities, particularly the agricultural colleges about which the students had lots of jokes. For example: One of the football (American football) players had failed "mathematics" so the football coach went with him to see the professor. "Give him another try, Professor," the coach asked. "OK" said the professor: "What is 5 plus 8?" There was a long pause as the football player tried to work it out. "13", he

327

finally said, to which the coach interrupted and said: "Oh, give him another try, Professor, he's no *Henry* Einstein".

Football in many American universities is considered one of the most important activities because of its fund raising potential although this is now occasionally being questioned. Salaries for coaches were, and still are, astronomical compared with professorial salaries. This is not unlike current ones for senior administrators in universities the number of which has grown exponentially. More and more people now voice the adverse affects of such bureaucratic growth. When a colleague and close friend complained to me about a legitimate problem he was having in his department in Oxford I suggested he go and talk to the Vice Chancellor (equivalent of the President in the US) to which he replied: "He doesn't have the time, he's too busy counting his salary."

After Southern Methodist University I had been invited to be the first University of California Stanislaw Ulam Visiting Scholar at the Los Alamos National Laboratory so we drove up to Santa Fe in New Mexico and on to Los Alamos. Ulam was a major figure in the Manhattan Project which developed the first atomic bomb. It was literally a bit of a head-aching first week since Los Alamos is more than 7,000ft above sea level. Although my appointment was not "inside the fence" where classified research was carried out, I had to go through the required medical and fill out a lengthy questionnaire on the computer. One question was: "Do you ever drink alcohol?" to which I clicked "Yes". The programme on the computer then moved over to a different set of questions, the first of which was "Do you drink: (i) once a month? (ii) once a week? (iii) once a day?" I clicked (iii) which launched another series of related questions of which the first was: "Do any of your family or friends worry about your alcohol consumption?" The answer was "No" so I was shunted back to the original questionnaire. The last part of the medical involved having a consultation with one of the doctors. I mentioned my surprise at the alcohol questions and wondered about the reason. He said that alcoholism was not at all uncommon if a family actually lived in Los Alamos (as opposed to Santa Fe where many lived and commuted) and only one spouse worked in the Laboratory.

Los Alamos is a very quiet little town spectacularly situated in the mountains with dramatic deep valleys. It adjoins several national monuments, parks, Indian reservations and so on. It is certainly not a great cultural centre which is why so many of the permanent people in the Lab commute from Santa Fe just under 20 miles away. It is, however, close to beautiful walking mountainous country which includes one dramatic ancient hill top Indian village site which you could only reach by climbing up ladders, which looked like they had been made from trees and branches by the Indians centuries ago. On the large plateau you have spectacular views which varied dramatically as you walked around. It was difficult not to walk on ancient pottery shards which were all over the place. The site had not yet been excavated, although that is not perhaps the right word since so much was simply lying around on the ground. Los Alamos is also near some small, formerly Mexican, villages with old churches and pilgrimage sites celebrated on various Catholic religious days, which give a view of how religion is practiced there. Some of the people working in the Laboratory were of Mexican heritage and their families had been in the area long long before it was settled by Americans. One such festival, I was told by one of the secretaries, an ancient Mexican descendent, which involved crawling on one's knees for more than 10 miles, was still regularly done each year.

Walking around in the country was not without danger, albeit rare. There are the occasional bears and the possibility of catching rabies from infected animals. As well as rabies, bubonic and pneumonic plague is present in the area as it also is in other areas of the western USA. During our time in Los Alamos a 14 year old boy in White Rock, a small town about six miles away, tragically died from septicaemic plague which he got from fleas from dead plaque-carrying rodents in their wood pile. The terrible Rocky Mountain spotted fever also exists. We were incredibly ignorant about such things, even ticks. One weekend morning Sheila and I had walked up into the wooded mountain area close to Los Alamos and had sat on a log to have a rest before going back down to then drive to Santa Fe to go to one of the museums. As we registered at the high desk of the museum surprisingly a lot of what I initially thought were lice fell out of my hair which I'd never ever had since I was a very young boy in Moffat when, as I described in Chapter 2, most of us got them from the Glasgow evacuees during the war. It turned out they were ticks which had detected the temperature difference because of these "animals" below them and they dropped on my head, or alternatively they crawled up my body although I would have thought they'd have stopped on the way up. Surprisingly none of them went on Sheila – certainly sexual discrimination.

329

JDM explaining his ideas and mathematical model about foxes and the spread of rabies to a small research group in *Los Alamos National Laboratory*, 1985.

During my time in the Los Alamos Laboratory I worked mainly on the modelling of the spread and control of rabies, although primarily associated with it in Europe and, particularly, if it somehow reached England which is still free of it. We showed how quickly, and where, it would spread up through the country and, with my colleagues, we developed a control strategy based on fox behaviour. One day, when in the men's toilets, a man who worked in the Los Alamos Laboratory, clearly very agitated, rushed in and lifted his foot into one of the wash-hand basins and started to wash his leg. When he saw my somewhat surprised look he said "I've just been bitten on the leg by a dog which is very worrying because of rabies." He then asked: "Do you know anything about rabies?" I was possibly one of the experts in New Mexico at the time! I said he should forget about wasting time washing his leg but get out, find the dog and its owner as quickly as he could and ask if the dog had been vaccinated. About a week later I saw him again, very much less agitated, and he told me he'd found the woman who owned the dog and she had assured him it had been vaccinated.

Foxes are the major carriers of rabies, in Europe, particularly in France where it was more common not that long ago. Some time later on returning to Europe, after giving a lecture in Paris on rabies, at dinner

330

with colleagues from the university, we talked about the problem of getting data associated with modelling the spatial spread. I said: "What would be enormously helpful would be if we could have some way of quantifying the movement of rabid foxes in the wild. But of course, who's going to tag a rabid fox and let it go." One of the people across from me said: "We did." I thought he was joking, but in fact the research institute where he worked had indeed electronically tagged six rabid foxes and let them loose, following them closely to get information on how they moved. It was completely random, as I expected, and exactly the rabid fox spatial movement behaviour I had incorporated in the model. Random movement is totally different to normal fox behaviour.

The year 1992-3 was certainly one of major change in our life. We had moved permanently to the Seattle area and the University of Washington. It was also the year I was back in Japan, this time with Sheila, to give various lectures as the Japan Society for the Promotion of Science Fellow. I also travelled widely to various universities giving a lecture or two in the US and Europe. It was the year I was invited to give a lecture to the Annual Scientific Meeting of the *Assoc. of Surgeons of Great Britain & Ireland* which was particularly gratifying since it was an indication that some of my medical research was filtering through to the medical profession. After it one of the doctors said he had never heard a scientific medical lecture before when the speaker also told a relevant joke, particularly one a touch critical of his profession: it wasn't a very serious one.

A particular warm family friendship we made in Santa Fe was with the Goldstein family, Byron, his wife, Carla Wofsy, and Byron's daughter Danielle: there are photos of Byron and Carla in Chapter 9 when they spent time at the Centre for Mathematical Biology in Oxford. The photo of Byron and me below is at their home in Santa Fe in 2004. Byron and I share many similar tastes and humour as well as for excellent wine. Byron was a permanent researcher in the Los Alamos Lab but in a different field to mine while Carla was a professor of mathematics at the University of New Mexico in Albuquerque.

University of Angers and the *Abbaye de Fontrevaud*, France 1993
As well as spending the occasional month at other universities in the US I also spent time as a Visiting Professor at various places in Europe, the longest being for a few months at the Institut de Biologie Théorique, Université d'Angers in Angers. Four of my graduate students from the

University of Washington came with me. Universities in France are very different, most with no campus as such but buildings grouped together in

Dr. Byron Goldstein and JDM, Santa Fe, 2004.

the city. My students stayed at various places around the city, one actually in a nunnery, not that she was religious. My host, a colleague and friend,Professor Gilbert Chauvet, the Director of the Institute, lived in a small moated mediaeval chateau he and his wife had renovated, about an hour's drive from the university. The chateau had previously been inhabited by two sisters. They had built a solid wall through the middle of the chateau literally from the ancient basement to the roof. They had done it so they would neither see, nor have to speak to, each other. Apparently they had lived like that for years.

During our time we got to know the area around Angers very well, including the magnificent Loire Valley. I also learned a lot more about the incredibly powerful French bureaucracy. The lively and very nice personal secretary of Gilbert Chauvet said that 1993 was the year she had been employed by the state for 25 years and so could retire with a pension. She and her partner, a teacher, decided to get married so they could move to Vietnam. We all got a formal invitation to the wedding, sent by their children, the eldest a 14-year old.

The other wedding during our time in Angers was of Gilbert and his wife Babeth's son, Pierre, which was held in their mediaeval castle. Pierre's new wife, Eva, came from Poland and her parents were at the wedding. Unfortunately they could not speak any English or French. We were all very surprised by my graduate student, Paul Kulesa, who was with the group in Angers at the workshop. Paul who whenever he had tried to say something in French it always resulted in friendly laughter because of his accent. At the wedding he put us all to shame by starting to speak fluently in Russian with Eva's parents: Russian was the only foreign language they spoke. It changed the whole atmosphere for them that someone, other than just their daughter, and, particularly someone as considerate as Paul, could talk to them and help them mix with other people at the wedding.

During our visit Gilbert and I decided to organise a practical two week "hands-on" Study Centre involving twenty bright enthusiastic young graduate students from around Europe (although there was one from the US and one from Mongolia) who were interested in research in mathematical biology. The concept and format of this Study Centre was similar to what had been done before with considerable success. I thought such a meeting could have a major influence on the future research attitude of the students of mathematical biology by then such a very rapidly developing interdisciplinary field. The idea included inviting several distinguished academics each of whom would pose a research problem and be involved with a subgroup of students for the two-week period of the meeting. Several others were invited to give a lecture. The workshop format (and probably the list of well known speakers) clearly appealed to young researchers since there were more than three times the number of applicants for the number of available places which meant that the academic quality (and, as it turned out, also their enthusiasm) of the research students was exceptionally high. None of them had been to a conference before so, being told it would be held in the mediaeval *Abbaye de Fontevraud* did not seem exceptional. As they later found out it certainly was.

What the students did not know was that they would be staying in the prestigious 5-star luxury hotel in the grounds of the 11th century *Abbaye*.

The grounds and cathedral are closed to the public at 5pm but not to anybody staying in the hotel. All expenses, including travel were paid for. We had been given money for the meeting by the *Département de Maine-et-Loire*, the Wellcome Trust and the European Science Foundation. It was one of the most enjoyable, lively and productive meetings I have ever been to. The food and service were indeed 5-star as was the unlimited amount of superb vintage wine at dinner. The students thought this was what all academic meetings were like! Without question the most exciting part of the meeting was the "hands-on" research by the various groups working on specific research projects. The students spent hours talking about their project. At dinner one evening one of my lively doctoral students, Daphne Manoussaki (the student who stayed in the nunnery) from Greece, had everybody doing Greek dancing. Around 11pm, however, they all went off to their specific study group: they often worked well into the night. The next day they worked just as hard, and enthusiastically as usual, even without much sleep. This went on for the whole two weeks. In the programme specific times were set aside for work on these projects but they were totally ignored by the groups: they worked and talked about their ideas at almost every available opportunity, including meals. The atmosphere and the students' participation was one of total involvement. We were also fortunate in having a group who all got on extremely well together. The experience has had a lasting effect on the subsequent careers of some of the participants who went on to become academics and certainly unforgettable for all the lecturers. If there is a justification of high thinking through high living this was an excellent example. Several research papers were written by the groups and later published in highly respected scientific journals.

During my time in the University of Angers I was asked to give a public lecture, unfortunately in French, on animal coat patterns: it was immensely time consuming, and nervous making in its presentation. Because it was a public lecture one of the area's major newspapers sent a reporter to interview me (in French). Among the questions he asked was whether I knew many French applied mathematicians to which I jokingly replied: "*Mais bien sur, tous les deux.*" (But of course, both of them.) To my surprise, and admittedly a little embarrassment, this quote was included in the newspaper article. There was, and even now, a remarkably small number of applied mathematicians in France as compared with the UK: in France the field is totally dominated by pure mathematicians.

The 1990s, and in effect ever since, has been a time of travelling all over the world, particularly in America and Europe but some others, for example, in Mexico, Canada and Hong Kong giving lectures many invitations of which I accepted since Sheila almost always was able to come with me, certainly all of them from 1990 on. Because of the generous conditions given me at the University of Washington, in effect I had a leave of absence every year for several months at a time until I formally retired in 2001 when we spent a complete year in France in our ancient property in the Dordogne.

XII

Prizes, Honours and Honorary Degrees

Election to national societies, depending on their international standing, can be very prestigious, particularly if one is elected as a Foreign Member or Honorary Member. In 1979, for example, I was elected to the Royal Society of Edinburgh, Scotland's National Academy of Science and Letters founded in 1783 during the Scottish Enlightenment which was an exciting intellectual time with such as Adam Smith, Robert Burns, David Hume and many others living and mingling in Edinburgh. Appointments to named professorships, named public lectures, are much more widespread and carry considerably less academic prestige. I have had many of these. Elections to societies, prize award ceremonies, in fact all such honours, are always very friendly, very social occasions and for me, Sheila and I rather, have involved visits to universities around the world.

With most honours there are formal certificates and medals. I've never known what to do with them: they simply sit in a box. Recently the Mathematical Institute in Oxford University thought it would be a good idea, however, if all Oxford University recipients of the Gold Medal of the *Institute of Mathematics and its Applications* would give their medals to be exhibited in a case in the Institute: I gather we all did. The most impressive diplomas I have been awarded are the degrees from my *alma mater*, the University of St. Andrews, which have the ancient dramatic crest dating from the early 15th century, when the university was founded. They are written in Latin, with your name translated into Latin if possible (James was *Jacobus*) and signed personally by all the members of the committee or council who approved the degree or award.

Honorary degrees

In the academic community and learned societies, subject prejudice is less prevalent than within the field of mathematics. Honours generally depend on having made some impact in the field or, of course, some contribution which non-specialists recognise or have been personally involved in. There are still major hurdles with interdisciplinary candidates since it can often be more difficult to assess the impact of the candidate's research in the different disciplines. It is, however, getting more recognised, which from my long-term belief in interdisciplinary research is somewhat deferred gratification.

Honorary degrees are traditional recognition of success in some context but they are, of course, also sometimes political. With so many of the leading politicians in Britain graduates of Oxford many more of them have been awarded honorary degrees. To be awarded one for academic achievement generally requires an academic, generally not a local, who submits a detailed proposal, backed up by the candidate's academic standing and achievements, to the university or appropriate academic society. Self-nominations are never ever considered otherwise universities would be flooded with nominations.

Usually the first you learn of such an honorary degree and other awards is when the university or society's President writes you a formal letter. Unusually in the case of the honorary degree from the University of Milan it was an informal letter from a friend and colleague, Professor Vincenzo Capasso, who told me. The University of Milan had wanted to award me two honorary degrees at the same ceremony, one in mathematics and the other in biology. Honorary degrees in bureaucratic Italy have to be approved by the appropriate national government body. Apparently the award of two honorary degrees in different subjects at the same time had never been done before in an Italian university so, the university was told it had to decide on only one: the university decided on a Doctorate of Mathematics, *Dottore Matematica* (*Dott. Mat.*) which was awarded in 2004. The ceremony was quite informal in a large lecture room in the beautiful spacious 16th century building which encircles the huge quadrangle in the old university. In Italy honorands have to give a short 20 minute lecture to the audience with the university Honorary Degree Committee seated in the front row. Just before the lecture at the beginning of the ceremony I was told, not very seriously, that officially if the committee did not think the lecture was worthy of somebody being awarded an honorary degree then they could rescind it. None of the committee, however, had ever heard of a degree not being awarded as a result of that rule. It was a particularly warm and friendly atmosphere during our whole visit. Of course with all honorary degrees one's wife or partner and any other family member there are included in all the social occasions.

My first, longest, very friendly, and particularly enjoyable one, with many social occasions, was associated with an honorary degree, an

Honorary Doctor of Science (D.Sc.), which I received in 1994 from my *alma mater*, the University of St. Andrews. It is an ancient university, and, as mentioned, the third oldest in the English speaking world, founded in 1410-13. The occasion lasted five days with highly organized large splendid formal lunches and dinners with senior members of the university and invited guests where the seating was all highly organised. It gave you a chance to meet a large number of interesting and lively people. There are now generally several graduation ceremonies each year in universities: there was only one each year when I graduated in 1953 and in 1956. There were so many fewer university students then. Now, at each ceremony, only one or two honorary degrees are given. The university faculty member who has been assigned, and has agreed, to deliver the laureate oration, describes the academic reasons for the award and other than academic facts: it can occasionally be very amusing – intentionally so. Usually the oration is given by someone in your academic discipline. St. Andrews interestingly had a faculty member from a totally different discipline write and give the oration. Before formally being given the degree the oration was read out by the faculty member, Dr. Ann Kettle, a mediaeval historian, who had been assigned the task of writing it and giving it: she did a superb and very impressive job of both. She had clearly done a lot of background research on me and my career. Among other things she incorporated some very amusing and very apt quotes related to some of my research, my time as a student, and much more, not all academic. Many who talked to me during the week, commented what a superb, highly original and amusing oration Ann gave and, as several said it was the most original and enjoyable they'd ever heard – I agree.

1994 Laureate address:
Dr. Ann Kettle, Department of History, University of St. Andrews

"Chancellor, I take great pleasure in presenting for the degree of Doctor of Science, honoris causa, Professor James Murray, Fellow of the Royal Society.

Chancellor, I present to you a graduate of this university who is a leading applied mathematician and perhaps the world's foremost mathematical biologist. Jim Murray came up to St Andrews from Dumfries Academy in 1949 to read Mathematics and graduated in 1953 with first class honours and the Miller Prize for the best graduate in the Faculty of Science. He came under considerable pressure to go off to Oxford to do his research (in those days research students were few and far between in St Andrews and not encouraged and cherished as they are

*today) but he was a very strong-minded young man and he insisted on staying here
and doing a Ph.D. in fluid dynamics under the supervision of Professor Ron
Mitchell who characteristically remembers his prowess on the football field - "better
to have him on your side than playing against you". Dr. Murray's was the first St
Andrews Ph.D. in Applied Mathematics to be awarded to a postgraduate student
and it was completed in two years - a shining example to today's research students.
He went straight to a lectureship in the University of Durham but then persuaded
Professor Sydney Goldstein, the leading expert in his chosen field of aerodynamics,
to take him under his wing at Harvard, beginning a career which has criss-crossed
the Atlantic: from Harvard to University College London, then on to Oxford for
the first time; back to Harvard and on to Michigan, followed by a spell in New
York. In 1970 he returned to Oxford as Fellow and tutor in Mathematics at
Corpus Christi College (a place not unknown to you, Chancellor). He became
Reader in Mathematics and in 1986 Professor of Mathematical Biology. In 1987
he was made an offer that he could not refuse and he left Oxford[1] to take up his
present post of Robert F Philip Professor of Applied Mathematics and Adjunct
Professor of Zoology in the University of Washington, Seattle. As a Scot who enjoys
living in North America, he is in the fortunate position of having an American
wife who enjoys living in Europe.*

*During his second spell in Oxford Professor Murray established himself as the
leading expert in the new field of Mathematical Biology and his distinction was
recognised in 1985 by his election to the Royal Society. He became the Director
(and was largely the creator) of Oxford's Centre for Mathematical Biology and in
1989 he published his immensely successful and influential work, Mathematical
Biology. Professor Murray gratefully acknowledges his debt to Professor D'Arcy
Thompson, whom many of today's graduands will know only as a character in the
Kate Kennedy procession: the one with the long beard and the parrot on his
shoulder, but to Professor Murray he is one of the great luminaries in the field of
mathematical biology - a man born well before his time. In the preface to his
monumental Growth and Form, written in the University of St Andrews during the
first world war, D'Arcy Thompson predicted that, 'It is not the biologist with an
inkling of mathematics, but the skilled and learned mathematician who must
ultimately deal with the problems of organic Form' and in the epilogue (after 1100
pages) he wrote, 'I have tried to show the mathematician a field for his labour - a
field which few have entered and no man has explored.' Professor Murray took up*

---

[1] I actually went to the University of Washington for the 1987-8 year on a leave of
absence from Oxford. It was not until 1992 that I retired early from Oxford to go
to the University of Washington.

D'Arcy Thompson's challenge and entered the exciting field of mathematical biology with a full awareness of the problems of genuine interdisciplinary research and the difficulties of communication between mathematicians and biologists. He once wrote that, "A remark such as "It's probably a secondary Hopf bifurcation in the p.d.e. parameter space" does not have biologists on the edge of their seats - unless to leave." He has shown how mathematical modelling can play an exciting part in the unravelling of the mechanisms of growth and development. He has explored the complex patterns of nature in such areas as the spread of epidemics from the Black Death to AIDS, wound healing, fingerprints and temperature dependent sex determination. Perhaps his most accessible work has been on colour patterns on animals. It is asked in Jeremiah, 'Can the leopard change its spots?' - not according to Professor Murray because they are genetically determined. Remember William Blake's poem:

Tyger! Tyger! burning bright
In the forests of the night
What immortal hand or eye
Could frame thy fearful symmetry?

Well, Professor Murray can tell us how it was done. He has also unravelled, to misquote Shakespeare, 'the cunningest patterns of excelling nature', the colours and patterns on the wings butterflies and moths, Just one more apt quotation of - with a bow towards Professor Murray's American connections: Amy Lowell: 'Christ! What are patterns for?' - Professor Murray can tell us.

Although he does not list his recreations in Who's Who Professor Murray has varied and humane interests, ranging from 18th and 19th-century water-colours to mediaeval history: Professor Murray, to some of us mediaeval history is a whole career. His fascination with mediaeval history is reflected in the quotation at the front of Mathematical Biology. It is a remark attributed to Alphonso the Wise, King of Castile and Leon in the mid 13th century: 'If the Lord Almighty had consulted me before embarking on creation I should have recommended something simpler.' Nature is anything but simple and by modelling its complex operations Professor Murray has revealed the art in nature and persuaded biologists to overlook St Augustine's warning to 'Beware of mathematicians and all those who make false prophecies'.

Jim Murray did not forsake St Andrews nearly forty years ago; indeed it was only two years ago that he revisited with his supervisor his favourite pubs and student bunks (remember 27 North Castle Street, 15 Church Street, 33 Bruce Street and *that cramped room at the top of Edgecliff). But now, 40 years on, we welcome back in state this master of the small world of the high-powered academic to the smaller world of his alma mater which nourished him and launched him on his distinguished career.*

Chancellor, I invite you to add to Professor Murray's B.Sc. and Ph.D. the honorary degree of Doctor of Science."

Honorary degree, University of St. Andrews 1994. From left to right: Sir Kenneth Dover, University Chancellor, Dr. Ann Kettle, who gave the laureate address, JDM, Professor Struther Arnott, Principal and Vice-Chancellor of the University.

Graduation ceremonies are held in the large Younger Hall in the university now with only one laureate a day since each graduating student has to go up on to the stage to formally have their degree conferred. Honorands sit on the stage. When called, you stand as the oration is given after which the conferring of the degree consists of kneeling in front of the Chancellor of the University, in this case it was Sir Kenneth Dover a

341

colleague from his time as President of my college, Corpus Christi, in Oxford.

The procedure is exactly the same as for each graduating student. While kneeling in front of the Chancellor the degree is conferred with the Chancellor patting you on the head with the reputed cap of John Knox. It is a very long tradition so it must be rather grubby by now. As you are getting up the degree hood is flipped over your head.

Knox, the great, narrow-minded and prejudiced reformist, contemporary of John Calvin, had an enormous influence in promoting the rigid, intolerant Calvinist view of religion in Scotland which still dominates much of Scottish church life and the daily life of many. In 1558 Knox wrote *"The First Blast of the Trumpet Against the Monstruous Regiment of Women"* which attacked the women rulers of the time, all Catholics, and which he viewed as against the Bible: "Monstruous" is not misspelled it means unnatural. He was certainly not overly popular in the university when I was a student. In his time though he certainly had justification for his criticism of the established Catholic Church and its practices. As a student, irrespective of the discipline studied, one was well aware of this period. The stone cobbled front of the ancient St. Salvator's College, founded in 1450, dates from this period. It is where the initials PH are on the ground to mark where Patrick Hamilton had been martyred in 1528. Scotland finally threw off the Catholic yoke around 1568.

In the photo above Sir Kenneth Dover, on the left, is wearing the elaborately gold encrusted incredibly heavy gown of the university Chancellor. By the end of each graduation ceremony he was exhausted and couldn't wait to take it off. The Principal Arnott Struther (later Sir Arnott Struther) on the right was immensely influential for the university. He had spent many years in the US. He recognised that the university had to become, not only a major arts university, which it was, but also a major science university which it now is. He was certainly very focused on doing so which, not unexpectedly gave rise to some criticism from the Luddites of which there is always quite a number, not only in universities, of course.

The lunch after the ceremony on the day I formally graduated was held in the Principal's house and I was seated beside the Principal's wife Greta Struther, who later was deservedly awarded an honorary doctorate for all her innovative work for the university. It was one of the pleasantest and liveliest lunches of the week. Towards the end she said that she had worried about having me on her right since she did not know what she would be able to talk about to a mathematician. Perhaps she had to sit beside a pure mathematician in the past.

At another lunch I met and talked a while to Harold Pinter, the playwright who was later awarded the Nobel Prize. He was there in his role as the husband of another honorand, Lady Antonia Fraser, whose books I had always enjoyed, but whom I found a touch arrogant and condescending, so unlike Pinter. I asked him if he, like Ted Hughes, a friend of his also, had been threatened by some of the crazy women's movements in the US that he would be murdered if he ever put foot in America. He had also received similar threats.

Another warm, more scientifically descriptive, honorary doctoral laureate oration was given by a colleague and friend Professor Mark Chaplain when I was awarded an honorary *Doctor of Laws* (LL.D.) at the University of Dundee in 2011. It was also a very enjoyable several day occasion. The only unsettling time was at drinks before the formal dinner for the laureates and invited guests. The Vice-Chancellor (Principal), Professor Sir Pete Downes who has made such an enormous difference to the university and its international standing, asked me if I would give the Laureates' after dinner speech. It made it an exhausting dinner since, naturally, I had to be very sociable throughout the dinner while, at the same time, think about what to say after it which would have to be interesting and with some relevant humour.

Other honorary degrees (D.Sc.) I received at the University of Strathclyde in Glasgow and Waterloo University in Canada with very kind, well researched and original orations given by long time friends and colleagues Professor Sean McKee at Strathclyde University and by Professor Sivabal Sivaloganathan at the University of Waterloo. These were very much shorter occasions, essentially the graduation ceremony and an elaborate lunch afterwards.

Endowed Professorship in Perpetuity: James D. Murray Chair in Applied Mathematics in Neuropathology

In the early 1990s, just after formally moving to the University of Washington in Seattle the Chairman of the Department of Neuropathology in the University of Washington Medical School, Dr. Ellsworth Alvord, always known as Buster, contacted me to see if I would like to try and model the growth and control of brain tumours, a field he had worked on for about 50 years. It was a challenging project and one I thought was of much more importance and direct human help than many of the projects I had worked on: it has certainly turned out to be so. Our first meeting, lunch in the Faculty Club, launched one of the most important and longest collaborative research projects I have worked on and a friendship which lasted until Buster died of a stroke in 2010 at age 86.

A very much rarer, totally surprising honour, rather than a prize, was a consequence of the many years I worked on brain tumours with Buster. This area is just one of the diverse fields in which I have done research. This honour, one of the most flattering, was totally unexpected and one of the most distinguished I have received. The correspondence regarding it was an email from Buster Alvord to ask if I would agree to have an endowed professorship named after me. The email is the most low key correspondence about an honour I have ever had. It was due to the generosity of Dr. Ellsworth Alvord and his wife Nancy Alvord. They endowed the *Nancy and Buster Alvord Brain Tumor Center* which was founded with six endowed professorships in perpetuity in the University of Washington of which the *James D. Murray Chair of Applied Mathematics in Neuropathology* is one:

http://depts.washington.edu/givemed/prof-chair/endowments/james-d-murray-chair-of-applied-mathematics-in-neuropathology/

I heard about it via the incredibly casual email, reproduced exactly here, typos as well:

11 Oct 2006, at 8:13 pm, Ellsworth Alvord wrote:
"dear Jim, I hope you won't be too embarrassed to alow a chair to be named in your honor, a chair of Applied math in neuropath, joint with the two depts, at least at first as part of a new center of excellence in the study and treatment of brain tumors. This has been incubating for several years and i finally decide that, if no one else was going to step up, we might just as well get the ball rolling! So, i hope you will accept the naming in your honor, in perpetuity as the saying goes - but of course, as time goes on, the subjects to be investigated need not be limited to tumors!! There are, after all, many other projects that math can contribute to. Many thanks in advance, best wishes, buster"

Since Buster and I started to collaborate together we published many research articles on the modelling and genuinely practical medical application to such brain tumours, mainly gliomablastomas (generally known as gliomas). His emails were always sloppy, the very opposite of his drafts and corrections to articles we wrote together.

In most of the major universities, particularly in the US there are many such named professorships but practically always with the financial donor's name, or an historical character's, attached to it, as it is with many buildings around campuses. There is, in most universities, a de facto financial scale which determines what can be named after the donor depending on how much money is given to the university. It can be a plaque on the outside of a building, the name of a lecture hall, a prize, a public lecture, an endowed professorship and so on. Some professorships and buildings are named after distinguished people, usually the donors, sometimes dating back centuries. The 18th century Lord Crewe's Benefaction in the University of Oxford described in Chapter 9 is rare, unique rather, and annually widely appreciated.

Election to the Royal Society and the French Academy (*Academie française*), *Institut de France*

During the spring of 1985 when we were in Los Alamos I was elected to the Royal Society giving the academically coveted FRS after your name. One of the Vice-Chancellors of Oxford University, Sir Richard Southwood, a zoologist and friend, told me I had been the first choice of the mathematics committee the year before, which was the first year I was on the candidate list, but for political reasons in the Society the second choice was elected. The actual election is a fairly formal occasion. When elected a Fellow of the Royal Society you have to sign the book of Fellows. The original book from the Society's foundation in 1660 was not yet filled so, on signing, it was interesting to look back on some of the signatures of the great names in the history of the Society, such as Isaac Newton and Albert Einstein. I had to sign the book with an ancient incredibly basic pen, like the cheapest I used in primary school, after dipping the nib into an inkbottle, the kind of ink which lasts for centuries. Blots were common. It was a dreadful scratchy nib which seemed like it had not been changed since the Society's foundation. My signature reminded me of my time in primary school when, at age 8, I was learning to write script with such pens and having my knuckles rapped with a ruler for it's lack of clarity and regularity, and the frequent blots.

In 2000 I was elected a Foreign Member (*Associé étranger*) of the *Académie française* (French Academy) at a resplendent formal ceremony in the *Institut de France* on the *quai de Conti* in Paris. Splendidly dressed trumpeters with their long trumpets heralded the entry of current *Academiciens* in their gold encrusted uniforms, and those to be elected, into the huge dome. A short oration was given about each candidate who, after it, walked up the few steps to be formally elected and presented with your Academy medal. I awkwardly tripped, not at all seriously, going up the steps. Highly unusually I was given the choice of being elected to the *Academie* as a mathematician or as a biologist. My primary Academician sponsor, Professor Michel Thellier, the renowned biologist, with his wife Suzanne, became close family friends. My French academic colleagues felt it would be helpful if I chose biology, which I did, since several in the *Académie* were trying to get it to become more interdisciplinary – not an easy task anywhere, particularly in France. After the formal event, officers of the *Académie* and the newly elected Fellows retired to an informal reception and superb lunch.

Institut de France, Paris

Election to the French *Académie* is very much more prestigious than the Royal Society in that it has less than 300 science *Académiciens* and less than 150 Foreign members (*Associés étrangers*) compared with around 1600 Fellows and Foreign Fellows of the Royal Society. The list of historic figures who have been elected is very impressive, such as Isaac Newton, Benjamin Franklin, Charles Darwin and Albert Einstein: a very distinguished group to be in!

After the *Académie* celebrations and the social events for the new Foreign Members, the British Embassy held a reception to which Sheila, our son Mark, who had flown over from New York, and Michel and Suzanne Thellier were also invited. We had previously met the then ambassador Michael Jay (later Baron Jay of Ewelme, a lovely little old village near Oxford) at dinner at some mutual friends in the Dordogne where Sheila and I had our old mediaeval manor house and farm.

Foreign members elected to the *Academie française* in 2000. The President is in the centre in the traditional heavily gold encrusted suit of *Academiciens*. JDM is the farthest left.

One of the unusual privileges of being an *Académicien* is that when you go to any of the national museums, historic castles and so on, in France if you show your formal card as an *Académicien* you never have to pay. It also includes any number of guests you have with you. Not only that, you simply walk to the front of any queue, where you are respectfully ushered in.

International academic prizes

For the vast majority of academics, prizes play little role in their lives. In academia, the number of smaller prizes, from medals as undergraduates to research awards, is legion. Many of those for academics in faculty positions have an upper age limit so they can play a significant role in promotion. Candidates for prizes, honorary degrees, election to national academies cannot submit personal nominations so such awards carry more weight. This injects some unfair consequences since difficult, sometimes obnoxious, but brilliant academics are less likely to be nominated, but surprisingly not as much as might be expected which is an indication of the reasonable objectiveness of much of academia. I have seconded several nominations for awards and elections for a few people whom I hoped I would never have to sit beside.

347

I have been privileged in having been awarded a number of academic prizes, other than student awards, each with their own idiosyncrasies, and which gave various levels of pleasure. One, the *Akira Okubo* Prize, is awarded by the *Society of Mathematical Biology*. The prize consisted of a plaque and, because it was at the beginning in the prize's financial life, I was given a cheque for $300; it is now very very much more. It gave me particular pleasure since Professor Akira Okubo was a man of immense human warmth, a distinguished, universally liked and admired theoretical ecologist. He had moved from Japan to the US after the war, had been a friend for many years and, when he spent some months in the Centre for Mathematical Biology in Oxford, a research collaborator: we published a paper, with two other colleagues, on the reason for the demise of the red squirrel in England. A photo of Akira when he visited the Centre for Mathematical Biology in Oxford is in Chapter 9; it captures his warmth.

One particular prize had a major effect on my subsequent career, and our life, namely the (US) Guggenheim Fellowship in 1967-8 which I mentioned before. This award lets you go wherever, and do whatever, you want for anything from a few months to a year. A particularly civilised aspect of it, certainly at the time, was that no final report whatsoever was required which I feel encourages more original and often more productive research, as certainly was the case for me. I described what I and our family did that year in Chapter 7.

Prizes in Applied Mathematics areas are determined by committees whose members are generally chosen for their academic distinction. In pure mathematics, on the other hand, many committees consist only of previous winners of the prizes which, of course, propagates the prejudice against those outside their field. The award of prizes often involves giving a prize lecture. I have always felt these lectures should be understandable to the general public but that is quite rare. Such public lectures from around the end of the 1990s have often been filmed but with the early ones sometimes rather amateurishly, depending, of course, on the university or society's filming group. Even as recently as 2012 some of the filmed lectures I gave in major universities were quite amateurish; the Turing Centenary plenary lecture in Princeton University was an example. The inaugural *Hooke Lecture* (Thomas Hooke 1645-1698) I gave in Oxford in 2014 was much more professional. Compared with many public television science programmes, however, they were at least scientifically sound with only the speaker involved. I am always surprised that some of the academics involved in such television programmes are so uninformed of the science, which is sometimes wrong, behind the programmes and about what they have to talk about. That's not new of course nor is it just restricted to science.

The most professional filming I have had was the PBS (Public Broadcasting Service, WQED Pittsburgh) film in 1998 about mathematics in the real world as described in Chapter 10 called *Life By The Numbers: Math Like You've Never Seen It Before*. A much longer film, a 3-hour series on Alan Turing's work for his centenary in 2012, involved a day with a Korean film team flown over specifically to film me talking about my research on animal coat patterns in our home in Litchfield, Connecticut. It was interesting to see the different approach. It is not as good as the PBS film, being a little disjointed since the final cut involved adding parts in sections where I was talking. There are some beautiful sections, however, on wild animals in Africa.

One unique and recently created new prize is, highly unusually, specifically for Applied Mathematics, namely the *William Benter Prize in Applied Mathematics*, which is awarded every two years. The Benter Prize is now recognised as the major Applied Mathematics Prize. The prize consists of an award of $100,000 and involves giving a plenary lecture at the award conference in the City University in Hong Kong. I was honoured to be awarded it in 2012. The atmosphere at the conference was a very friendly one. This was to a large extent due to William Benter himself, the chairman of Applied Mathematics in the University, Professor Roderick Wong and particularly his personal assistant Sophie Xie who organized it superbly and ensured that all the local student helpers she chose were all genuinely friendly and immensely helpful. The photo below of us all makes the atmosphere clear.

William Benter, born and brought up in Pittsburgh, is himself a real, practical and immensely successful applied mathematician. He is universally respected for many things such as the widespread philanthropy of him and his wife, Vivian Fung. Bill founded the *Benter Foundation* (www.benterfoundation.org) in 2007. He is rightly starting to be mentioned in connection with Andrew Carnegie when Carnegie started his philanthropic career of which I personally benefited with the Carnegie Fellowship I was awarded to do my Ph.D. many years ago as a student in St. Andrews University. Bill Benter has an extremely successful business in Hong Kong betting on horse racing. He developed a highly original scientific mathematical method of betting very successfully.

From left to right, JDM, Professor Roderick Wong and Mr. Bill Benter, City University of Hong Kong, 2012.

Sophie Xie and JDM. City University of Hong Kong, 2012.

Scots have been leaving Scotland for centuries. There was no feeling whatsoever that one's responsibility was to stay for the possible benefit of Scotland or its universities. This was not the case in Oxford as I described in Chapter 8 when I decided to retire from Oxford a few years early to go back to American academia at the University of Washington. The *Edinburgh Mathematical Society* is one of the highly respected mathematical societies which dates from the mid-19th century. It is generally associated with the purer side of mathematics. One of the highest honours, even more so than most of the prizes and medals, in most academic societies, as I mentioned, is to be elected an Honorary Member. To my surprise, astonishment rather, and pleasure, I was elected such a member in 2008 to commemorate the Edinburgh Mathematical Society's 125th anniversary.

There are only three living Honorary Members and 25 in total from the Society's founding in 1883: I am the only Applied Mathematician. At the ceremony meeting, listening to one of the invited lectures, I was sitting beside a world-renowned Fields Medallist colleague from Oxford, Sir Michael Atiyah: he is one of the three living Honorary Members. I found the lecture totally incomprehensible and leaned over to ask him, if he was understanding it since the lecturer was a pure mathematician. Michael wasn't doing any better than I was.

In 2011 eight years after getting an honorary degree I was back in the University of Milan, even in the same hall, to receive the *European Academy of Sciences* premier award, the *Leonardo da Vinci* medal. This consists, not of a medal, but of a heavy crystal (6 inches in diameter and weighing about 1.5Kg, that is about 3.5lbs) with an internal engraving of the well-known one of Leonardo da Vinci's head and the engraving of the medal details and date. The ceremony was an even less formal than the previous one in Milan. When presented with the award in a padded box I thought it was a typical medal and so did not realise how heavy it would be since it was in a solid blue box and I accidentally dropped it on the floor: it fortunately did not break. There was laughter and much applause for that. The whole atmosphere was incredibly friendly which I have found on all occasions I have been at in Italian academia.

European Academy of Science premier prize: *Leonardo da Vinci Medal* presented in 2011 at the University of Milan by Professor Enzo Capasso is on the left with JDM on the right. The prize plaque is on the right.

In 2009 I was awarded the Royal Society's premier prize lecture and medal in the Physical Sciences, the *Bakerian Prize Lecture*, which has been given every year since 1775. It is a lecture for the general public. The last time it was given by a mathematician had been 34 years before. I wanted to show the public that mathematics can be genuinely useful in the real world as opposed to the public's customary view of its irrelevance. The title, published description and especially the abstract, resulted in a large audience of several hundred overfilling the hall and included quite a number of international media people who sought interviews. It was widely reported internationally. The main reason was that among the things I was going to talk about was divorce prediction for newly married couples. The report in the *Sydney Morning Herald* (27 March 2009) had a very funny cartoon accompanying the article "*Love by the numbers*" (see Chapter 14). The *London Telegraph* had: "*Will true love last? Mathematical model may provide the answer*". In the French *Libération* it was: "*Le divorce, c'est mathématique*". In the Italian *Libero* it was: "*La matematica dell'amore: elaborato in Gran Bretagna l'algoritmo del divorzio.*" There was a lot of world press even with an article in *Good Housekeeping!*

The Royal Society web poster with the Bakerian Lecture abstract is below. The recorded lecture web page is:

https://royalsociety.org/events/2009/mathematics-real-world/

"Mathematics in the real world: from brain tumours to saving marriages"

Bakerian Prize Lecture

Professor James Murray FRS

"Practical mathematical models are becoming an accepted part of most medical and scientific disciplines. They cover an ever expanding spectrum of topics. A few of the more unlikely applications are justifying intertribal warfare, the benefits of cannibalism, how the leopard gets its spots, how sex determination in

crocodiles has let them survive and demonstrating the connection between badgers and bovine tuberculosis. This lecture shall describe the modelling of two applications.

The prognosis for patients with high grade brain tumours is grim and the various treatment protocols such as surgery, radiation and chemotherapy cannot effect a cure. A simple model using patient data and brain scans quantifies the spatio-temporal growth of brain tumours. Analysis of the model shows how difficult it is to decide on the tumour volume to be treated and shows why such treatments have so little success. The model simulations can estimate life expectancy for the patient and show how it might be possible to use a patient's past record to quantify possible treatment efficacy.

The rise in divorce rates in developed countries is a widespread but poorly understood phenomenon. A simple but surprisingly predictive mathematical model, based on only a few parameters describing specific marital interaction patterns, has helped design new scientifically-based intervention strategies for troubled marriages which are proving encouragingly successful in clinical practice. In a 12-year longitudinal study on a large number of marriages, the model has predicted divorce with an accuracy of 94%."

Named public lectures in universities are legion. You are always treated royally. The many that I have given meant travelling all over the world with all expenses paid. Looking back, the lecturing system has changed out of all recognition from the time when one wrote with chalk on a blackboard to sophisticated computer programmes which let you cover much more, show photographs, short movies and so on. Now one has to get formal permission to use certain illustrations, photos, cartoons and so on and in many cases there can be a significant fee for a single use. The legal world has certainly had a significant negative impact. Not surprisingly university museums are the easiest to deal with while national museums are among the worst: I have found that most of the time they never reply, such as the Smithsonian in Washington on the two occasions I wrote to it. On the other hand some are extremely helpful, like the National Bibliothèque in Paris, but, admittedly, only after it was informed by the Académie française that I was an Académicien.

Every two years the University of Washington awards a professor, chosen from all the university faculties, to give a public lecture. In 1998 I was awarded this honour. It was filmed but at that time not very professionally. I wrote just a few years ago to see if I could get a copy: I was told I could and what it would cost me! A more unusual lecture invitation when at the university was in 1992 and again in 1998 when I was asked to give a Pinkham Lecture in the Swedish Hospital in Seattle. It was a lecture primarily for doctors and medical practitioners in the wide Seattle area and King County in Washington State to tell them, without great technical detail, about new treatment or discoveries in medicine or new developments in the sciences. The audience filled the enormous lecture hall. I was very impressed, although somewhat less so when I found that, for some, their attendance was part of a necessary yearly updating of their practicing license and attendance was a requirement. It was not all science and medicine and on the second occasion one relaxing break "lecture" consisted of some actors enacting a scene from a play about mathematics. Unlike all other such meetings of simply lectures, at the end of the day the audience had to fill out a form grading each lecture and lecturer. I must have done ok since I was invited to give another one a few years later.

Academic World of Mathematics

Mathematics has had an excellent, often undeserved, press for at least the past few centuries. Here I want to briefly put a common view of mathematics in perspective and as conceived in the real world. As mentioned, mathematics in academia is almost universally considered as pure mathematics. I do not mean it is trivial but it is, in effect, generally of little practical use whatsoever. One can almost say that it is unfortunate that Applied Mathematics shares the same word "mathematics". The essence of applied mathematics is in applying mathematics to problems in the real world. The myth that was propagated for many years among pure mathematicians, was that Alfred Nobel did not fund a Nobel Prize in mathematics because a Swedish pure mathematician called Mittag-Leffler had gone off with his wife. Nobel was never married and, in fact, emigrated from Sweden when Mittag-Leffler, who was supposed to have done it, was a student. Apparently Nobel never thought of a prize in mathematics. As a scientist himself he believed that mathematics was indeed important but as a useful tool in subjects like chemistry and physics: in other words Applied Mathematics. He also wanted the prizes to recognise individuals who had done something useful in the world which, of course, excludes practically all "pure" mathematics. Nobel was certainly right.

The fact that there is no Nobel Prize was the motivation for the Fields Medal which is a major prize in mathematics, which everyone in academia knows means "pure mathematics". I can name a few applied mathematicians, not even major international figures, who have done more for the world and mankind than practically all the Field Medalists put together. A typical example of the total incomprehension, of pure mathematics to other than a few (pure mathematicians) is the 2012 citation for the US National Academy of Sciences prize in mathematics: the prize citation reads: *"for the proof of the nilpotence theorem: if f: K~K is a pointed map from a finite CW complex to itself that is trivial on a complex bordism, then some iterate of f is stably nullhomotopic."*

In my final two years as a mathematics undergraduate I took several courses in pure mathematics which were a little interesting but more like just a complex intellectual game. One of the younger permanent faculty tried to convince me to do a Ph.D. in pure mathematics since he felt applied mathematics was less intellectual and not as respected. He was right about the latter and certainly not about the former. I decided to do applied mathematics because I enjoyed it and, even as a student, liked the fact that it could have practical relevance in the real world.

There was, and still is, a belief that pure mathematicians often cease publishing research in their mid to late 30's because they are burned out. Among the applied mathematicians, active researchers continue publishing until retirement and many of them long afterwards. Many of us, if we thought about it, felt that the pure mathematics colleagues who stopped doing research were not burned out but were just bored and did not see any point in it.

Publishing research articles, books and so on, and getting research grants was not an essential part of academia in Europe, certainly prior to the early 1980s, as is universally the case now with ever more rules in the application procedures. Pure mathematicians traditionally never consider their research has any practical use or application of any kind, so getting grants is less important. One of the major pure mathematics world figures in the mid 20th century, G.H. Hardy of Cambridge University, felt that the most beautiful mathematics was mathematics which had no practical use whatsoever and he would have been appalled if he thought his had. His specialty was number theory.

Even in France, particularly, where mathematics means pure mathematics and is considered the peak of intellectual ability, the Education Minister in 2008 wanted to stop the pre-eminence of mathematics in the *Baccalauréat* because of its lack of relevance in the world. The arrogance of mathematicians in France is closely matched by that of physicists in America. From the beginning of my academic research career I have been fortunate to have been totally unconcerned about what pure mathematicians thought about my work – most couldn't, nor would want to, spend the time to understand it anyway. One email I recently received, sent to me certainly in error, had attached to it a copy of a pure mathematics research article the title of which was completely incomprehensible. I forwarded it to my friend, Professor Philip Maini in Oxford and jokingly said: "*I doubt if 7 people in the world will read this.*" He emailed back: "*That many?*" Not surprisingly pure mathematicians have been the butt of jokes by those in the sciences and applied mathematics for as long as I can remember.

The renowned well-known 19th century applied mathematician (and physicist) James Clerk Maxwell ((1831-1879) was not a great fan of pure mathematicians. He said: "*Mathematicians may flatter themselves that they possess new ideas which mere human language is as yet unable to express*". He was a Scot, a very wealthy one, whose huge country mansion (called *Glenair*) was in the country not far from Dumfries in Scotland, about an hour from Moffat where I grew up. It is now a ruin but spectacularly situated with incredible views over its enormous grounds. He was born in Edinburgh in the impressive Georgian house which is now the *James Clerk Maxwell Foundation* and the *International Centre for Mathematical Sciences*. There is a very nice statue of Maxwell in George Street, one of the main streets in Edinburgh. In 2008 a former graduate student of mine, Professor Jonathan Sherratt kindly organised an *International Symposium* in my honour in the *International Centre for Mathematical Sciences* in the Maxwell house. Jonathan, a brilliant applied mathematician, is the second youngest person to have been elected to the Royal Society of Edinburgh.

Dr. Richard Feynman, the brilliant 1965 Nobel Prize winner in Physics, remarked at lunch one day at California Institute of Technology (Caltec) after listening to me give a very simple explanation of something he hadn't heard about, commented: "*Even a mathematician could understand that!*"

To give an easily understood example let me describe a classic pure mathematics problem which many pure mathematicians have spent their life trying to prove as opposed to just verify. It is called *Fermat's Last Theorem* the name of which is relatively widely known to the general public. Pierre Fermat (1601-65) was a very bright and clever lawyer who was also interested in mathematics. He was quite a politician, changing his name to Pierre de Fermat, and was often involved in disputes as to who discovered what first. Fermat is remembered as one of the well known mathematicians, a very pure one, in the first half of the 17th century.

Fermat had written a note, in Latin of course, in the margin of a book in which he claimed to have found a proof for a classical problem. The note was found posthumously but the proof was never found. With elementary school algebra it is easy to understand what the theorem actually says. Suppose you have an algebraic equation $x^2+y^2 = z^2$ and ask for integer numbers x, y and z which satisfy this equation. They are easy to find. For example, if x=3, y=4 then z=5 is one solution. Substituting these into the equation gives 3^2+4^2 = 3x3+4x4 = 25 = 5x5 =5^2 and so z=5. In other words one solution of the equation $x^2+y^2 = z^2$ is x=3, y=4, z=5. Another solution is x=6, y=8, z=10. In fact there is an infinite number of solutions.

Now consider the equation $x^n+y^n = z^n$ where n is an integer larger than 2, for example, $x^3+y^3 = z^3$, then Fermat's last theorem says that there are no integer values for x, y and z which can satisfy this equation. That is for n=3, 4, 5,..... and all subsequent integers, there is no solution. There are countless numbers of pure mathematicians who have spent their whole academic career over the past few centuries trying to prove this result rigorously but with no success until the mid-1990s. With current computers billions of integers can be tried in a second and none will be found. But that is not a mathematical proof even if it would convince all the scientists and non-scientists I've ever known.

As an applied mathematician such a career and lifetime endeavour to prove such a problem are incomprehensible. Imagine looking back on your career and life and reflecting on what your research has been for decades and what use it has been to anybody. Applied mathematics is such a very different discipline. I describe several examples of some of the practical mathematics research I have personally done in Chapter 14. Applied mathematics as a discipline suffers somewhat, as I mentioned, from the fact that it has mathematics in its title. Mathematics departments, particularly in France and the US are almost universally primarily departments of pure mathematics with little to no interest in applying mathematics in the real world. Some years ago the mathematics department in one of the upstate New York State universities was going to be closed because of its irrelevance. British and Commonwealth universities however have traditionally been very much less rigidly focused:

practically all mathematics departments in these have applied mathematicians – a heritage from Britain.

The justifiable belief that mathematics, as generally studied and taught around the world, is of little use is actually a view that has been echoed for centuries. Its use in the real world, until the 19th century, and even then, was limited to applied scientists. Mathematicians have had a critical press for a very long time. The general view was succinctly stated by Nicolas Copernicus (1473-1543) who said: "*Mathematics is written for mathematicians*" which is an accurate description of what is universally published in pure mathematics journals today. Genuinely practical applied mathematicians are generally still held in rather low esteem in the world of mathematics which has never ever bothered me nor the many applied mathematicians and scientists I have known and particularly those with whom I have collaborated around the world. Sitting beside a distinguished pure mathematician visitor at dinner in Corpus Christi College one evening in the 1970s I had a very difficult time trying to keep a conversation going as did the person on his other side. It brought to mind a view expressed by Bernardino Ramazzini (1633-1714) a famous medical figure who used cinchona bark in his treatment of patients with malaria: quinine is extracted from it. He said of mathematicians: "*Mathematicians have to ponder the most abstruse problems far removed from material existence, and to this end the mind must be kept detached from the senses and have hardly any dealings with the body; hence they are nearly all dull, listless, lethargic, and never quite at home in the ordinary affairs of men.*" Saint Augustine (354-430) was not a great fan of them either: "*Beware of mathematicians and all those who make empty prophecies. The danger already exists that the mathematicians have made a covenant with the devil to darken the spirit and confine man in the bonds of hell.*" Another example is the 18th century philosopher George Berkeley (1685-1753) who wrote in his private notebooks: "MEM. *Upon all occasions to use the utmost modesty - to confute the mathematicians with the utmost civility and respect, not to style them rather Nihilarians .... N.B. To rein in ye satirical nature.*"

For applied mathematicians, who are genuinely interested in the real world and its people, to be excluded from any prize, however prestigious it might be in the mathematics world, does not bother them – except they would not mind getting the hundreds of thousand dollars of the prizes! I feel immensely fortunate not to have listened seriously to the pure mathematics lecturer in the University of St. Andrews, when I was an undergraduate, who wanted me to do research in his pure mathematics area. When I mentioned to my friend and colleague, Professor Philip Maini (University of Oxford) that I had recently been sent another research paper by mistake which I found totally incomprehensible he said: *"Oh, it must be a pure mathematics one."* Almost all the applied mathematicians I know in the world practically never give pure mathematics a thought, unless to joke.

XIII

Our Other Professions, the Arvon Foundation and Our Life in France

Disease of historic old stone houses
In my long life in academia I have found it surprising how incredibly few academics ever wanted to live in the country, far less in old stone houses completely on their own and to be as much there as possible with their family. The number who wanted to, and who also had to renovate them, I found were practically non-existent. The norm for academics has been to buy moderate to small houses with close neighbours even when in villages commutable to their university. It is even more so now with the escalating house prices of country houses in Europe, and also houses in towns in Britain, particularly in Oxford. Sheila and I have always wanted to be in the country and live in ancient period houses: we have frequently and fortunately been able to do that. It has, in effect, meant of course that we had to have another profession, namely restoring such historic properties. All the ancient houses we have had and renovated in England are now *Grade II Listed Historic* buildings while in France the mediaeval one is now registered with *Bâtiments de France* which are buildings considered part of France's heritage.

As described in Chapter 6 it was buying an ancient thatched house which needed total renovation that we sold without completing the purchase, which gave us the money to buy an even more beautiful ancient house in 1960 in a small village called Hempstead about 50 miles from University College London where I was a lecturer. The Hempstead house shown in Chapter 6 needed some internal renovation. When my parents visited us, my father, who certainly did not have our love of old houses, quite the contrary, thought we were silly, irresponsible rather, to have bought it, as well as all the other ancient houses we bought later. He felt he was right since the very first time he stepped into the house in Hempstead he said: "You've got dry rot somewhere." In Scotland it is considered one of the worst things a house can have and often made a house un-saleable. So much so that if it was found in a house, for example, in Moffat, the owners often had it removed in the middle of the night so that nobody would know. It is widely believed, in Scotland, that the spores can actually diffuse through as much as 2 feet of sandstone. In fact in the Hempstead house there was a small amount of dry rot in the entrance hall which my father found (by smell) and we had it removed – not in the night! It does not confer the same stigma in England. We only had the house a year, selling it in early 1961, since I had been appointed to a permanent faculty position in Oxford.

Sheila and I simply loved the atmosphere and feeling of old, particularly stone, houses and, unrealistically and irrationally, never ever thought of all the work involved in their renovation. It was certainly Sheila's and one of my other professions. During the renovations, which usually took as much of my time as my academic responsibilities, it meant, of course, that I tended to work practically all the time. I never ever thought of that and never felt it was a burden, just normal. The first house, which needed major renovation, was in Woodeaton, a tiny ancient village a few miles from Oxford, and which is described in Chapter 6. The other important thing about wanting to live in the country is that Sheila and I simply have always loved being together and on our own as much as possible.

The summer of 1963 before moving back to America we tried to buy a house near Moffat, where my parents lived and I grew up, to keep a foot in Europe and I also knew how much it would please my parents. House prices were still comparatively low. We tried to buy a rather large house with a lodge cottage called *Craigieburn* a few miles outside of Moffat in the country. It had once been owned by the father of Jean Lorimer a beauty whom Robert Burns the Scottish national poet adored: he called her *Chloris*. He wrote many poems and songs to her perhaps the best known of which starts with:

> *Sweet fa's eve on Craigieburn,*
> *And blythe awakes the morrow;*
> *But a' the pride o' spring's return*
> *Can yield me nocht but sorrow.*

(fa's – falls, a' – all, o' – of, nocht – nothing)

It is certainly not one of his best nor are any of them related to Craigieburn, but she was an inspiration for him. Jean went off with a loser who spent all her money and who left her three weeks after their runaway marriage in Gretna Green about 30 miles south of Moffat. The house was actually rather unattractive with the old stone walls plastered but it was very much in the country. Anyway it did not work out which was a good thing.

The other place we then tried to buy, which was even more irrational but which suited our tastes much better, was a very romantic ruined ancient 16ᵗʰ century stone fortress called *Spedlin's Tower* replete with its bottle dungeon prison and a magnificent stone arched large room with an old fireplace. It has its own ghost, a miller who had worked for the Baronet owner, called Jardine, well known as a difficult man. The miller was imprisoned in the dungeon after a fight with the owner and died of starvation, after eating one of his hands: the owner had gone off and had

15ᵗʰ century *Spedlin's Tower*, Scotland 1965, with a photo of a window and its fireplace in the large room before any restoration.

forgotten he was there. The Baronet's family were supposedly tormented by the miller's ghost and shortly after moved out of the tower. There are some photos we took of it above. It is about 13 miles from Moffat spectacularly situated on a bend of the River Annan the source of which is up in the hills close to Moffat. The walls are about 10 feet thick. The roof had collapsed and the exposed top floor covered over with tar. It had not been lived in for a few hundred years. The upper class owner lived in a large estate in a village a few miles away. He said he did not want to sell it. Perhaps he had clearly never thought about it and our interest put the idea into his head since not long afterwards it was sold and renovated. It is now an elaborately gardened renovated country house. Of course, another possibility is that the owner did not want to sell it to us with my local Moffat accent, which very much implied the wrong class in those days. With our later rather peripatetic life it was a good thing we did not buy it but we certainly thought about it very seriously.

North Devon, England: *Totleigh Barton Manor* and the founding of the *Arvon Foundation*

I formally moved from the University of Michigan to New York University in the summer of 1967 but on leave of absence from New York for the year 1967-8. When we were in France in 1968 we travelled widely around the country as tourists, to visit colleagues in various universities and to give some lectures. It was, however, also essentially a pilgrimage to old towns, mediaeval cathedrals, isolated villages with ancient churches, all over France. Subconsciously, I think, we were looking for another old house. Because of the violent student protests of 1968 in Paris, particularly near, or rather in, the *Place Maubert* where we were living in an apartment, as described in Chapter 7, we decided to spend the rest of my fellowship time back in England. We made a preliminary trip primarily to look for a house in the country which would be our regular summer escape from New York. Devon was particularly appealing since there were still a significant number of old isolated stone houses in the country. We systematically scoured the countryside moving all over but increasingly farther north in rural Devon. We thought the very small hillside market town of Hatherleigh would be a particularly nice place to be near and we eventually found an isolated, incredibly ancient, thatched stone house called *Totleigh Barton*. Barton is an Anglo-Saxon word meaning lands of the manor. The house was pretty much a complete wreck: the old barn and pigsties were actually in a better state. The area around *Totleigh* is one of the most beautiful and untouched parts of central Devon about 5 miles from Hatherleigh along a very tiny road leading out of Hatherleigh towards the small uninspiring village of Sheepwash about 2 miles from the house. The house is about a mile down a narrow dirt farm road through some fields ending about 200 yards across a field from the very much unspoiled, River Torridge.

To get to the house you had to drive through the farmyard the farm owner of which had decided to sell the old house. It had been empty for years and was in a dreadful state with a collapsing thatched roof, no sanitation in the house, a primitive kitchen, scary old primitive pre-war

View of *Totleigh Barton* from the hill, 1969 - now the *Arvon Foundation's* Principal centre.

electrical wiring, some dangerous floors upstairs and so on. The house was in a worse state, other than Spedlin's Tower, than any we had ever considered before but, irrationally, it was love at first sight. The farmer, not our favourite Devon person, had put what we thought was a relatively low price on the house since he had no appreciation, and certainly no romantic feelings, for such ancient buildings. It had also been for sale for a long time. He later regretted the price after we had renovated the house so he came up with the idea of trying to get planning permission for houses in the woods across the field which would have totally changed the character and atmosphere of the old house and which he knew we would have to buy. We bought the woods for more than we paid for the house and very much more than they were worth but it preserved the rural atmosphere and views which were so important to us. The farmer acquired the nickname Greedy Goaman. In fact when we started working on it and realised the extent of the basic structural renovation required the price we paid for it was certainly not at all too low. Even so we certainly did not regret buying it. We were particularly fortunate that I had a background in plumbing, carpentry and a general practical bent, and Sheila and I had already acquired considerable renovating experience with the old stone house we had in Woodeaton near Oxford described in Chapter 6.

So, once again we started on yet another old period stone house renovation. The house had to be rerofed, rethatched rather, plumbed, an external septic drainage system installed, a buttress built outside to hold up a dangerous looking wall, complete electrical wiring, oil fired central heating, a new floor for a bathroom, a lot of structural stone work inside the house and much more.

Of course there was no telephone. Very few of such country houses had one at the time and certainly not one such as Totleigh. Getting one was quite an undertaking, and expensive, since it could only be installed with actual telephone wire which had to be brought from the closest pole about a mile away and across the wide River Torridge. The wire also had to be buried around 3ft underground since poles were not allowed on the farmland. This was done using a mole digger. This is a long, about 4ft, metal cylinder, a few inches in diameter, which was first buried in the ground and to which was attached a very strong chain with the telephone wire at the back. A tractor dragged the chain with the cylinder front designed so that it stayed approximately the same distance under the ground. It had to be this far under the ground so as not to be disturbed by any farm ploughing and harvesting. Not only had it to be drawn underground for almost a mile including the same depth under the bottom of the river which, fortunately, although wide (about 50 feet) it was not very deep so the tractor simply drove across the river. Watching the whole process was like a family outing. After the first rain you could hardly see where the chain had been pulled.

We did most of the renovation ourselves working like slaves, doing the usual stone mason work ourselves, replacing floors, decorating, removing ceilings to expose and repair the old mediaeval beams behind, plumbing and so on. Although exhausting it was immensely satisfying. Our young children Mark, then 6, and Sarah, 3, loved *Totleigh Barton* and roamed freely on their own about the countryside around the house, farm and the River Torridge. They also made friends with the kind young farm worker who often took them around the farm on his tractor or sitting on the back of the trailer. Mark and Sarah were genuinely warm friends and loved being together: they walked holding hands much of the time. Mark felt completely responsible for her.

The tradesmen we had were not the best but it was difficult to get any to travel as far as the house, sometimes as much as 10 miles away from their base, which they very rarely did. I had to describe to the plumber, Mr. Sing, nicknamed Simple Sing, exactly what and how to do what we wanted which was not too difficult with my family background, while the young man who had just finished his electrician apprenticeship was not the most professional but so much nicer than his boss, Mr. Sluman, whom we rightly nicknamed Slimy Sluman.

Sarah watching Mark running with the view across the valley.

Sarah in impish mood 1968.   Sarah under the gutter leak.

Mark and Sarah on one of their regular walks 1969.

Mark and Sarah on another of their regular walks from *Totleigh Barton* 1969.

Mark on the wall in front of the house with a bright red shirt Sheila had made, 1969.

Sarah running on top of the wall in front of the house, 1969.

Mark and Sarah 1968-9 at *Totleigh Barton*.

Mark with the cows at *Totleigh Barton*, 1968.

Some of the people who worked for us were from a different era. The thatcher, a totally unsmiling, but not unpleasant, man, Mr. Rodd, was in his 70s and had been thatching ever since he was a child. He lived alone some miles away in the country in a small derelict looking house with an earthen floor in keeping with farm workers' houses of the 19th century and earlier. I had to pick him up since he only had a bicycle. He made his own ladders from branches of trees, the treads of which quite often broke as he climbed slowly up them to the roof with a heavy bundle of thatch, called a nitch, on his back. We had no idea how he had not had major accidents. As was the custom in those days, of course, everyone was referred to as Mr or Mrs or Miss. We never knew the first names of the workmen.

Sheila felt sorry for the thatcher and on one occasion decided to try and help by carrying a bundle of thatch up to the roof for him. She never got beyond the first two steps since the nitches weighed at least 50lbs (c20Kgs) each after they had been sprayed with the necessary water which was always done before taking them up to the roof. So, instead we just supplied him with tea every couple of hours. Mr. Rodd had lived all his life outside the village of Sheepwash. This was almost the norm for the people in the area; they hardly ever left the neighbourhood.

At the time, North Devon was still very rural and very isolated. One day a group of three men, clearly three generations, walked down the

Renovated *Totleigh Barton* (front) with its barn on the left, 1970.

370

Totleigh Barton renovated back with the tower door, 1970.

narrow old farm dirt lane, from where the hill photo above of the distant house was taken. They had walked from their farm some miles away to see who these "foreigners" were and, more interestingly, what we were doing with the old buildings and all the disruption in the land around the house about which they had heard. We were clearly a subject of local gossip. The land disruption was because we were installing a septic system with a large complex drainage system. They introduced themselves, in the very strong very nice Devon accent: "We be Gilberts." They were fascinated with the septic system and its drainage system wondering what it was for. They had never seen anything like it before and had, all their lives, only an outside privy, which was the same as for *Totleigh* when we bought it. They wondered what all the trenches were for and asked what a septic system was, how it worked and why we needed one.

Most of the local people we had help, or try to help, were very willing if not always the most useful. The blacksmith in Hatherleigh on the other hand was particularly nice, helpful, practical and loved his work. The mason, Mr. Bolsden, although that is a little too flattering for his trade ability, always wanted to help. We took out the ugly old 19ᵗʰ century fireplace, and the large broken wood lintel above it in the main room so as to expose the mediaeval stone one behind. Unfortunately when we did it he did not put in the wall support properly, which he was supposed to do while we propped up the wall above the fireplace with metal acrow props. The consequence of that was we not only had to install another old antique wooden lintel, which we personally did and had planned, but also had to repair the stone wall above it all the way up to the first floor because of the large crack that had appeared in the wall. As a mason, Sheila was in a different (and certainly superior) class to Mr. Bolsden after our apprenticeships in *Old Upper Farm* in Woodeaton near Oxford. Mr. Bolsden's other problem was drinking. Prior to returning to New York in September 1969 we left money for him to do some specific jobs around the property. This was all too much of a temptation for him and he drank it away, with some boasting, in the Sheepwash village pub. When we saw him again the following summer he had not done any of the simple work he had been asked to do. He was clearly rather ashamed and tried to make up for it but with his practical incompetence it would have simply caused more problems. By the time we left in the autumn of 1969 to go back to New York, the house was only just habitable.

We had learned a little about the history of *Totleigh Barton*. Although I have not seen the original, it is listed in the late 11ᵗʰ century historic *Domesday Book* and was supposed to be one of King John's (1166-1216) hunting lodges. Parts of it are certainly ancient with some of the stone walls several feet thick in parts. When we took out the small ugly late 19ᵗʰ century fireplace in the main room we found the original ancient stone fireplace behind it buried in the wall: it was enormous, around 9ft in width with an ancient stone oven, in not unreasonable condition, on the left side. What made us think that there perhaps was something in the hunting lodge legend was that we discovered a hidden, very steep narrow stone staircase, on the left in the photo below, which went up to the single room tower the entrance to which we had assumed was only accessible from the outside with a ladder. It was possibly a priest's room, or a hiding place, during the time of Cromwell and the Restoration in the 17ᵗʰ century. We also found in the staircase a small, somewhat broken, wooden double-sided mediaeval wood comb, hand made of course, together with a small, rather badly torn and eaten, very elegant soft leather doll's dress, obviously well loved and very much the worse for wear. Both of these, particularly the doll's dress, clearly came from upper class inhabitants. The house had certainly been upmarket in earlier centuries and had seen very much better days so it could perhaps have been a hunting lodge for the aristocracy in earlier times. Irrespective of the vintage of the house it is a lovely place, beautifully situated as in the photo from the hill up the small lane behind the house.

Totleigh Barton: old hidden fireplace and the ancient stone staircase on the left, 1969

Mediaeval comb in the hidden staircase.   Thel and Wyatt McDowell at home, 1970.

A very rare upset Sarah   Dr. Wyatt and Thel McDowell, Sheila and JDM in the country behind their home in Hatherleigh, Devon 1970.

As in our house in France many years later, we started to get to know other people in the area who had similar feelings about old houses and the country. Ted Hughes, as mentioned before, a particularly close friend from long before when we were both in the Boston area in 1958, lived only a few miles away. We got to know and became friends with several of Ted's literary and artistic friends such as the well known American sculptor Leonard Baskin whom I talked briefly about in Chapter 5. After cutting my hand and needing a few stitches we met the local doctor, Dr. Wyatt McDowell and his wife, Thel, who lived in Hatherleigh. Wyatt never believed in the increasing norm of being part of a multiple doctor practice and always practiced on his own, feeling incredibly responsible for all his patients in the town and neighbouring villages. We became particularly close friends and saw them often, long after we had sold *Totleigh Barton*.

Thel and Wyatt, of course, knew everybody for miles around and we met many of their friends at dinners which enlarged our social life in a very wide area around. We occasionally went to a neighbouring village to have dinner in an old local inn where the McDowells were, of course, well known. Then no one cared about age limits when sitting in the small pub of the ancient stone inn so our children Mark and Sarah of course were always with us. Not surprisingly they particularly liked Wyatt and Thel. On one occasion the owner/bartender went round our group asking what we would like to drink, which customarily was sherry or wine. When he got to Mark, who was about 7, he asked him what he would like. Mark had recently tasted sweet vermouth at some friends' house, so he said "Sweet vermouth, please" which the owner, as if it was the most natural thing in the world, wrote it down and duly brought Mark a very small glass of vermouth on the house.

The *Arvon Foundation* – the early days

At dinners at Ted Hughes' place, *Court Green*, in North Tawton, in 1969 and, after he had married Carol Orchard, in late 1970, we met some of Ted's writer friends, particularly the poets and authors John Moat and John Fairfax. Since John Fairfax did not live in the area we saw much more of John Moat and we became family friends with John and his wife Antoinette (Annie): they lived in a romantic old mill in North Devon on the coast and we usually also saw them socially whenever we were down in Devon. On several occasions we discussed John Moat's and John Fairfax's original idea put forward in 1968 of a non-profit writing teaching centre in Devon to promote the interest, particularly in poetry, of budding young writers which they called the *Arvon Foundation* and which we hoped would get the backing of the *British Arts Council*. It was initially thought of, not only as a retreat but where people could take live-in courses, give performances and generally be literary and creative. Their idea was to have small groups, initially of young people, attend a writing course for a few days, run by an established author or poet, and to discuss their work and do some writing. The first courses were immensely successful. It was certainly not clear in the early days, however, how successful the Arvon would be. Ted Hughes played a major role in many ways, including raising money, in its subsequent success.

Funding was certainly one of the major problems. When we all got together in the early days we certainly wondered if it would make it. It was certainly not obvious how successful it would be nor even whether or not it could get going at all. Since I had been involved in many of the discussions and was a permanent faculty member at the University of Oxford and a Fellow of Corpus Christi College they felt that it might help in attracting recognition and financial support if a permanent University of Oxford academic was listed among the small original group as an Advisory Director so I was listed on the Board of Directors in the headed notepaper. I officially became one of the two *Advisory Directors* in the *Arvon Foundation* in 1969 and during the early 1970s. John Moat, in a letter he wrote to show me the new notepaper which had just been printed, was clearly very pleased with it. He also bounced ideas off me and in one of which he wondered what I thought about having a poetry course for young scientists from Oxford, possibly mixing them with non-scientists. Unfortunately I couldn't be very encouraging with my experience of most science students whose interests and talents were generally not literary.

THE ARVON FOUNDATION   *TOTLEIGH BARTON MANOR SHEEPWASH BEAWORTHY DEVON*

Tel: Black Torrington 338

CHAIRMAN: THE HON. ROBERT GATHORNE-HARDY   DIRECTORS: JOHN FAIRFAX JOHN MOAT   SECRETARY:
ADVISORY DIRECTORS: JOHN LANE, Director of the Beaford Centre & Dr. JAMES MURRAY, Fellow of Corpus Christi College, Oxford.
Full Member of the South Western Arts Association and of the Southern Arts Association

Original letterhead of the *Arvon Foundation* and the Directors 1970.

An indication of the early problems is in the draft of the Directors' Report 1970-1971 which John Fairfax sent me. It was very worrying with the disastrous appointment of the first organizing secretary who stayed six months the second three months of which was the period of his termination notice. I did not personally meet him but the beginning of the report describes in detail how unsympathetic and what a complete lack of understanding he showed about the whole process of recruitment for courses. John, a particularly warm and sensitive man, said the only positive thing the secretary did was to develop a reliable system of accounting. It was certainly a depressing and discouraging report but as usual John Fairfax and John Moat tried to be optimistic. We all thought that writing, particularly with the enthusiastic participation of young people, could be nothing but successful so this report brought some realism to us in those early days as reflected in the following excerpt from the draft report John Fairfax sent to me for comments and suggestions.

XIII. Our Other Professions, the Arvon Foundation
and Our Life in France

Major excerpt from:
THE ARVON FOUNDATION
DIRECTOR'S REPORT 1970-71:

"The importance of this year to Arvon undoubtedly lay not in the new determination of its work so much as in its somewhat rigorous confrontation with its own facts of life.

Over this last year I think it would be true to say that a new realism has entered Arvon's management. It has been recognised that there are two main areas of difficulty which will have to be squared if the <u>progressive</u> future, which is felt to be vital, is to be achieved.

The first, inevitably, is the area of finance. The generous grants that have come to us privately and from charities (in particular the Chase Charity) have bought Arvon breathing space. But these are short-term grants, and clearly the future is dependent on our solving the problem of our sustained long-term viability.

The second is the area of public relations. Our experience has shown that there is little difficulty in stimulating initial interest in our work, and even promises of cooperation. But it is going to require really considerable administrative ingenuity and energy if this initial interest is to be sustained into action. I think it is true to say that we have found that while there is an unexpected amount of willingness among educational authorities to accept new ideas and experiments, this willingness overlies a really staggering inertia; too often the energy goes into welcoming the idea, but when the action is called for then the system yawns – the energy is spent! However, we have proved that the inertia will yield – to energy.

One other thing should be mentioned here. In the last months the possibility of the Beaford Centre becoming on its own terms a residential centre for the Devon L.E.A., and linking its work with Arvon has moved from possibility to probability. This new scheme would come into operation in September or January. The implication of this are too manifold and too conditional to warrant an airing here, but it is felt that if this is a genuine departure then it affords Arvon a way of real promise in squaring the two areas of difficulty outlined above.

In sum it should be said that Arvon is more substantial now than at any time – and that this is in part due to the astonishing generosity of its friends and those who have been prepared to involve themselves with it (to all of whom the directors are inexpressibly Grateful); and in part due to the increasingly realistic awareness of its potential. It remains that perhaps the greatest danger to Arvon lies in the multiplicity (potentially dissipating) of the ideas it might pursue."

It was not all discouraging since there had already been several courses which proved very successful due primarily to the enthusiasm, effort and thoughts John Moat, John Fairfax and Ted Hughes put into the *Arvon*. The *Arvon* has proved to be immensely successful and is now very well known. When we all got together in the early days we certainly had considerable doubt.

When I was appointed to a permanent academic position in Oxford we were given a college house, described in Chapter 8, to live in. We had not been able to spend as much time in *Totleigh Barton* as we had hoped which enforced our decision to sell it and look for a house to buy near Oxford. It came up at dinner one evening at Court Green, Ted Hughes' house, and also with John and Annie Moat at their place. Later in 1970 John and Annie decided to buy *Totleigh Barton* for the permanent Centre for the *Arvon Foundation* and to which Sheila and I contributed ten per cent of the sale price. John Moat published a short book: *"The Founding of Arvon"* in 2005. *Totleigh Barton* is the primary Centre but with two others, one of which is Ted Hughes' old, large, mill owner's country house, *Lumb Bank* in the beautiful countryside of the Pennines in Yorkshire and the other, *The Hurst*, a manor house in splendid country grounds in Shropshire.

Sletchcott, King's Nympton, North Devon

We knew we were going back to Oxford in early January 1970 and were going to move into the large Corpus Christi College house, *Pinsgrove*, which no one in the college wanted - it was much too large and grand - as described in Chapter 8. We decided it was impractical to keep *Totleigh Barton* so we reluctantly decided to sell it as mentioned. Since *Pinsgrove* belonged to the college, that first year back we thought that we should try and find a house to buy and, as usual, a place in the country, so we duly scoured the countryside around Oxford looking at various old houses but found none that appealed or that we could afford. The area around Oxford, of course, is nothing like as rural as Devon but it does have some lovely small towns and countryside. Woodeaton, where we had bought *Old Upper Farm* and renovated ten years before, now had a group of tasteless new houses in the middle of the village, developed by the *Oxford Preservation Trust* which to me violated the whole concept of a preservation trust. Woodeaton had totally lost its untouched rural atmosphere. Sir Douglas Veale, the University Registrar, the most important permanent administrator in the university, coincidently was an Honorary Fellow of my college Corpus Christi. He was also the President of the *Oxford Preservation Trust* from whom we had bought our house in Woodeaton. At dessert after dinner one evening in college I met him for the first time. I started, perhaps a little disrespectfully as a new faculty member, to criticise the Trust's development plans for Woodeaton which would ruin the old traditional atmosphere in the village, which it certainly did. He was immensely patient and not totally unsympathetic to my view. It was actually the start of a friendship between us until he sadly died of cancer in 1973. The last time I visited him in hospital he made a huge effort, clearly very tiring, to be the usual warm and considerate person I had always known.

By the end of the year it was clear how much we missed Devon so we wanted to have a house to spend time there again, an ancient one of course. Had the Arvon Foundation not been successful John Moat said he would have been pleased to have sold *Totleigh* back to us. We started looking for another old house, again in the area around Hatherleigh which we knew well and already had several very good friends only short drives away. We found one, another ancient thatched house with even more outbuildings which, as usual, required considerable renovation but less than *Totleigh* and *Old Upper Farm* in Woodeaton although the latter was relatively new in comparison, dating only from the beginning of the 17th century. The house we found is called *Sletchcott* and is just over a mile from the tiny village of King's Nympton. It is in a spectacular position on top of a hill with distant views over its fields to the empty country towards Dartmoor National Park and to the village. It is the oldest house in the village. The renovations, although certainly not trivial, were less arduous for us but it also required re-thatching, this time done by a bunch of young very professional thatchers, a rare trade even in Devon at that time particularly for young people. As we, by now, expected in such houses we had to remove the ugly early 20th century fireplace to expose the old mediaeval one behind. The major structural work we personally did was to add a dining room by incorporating an attached old small stone barn by inserting a door in the ancient thick stone wall into it from the kitchen. With our previous masonry experience it was not difficult, just time consuming. The door lintel we used of course was an old wooden lintel we found. Rather than dig up the floor to lay flagstones we discovered an old graveyard where the church was selling off large 18th and 19th century slate headstones which had been piled against the outside back of the church for many years. They sold them at a ludicrously low price to get rid of them. We thought it would be interesting to use these with the names and details facing up. Some were very interesting and certainly gave the people a somewhat longer immortality than if they had been simply broken up or put in upside down. Unfortunately the people who later bought *Sletchcott* from us a few years later did not like the idea so they removed them.

Aerial view of the *Sletchcott* property, King's Nympton in the 1960s.

Sletchcott had always had a thatched roof. The walls were built of traditional cob a building material which had been used for centuries, particularly in Devon. Cob is mainly a mixture of clay, soil and straw which are mashed together with water, and was traditionally trampled on by oxen until it was like a smooth clay. When hardened it is very strong and solid unless it gets rain on it. We learned from the owners after us that they had had a problem with a small part of the thatching at the back of the house above the main wall of the house the consequence of which was rain leaking onto the top of the wall. The result was that an extended section of the cob wall under the leak disintegrated and a large section of the wall had to be rebuilt which they did but not with cob.

With much less renovation to do we had many more friends visit, from America such as our close friends, Professor Chia-shun and Shirley Yih from Ann Arbor, Professor Sydney and Rosa Goldstein, my post-doc supervisor from Harvard, as well as others from Oxford. We also had much more time to indulge our love of the countryside. We saw much

more of our Devon friends particularly the McDowell's and Ted and
Carol Hughes with Ted's children with Sylvia Plath, Frieda and Nicky.

When we were in *Totleigh Barton*, through our friends the McDowell's,
we were invited to a garden party of friends of theirs who lived not far
from Hatherleigh. It was where we met a son of their friends, Johnny
Sturt, his wife Alex and their young daughters Claire, Emma and Claudia

Sletchcott, King's Nympton, renovated with some of its barns on the left, 1972.

Sletchcott our family in the front lawn, 1972.

with whom Mark and Sarah had an immediate mutual warm rapport. They have been family friends ever since. We saw them often when years later we lived in France since, after Johnny retired as headmaster of the grammar school in Newton Abbot in south Devon, they moved permanently to France eventually moving within easy driving distance from our French house, *La Combe*. We saw the Sturts every time we were down in Devon. The photo is of us all at *Sletchcott*.

The Sturt family: Alex (back left, Sheila and Johnny behind the children Claudia, Sarah with Claudia, Emma, Claire and Mark on the grass, c1973.

Mark is now godfather to Emma's son. Sarah and Claudia were particularly close, roughly the same age. Claudia, very lively and fun, eventually went to Oxford University and on graduating, surprisingly to us, went into the Prison Service. She feels very strongly that the service should try and genuinely help prisoners, something she has tried to do ever since. In 2003 she was appointed the first woman governor of a prison, the notorious Dartmoor Prison, a huge granite prison and one of the grimmest and toughest in England. She was subjected at the beginning of her time to wolf whistles. It is situated literally in the middle of Dartmoor National Park, the huge dramatic bleak moor of nearly 400 square miles about 20 miles from where we had our Devon houses. The prison looks like a mediaeval granite fortress. Claudia was immensely successful in changing the whole atmosphere of the place because of her highly original methods and

Claudia Sturt
France c1993

genuine concern for the prisoners. Her appointment caused a lot of stir in the press because she was a woman. Not surprisingly Claudia moved up in the prison hierarchy in Britain becoming Deputy Director of the whole Prison System in 2011. Claudia is now the Anti-terror chief in British prisons to try, among other things to stop prisoners being radicalised when in prison. Mark's early artistic eye for beautiful paintings was shown the first time we went to the Sturts' home for a family lunch. The children all went off into the formal drawing room. Mark came rushing out to tell us that there was a Turner watercolour painting on the wall that we should see. We didn't think it was but Johnny said that it was in fact possibly a Turner which his parents had bought many years ago. Johnny and Alex were very impressed – Mark was 10. Many years later, when we were living in France, we visited Alex when Mark was spending a week with us at our French house, *La Combe*. Mark, by then a well-known art expert with his own art gallery in New York (*Mark Murray Fine Paintings*) recognized the old watercolour he had seen as a child. He immediately realised it wasn't a Turner but told Alex that, if she would like, he would take it back to New York to make sure. Alex still has it in her house in the commune of the small village of *St. Crepin De Richement* in France. Sadly Johnny had died of cancer some years before.

Oxford friends Sir Tom Bromley and his wife, Allison, at *Sletchcott* with Sheila and our children Mark, seated, and Sarah on her knees playing with Tom and Allison's dog, 1972.

View from *Sletchcott* to the southeast across the valley 1975.

View from *Sletchcott* south, across the sheep filled field, to King's Nympton village, 1975.

One near neighbour, who also became a friend and lived a short walk up the hill behind *Sletchcott*, was Miss Owen, a fascinating, highly intelligent 90-year old retired teacher who had spent her short career, until she was 45, in South Africa. We never knew her first name which was not at all uncommon then. With her accent, and simply how she interacted, she had clearly belonged to the upper class many of whom had gone to

South Africa on educational non-religious missionary work particularly in the beginning of the 20th century. Miss Owen lived in a tiny wooden house in the middle of five acres. She kept several animals and each year gathered the hay on her land. She worked essentially full time looking after the land, did not have a television and spent her evenings mainly reading. Except for shopping for food her life was totally within her small "farm". She had no relatives alive and in her will left the property and everything she owned to the *Ornithological Trust* which gave her a ridiculously difficult time as a result. She was, for example, not allowed to make any changes whatsoever, such as updating plumbing, changing the small wooden deck and so on. She felt that the Trust could not wait for her to die and only tolerated her living there because she had the legal right. Our other close neighbours, were the family of a retired farmer, Mr. Turner, a very gentle kind man, who felt he had been given a new life as a result of a recent hip replacement, not a common operation at the time and with the medical belief that it could last only a few years. Mark and Sarah were friends with his very nice lively young children who lived on his farm a short walk down the hill towards the village.

Sarah and Mark helping with the harvesting at Miss Owen's, 1973.

Sheila helping with Miss Owen's harvesting, c1975.   Mark, c1975.

Our farmer neighbour friend, Mr. Turner, Sheila and Sarah, c1975.

While we were living in *Sletchcott* Miss Owen fell over her dog and broke her leg which necessitated her having to be in hospital in a ward for some days. She told us that the strongest incentive to get out was to get away from the unbelievably banal uneducated conversation of the other women patients: they could not understand what she found so interesting in books.

Sheila and Mark on our old granite farm roller and the large mainly cob walled barn on the left, c1975.

Our family beside the old mediaeval fireplace with Mark and Sarah each with one of their favourite animals, Christmas, 1974.

We decided that for one academic term Sheila and Mark and Sarah should stay in *Sletchcott* and get on with the renovations while I stayed in college, teaching and doing research, only going down to *Sletchcott* at weekends. I was incredibly well looked after in college with my personal "scout" (servant), all meals provided and accommodation in one of the nicest historic rooms in Oxford, the founding President's living room, as in the photos in Chapter 8, and his adjacent bedroom and bathroom which in my time had running water! We enrolled Mark and Sarah in the small village school in King's Nympton which consisted of about 30 children. Mark and Sarah walked to school each day about a mile and a half along the small road to the village situated on the opposite hill to *Sletchcott*. They had a lovely time, with the local children in the school being particularly friendly and with the two women teachers totally devoted to the children's education. Each teacher covered several age levels, not unusual in small country schools at the time. Towards the end of the school year there was a regional competition for the best short story in the two classes in the school, the younger group less than 8 and the older group older than 8: the school only had children up to 11 years old. All the children were required to write a short story and, so as not to cause accusations of favouritism, the stories were judged by an outsider. Mark won the competition for his group of classes while Sarah won it for her group. It caused no resentment at all perhaps because they were both outsiders and particularly well liked in the school. They both had good particular friends at the school. At an unusual early age Mark had already shown his remarkable gift and love for elegant copperplate penmanship, superb writing as well as a natural talent for playing the oboe.

The village of King's Nympton was a very small isolated village, like so many in Devon, with all the children local and with long established village parents' families. One exception was the daughter of the lively vicar of the church in the village. She was the first "girlfriend" Mark ever had. So that he could be with her he took to walking the almost two miles each way along the very quiet small country road to the beautiful old 14th century church every Sunday. They clearly liked to be together and after church would walk together around the country.

Even with the increasing population in England, the "Green Belt" around towns and villages, where no new houses were permitted, was generally rigorously preserved. It was almost impossible to get building permission in such areas except for farm buildings on existing farms and even then they were very limited. The effect has been to ensure much of the rural quality of the countryside with the side effect, of course, that the price of houses in England has increased enormously since towns were so contained. The lovely rural views from our house across the valley as in the photographs above benefitted from such laws. Not surprisingly in such remote rural areas, particularly those with no large town close by, if someone had the right friends, local standing, or perhaps enough money -

although the latter is very much less common in England - it was, very occasionally, possible to get planning permission. We discovered, purely by accident, and to our astonishment that someone had obtained building permits for a group of houses in a large field on the opposite side of the valley from *Sletchcott* in the official green belt. As outsiders, or even if we had been long time locals of no standing, there was little we could have done about it. With the blessing, of course, of Miss Owen and our farmer friend, Mr. Turner, we decided to write to the *Member of Parliament* for North Devon, Jeremy Thorpe, who was the leader of the Liberal Party at the time, and ask how such a permit had been obtained and to solicit his help in getting it rescinded. He was a particularly popular member of parliament. He genuinely loved North Devon and within a few months the planning permission had been officially revoked. Shortly after we sold *Sletchcott* in 1975, Thorpe suffered from the sexual rigidity at the time. An acquaintance claimed to have had a homosexual affair with him in the early 1960s when homosexuality was still illegal and which Thorpe denied but as a result of which he resigned from the Liberal Party in 1976. Thorpe was later charged with conspiring to murder his former acquaintance but was acquitted of the charge in 1979.

Back in college in Oxford I was starting to find the 12-hour tutorial requirement once again too intrusive on my research time and I started to wonder if I should stay in Oxford. Fortunately, because of my international research standing, after two years, in 1972, I was promoted to *Reader in Mathematics*, which halved my tutorial load so that I could devote more time to research. It was then clear to us that I would likely stay on in the University of Oxford for the foreseeable future and that we should really buy a house in Oxford which at that time were still affordable for an academic. So, sadly we put our old house, *Sletchcott*, up for sale in 1975 and it sold very quickly. We had already scoured the countryside around Oxford some years before and realised that the best alternative for the family, with Mark and Sarah's schools playing an important role, was to buy one near Oxford. So, I approached the college to see if it would sell *Pinsgrove*, the college house we had lived in since 1970. Although Corpus Christi College owned property all over England it decided that owning a college house, particularly a large one, a few miles outside of the town was not a good thing so it agreed to sell it to us. The College Bursar, and Sheila and I, obtained formal valuations from different real estate agencies. The college agreed to sell it at the lower evaluation when I told the college that its assessor, a rather inexperienced one, had asked, unprofessionally, what figure our assessor had put on the house so that he could make his higher which he felt was expected of him. So we bought *Pinsgrove* in 1976 and continued to live there until we sold it in 1990 when we had decided that we would go back to the USA as described in Chapter 8. It is the only house we bought which did not need major renovations since it was not old, built around 1920, and the college had already done most of what had been required when we first moved in, in 1970.

Our Life in France: *La Combe*, Dordogne, France

Some years after Mark and Sarah had left home, finished college and were working - Mark in 19th century art in Sotheby's New York with Sarah a newspaper photographer in London - we realised, or rather realised afresh, how much we missed living in an ancient house in the depth of the country. It also coincided with our deciding that I would retire five years early from the University of Oxford, as described in Chapter 8, to return to academia in America where several universities were interested in having me join the faculty to help start up a research group in mathematical biology. When we were finally going to move back to America permanently in 1992 we found the thought of having no foot in Europe rather discouraging so, in 1990, we started the familiar process of enthusiastically scouring the countryside for yet another old stone house. This time, however, it was in the Dordogne in southwest France. We knew much of France from our time there in 1969 but not that part as well, although, of course, we knew of its ancient history and pastoral beauty. We finally found a marvellous mediaeval 14th century property called *La Combe* about two kilometres from the ancient tiny village of St. *Laurent des Bâtons* which had been one of the stops in mediaeval times on one of the pilgrimage routes to *Santiago de Compostela*. The St. *Laurent* commune is very large for its very small, approximately 200, population, about 10 inhabitants for every square kilometre.

La Combe is situated in its 50 hectares (about 125 acres) with not another house in sight. There are several photos below. About a quarter of the land was woodland with ancient small paths through them. There is an ancient stone barn, which was part of the property but well away and totally out of site of the main house. The old barn, *Le Barry*, had a basic house converted at one end. Of course, as usual, the main house and all its outbuildings needed major renovations. An indication of what the state of the property looked like when we bought it, and after the cement

plaster had been removed, is shown in the two photos below of one of the
long buildings in the courtyard known as the *maison des colons* (house of
the colonists) which is one of the buildings where the farm workers had
lived, typically very primitively.

Maison des colons before renovation, 1991.

Maison des colons after renovation, c1993.

The *Maison des colons* has a barn at the left and two very basic farm
worker houses used until well into the 20th century. Practically all the
buildings on the property, other than *Le Barry*, were similarly cement
plastered, the removal of which was arguably the major work in the

renovation. It was a tedious job and unfortunately we were not able to get enough workmen to help and those who did were not the greatest, albeit pleasant and who tried to be helpful. We were fortunate, however, that much of it on the walls turned out to be plaster, rather than cement, and it had been rather badly done which made it so much easier to remove than we had first anticipated. So, the underlying ancient stone structure was restored to its original with all the stone patina exposed. There was a lot of other renovations required, such as moving the old septic tank (in the basement) outside the house, adding a new drainage system to the old one, installing central heating, structural changes, reroofing much of the main house, interior renovations, plumbing, fixing the ancient ceiling beams, decorating, and so on, much of which we personally could not, nor wanted to, do but in the end we did a lot of it. Fortunately the entrance hall had been left as it was in earlier mediaeval times with what is called a *pisé floor*. Such flooring is made by inserting long thin hard stones, polished on the top, vertically into the earth as close together as possible. Such floors, if done properly, last for centuries. The photo shows what it looks like.

La Combe entrance hall with the *pisé* stone floor.

This time we kept the property for 15 years, loved the time we spent there, made many new lifelong friends and got to know the southwest of France, in particular, and French ways extremely well.

With the very generous arrangement and freedom I had with the University of Washington, together with a full time personal secretary, we were able to spend several months each year in France. The Dordogne *Département* for a very long time has been an enclave for people from all over Europe who wanted to live, sometimes to work and sometimes to retire, in the country in lovely surroundings of which the Dordogne is one of the most beautiful areas. The largest number came from England and the Netherlands. We had friends over a wide spectrum and area. Social gatherings, dinners most often, were frequent and lively where we met an incredibly diverse and fascinating group of people.

La Combe across its valley and much of its land and Sheila and JDM, 1995.

The first friends who visited us in 1991, and before the renovations had really been started, were Professor Lewis Wolpert FRS from London who had been a science colleague and friend for several decades, together with his, then, very lively and warm girlfriend, Jill Neville, the renowned Australian author, and his future wife. Sadly Jill died in 1997 of liver cancer just four years after she and Lewis were married. They spent a few days but since we still did not have all the furniture moved from Oxford and the renovations had not been started they had to sleep on the floor of one of the rooms. Their visit was a very relaxing time for us during the usual house moving and renovating stresses.

La Combe courtyard entrance and house front (after renovation), 1995.

La Combe house front (after renovation) from the field beside the house 1995.

Large 15th century Corpus Christi College elm table in the kitchen of *La Combe*, 1992. The lavender on top, from the courtyard, is drying.

Professor Lewis Wolpert, Sheila and Jill Neville (on the right) at *La Combe*, 1991.

Other close family friends from Oxford, Malcolm and Sheila Gough, whom I talk about in Chapter 8, visited us in the early 1990s. Malcolm recently celebrated his 90th birthday.

Sheila and Malcolm and Sheila Gough, on a visit to *La combe* c1994.

Our close friends, who became life-long friends, in the Dordogne, including local French, were immensely varied: we would never have met them in academia. Our non-French friends were mainly retired and lived permanently in France. To mention just a few of our particularly close ones there was a retired British army Colonel, Ronald Gower and his warm and lively wife Barbara. Ronnie had been in the D-day landing, flown planes in later wars in the Far East which is where he met Barbara. Another was Sir William Harding who had been the British Ambassador to Brazil and had been an important figure in some of the sensitive problems in the Foreign Service since the1960s, such as the Falkland Island saga with Argentina. Bill, and his wife Sheila, had moved permanently to France when he retired. Another was Gordon Ramsay a well-known English surgeon and his wife Christine, an anaesthetist. Wierd Minzinga-Zylstra and his wife Rijkje, are originally from Holland. Wierd had been a major figure in *Shell*. He had been the Head of it in La Jolla, California and had worked for many years for the company in Indonesia, Venezuela and Japan. There were also several retired very successful business magnates. Some of our French friends are the Mayor (*Maire*),

396

Claude Secret, of our village, St. Laurent des Bâtons, and his wife, Monique, a retired Judge, a French couple from North Africa, the kind farmer Laurent Escarmant, who cultivated our land, and his whole family. There are many others –now sadly "were"– since they were generally older than us.

The frequent social occasions, usually for dinners, lunches or garden parties, were always very lively with superb cuisine and wine. When we had such social occasions at our home we had to be aware of some, albeit very few, of the tensions between of some of our friends who lived permanently in France: we kept a list of who not to invite with whom.

Most of our friends had been personally involved in renovating their old properties after very successful careers. Even with such diverse and different backgrounds we had many common interests. We were immersed in the culture, loved ancient buildings, untouched small villages, and, compared with England, open mediaeval churches in which concerts were often held. Practically all of our friends lived in ancient stone houses in the country or in very small lovely old villages. Our house was by far the oldest and particularly liked and appreciated by all our friends. Our life and social world we lived in France for nearly 17 years was such a different one to academia and for which we are immensely grateful and look back with nostalgia.

The whole area in this part of the Dordogne is a summer tourist one, particularly the small towns on the Dordogne River. *La Combe*, for example, is about 20 kilometres from the lovely old small hillside village of Limeuil where the Vezère river joins the Dordogne river and where several of our friends lived. The ancient prehistoric caves of *Lascaux* are an easy drive: they are particularly well known although for years now tourists can only go into a replica to preserve the original ones with the prehistoric paintings. The tour we took was rather boring. A French friend said he could arrange for us to see the original Lascaux caves but we passed it up.

Our house, *La Combe*, had originally been a 14th century fortified manor house. The old entry, now filled in, is half way up the front wall. The property has an ancient stone dovecote (*pigeonnier*), about 10 metres high: it was built on the side of a small stone cliff about 5 metres high. We decided to renovate it and make it into a small, single bedroom, en suite guesthouse. It was certainly a major undertaking. We first had to build a stone staircase from the courtyard with an iron rail because of the cliff on the right as in photo below: the photo shows the dovecote before the plaster had been removed from the walls. We built a rather clever door which let a lot of light through: there was only very small windows inside We replaced the rotten old top floor, built a balcony, repaired the plaster on the ceiling which is in the photo below. We also constructed a curved wooden staircase, made windows out of some of the pigeonholes, installed a small bathroom with it's own external septic system, although for that we had it dug by a workman. When looking in the archives in the library in the major town of the area, Périgueux, about 30 kms north, we found a 19th century booklet describing rural life in mediaeval times and which included a mediaeval marriage contract for someone in our commune. From the description it was probably *La Combe* which was, particularly in those times, a major property of the commune. The contract listed what the bride would bring to the marriage, such as how much manure per year for the fields. It also said that for each pigeonhole in the dovecote you were required to have half a hectare (about 1¼ acres) of land. The mediaeval dovecote in *La Combe* has 50 pigeonholes. The guest suite used the two floors which had been constructed so that the pigeon eggs could be easily gathered in its original *pigeonnier* use.

We also decided in the late 1990s to completely renovate *Le Barry*, the old barn, and enlarge the basic house to include the whole of the barn which made it into a rather large house, with a soaring beamed ceiling in the living room. It had its own dramatic view over the land, again without another house or building in sight. We thought of eventually moving there since there was less to look after.

Sheila walking up the farm lane above the renovated *Le Barry*, c2002.

XIII. Our Other Professions, the Arvon Foundation and Our Life in France

The commune is the area around the village, or small town, which comes under the aegis of the mayor. For the first few years in *La Combe* the mayor in *St. Laurent des Bâtons* had been mayor for several decades and was, among other things, noted for bending rules etc. When he finally retired the new mayor, Monsieur Claude Secret, was considered a "foreigner" since he had spent much of his career in business in Périgueux about 30 kms north and whose wife, Monique, was a *Juge d'Instruction* (Investigating Judge) in Bergerac, about 25 kms from *St. Laurent*. Being the mayor, particularly in small villages in France, can be extremely complex, difficult and tense: to us it is totally incomprehensible why anyone would ever want to do it. Our farmer friend, Laurent Escarmant, had he wished, would have got practically all the votes in the commune but he shared our view of the position and would never have dreamt of it. We became friends with Claude and Monique Secret who surprisingly spoke no English. One evening at dinner at their house, Sheila asked Claude why on earth he ever wanted to be *Maire* to which he replied "*J'aime le combat*" (I like the fighting). Unfortunately he was not considered a very good mayor by the village and many decisions were effectively shelved. We experienced one when we wanted to move the small country lane farther away from our house, oddly the process is called a *changement d'assiette* (change of plate). Even most French people have no idea what the phrase means legally. The application languished when Claude was the mayor but

Dovecote (*pigeonnier*) on the left, the garage barn and one of the former workman's cottages on the right with its large one armed iron cross.

when the new mayor was elected it was approved within a month, with the commune generously contributing half the legal fees, not that they were very large. Claude Secret was not re-elected which so upset him that they sold their house and sadly left the area to move farther south but also to be closer to their grown up family.

Unrenovated dovecote with the steep drop on the right. The balcony guest room in the converted upper floor with the original beamed ceiling and now glassed in pigeon holes.

We heard from the mayor, Claude Secret, some of the problems in the commune, mostly a result of disagreements over land boundaries which had lasted in the village for as long as anyone could remember; some at least since the mid-19th century. The family feuding also lasted as long and very very occasionally resulted in a fight between two of the young men, usually intoxicated, from the two feuding families without much injury to either of them. The village had several get-togethers each year for a lunch or dinner which people in the village prepared. We were always invited and warmly welcomed: they were always very friendly hospitable occasions with superb food and reasonable wine but rather loud music.

As friends of the most respected family in the commune, the Escarmants, we learned of some of the very local affairs which went on and which our non-French friends around the Dordogne never ever heard of in their villages. One example was of a French couple who lived for many years in a property a few minutes walk up the small hill behind *La*

Combe: they had four children but had never got married. The father, around 50, died suddenly of a heart attack. His mother then immediately had the children' s mother with her son's children evicted from the house because they had not been married and so she had no right to live there. The subsequent effect was a spate of marriages among several unmarried couples in the commune.

It was also at dinner at the Secrets' house one evening I realised how easy it is to make a mistake in meaning and implication by translating too basically from English to French. I had been told by a friend in the village that Monique Secret had just retired from her position as a *Juge d'Instruction*. I said to Monique "*J'ai entendu que maintenant vous êtes finis*" as a translation for "I heard that you're now finished (as a judge)." There was a hushed silence and then she burst out laughing. In French that means you're now effectively dead. I should at least have said "*avez finis*" (have finished). It was always very much easier to understand the French of French friends from further north. The southern and Dordogne country accent we often found difficult to understand but, without exception, everyone was always incredibly patient with us and clearly were often greatly amused by our French.

Our friends were in two very different groups, one local French, and the other international. Our French friends were mainly in, or neighbouring, the commune of St. *Laurent des Bâtons* and colleague friends in universities around France. Our close friends Gérard and Fanny Trotet lived just outside the village. Gérard, the only academic among our friends in the Dordogne, had been a professor of biology. He had spent his career in academia in North Africa which he and Fanny greatly missed. They talked longingly and nostalgically of Tunisia, its people and the country. Gérard had been a professor in the university but after the Algerian war of independence they had to leave and he got a position in a French university. The French in North Africa were always referred to as *Pieds noirs* (Black feet). We never knew the origin of the name: Gérard told us it was because the French soldiers had always worn black boots. A friend, as a consequence of our friendship with the Trotets, was a very kind, gentle and always elegantly dressed elderly lady, Madame Cecille Anlouer. She wrote a fascinating *Fil de Mémoires* (*String of Memories*) which is like a memoir and which, unfortunately, we were unable to convince her to publish. We tried several times but she said nobody would be interested. She just thought we were being kind. Her parents had spent much of their working life in China. When she was 9 years old they decided that she must go back to France to be educated in the traditional French way. She and her mother travelled by train (which took about a week in those days) but they stopped for a rest at a hotel in St. Petersburg, planning on getting the train to Paris the following morning. It was literally the beginning of

Laurent and Jeanine Escarmant with JDM and our son Mark, *La Combe* c1993.

Fanny and Gérard Trotet, c2000,
St. Laurent des Bâtons

Laurent Escarmant, c1993.

the 1917 Russian Revolution. Reading how a 9 year old viewed such a major event was fascinating, such as how she watched the soldiers march on the road immediately below her window singing enthusiastically and all of them waving to her. Cecille and her husband, when he retired (he had also worked in Tunisia which is where they became friends with the Trotets), moved to a nice old property a few kilometres from where we lived: we never knew her husband who had died many years before. Cecille, when in her early nineties, moved into a very comfortable and very kindly run retirement home in *Ste Alvère*, a very small neighbouring town about 8 kilometres from *St. Laurent*, where she was still always elegantly dressed and as lively and interesting every time we went to see her or she was brought to *La Combe* for tea by Fanny Trotet.

One of the pleasures of *La Combe* was that we had time to enjoy many of our lifelong friends and academic colleague friends who visited us in *La Combe* over the years. The dovecote guest quarters were often used. One visit in the early 2000s was by our oldest close friend from my Harvard days, Bill de Spoelberch with his incredibly nice and warm new Italian wife, Ludovica Serafina. As I mentioned earlier, sadly Choupette had died of cancer in the 1990s. A particular pleasure of our time in France was that we saw more of Bill and his family on trips to Brussels for various extended family occasions. Bill and Ludovica visited us for a few days when we were living in Princeton in 2012. Ludovica, before retiring, had been a biologist in the *European Union Science Bureau* Control of Infectious Diseases. She travels with Bill on some of his trips on Aga Khan Foundation business and on one occasion wrote a very lively splendid report of their trip. The photo below is on one of these to Pakistan and India in 2015 with Ludovica's head appropriately covered. It is such a pity we do not see each other much more often – Brussels is not quite next door.

Laurent Escarmant and his wife Jeanne (whom we always called Jeanine) firmly believed in education for their children even though Laurent had left school at 14 and had lived in *St. Laurent* practically all his life. Towards the end of the war he was forcibly transported to Germany to work (effectively as a slave) in a factory. Philippe their son went to agricultural college while the youngest, Évelyne, went to the University of Bordeaux. Évelyne is the only member of the family who does not live in *St. Laurent des Bâtons* but in Paris where she is married to a particularly gentle, kind and highly intelligent practicing Muslim called Youssef Abaoubida. As is well known, Muslims in France are frequently subjected to irrational prejudice, and often have difficulties getting jobs since, irrespective of their education, such as a university degree, as soon as their name is given they are often immediately dismissed from consideration. Youssef did not have this problem since he is a very clever information technology scientist and France does not have enough of them. The gentle former husband, Ashraf Zogheley, of one of the other Escarmant daughters, Cecille, a nurse, came from Egypt, is totally trilingual with a

Bill de Spoelberch and his wife, Ludovica Serafina, in Pakistan, 2015.

degree in engineering. He has had such problems as soon as his name was read.

Sheila and I were always kindly invited to the major Escarmant family events and dinners with their extended families and friends in the area. They were always extremely warm and lively occasions. The last time we were in that area of France (we had sold *La Combe* some years before) the whole family and all the grandchildren came to a superb dinner which, as always, exuded the customary informal and warm atmosphere. The dinner was specifically for us, on Jeanine's long narrow terrace which is in the tiny village centre with a view of the old church and the old farm complex, dating from the middle ages, across the valley, which was where pilgrims could stay on their pilgrimage to *Santiago de Compostela*.

Laurent absolutely loved the country and being a farmer. Farming and his family were everything to him. When having to sit on his tractor waiting for something he would take out a book to read. One day when he and I were talking in our courtyard and looking up to the field beside our house where there were three of his cows quietly grazing, Laurent said, with warmth in his voice: *"Elles sont si belles."* (They are so beautiful.). He also loved old buildings, the sense of ancient history and prehistory. The Dordogne area is full of ancient fossil sites, with fossils common in the fields around *La Combe*. The *Lascaux* caves (*Grotte des Lascaux*), as mentioned, are about 50 kms away with the Neanderthal caves in *Les Eyzies-de-Tayac-Sireuil* about 35 kms from *La Combe*. The tourist shops in Les Eyzies are filled with hundreds of polished fossil shells. I couldn't resist making some earrings for Sheila from two of the small ones and which she still wears. While ploughing one of the fields Laurent regularly found fossils and on one occasion found an enormous fossil ammonite shell, about 15 inches in diameter which he kindly gave to us. We felt it should not leave the area so we made it part of the wall restoration above the front door of the main house. When we took the old plaster from the various buildings we found several fossil pieces buried in the old stones but none as dramatic as the ammonite one.

While we were in *La Combe* in the early 1990s the French government encouraged every French person over the age of 60 to have a free medical examination. Laurent had undoubtedly inhaled harvesting dust for decades and decided to have one. He was found to have a major potential heart problem and was convinced to have heart surgery in the highly respected hospital in Bordeaux. A few days after the surgery he was moved to a rehabilitation unit, surprisingly without any constant medical monitoring, and where he sadly died of a heart attack. He was mourned by everyone in the area. Jeanne, his wife, was devastated and did not recover any life for herself for about three years. The funeral brought an enormous number of people from all over the commune and beyond to pay their respects. Sadly other of our French friends and non-French friends also died during our time in *La Combe*. The last time we saw Jeanine was when she and her eldest daughter, Hélène, spent a week with us in our home in Pennsylvania two years ago.

Our experience of hospitals in France was minimal but the atmosphere, once you got past the dragons at reception, was very much more casual and friendly than in Britain and the USA. Our friend Dr. Peter Berczeller, a retired New York University Medical School professor, felt responsible for us and on one occasion said I must go into the main hospital in Périgueux for a problem which turned out to be due to a kidney stone. I was supposed to have very light food. The nurses either had not read the instructions or did not believe them since I was served excellent meals and each day asked what kind of wine I would like with

405

my lunch and dinner. I was in hospital a few days since our doctor friend, Professor Peter Berczeller, thought I could perhaps have developed diverticulitis which required immediate intravenous antibiotic treatment.

Another French couple, Mimi and Peter Chatenay, whom we met at dinners at some of our friends and who became friends, were considerably older than us. Mimi had come from an upper class family and was ostracized by her family for many years for marrying Peter considered to be from a much lower class. Mimi had been a nurse in the war while Peter had been a French-English translator with the free French in England. They spent a lot of time in England and America during the war. Peter, a very funny anecdotal storyteller, had been with American troops in the Normandy landing. The day after they landed his Captain pulled him aside and said: "*Ok Peter. Now we've landed I want you to get me a bottle of wine and a woman.*"

As a foreigner living in France you have to be careful to respect the local customs. These included, in our case, allowing one of the local village hunts to hunt wild boar on our land. Tensions in the commune were reflected in the number of hunts in the village: in the case of the small *St. Laurent* commune there were six. The one on our land was, of course, the one with Laurent Escarmant, and his son Philippe. Every year on returning to *La Combe* one of the members of the hunt would appear with a number of choice pieces of frozen wild boar which we always much enjoyed. While going and coming from dinners with friends we often saw wild boars, with twelve young on one occasion, crossing the roads. We always gave the boars a wide berth. The boars gave the clear impression of supremacy and walked slowly with what can only be described as a confident arrogant swagger. The actual hunts had often been undisciplined. On one occasion, we were told, a doctor who belonged to one of the local hunts was accidently killed when the hunters had gathered round a wounded boar, fired at it and one bullet ricocheted off a stone and killed him.

In a village about 10 kilometres from *St. Laurent* one English couple, whom we did not know, did not approve of hunting and refused to give their village hunters permission to hunt on their land. The villagers, who had hunted on it, no doubt forever, discovered there was an official right of way through their land for vehicles, it went past the side of their swimming pool. So, some of the young villagers took to riding their motorcycles regularly and noisily past their pool. Within a year the property had been sold and hunting resumed. In France people are legally allowed to walk anywhere through your land but not drive a vehicle except on authorised roads and tracks.

One aspect of France, which we found was unknown to most of the foreigners, and indeed many French, was the presence of government spies in the villages and towns. It has been going on for centuries of course. In *St. Laurent* we were told it was the local postman, who retired like so many in France in his early fifties during our time in *La Combe*. His successor, clearly not a spy, eventually got fired for drinking too much and driving under the influence. Police also flew over your land in helicopters to make sure there are no fires in the summer (not unreasonable) but also to ensure that no paid workmen are working on Sundays which was illegal. They would fly low enough to see if there was a workman's truck parked. In some villages where there were interfamily tensions one would occasionally anonymously report on a neighbour breaking the law, usually in a letter, called a *corbeau*. We had one very helpful, very professional and very literate nice electrician who did some work for us and with whom we often had coffee. Associated with this aspect of government spying when I asked him whether he really believed in *Liberté, Égalité, Fraternité*, (*Freedom, Equality and Brotherhood*), he jokingly replied *"Oui, bien sur - Liberté avec surveillance"* (Yes, of course - Freedom with surveillance).

There are official government rules and laws about privacy which the government agencies regularly ignore. We had personal evidence of this when we had a bizarre burglary at *La Combe*. The Escarmant family felt responsible for us and *La Combe*, and, of course, had keys to the house. When we returned to France one year we arrived at *La Combe* around midnight and found Philippe Escarmant waiting in the courtyard. We had written, as usual, to say when we were returning and we found that he had been waiting there for several hours. It turned out that there had been a burglary with the burglar having broken in through a shuttered front window, doing surprisingly little damage however. He was clearly very professional, highly specialized and knowledgeable. The only thing he stole was the actual clock mechanism of a 19th century grandfather clock which was in its tall antique wood case. This was clearly his specialty, or at least one of them, since the mayor of a neighbouring village, the father of Mireille, Philippe Escarmant's wife, also had one stolen shortly afterwards. The burglar went through our house and picked up a small antique Seth Thomas-looking clock. By the time he got downstairs he had realised it was only a rather good modern copy so he left it on a chair in the entrance hall. He also saw what looked like a mediaeval religious ivory carving and tried to pull it off the wall and realised it was only a very good plaster copy so he left it hanging. Fortunately I was able to restore it. Philippe had not gone into the house because the *gendarmes* had said nobody should go in until they had time to look for clues.

It was the sequel which was one of the amusing aspects of the affair. We ignored the suggestion, of course, about not going into the house until the gendarmes came from the larger but also small village, *Ste Alvère*, the following morning. There were several of them, all very sympathetic, who came into the house and sprayed the antique case of the grandfather clock with talcum powder. They then pulled out a small camera, one of the strongest competitors for the cheapest I had ever seen, and took a number of photos which could not possibly have shown fingerprints. I was asked to go along the next morning to the police station, the *gendarmerie*, and give relevant details of what had been stolen, damaged and so on.

The senior gendarme in the *gendarmerie* in *Ste Alvère*, a particularly nice and friendly man, who spoke not a word of English, sat in front of an old computer and started to type, laboriously and incredibly slowly, with two fingers, one on each hand, my answers to his questions. I suggested that I could do the typing; he immediately accepted with obvious relief. After it we chatted a little and at one point he asked if I was married. When I said: "*Yes*", he said "*But I don't have a card on file for your wife, only one on you*" so I supplied the required details on Sheila. It is officially illegal to have such cards on file but it clearly made absolutely no difference. A sequel to all this was some months later when driving back to *St. Laurent* I saw a group of *gendarmes* up the hill above the village near a wide part of the road where cars could pull off. They were doing a random breathalyser check of all drivers. As I moved up the queue to the gendarme ministering the breathaliser the senior gendarme, who was in charge, saw me when I rolled down the window and immediately came over, shook my hand and said: "*Ça va bien?* (colloquially means: "Are things going well?") and waved me on with: "*Allez, allez!*" (On you go!). I was not at all over any alcohol limit but I could have been a little with some of the lunches we were often invited to. Locals, as we were clearly now in effect considered, are often treated very differently.

The neighbouring village, *Ste Alvère*, is the local "capital" of the truffle region. Sadly the ancient commune of *St. Laurent des Bâtons* has recently (2016) been made officially part of *Ste Alvère*. We were often given truffles by our friend Laurent Escarmant who regularly searched for them in his and our woods; he was extremely skilful at finding them. *Ste Alvère* is also where there is a small local medical group practice the senior person of which is a doctor called Dr. Ducène. He had been the mayor, somewhat dictatorially, for years. He clearly felt destined for more national recognition which we learned he later got. For anything serious he was a very good and caring doctor and still did home visits. When we were first looking for the clinic we stopped and asked a retired garage mechanic where Dr. Ducène's clinic was. The man, who regularly sat outside his house and old garage close to the clinic jokingly said: "*Ah, vous voulez dire Saddam Ducène!*" (Ah, you mean, Saddam (D)Hussein!). Although I found the doctor sometimes a touch arrogant, condescending and at times a bit rough with routine things on the rare occasions we went to the clinic he did care about the village and managed to get all manner of positive things done for it.

One minor thing, the *Maire* arranged was for an official postcard, copied below, advertising *Ste Alvère* as a centre for truffles (*Terroir de la truffe* (Territory of the truffle) with photos of several of the ancient buildings in the area where they were found. The one in the bottom left of the postcard below is a winter photo (not a very good one) of our long old stone barn and workman's house in the front courtyard, the "*maison des colons*" as I described above. It is in the two photos above of the "before" and "after" renovation. The wooden contraption on the bottom right is an old cow "raiser" which lifts cows off their feet for various treatments.

Farm workers in the commune had worked on the village farms for generations and only had one name. When surnames were required they often simply adopted the name of the farm where they worked. In the village of *St. Laurent des Bâtons* there was an old man, a *Monsieur La Combe*, who occasionally walked from the village, about two kilometres along a small country lane and called in to *La Combe* to reminisce. His father had worked on the farm in the 19th and early 20th centuries and had taken the surname *La Combe*. He had actually lived in one of the *La Combe* workmen's houses with his parents as a child. It is also behind in the photos below of Sheila with flowers and the other of Sheila and me sitting.

We thought the building rather a poor choice with all the other, much more beautiful and historically important, buildings to choose from on the property. The centre photograph in the postcard, however, was a very good choice. It is a few minutes walk up the hill of the tiny country road behind *La Combe* and adjacent to the boundary of our property. It is

le patrimoine de pays de la communauté de communes du

Terroir de la truffe

Sainte Alvère postcard illustrating the ancient territory of truffles. The *Maisons de Colons* in *La Combe* courtyard is the small photo on the bottom left.

an ancient dovecote with a traditional *lauze* roof. These old roofs (*toits en lauze*) are made with flat stones traditionally laid practically horizontally on top of each other and so are unbelievably heavy but surprisingly require less wood structure support below it since the gravitational forces are spread differently to those which are laid on a slope. When the minimal wooden structure starts to rot the roofs do not always simply collapse because of the way the forces act. It is a very clever design and incredibly long lasting.

Our family in the front of *La Combe* on one of our old antique granite rollers. Sarah, Sheila and JDM are seated on the roller with Mark in front – again with one of their animals, c1992.

Sarah, Sheila and JDM under the *Maison des Colons* vines, c1993.

411

Mark, Sheila and Sarah, in *La Combe* with their childhood animals, c1993.

Sheila gathering wild lupin on the hill above the courtyard of *La Combe*, c1995.

Sheila and JDM in the evening in front of the vines and the *Maison des colons*, c1998.

Sheila and JDM on the terrace on the old Devon granite roller, c2000.

Sheila in the upstairs library, early evening, c2000.

JDM and Sheila in the living room in *La Combe*, c2002.

Eventually in the early 2000s we started to find *La Combe* getting rather too much for us to look after and we sadly, but sensibly, decided that we should sell it, which we did personally without any agent, in 2005 with an advertisement with some beautiful photos in *Country Life* magazine. The English couple who bought it were rich and sadly decided to make major tasteless changes, including a large swimming pool with buildings in the back of the house which make it look a bit like a cheap holiday site. Of course, we never ever got involved or commented on any subsequent changes in the houses we have renovated but in the case of *La Combe* we were particularly saddened to find, when invited to dinner once, that the old original mediaeval ceiling beams, for example, had been painted, and, even worse, a bright light blue which together with the swimming complex we felt had destroyed so much of the original mediaeval character of the property. It was, of course, none of our business.

Philippe and Mireille Escarmant had also been invited to the dinner since Philippe was going to continue farming the land. We were invited to help with translating since the new owners did not speak any French. What the new owners did not realise was that such an invitation normally included the whole family so their three children also turned up which made it a rather Spartan dinner. The eldest daughter, Elisa, 14 at the time, realised what had happened and took over the kitchen to help, and, to save the owners' being embarrassed, kindly made it seem as if everybody had been invited and that there was plenty of food. These owners sold *La Combe* about three years after they bought it and had destroyed so much of its ancient character.

We found it so hard to think of leaving France after selling *La Combe* that we irresponsibly bought another, very much smaller, old property, called *Fondarrière*, only a few kilometres away in another commune, but also totally isolated in the middle of its own 12 hectare piece of land with our now accustomed requirement of a dramatic distant untouched view south across our large valley. It is about two kilometres from *Cendrieux*, a small, not particularly interesting village, but with an old interesting 16th century church. We became friends with the very nice and hospitable couple, Jacques and Geneviève Nups who lived across the valley from us, in an enormous property with a small lake. We gave them our old granite rollers. *Fondarrière* needed some renovation, as usual, but it never became anything other than just another house and we sold it, again very easily, two years later when we decided to return and live full time in America. The retired couple who bought it had lived in Paris all their careers. They clearly love it. Their daughter and her family moved into the old barn west of the property which we had used as a garage and which they renovated.

Fondarrière: the old west wing with its traditional Perigordian roof, 2007.

Salon and dining room in *Fondarrière*, 2007.

The old house, *Fondarrière*, in the photo above is the west wing with the entry to the courtyard with the late 19th century east wing through the arch on the left. Very high and steep roofs like this are common in the

416

Dordogne and known as *Perigordian* roofs. The large salon and dining room, which covers the whole of the west wing, had a very high soaring ceiling with a huge multi-candle candelabra which was lowered from an incredibly strong pulley system from the upstairs landing so you could light the many candles, about 30. In the photo the large French doors on the right opened onto the courtyard with the other wing of the house.

One of the surprises when we first walked around the woods was the fun carving some previous owner had done on a tree stump in the middle of the wood and which is nowhere near any path. The former property of our dear friend Cécille Anlouer, who wrote the fascinating *Fil de Memoir* described above, literally bordered ours but sadly she had died some years before but, seeing her house, always brought back warm memories.

Artisan life

My curiosity in learning how to do practical things started as a very young child, whether it was repairing burst lead pipes, making iron horse shoes in the blacksmith's workshop, literally next door to our house, carving airplanes during the war, repairing boots and shoes, making catapults, bows and arrows, skinning rabbits and curing the skins to make a Daniel Boone hat and so on. None of my brothers surprisingly ever made anything, although my sisters knitted sweaters and animals for Mark and Sarah when they were very young children and socks for our father. In fact none of my later academic friends did either. I simply had an insatiable curiosity, which included learning about other people's expertise. As a young child I also collected stamps, for example, for a few years before the war. It was a time when all German stamps had a picture of Hitler on them. So, many years later, even when our house renovations were still going on the urge to make different things had in no way abated. During my time at New York University the facilities for making anything in an apartment were limited but with a relatively large three bedroom, two bathroom university apartment the second bathroom became a darkroom, where I continued my enthusiasm for photography, and used it as a simple workshop for making silver jewellery which I found satisfying and surprisingly nothing like as difficult as I had imagined. I have continued the latter ever since giving me constant pleasure making pieces for Sheila, friends, Sarah and our granddaughters. The photographs below are just a very few of the jewellery pieces, such as earrings, necklaces and so on that I have made.

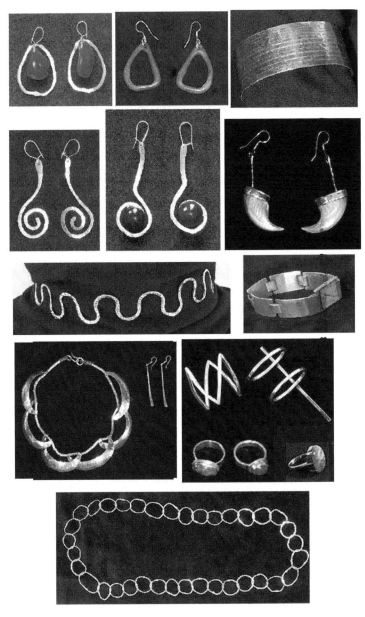

A small selection of silver jewellery pieces.

Sheila had a practical bent as well, having learned dressmaking as a young teenager from a neighbour in Essex, Connecticut. She made some lovely, fun, highly original and tasteful clothes for Mark and Sarah when they were young children: they loved them. She always found elegant, often antique, buttons for them. Mark, when at prep school in Oxford, had to wear the school uniform so he particularly liked the clothes Sheila made. When Sheila found some interesting very nice cloth, often at country antique fairs in rural Devon and in the Dordogne, she made, very professionally, fun and highly original clothes for all of us. I still wear two of the elegant waistcoats she made for me. The children particularly loved the original animals she made for them as children several of which they still have and treasure with their original names, like Leonardo for the long lemur which was as almost as tall as Sarah when Sheila made it and another of an elegant "wife" of a favourite bear of Mark's called Eboo now very much showing his age. With all our time in the country with just the family Mark and Sarah developed complex and very funny games with the animals, known as the "Ans", talking to each other. The "Ans" had very different personalities – not always predictable or respectable.

As I mentioned, even as a child I enjoyed working with wood, pretty well any material in fact. My real furniture making, however, started in Ann Arbor, Michigan in the early 1960s, when I discovered how beautiful American black walnut was. As described in Chapter 7 we bought wide raw planks in an old sawmill a few miles from Ann Arbor. I had the idea of cutting the widest one in half and inserting two flat edged ones in between, the effect of which was to have a table top which looks like a slice of an enormous walnut tree over a yard in width: it is over 8 feet long. We had already made two such natural coffee tables but from one very wide slice of wood, the idea of which we thought of when driving along a country road past a sawmill which made coffins when Sheila met me when I embarked from the liner in Southampton returning to England from America in the autumn of 1959. A large walnut table with its walnut carved legs which we still have is a larger version (in the style) of the smaller walnut coffee table in the photo below.

At a farm auction in Devon when we lived in our house *Sletchcott* I bought an ancient oak fire lintel for a few shillings (there were 20 shillings in a British pound). The British coinage was decimalised in 1971. We carted it around all our houses until we moved to our French house, *La*

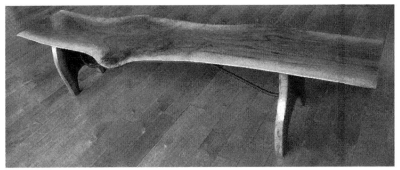

Natural walnut wood coffee table.

Combe. We continued our occasional Sunday tours to antique, junk rather rather, fairs around the area in the Dordogne where we lived and on one occasion found some antique iron fire dogs and we had the idea of using them as feet for a coffee table using the old fire lintel we had found in Devon more than thirty years before. The result is in the photo below and which we have used ever since.

Coffee table made from an antique English oak fireplace lintel with its antique French iron firedog legs.

In 1976 I visited the University of Florence for a month at the invitation of the mathematics department. A friend and colleague, Professor Aldo Belleni-Morante, who had spent some time visiting my research group in the Mathematical Institute in Oxford, knew of my interest in "making" and repairing antique furniture so he took me to see a friend's workshop in Florence. His friend specialized in antique furniture repair and, I suspect, faking antiques. His friend showed me an interesting wood drill he had invented: it consisted of a short very thin drill welded on to a strong but very flexible thin steel wire. He drilled a small shallow hole in the wood, the typical diameter of a woodworm hole, and then inserted this flexible drill and drilled it into the wood. The resulting hole was not straight but varied wildly exactly like a woodworm bores a hole. He said that it was common for people, particularly dealers, interested in his antiques to pull out a thin solid needle and poke it into the "worm" hole to see if the hole was straight and therefore a fake since woodworms, of course, never eat straight holes in wood unless they are extremely focused! Faking antiques, of course, has a very long history. When in Taiwan and being shown round the National Museum some of the beautiful 18th century pottery we were shown were superb copies of Ming dynasty (1368-1644) pottery. We also occasionally did the rounds of antique shops in the Dordogne and on one occasion, in the small town of *Lalinde*, not far from our village, *St. Laurent des Bâtons*, we saw a rather elegant old oak cupboard part of which was painted decorously in the traditional way but with the paint in surprisingly good condition. We learned later that the "antiquing" had been done by an artist friend we knew socially who lived in the area. She was outraged when we told her the dealer had said it was the original 18th century painting thinking we would not know the difference. The dishonest antique dealer had been in business for a long time. Of course it is not unusual to be thought not very bright or knowledgeable if speaking a foreign language with a strong accent and grammatical errors.

With all the moving from one university to another and the house renovations, furniture making took a back seat until we were settled in Oxford from 1970 on until we sold the house, Pinsgrove, twenty years later. Finally, after being promoted and with so much less teaching, I felt that Oxford was going to be my academic home from then on. After buying Pinsgrove in 1976, we built a barn for a workshop and beside it an external covered wood storage lean-to on the edge of the 3-acre property hidden behind the garage and a huge hedge. So once again I was motivated to indulge in making things, not just carpentry but bronze and and pewter work, carving, leather pieces such as briefcases, music cases, silver jewellery, of course, picture framing with watercolour mounts and others. Many years before, when I was around 13, I made the leather sporran for the kilt I got when going to the international scout jamboree in France in 1947. I am wearing it in the photo in Chapter 2 along with the small bone necktie holder which I made from a piece of an animal's leg bone by removing the inside and polishing it. I also made a decorated leather sheath, for the old leather handled sheath knife I had been given, replete with long leather ties to simulate what I thought was how American Indians would have made it.

Our children Mark and Sarah also loved to do things which required serious concentration but with such very very different tastes and pursuits. Sarah loved to try and make things in the workshop with me. Her drawings, for example, were also always incredibly original, often very funny, usually of fantasy animals in unusual situations – she still draws them in cards she sends and we still use the bookmarks she drew and painted. I remember the occasion when she was about 4 or 5 years old she wanted to use a saw and a hammer so I gave her a small piece of wood and some nails to play with: the result is in the photo below along with two of the wild animals she made by twisting wire that was lying around when she was about the same age. They still give us a lovely sense of warmth and amusement.

Sarah's activities, interests, and commitment, as a child were so different to Mark's. Mark's interests, even as a young child, were primarily art and music. He liked elegant ink pens and spent hours learning to write in beautiful 19th century copperplate script. He became an outstanding oboe player, again practicing for hours, as described in Chapter 8.

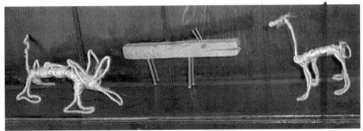

Sarah's wild animals when she was around 4 years old.

Sarah's Christmas card 2008.

With such a workshop I could not resist making some larger pieces of furniture because I had so much of the old 16th and 17th century oak from the college barns which had been demolished, vandalised I felt. Two examples are a table and writing desk below. The dark walnut rocking chair below was made from walnut wood we had got in Michigan years before when I was on the faculty of the University of Michigan and which has been moved to all our houses ever since. The "antique" coffer was made from pieces of the 16th century muniment cupboards which my college Corpus Christi College decided to throw out which greatly shocked me as described in Chapter 8. The magazine rack, joined with some of the muniment cupboard iron hinges, and the bookstand are made from parts of the mediaeval floor boards which had to be removed when we renovated *Totleigh Barton* as described above and which we couldn't bear the thought of throwing away. The writing desk below has a traditional secret place behind the back of the small cupboard in the centre at the back between the curved letter racks. All of the wooden pieces bring back fond memories from our peripatetic artisan life.

"Antique" oak dining table, 9.5ft by 3.5ft, made from antique oak wood from an old 17th century barn.

Desk made with the antique oak wood from the Corpus Christi College barn.

Walnut wood rocking chair.

Stands made from the antique floorboards from *Totleigh Barton*.

Coffer made using the college's antique muniment cupboard doors with their 15th century antique hinges , locks and handles.

Making walking sticks, which unrealistically I never thought I would ever need, was, unlike the polycandelon below, enjoyable and relaxing. I had, over the years, acquired a few pieces of exotic hardwood but not having a lathe I had to make the sticks by eye which turned out not to be nearly as difficult as I had imagined. It made me understand that in the pre-lathe days it was not that difficult to make them visually uniformly round and straight. As a child growing up in very rural Scotland I was occasionally given an old sheep and cow horn from friends of my father - all part of my innate curiosity, or rather appreciation, of natural things. I was able to use them for some of the cane handles which now remind me of that very distant and very different life I might have had to have.

It is interesting how to bend long horns into curved walking cane handles, such as the two black ones in the photos below. You first subject them to steam for a considerable time, which softens the horn a little, and then bend them in a vice, but only a certain amount at a time so as not to cause cracks, and keeping them bent until they dry in the curved shape. It has to be done many times so the curve retains its horn smoothness and is as round as you want it. With canes it is necessary to have a round metal junction between the wood and the handle not just to be more professional but to stop the uncontained wood splintering with pressure on the handle. With my plumbing background brass pipe couplings, which I filed round, seemed made for them although I did make a few in

425

silver. When I finally got a small lathe I made some canes in three parts so they could be unscrewed and put in a case when travelling.

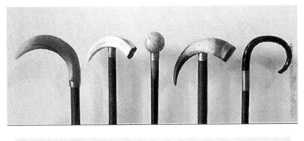

Selection of walking sticks. The ball handle in the round headed one in the handle is a 19th century ivory billiard ball.

With the lathe I also made a bunch of salt and peppershakers and pens because I still had some lovely old exotic hardwood around which was burning a hole in the drawers. We still use the pens as does Mark.

Selection of salt and peppershakers and pens of various kinds.

I started to use a walking stick for steep climbs on walks in the late 1980's but only regularly in the 2000's. This was when I started to be affected by the phenomenon called post-polio syndrome which affects muscles and starts many years after contracting polio. It is not known why nor when it will occur. Basically when the muscle cells die they do not regenerate as in normal people. Most medical people have never heard of it, surprisingly even orthopaedic specialists but then they're not considered at the top of the medical profession. I got away without it longer than the norm, roughly 65 years after I got polio. It could perhaps have been the problem with President Franklin D. Roosevelt since he contracted serious polio in 1921 and died in 1944. Polio certainly did not stop him from running for, and winning, major political offices and the presidency four times. Perhaps polio's side effects include a commitment to try and excel at whatever one decides to do.

The "Byzantine" polycandelon, in the photo below, is nearly two feet in diameter and is a copy of the larger of the two mediaeval Byzantine bronze polycandela in the University of Oxford's Ashmolean Museum. I knew the Director whom I met at High Table in Corpus Christi College and so easily got permission to take photographs of it outside its case. Polycandela were used to hold lamps and were particularly common in the Byzantine period and in the mediaeval Islamic era. The one I tried to copy is from AD 500-600: it is in almost pristine condition. To make as realistic copy as possible this necessitated finding out how to antique modern bronze. It is a terrible process; you have to paint the bronze with strong warm acid and leave it a specific, fortunately a short, amount of time, while desperately trying not to breath in the horrible fumes while at the same time roughly rubbing the acid on the surface with steel wool so that the final effect is one of rough antique looking surface. It is the only "antique" bronze I made. As with all the "antiques" I made I learned a lot about the history and background of the pieces which, of course, was one of the key motivations and pleasures. With large candles in the polycandelon and hanging from the ceiling it required a long handled candle snuffer which was the excuse for making one out of pewter. Soldering pewter can be a little delicate since it is so easy to melt the pewter. The one I made works very well as a snuffer. The curved handle was intentional since it makes it easier to use.

About 10 miles from our house, *Sletchcott*, in North Devon there is a beautiful old mediaeval church with dramatic ancient stone bosses which captivated us with their originality and dramatic, imaginative, yet simple, stone carvings. One small head sparked an enthusiasm to try sculpting, something I had never done before. With the limited time available from renovating houses, academic research and teaching I thought of trying stone coloured white cement carving. With this process you mix white cement with, for example, red sand the result of which looks almost like sandstone when it dries as in the photos below of the head I made which

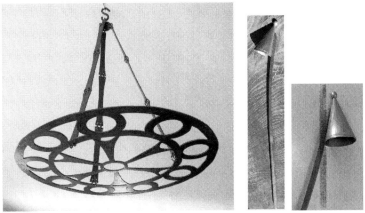

"Byzantine" polycandelon and its pewter candle snuffer.

is on a window sill in our French house, *La Combe*. Alternatively with just white cement and sand it can resemble stone. It started Sheila and I off on yet another "profession" namely "stone" sculpting with the lantern examples below. The head I made is also on the wall in the photo of Sheila and I in our French house, *La Combe*, sitting on the enormously heavy granite farm roller two of which we bought for £1 at a farm auction near *Sletchcott* and on which Sheila is sitting with Mark in the photo in the *Sletchcott* section photos. The rollers had been made in the 19th century by prisoners in Dartmoor Prison which is only a short drive from *Sletchcott*. Needless to say they were not paid for their work. We left the rollers with friends in France. Our "stone carving" profession did not last long, only long enough to design and carve two Japanese lanterns which I had always found romantic ever since going to Japan in 1975 and later with Sheila in 1992: they are in the photos below and both are around 5 feet high. Such sculpting certainly does not take much time. After mixing the sand and cement you put it in a container slightly larger than the piece you want to sculpt and let it dry enough (about 2 hours) so that it stays as a unit but is not yet set. You then remove the container and have about two hours to carve whatever you want after which it is too hard. The limited time certainly focuses the mind. The green mould on the lantern was a result of trying to age it by putting manure on the top – it worked. The square one had a round hole where birds regularly built a nest. The engraving on the side of the square lantern is my name in Chinese from our time in Taiwan.

JDM with one of our sculpted "Japanese" lanterns, c1985.

Our sculpted "Japanese" lanterns: they are about 5 feet high.

As I mentioned in Chapter 3, I became interested in glass blowing when a student at the University of St. Andrews and spent some time, not very much, learning how to blow glass, mainly for chemistry experiments. The only personal things I made were a few glass bowls and a set of sherry glasses, two of which are all that have survived: they are certainly not our taste now – the glass stems are a light green. Later Sheila and I became enthusiastic pottery makers and took lessons when I spent the 1963-4 year at Harvard. We only had time to take the initial lessons in which we had to learn how to make pieces without turning but with thick strings of the clay which you rolled and wound round to make the shape you wanted and which you squeezed together and smoothed the piece by hand: it is a very much slower process. It is also much easier to lock in small air bubbles which can explode when firing them in the kiln to make the clay hard and durable. Such an explosion, of course, breaks everything that's being fired in the kiln. Firing also embeds any design or colouring you have added. Like the blown glass pieces little has survived. The two we still have are the pot I made and the large bowl Sheila made with its interesting, original and tasteful inside colouring.

After returning to Oxford in 1970 we developed, for a short time, an

Sheila's pottery bowl, 12 inches diameter.

JDM's blown sherry glasses.

JDM's pottery c15 inches high.

JDM's concrete sculpture of a "mediaeval" head: c12 inches high.

enthusiasm for brass rubbing because there were so many ancient churches around Oxford with some lovely mediaeval brasses. Brass rubbing of the mediaeval brasses is now almost universally not allowed with such brasses encircled by low iron railings. There are several dramatic 14th-16th brasses in the chapels of the older university colleges. The one in Corpus Christi chapel is not particularly interesting being too modern, only 16th century. We still have several of our favourite ones hanging in our house: there are photos of four of them below.

The bishop (around 8 feet high) and dated 1417, is of Thomas Cranley who was the Warden (the name of the President) of New College two years after it was founded in 1337 and is in the college chapel dating from that period. He became the Bishop of Dublin which is the reason for the religious attire in the brass although most colleges until the founding of my college, Corpus Christi College, in 1517 were essentially religious foundations. The brass rubbing of the knight is a fairly typical one with the knight standing on top of a mythical lion. The skeleton, also a fairly common type is a very unusual one in that it is grinning wildly. There are always the names of the people they represent and some inscription below the brasses together with brief descriptions, always religious. In the one of the skeleton it is a particularly long inscription. Mediaeval brasses were generally made for the wealthy and major church figures (also very wealthy then) in the hope that it would elicit prayers from the people walking past them in the church and which would therefore help to ease the suffering of the soul in purgatory. We saw one mediaeval brass which had been done before the person died with the name and dates to be filled in after their death: they had been forgotten to be added so the blank space is still there. Many brasses are of kneeling "supplicants" looking up to the Virgin Mary. Often prayers are included in the writing but so very few people who saw the brasses could read at the time, and even less since they are almost all in Latin.

I believe all these extracurricular activities I have been involved in have been beneficial to my research. I was totally detached for long periods from thinking about the scientific problems I was working on, or in trying to solve specific problems. Going back to them again I found I often had totally new ideas. With the latter, I occasionally would wake up in the night with what I thought a brilliant new idea about how to solve some of these mathematical problems. I kept a notebook beside the bed to write them down in case I forgot these original new insights. On reading them the next day they were, with rare exceptions, complete rubbish. In between times of starting some new research I often made a few practical useful things which were not very time consuming and which I used continually for much of my career, such as leather briefcases (suitably antiqued), countless picture frames of all sizes with watercolour mounts I painted, and so on. The one activity I necessarily have never stopped is repairing my shoes and leg brace which I wear and which I have done since childhood. I have to do it even now, since with increasingly less polio around it is beyond the experience of practically all of the orthotics professionals - but then I have done it for so much longer. Looking back not only do I not regret for a minute the time I have devoted to all these non-academic pursuits, but remember them with much pleasure. Sheila and I warm at the memories of them and the things we made and still have and use around our home.

Brass rubbings: Typical 14-15th century Knight.   An unusual grinning skeleton.

Brass rubbings (over 8 feet high):
Henry Sever, Warden (that is President) of
Merton College (Oxford) 1456 – 1471.

Bishop Thomas Cranley, Warden of
New College (Oxford) founded in 1337.

XIV

Mathematics in the Real World -from Animal Coat Patterns to Brain Tumours, Divorce Prediction and Others

A widely held view of mathematics by the general public (and by those in most academic disciplines) is that it is of little use or relevance in the real world and that you are either good at it or not. There is also a widespread phobia about mathematics and the feeling that there is nothing much you can do to improve your understanding or ability even if you want to. This has been the general view for centuries. The major national and international societies do little to help. I have found, however, that the audiences, in public lectures I have given around the world, are genuinely interested when you describe how incredibly useful mathematics can be in the real world. I describe in this chapter just a few of the very practical uses of applying easily understood non-technical mathematical concepts to problems in the real interdisciplinary scientific world which I have personally been involved in - two in biology, two in medicine and one in psychology.

An indication of how completely out of it the typical pure mathematician is in the scientific world, not only in biology and medicine, is from a book written by a French pure mathematician and philosopher Auguste Compte (1798–1857) who said: "*In mathematics we find the primitive source of rationality; and to mathematicians must the biologist resort for means to carry out their researches*". This is hardly the best approach to initiate interdisciplinary collaborative research which is increasingly important. More recently, Professor René Thom, who was one of the major French pure mathematicians in the latter part of the 20th century, and a Field Medallist, said: "*I agree with P. Antonelli when he states that theoretical biology should be done in mathematical departments; we have to let biologists busy themselves with their very concrete - but almost meaningless - experiments. In developmental biology, how could they hope to solve a problem they cannot even formulate?*" The last time I heard Thom give a lecture was in the University of Oxford in the 1980's which supposedly was related to biology. The lecture was very well attended, appallingly given and totally incomprehensible. Many more people got up and left the lecture theatre than I have ever seen in any lecture.

Genuinely practical applied mathematicians try to construct realistic mathematical models of the phenomenon, biological, medical or whatever, that they are studying and trying to understand. It is certainly not always possible to solve exactly the resulting mathematical problem so you have to make approximations and realistic assumptions which make the basic mathematical analysis possible so as to gain some biomedical or physical insight. It is a view succinctly expressed by Michel de Montaigne (1533–1592) in his essay: *De l'utile et de l'honnête*: "*À la verité, et ne crains point de l'aduouer, je porterois facilement, au besoing, une chandelle à Saint Michel, l'autre à son serpent.*" (*On usefulness and honesty: In truth, and I'm not afraid to admit it, I would, if needed, just as easily light a candle to Saint Michael and another to his serpent.*) From all I have read, and know about Montaigne, had he been

a mathematician he would certainly have been an applied one and certainly involved in the real world. The photo of Montaigne is an unusual one: it is of a portrait in the Bodleian Library in the University of Oxford. Practically all portraits of Montaigne are when he is much older and already of international renown.

I managed to do enough research for a mathematics Ph.D. degree in the applied mathematics field of fluid mechanics in 18 months. The field is the study of fluid flow, quantifying, for example, the effect on bodies immersed in fluids, what forces it exerts on such bodies, how they affect

A portrait of Michel de Montaigne in the Bodleian Library, University of Oxford

the flow and so on. It was one of the largest research areas of applied mathematics for much of the previous fifty years. With all its ramifications and extensions it is still a major field and of major practical importance in a vast array of applications. At the time I did my Ph.D. in the field you essentially started with a set of mathematical equations known as the *Navier–Stokes* equations which were proposed in the 19th century and the solutions of which describe a wide range of diverse real world fluid motions and how they affect a wide range of phenomena. The mathematics involved solving the equations for specific physical problems and making practical predictions. There was, and still is, a large number of researchers who study such equations primarily for their mathematical challenges but with little or no interest in applications, an approach which never appealed to me. The applications specifically associated with my research were closely related to what are called pitot tubes: these are appendages to aircraft wings which are used to measure the aircraft's speed accurately. The British *Air Ministry* at the time had listed the problem among the top ten research problems it had and wanted solved.

Although I initially found the research in fluid dynamics interesting and challenging I knew that I did not want to spend my research career studying essentially the same equations even with original applications. So, when I went first as a post-doctoral student to Harvard to work with one of the accepted major people in the field at the time, Professor Sydney Goldstein FRS, I said I would like to work in a totally different area which I did, namely how to quantify certain phenomena in biochemistry called ion exchange processes. Goldstein wanted me to work on a problem in aerodynamics but he didn't push it. The ion exchange problem was challenging mathematically but the applications, although experimentally practical, were not very exciting to me so, on returning to England in 1959, I became involved in a process called fluidization which I very briefly described in Chapter 6. I also got involved in a new application of fluid dynamics to what was called magnetohydrodynamics which includes adding electromagnetic elements to fluids. I felt it was just using the same mathematical techniques and ideas so my involvement did not last long. Later, back in America, by the end of the first year on the faculty of the University of Michigan it was clear to me that I wanted to try and use my mathematics in other fields, particularly the biological and medical sciences which seemed to me to be the most exciting and important fields of science for the foreseeable future, something I still strongly feel to be the case. I published my first book on mathematical biological problems in 1977 with my second, the first edition of my major book, *Mathematical Biology*, in 1989 flatteringly often referred to as the Green Bible because of its green cover with a lovely photo of a leopard (as in the covers at the end of this chapter). It is now in its third edition in two volumes and translated into several foreign languages. These books, written for practical minded applied mathematicians interested in the real world, give a spectrum of the wide range of biomedical problems I have found exciting and in which I have tried to make a genuine practical contribution.

Some diverse examples of my research are modelling how pilot ejection seat back injuries are caused and could be prevented, how enough oxygen can get into muscles, why sea snakes do not get the bends, ecological predator prey problems, animal population dynamics, the spread of epidemics, liver disease in obese patients, why we cannot design a better breathalyser, the spread and control of rabies among foxes if it comes to England, sex determination and survival of the *crocodilia*, wound healing and scar formation, comb formation in honeybee colonies, pigmentation pattern formation on snakes and butterflies, wolf-pack formation and wolf-deer survival, formation of vascular networks and many others. I briefly describe below the research I did on the benefits of cannibalism and its modern relevance. In this chapter I describe, in a non-technical way with a little detail, just five examples of interdisciplinary research which partially illustrate the scientific diversity I have had the good fortune to have been involved in. My research career has given me enormous pleasure, nourished my fascination with science and the world about us, and the desire to understand, and hopefully be useful, in the real world.

By the end of the 1970s I felt that the field of mathematical biology was now well established and, as an indication of its standing, importance and fascination, it would be beneficial to organise a conference in the field in the Royal Society in London. I talked to my friend and experimentalist colleague, Professor Lewis Wolpert, even though we did not agree on much of the modelling in biological development, and asked if he would like to join me in putting in the application to which he enthusiastically agreed. He had been a strong supporter of my interdisciplinary research for many years. At the time Lewis was not yet a Fellow of the Royal Society (but was elected just before the conference started): I was elected in 1985. At the time to help increase the chance of the meeting being accepted, and financed, the feeling was that you had to have a Fellow of the Royal Society among the applicants. Lewis knew Professor Sydney Brenner, who was an experimental biologist who had been a Fellow of the Royal Society for some years and he agreed to be listed as one of the proposers in our application. The application, written by Lewis and I, was accepted and in 1981 we held the first major conference in the field of mathematical biology in the Royal Society in London. The meeting was very successful and attracted major speakers in the field from around the world. The only negative, highly embarrassing rather, part of the meeting was the totally unexpected closing speech by Sydney Brenner who launched into an unpleasant, sour tirade against the use of any mathematical modelling in biology. The audience was astonished and highly embarrassed for him. There was a lot of discussion afterwards as to why he had done this, particularly having agreed to be officially listed as one of the organisers – not that he did anything – and we could only think the bitterness was perhaps associated with the fact that he had not yet been awarded a Nobel Prize for his research. He was eventually awarded one twenty years later in 2002. Alternatively perhaps it was because he had recently broken his leg and it was taking a long time to heal. Or maybe it was just because of an acerbic nature. I never saw him again after the conference.

There are always major problems starting a new discipline, particularly an interdisciplinary one, even though researchers had worked on such problems for many years. An important, very early research article about the benefits of smallpox vaccination, was published in 1760[1] by a well known mathematician, Daniel Bernoulli. The paper, in which he proposed a very basic, but very practical, mathematical model, is not at all well known since it was written in French. Bernoulli, or rather the Bernoullis, since several in his extended family were mathematicians, actually genuine applied mathematicians, are well known for their work in fluid mechanics. There is a classic, widely researched equation called the Bernoulli equation. When Daniel Bernoulli could not get an academic job as a mathematician he took a medical degree and went to Venice to practice, which is why he was concerned with smallpox and saw how very useful applied mathematics could be.

Traditional discipline-focused researchers sometimes feel threatened and react in diverse ways. It is, not surprisingly, students and younger scientists and imaginative established faculty, who are usually most interested and enthusiastic about a new area or applications related to their field, or simply because of their natural curiosity. There were many such participants at this Royal Society meeting so I felt it might help to

---

[1] D. Bernoulli, *Essai d'une nouvelle analyse de la mortalité causée par la petite vérole, et des avantages de l'inoculation pour la prévenir.* (Essay on an original analysis of mortality caused by smallpox, and the advantages of inoculation to prevent it.) *Histoire de l'Acad. Roy. Sci. (Paris) avec Mém. des Math. et Phys.* (1760),1-45.

voice some of my own feelings about the field in the introductory remarks[2] which are relevant to the rest of this chapter:

"*Genuine interdisciplinary research and the use of models in general can often produce spectacular and exciting results. It is now less common to hear a bioscientist dismiss their use, although they may still privately do so. For those souls who are promoting the field in the face of vocal pre-prejudiced opposition and criticism there is the apt north African proverb: ' The dogs may bark but the camel train goes on'.*"

As I mentioned at the Royal Society conference in 1981, there are many reasons for the increased involvement of mathematicians and physical scientists in the biomedical sciences. For example, there is on the one hand the genuine scientific interest and excitement of people becoming involved in new fields and new applications, and on the other, a realisation that some of the traditional areas, in Applied Mathematics at least, were becoming moribund. Certainly from my experience in America and Europe, when mathematics courses are offered which discuss bio/ecological/medical modelling, students (and some of the faculty) give them major support. I have always found that the strongest interest and enthusiasm comes when the problems discussed are practical and relevant in the real world.

As a consequence (of this Royal Society meeting) I hoped that the uncommitted mathematicians would take away with them the view that not all mathematicians or theoreticians are out of it, unrealistic, and so on, and that not all biomedical scientists are unsympathetic to modelling and interdisciplinary collaboration. Mathematics–biomedical research, to be useful and interesting, must be relevant biologically, and medically, and not obvious. Real parameter values in the models, for example, have to be put in or assigned by people who know or can learn something about the problem. The best models should show how a process works and then what may follow from original predictions of the modelling. An acceptable first step is a model which phenomenologically describes the biology. Suggestions as to how a process works may evolve from it. What is neither wanted nor appreciated are models whose aims are to show mathematical colleagues how clever the mathematics is. Nor are trite phrases that do not explain or enlighten the mechanism studied. For example: "*it is an elliptical*

---

[2] Introductory remarks: Royal Society Meeting on *Theories of Biological Pattern Formation* (J.D. Murray). *Phil. Trans. Roy. Soc. (Lond.) B* 295: 427–428, 1981.

umbilical catastrophe" (which I actually heard from a pure mathematician) sounds more like a complicated birth by an incompetent doctor.

From a mathematical point of view I feel that the art of good model building relies on a sound appreciation and understanding of the problem in whatever discipline it is in. The five examples I describe in this chapter come from biology, medicine and psychology (a very novel one). In all of them it was essential to: (i) construct a realistic mathematical representation of the important phenomenon being studied; (ii) find the solution, quantitative if possible, of the resulting mathematical problem; and, finally, very importantly; (iii) give an easily understood practical interpretation of the results with biomedical and psychological insight and predictions. The mathematics is dictated by the biology, the medical science and the psychology, not vice versa. If the mathematics is trivial, so be it. The research is not judged by mathematical standards but by different and certainly no less demanding ones.

Of course, there are still the Luddites in all of these disciplines but they are generally not as vocal anymore and certainly not listened to, except out of politeness.

1. How the Leopard Gets Its Spots[3]

Research problems I have worked on have come about from a wide, and often chance, diversity of reasons. For this one on animal coat patterns it came from our daughter Sarah when she was around four. I had read to her Rudyard Kipling's "*How the Leopard gets its Spots*" from his "*Just So Stories*" which our daughter loved. Afterwards she asked: "*But how do they get their spots?*" I admitted I did not know but, being in the University of Oxford at the time, I said I would talk to some colleagues in the university and find out. I asked several biologists about skin patterning and it was clear no one knew how animals got their spots so I thought, why not try. So, I worked on the problem of animal (and snake and butterfly) coat patterns on and off from the late 1960s until the late 1970's. Experiments on such animal markings were extremely rare. One of the first, and very

---

[3] The research was first published in 1979 with the major article in 1981: On Pattern Formation Mechanisms for Lepidopteran Wing Patterns and Mammalian Coat Markings. *Philosophical Transactions of the Royal Society. B 295, pages 473–496 1981*). Part of this section was described in a non-technical article I wrote for *Scientific American* (March 1988, Vol. 256, No. 3).

interesting experimental research studies on why the leopard gets its spots, was only published in 2011.[4]

Mammals exhibit a rich and varied spectrum of coat patterns but surprisingly there are very few suggestions as to how they are formed. Although genes control the processes involved, the actual mechanisms which create the patterns are still not known. It would be interesting from the viewpoint of both evolutionary and developmental biology if a single mechanism were found to produce the enormous variety of coat patterns found in nature.

In 1970 I had the thought that a single pattern–formation mechanism could underlie most, if not all, of the wide variety of animal coat markings found in nature. I started doing serious research on it the first year back in Oxford but, as often the case, I got side tracked into other problems several of which involved a variety of different pattern–formation mechanisms but applied to various physiological and ecological problems. I did not decide to publish my animal coat pattern research until after giving a lecture on the work at the Italian *Accademia Nazionale dei Lincei* in Rome and hearing the audience's positive reaction to it. Perhaps it was symbolic since the Italian Academy of Science is named after an animal, the lynx (*dei Lincei* - of the Lynx) which has incredibly sharp vision, a concept which is certainly required in good science. Here I shall briefly describe the simple mathematical model (in non–technical language) for how these patterns may be generated in the course of embryonic development. An encouraging feature of the model is that the patterns it generates bear a striking resemblance to those found on a wide variety of animals such as the leopard, the cheetah, the jaguar, the zebra, the giraffe and many others as illustrated below. The predictions of the simple model are also consistent with the observation that, although the distribution of spots on members of the cat family and of stripes on zebras, for example, vary widely, they are unique to the individual and each kind of distribution adheres to a general theme. Moreover, the mathematical model also predicts that the patterns can take only certain forms, which in

[4] William I. Allen, Innes C. Cuthill, Nicholas E. Scott-Samuel and Roland Baddeley, Why the leopard got its spots: relating pattern development to ecology in felids. *Proc. R. Soc.* B 278 (2011): 1373-1380.

turn implies the existence of developmental constraints, which has been a highly relevant and widely studied topic in developmental biology for a very long time, at least since the beginning of the 19th century. It is not clear as to precisely what happens during embryonic development to cause the patterns but the mechanism is almost certainly initiated by some genetic switch. The appeal of the simple model comes from the mathematical model's richness and its surprising ability to create patterns and general constraints, which correspond to those observed in nature.

Some facts, of course, are known about coat patterns. Physically, spots correspond to regions of differently coloured hair. Hair colour is determined by specialized pigment cells called melanocytes, which are found in the basal, or innermost, layer of the epidermis. The melanocytes generate a pigment called melanin which then passes into the hair. In mammals there are essentially only two kinds of melanin: eumelanin, from the Greek words *eu* (good) and *melas* (black), which results in black or brown hairs, and phaeomelanin, from *phaeos* (dusty), which makes hairs yellow or reddish orange.

It is believed that whether or not melanocytes produce melanin depends on the presence or absence of what are known as chemical activators and inhibitors. Although it is not yet known what those chemicals are, each observed coat pattern is thought to reflect an underlying chemical spatial pattern, called the prepattern. The prepattern, if it exists, should reside somewhere in, or just under, the epidermis. The melanocytes are thought to have the role of "reading out" the pattern. The model I describe below, a chemical one, can generate such a prepattern of chemicals, called morphogens. The biological pattern follows the morphogen prepattern. Even now, decades later, the concept of such a skin patterning procedure has only been confirmed experimentally in the last few years in one, or possibly two, situations. It was because of the experimental lack of knowledge of any patterning mechanism that we proposed the much more practical, and importantly, experimentally confirmed, biological patterning mechanism called the mechanochemical theory in the early 1980s and which is described later in a separate section below in this chapter.

With the chemical prepattern model I began with the assumption that morphogens can react with one another and crucially diffuse through cells and tissue. The mathematical model used shows that if morphogens react and diffuse in an appropriate way, spatial heterogeneous patterns of morphogen concentrations can arise from an initial uniform distribution in an assemblage of cells. These models are referred to as reaction diffusion models and are applicable if the scale of the pattern is large compared with the diameter of an individual cell. The models are applicable to the leopard's coat, for example, because the number of cells in a leopard spot at the time the pattern is laid down is probably on the order of 100. Examples of the mathematical equations had been studied for some years by various researchers, including myself. The original concept, albeit not for animal coat patterns, nor in fact for any specific biological system, had been suggested by Alan Turing in 1952.

I first proposed a specific model system in the early 1970s. In a typical reaction–diffusion model one starts with two morphogens which can react with each other and diffuse, that is spread, at different rates. In the absence of diffusion – in a well-stirred reaction, for example – the two morphogens react and reach a uniform steady state. If the morphogens are now allowed to diffuse at equal rates, any spatial variation from that steady state will be smoothed out. Crucially, however, if the diffusion rates are not equal, diffusion can actually be destabilizing: the reaction rates at any given point may not be able to adjust quickly enough to reach equilibrium. So, if the conditions are right, a small spatial disturbance can become unstable and a spatially heterogeneous pattern begins to grow. Such an instability is said to be diffusion driven.

One can get an intuitive idea of how such a mechanism can give rise to spatial patterns from the following, albeit a somewhat unrealistic, example. The analogy involves a very dry forest – a situation ripe for forest fires. In an attempt to minimize potential damage, a number of fire fighters with helicopters and fire-fighting equipment have been dispersed throughout the forest. Now imagine that a fire (the activator) breaks out and a fire front starts to propagate outward. Initially there are not enough fire fighters (the inhibitor) in the vicinity of the fire to put it out. Flying in their helicopters, however, the fire fighters can outrun the fire front and spray fire-resistant chemicals on trees; when the fire reaches the sprayed trees, it is extinguished so the fire front is stopped.

If fires break out spontaneously in random parts of the forest, over the course of time, several fire fronts (activation waves) will propagate outward. Each front in turn causes the fire fighters in their helicopters to travel out faster (inhibition waves) and quench the front at some distance ahead of the fire. The final result of this scenario is a forest with blackened patches of burned trees interspersed with patches of green, unburned trees. In effect, the outcome mimics the equivalent outcome of reaction–diffusion mechanisms which are diffusion driven. The type of pattern which results depends on the various parameters of the model, related to the reaction rates, diffusion rates and crucially the domain size and are obtained from the mathematical analysis. It is not even very sophisticated mathematics, essentially upper undergraduate level. There are photos below which show the practical results of the mathematical model applied to animal coat patterns.

Returning to the patterning mechanism I studied, there is a large number of reaction and diffusion parameters (as well as many real reactions) which can produce such spatial patterns. There are also, now, many chemical reactions known which react and diffuse in such a way as to produce spatially heterogeneous patterns. So that it was not in effect curve fitting, in my mathematical model I kept all of the chemical parameters fixed for all the solutions I obtained from the model equations I used. I varied *only* the *scale* and *geometry* of the domain (thus mimicking the shape and size of an animal coat). These do not affect the chemical reactions. As initial conditions for the calculations I chose random perturbations about the uniform chemical steady state. The resulting steady state spatial patterns which developed are coloured dark and light in regions where the concentration of one of the morphogens is greater than and less than the concentration in the homogeneous steady state: see the figures below. Even with such limitations on the parameters the wealth of possible patterns is remarkable.

The visually dramatic first example of a real oscillating reaction was the colourful chemical reaction discovered experimentally by a Soviet experimentalist, B. P. Belousov, in the 1950's. Such reactions can oscillate with clocklike precision, changing from, for example, blue to orange and back to blue again twice a minute. The concept of oscillating reactions was revolutionary and widely disbelieved at the time. When I mentioned it to the chemistry Fellow at dinner in my college one evening in the early 1970s he said: "They can't exist." Belousov had great difficulty publishing his results, got very discouraged and became rather reclusive. It was only when a graduate student, A. M. Zhabotinsky, some years later, managed to persuade him to try again that a brief abstract was finally published in 1959 in an obscure journal. The reaction eventually became widely known and is now referred to as the Belousov-Zhabotinsky reaction. The specific experimental reaction I used in my reaction diffusion model, and for the mathematical analysis, is another real oscillating reaction discovered by a

French chemist, Dr. Daniel Thomas. Thomas had discovered the process independently: it is one of the first practical reactions the chemistry of which is fully known and the experiments carried out and described with scientific rigour.

I first heard of Thomas' work when visiting his university, the University of Compiegne in France, as an external Ph.D. examiner. It was the first French doctoral examination I had been involved in. I naively thought it would be like in Britain and the USA so I had prepared several technical questions. I had, of course, also carefully read the thesis: it was very impressive. I had to start the oral questioning. When my French colleagues asked their questions it was clear that the examination was a pure formality. Afterwards I asked about it and was told that the decision had in effect already been made to award the candidate the degree. The main part of the occasion was the lengthy, superb lunch with fabulous wines which followed and comparable dinners the few days I was there. The candidate, of course, was also invited.

So, how do the results from the model relate to typical coat markings and general features found on animals? I started by using tapering cylinders as the chemical reaction domain to model the patterns which could occur on the tails and legs of animals. The mathematical results showed that if a two or three-dimensional region marked by spots is made sufficiently thin, the spots will eventually change to stripes as in the figures below. The black and white figures on the right of the various tails are the results from the analysis of the mathematical model. The tail drawings, which are typical animal examples (cheetah, jaguar, leopard and genet), are from the *Scientific American* article the reference of which is in the footnote above.

The results from the mathematical model, that is the reaction–diffusion pattern formation mechanism I used, exhibit patterns which bear a striking resemblance and the same general character to those found on many animals such as a few shown below.

I also applied the model to the markings on the cheetah, the leopard, many animals in fact. It was easy to generate a series of stripes with the model mechanism: the tails above are examples. In a striped animal the junction of the foreleg with the body is more complicated, but the mathematical model also predicted the typical idealised scapular stripe pattern where the front leg joins the body as in the figure of a zebra below which shows, below it, the solution from the mathematical model. The two types of zebra are illustrated in the photos below with Grévy's zebra on the top and the plains zebra mother and foal below it: the leg-body pattern is qualitatively as the mathematics indicates. Also, as predicted, each animal's markings are unique: the photo of the zebra and its foal is an example.

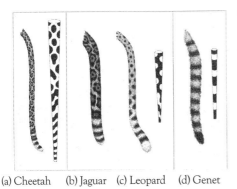 

(a) Cheetah   (b) Jaguar   (c) Leopard   (d) Genet   19th century Italian cartoon.

Cheetah photograph is reproduced with the kind permission of a friend, Professor Andrew Dobson (Princeton University).

Leopard photograph is reproduced with the kind permission of a friend, Henk Hoksbergen.

The patterning on the embryo determines the final adult patterning.
In the case of the Grévy's zebra, as in the photo below, the patterning
mechanism must be activated at a later stage when the embryo is larger so
more stripes can be accommodated on the embryo. The pattern, or rather
prepattern, is almost certainly formed when the embryo has already developed
early limb structures since the mathematical model suggests that the
patterning at the leg–body junction is ideally as shown in the mathematical
prediction in the following figure with an example of an actual zebra's leg–
body patterning: they are qualitatively similar. The top of the back stripe
patterns in the centre diagrams below are patterned solutions obtained
from analysis of the model pattern formation system.

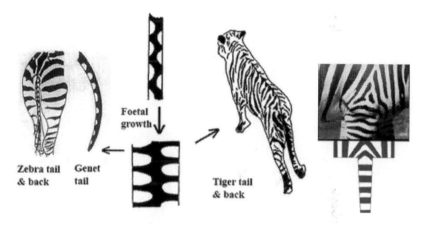

The results from the mathematics also indicate the more complex
familiar patterning on a variety of animals: the examples of the leopard and
cheetah above and the zebras below are only a few.

Grévy's zebra.

The photographs of the Grévy's zebra above and these two Plains zebras are reproduced with the kind permission of a friend, Professor Daniel Rubinstein (Princeton University), the well-known international authority on zebras, particularly in Kenya.

To study the effect of scale in a more complicated geometry, I considered a basic generic animal shape consisting of a body, a head, four appendages and a tail. I started with a very small shape and gradually increased its size, keeping all the parts in proportion. I found several interesting results. If the domain is too small no pattern can be generated as is predicted by the mathematical analysis. As the size of the domain is increased successive bifurcations occur: different patterns suddenly appear and as the "animal shape" grows larger they disappear with different patterns formed. The patterns show more structure and more spots as the size of the domain is increased. Slender extremities still retain their striped pattern if the embryo scale is not too large. When the domain is very large, the pattern structure is so fine that it becomes almost uniform in colour again as shown in the figure below: the largest figure is actually several thousand times larger than the smallest.

The scale affects the patterns generated within the constraints of a generic animal shape. Increasing the scale and keeping all the other parameters fixed produces a remarkable variety of patterns. The model results agree with the fairly universal fact that small animals, such as the mouse, have uniform coats, intermediate-size ones such as the leopard have patterned coats and large animals such as the elephant and rhinoceros are uniform in colour. The Valais goat, *Capra aegagrus*, shown below is an example of the first bifurcation. Examples of the second bifurcating pattern occurring naturally are found, for example, in the anteater and the Galloway cows below.

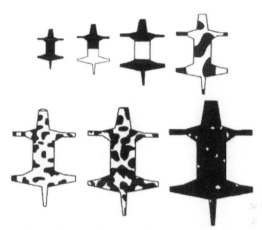

Scale effects on the general type of pattern.

Valais goat (Photograph is courtesy of BS Thurner Hof, Wikipedia).

Original etching of an anteater published by G. and W. B. Whittaker, February 1824.

Galloway cows. Photograph is courtesy of Alan Wright and was taken in the Lowlands of Scotland. It is another example of the second pattern bifurcation.

The leopard (*Panthera pardus*), the cheetah (*Acinonyx jubatus*), the jaguar (*Panthem onca*) and the genet (*Genetta* genetta) provide very good examples of the predicted pattern behaviour. The spots of the leopard reach almost to the tip of the tail. As shown in the above photos, the tails of the cheetah and the leopard (also the jaguar) have distinctly striped parts. The genet, for example, has a totally striped tail. These observations are consistent with what is known about the embryonic structure of these animals. The prenatal leopard tail is actually sharply tapered and relatively short, so one would expect that it could only have stripes near the tip, as is the case: see the photos above. The adult leopard tail is long but has the same number of vertebrae. The tail of a genet embryo at the other extreme has a remarkably uniform diameter which is quite thin. The genet tail is therefore not able to support spots, only stripes – just like the animal in the cartoon above.

The model's mathematical analysis also provides a genuine example of a developmental constraint, documented examples of which are quite rare although another, very different one, is described in the section below. If the pattern-forming mechanism for animal coat markings is a reaction-diffusion process (or any process which is similarly dependent on scale and geometry), the constraint would develop from the effects of the scale and geometry of the embryos. Specifically, the mechanism shows that it is possible for a spotted animal to have striped tail but not possible for a striped animal to have a spotted tail.

The effects of scale on pattern suggest that if the general model concept is correct (which I believe it is) the time at which the pattern-forming mechanism is activated during embryogenesis is of crucial importance. There is an implicit assumption, namely that the parameters are roughly similar in different animals. If the mechanism is activated early in development by a genetic switch, say, most small animals which have short periods of gestation should be uniform in colour. This is generally the case. For larger skin surfaces, at the time of patterning activation there is the possibility that animals will be half black and half white. The honey badger (*Mellivora capensis*) and the patterned Valais goat (*Capra aegagrus hircus*) are two examples (see the photo above of the latter). As the size of the domain increases, so should the extent of patterning. In fact, there is a progression in complexity from the Valais goat for example to certain anteaters, through the Galloway cow shown, common in Scotland (hence the name) when I was growing up there. More complex striping is particularly common on the zebra and on to the leopard and the cheetah. At the upper end of the size scale the spots of giraffes are closely spaced as shown below. Finally, very large animals should be uniform in colour again, which indeed is the case such as with the elephant, the rhinoceros, the hippopotamus and, no doubt, the extinct woolly mammoth.

The photograph of the giraffes (*Giraffa camelopardalis reticulata*) below is reproduced courtesy of a long time friend, Professor Andrew Dobson (Princeton University), a superb photographer of a wide variety of wild animals in the Serengeti. The small figures below the giraffes show spot examples from giraffes together with those from the mathematical model analysis of two different giraffe species, *Giraffa camelopardalis reticulata* (right) which has larger, closely spaced spots in contrast to the *Giraffa camelopardalis tippelskirchi* (left) which has smaller spots separated by wider spaces. All these different patterns can be accounted for in the mathematical model I proposed. The assumption is that the giraffe coat pattern is laid down when the embryo is probably around 35-45 days old and has an approximate length of around 8-10cms: the gestation period for a giraffe is around 457 days. Typically the time it takes to form the basic coat patterns during embryogenesis is of the order of a day or so.

Photograph is reproduced with the kind permission of a friend, Professor Andrew Dobson (Princeton University). The skin pattern examples and the figures below (solutions of the mathematical model) show how the mechanism reproduces the different but typical giraffe species coat patterns.

I am sure that the time at which the pattern-forming mechanism is activated is an inherited trait, and so, at least for animals whose survival depends to a great extent on pattern, the mechanism is activated when the embryo has reached a certain size, or rather time in gestation. Of course, the conditions on the embryo's surface at the time of activation exhibit a certain randomness. An important aspect of the model is that, for a given geometry and scale, the patterns generated by the model for a variety of random initial conditions are unique although, importantly qualitatively similar. In the case of a spotted pattern, for example, only the distribution and shape of spots vary. The finding is consistent with the individuality of an animal's coat markings within a species. Such

452

individuality allows for kin recognition and, crucially for survival, also for group recognition.

A reasonable candidate for the universal mechanism which generates the prepattern for mammalian coat patterns is a mechanism such as I used. Any reaction–diffusion mechanism capable of generating diffusion driven spatial patterns would provide a plausible model for animal coat markings. However, in spite of much research essentially only very very few reaction-diffusion mechanisms have been found experimentally in zoological development, and those only in the last few years. One is associated with ridges in embryonic palate formation and, more encouraging from the animal markings point of view, on fish stripes in a relevant article by my friends Professors Rafael Barrio and Philip Maini and their colleagues.[5] What I feel is not in doubt is that such patterns depend strongly on the geometry and scale of the domain where, and when, the patterning process takes place. Consequently the size and shape of the embryo at the time the reactions are activated determine the ensuing spatial patterns. Later growth, of course, can, and often does, distort the initial pattern. What I am also convinced of is that if the patterning system is not such a system as I studied, it has to exhibit similar pattern formation restrictions and behaviours.

There are numerous teratologies in the animal coat pattern area when the process is disrupted. Among cheetahs it is not that uncommon, nor among zebras. The striped sheep below, however, is the only one of which I have heard. A research collaborator from Australia who visited the *Centre for Mathematical Biology* for some months went to school with the owner.

In the drawings below (a) is of a coat pattern abnormality found on a cheetah in Zimbabwe (Rhodesia) in 1926. It was originally thought to be a hybrid between a cheetah and a leopard but then it was decided that it was a new species and was called *Acynonix rex*. It is not a new species. Such abnormal patterns are not that unusual. In (b) the photo of the striped black sheep is courtesy of *The Canberra Times*. The white striped black zebra in (c) is not that unusual.

---

[5] J.L. Aragon, C. Varea, R.A. Barrio P.K. Maini, Spatial patterning in modified Turing systems: Application to pigmentation patterns on marine fish, FORMA, 13, 213-221 (1998). (Cover article)

When I gave several public lectures on this topic some years ago and if the audience had a significant number of coloured people I occasionally asked the audience who thought a zebra was a white animal with black stripes and who thought it was a black animal with white stripes. Amusingly most of the coloured audience voted for the latter while most

454

of the white audience voted for the former. In fact, it is a black animal with white stripes.

Many factors, of course, affect animal coloration and patterning. Timing of the pattern initiation mechanism is crucially important in animals in the wild for their survival. The black zebra in the photo above with the few white stripes was generally on the edge of the group and its difference was clearly a sign of recognition of a non-normal animal. This was not the case, however, with the black striped sheep above – the domesticity of sheep could be the reason. In the case of domestic animals, of course, skin patterning is much less important for survival. Temperature, humidity, diet, hormones and metabolic rate are among some of the relevant factors. Although the effects of such factors probably could be mimicked by manipulating various parameters there is little point in doing so until more is known about how the patterns reflected in the melanin pigmentation are actually produced. In the meantime one cannot help but note the wide variety of patterns which can be generated with such a pattern formation model by varying *only* the scale and geometry. The considerable circumstantial evidence derived from comparison with specific animal-pattern features I find encouraging. The fact that many general and specific features of mammalian coat patterns can be explained by this simple theory, however, does not make it right. Only experimental quantification can confirm the theory.

Interestingly, the mathematical problem of describing the initial stages of spatial pattern formation by reaction-diffusion mechanisms (when differences from uniformity are minute) is similar to the mathematical problem for modelling the vibration of thin plates or drum surfaces. The analogous requirement for vibrations on the surface of a cylinder is that the radius cannot be too small otherwise only ring like patterns can form. If the radius is large enough, however, two-dimensional patterns can exist on the surface. As a consequence, a tapering cylinder can also exhibit a gradation from a two-dimensional pattern to simple stripes as is also shown in the figure above of various animal tails. The waves on water in a narrow channel are similar. If you throw a stone in, very quickly there are only one-dimensional propagating waves along the channel.

The results and predictions of the model were corroborated visually and dramatically, in a collaboration with colleagues. The vibration experiments were cleverly thought of and carried out by a colleague friend, Professor Charles (Chuck) Vest, later an innovative President of Massachusetts Institute of

Technology (MIT), and one of his students, Youren Xu[6] at the University of Michigan when I was visiting the university and had given a general lecture. They generated standing-wave patterns on a vibrating plate and changed the nature of the patterns by simply changing the frequency of vibration. The patterns were made visible by a holographic technique in which the plate was bathed in laser light. Light reflected from the plate interfered with a reference beam: the resulting patterns were recorded on a piece of photographic emulsion as shown in the examples below. We found that low frequencies of vibration produce simple patterns and high frequencies of vibration produce complex patterns. The observation is interesting, because we showed that if a pattern forms on a plate vibrating at a given frequency, the pattern formed on the same plate vibrated at a higher frequency is identical with the pattern formed on a proportionally larger plate vibrated at the original frequency. In other words, this experimental data, in a totally unexpected way, support, confirm rather, the conclusions above that more complex patterns should be generated as the scale of the mathematical model reaction–diffusion domain is increased. The resemblance between the patterns I found mathematically and the standing wave patterns subsequently produced by the plate vibration data is very striking as shown in the figures below.

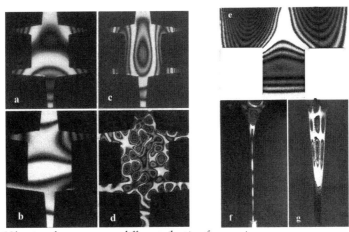

Vibrating plate patterns at different vibration frequencies.

---

[6] Holographic interferometry used to demonstrate a theory of pattern formation in animal coats. Youren Xu, C.M. Vest, and J.D. Murray. *Appl. Optics* 22: 3479-3483, 1983. (Cover article)

The more complex patterns in the figures (a–d) are achieved by vibrating the same plate at progressively higher frequencies rather than using larger plates at only one frequency: I showed mathematically that they give the same patterns. The leg body pattern (e) and the tail patterns (f) and (g) also exhibit the same general characteristics, such as, for example, if the tail is very narrow it can only sustain stripe patterns.

Perhaps the appropriate end of this section is a photograph of a cheetah which our daughter, Sarah, sent us many years ago, when she was visiting in Zimbabwe. It is clear it does not at all approve, nor agree with, the theory in this section.

2. Why are there no 3–headed monsters? Pattern formation in morphological development

The formation of spatial pattern has been a central issue in developmental biology for centuries. In spite of the extensive amount of experimental research in this area, little is yet known about the underlying mechanisms which lead, for example, to the cartilage patterns in developing limbs, the patterns of feathers, scales and hairs, how teeth are initiated, what really produces the spots on leopards or the myriad of patterns on butterfly wings and so on. Had we knowledge of the developmental mechanisms involved we could probably have prevented, for example, such tragedies as the thalidomide affair, in which the cartilage pattern–generating mechanism was corrupted. We shall also never completely understand evolution until we can take into account the developmental mechanisms which selection can act upon. The research we did on this, and described below, unexpectedly also increased our understanding of some evolutionary developments in animal limb bone structures.

The rich spectra of patterns and structures observed in the animal world evolve from a homogeneous mass of cells and are orchestrated by genes through the initiation and control of pattern-formation mechanisms. As mentioned above, these mechanisms are, even now, essentially unknown and the search for them has stimulated a vast amount of experimental and theoretical research. Although our understanding of developmental (that is morphogenetic) processes has progressed enormously in recent years, we still have a long way to go. Biological pattern formation was a major area of research at the *Centre for Mathematical Biology* in the University of Oxford, which was founded in 1983 to promote interdisciplinary research in the biomedical sciences in the broadest sense. The mechanism described below is, I believe, the first to be experimentally confirmed.

The complexity of biological pattern and form will certainly not succumb to a simple set of succinct rules, such as Newton's laws in physics, which explain and predict so many physical processes. Mechanisms of biological pattern formation are very much more complex and their elucidation still presents a vast number of the most challenging problems in science. The use of mathematical models as one of the techniques in trying to understand the mechanisms involved has increased markedly over the past 50 or so years. The basic philosophy behind practical modelling is, to me, simple. It tries to incorporate the observed biomedical and physicochemical events, which from observation and experiment appear to be going on during development, within a model mechanistic framework - analogous to Newton's laws but much more complicated- which can then be studied mathematically. The results from the analysis of these 'laws' are then applied to real and specific developmental situations with a view to providing insight into how embryonic patterns are laid down and to making predictions which, crucially and essentially, can be tested experimentally. An important element in this research is the close collaboration between the theoretician and experimentalist.

In this section I briefly describe the mechanochemical approach to developmental biology. It is known as the *mechanochemical theory of biological pattern formation*. Along with a friend, Professor George Oster (Berkeley), we proposed and developed the theory when George was spending several months at the *Centre for Mathematical Biology* in the University of Oxford in the early 1980s. We later applied it, along with some of our experimental co-workers, to other developmental phenomena, and also with Professor Philip Maini (Oxford) when he was a mathematics graduate student and post-doctoral of mine in Oxford in the mid-1980s. The Murray-Oster theory [7] of pattern formation has stimulated experimental programmes around the world. By way of illustration I sketch here in a little detail one of the specific problems we first investigated, namely developing cartilage patterns in the vertebrate limb.

In the previous section, to get some idea of how pattern formation can arise, I described what is in effect now a classic model. Such models have been and still are widely studied mathematically. Because of the paucity, or more accurately, essentially lack of experimental verification, the limitations of reaction–diffusion pattern formation models in biology was the motivation for this totally new approach and theory of developmental biology pattern formation.

Importantly the theory here is based on extant biological facts about cells in a developing embryo and the tissue in which the cells are embedded. This class of models captures the key experimentally observed interactions between the mechanical forces generated by the cells and their extracellular milieu. Together they give rise to developmental processes which we modelled. The analytical study of our model showed that a purely mechanical version of the theory could be responsible for certain observed patterns and how they are actually formed in embryonic development. These mechanochemical models are based on accepted fundamental mechanical biological concepts and do not specify the type of cells and matrix involved but rather only consider possible interactions between the various biological components. Importantly, and very encouragingly, the theory and many of our biological predictions have been confirmed by experiment.

---

[7] J. D. Murray, G.F. Oster and A.K. Harris, A mechanical model for mesenchymal morphogenesis. *J. Math. Biol. 17 (1983): 125–129.*

G.F. Oster, J. D. Murray and A.K. Harris, Mechanical aspects of mesenchymal morphogenesis, *J. Embryol. Exp. Morph. 78 (1983): 83–125.*

J. D. Murray and P.K. Maini, A new approach to the generation of pattern and form in embryology. *Science Progress* 70 (1986): 539-553.

G.F. Oster, N. Shubin, J. D. Murray and P. Alberch, Evolution and morphogenetic rules: the shape of the vertebrate limb in ontogeny and phylogeny. *Evolution* 42 (1988):862-884.

The basic model hinges on two key, experimentally determined, properties of *in vivo* embryonic cells called mesenchymal cells: (i) cells migrate within a tissue made up of a fibrous matrix, called the extracellular matrix (ECM), and (ii) cells can generate traction forces thereby deforming the tissue matrix. The basic mechanism models the mechanical interaction between the motile cells and the elastic tissue, called the substratum, within which they move. Mesenchymal cells, a photos of which are shown below, move by exerting forces on their surroundings, consisting of the elastic fibrous matrix and the surface of other cells. They use their cellular protrusions, which stretch out from the cell in all directions, gripping whatever is available and pulling. Due to the heterogeneity in matrix and cell densities, cell traction tension lines form between the cell clusters. These tension lines correspond to aligned matrix fibres along which cells actively move thereby defining cellular highways between the clusters of cells. One of the major roles of the modelling and its mathematical analysis was to indicate which features are essential for biological spatial pattern formation as observed in nature.

The actual models consist of three equations. (The specific type are nonlinear partial differential equations which require a relatively sophisticated applied mathematical background to solve.) The scenario reflected quantitatively in the model's equations is that you start with a given number of such cells involved in the patterning process. During development the cells multiply and move around: this is mimicked in one equation. Another equation quantifies the mechanical cell–extracellular tissue interaction which incorporates cell movement, called mechanotaxis

(a)   (b)

Examples of real cells: (a) single mesenchymal cell, (b) cells exerting tension on biological tissue. Photos are courtesy of Professor Albert Harris.

or haptotaxis, and which influences cell movement (a bit like climbing up a jungle gym) while the third equation quantifies the mechanical interaction of the cells and the biological tissue matrix. The model posed, and still poses, numerous challenging mathematical problems as well as diverse biological modelling problems, many of which have not yet been investigated in any depth. Although the model system is mathematically formidable its conceptual framework is quite clear, as illustrated in the figure below. The traction, which is generated by the cells, is crucial. The parameters associated with the model are all quantifiable from experiment. The mechanical cell-tissue patterning scenario is encapsulated in the figure below. The arrow directions from the boxes indicate what each influences.

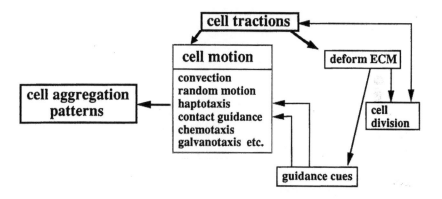

Here ECM denotes the extracellular matrix, the biological tissue, in which the cells move and distort it. There is an increase in the number of cells through cell division, called mitosis. Haptotaxis is cell movement directed by the deformed biological tissue matrix. The combination of all these phenomena results in cell aggregations which can give rise to cartilage aggregations, for example, which I describe in detail below.

Several factors affect the movement of these embryonic mesenchymal cells. Among them are: (i) convection, whereby cells may be passively carried along on a deforming tissue; (ii) diffusion, where the cells move randomly but generally down a cell density gradient; (iii) haptotaxis, where the cells move up an adhesive tissue gradient; (iv) contact guidance, in which the tissue on which the cells move around suggests a preferred direction; (iv) contact inhibition by the cells, whereby a high density of neighbouring cells inhibits cell motion; (v) chemotaxis, whereby a gradient in a chemical can direct cell motion: it can be both up or down a chemical concentration gradient depending on the chemical; (vi) galvanotaxis, where movement occurs from the field generated by electric potentials, which are known to exist in embryos. All of these provide a preferred direction of motion for cells. These effects are all well documented experimentally. The detailed mathematical study of the model equations, incorporating only the effects (i)-(iv), showed how typical spatial patterns of cells regularly found in development, bone cartilage for example, are formed.

From a physical viewpoint it is not difficult to see, qualitatively, how the model mechanism generates spatial patterns. Cell tractions pull the ECM (the tissue matrix), thereby dragging other cells towards them thus creating a denser matrix which makes it easier for cells to move on - they get a better grip. This aggregative tendency is countered by the elasticity of the ECM and other dispersal effects, like diffusion, which try to maintain homogeneity. Cell aggregation takes place when the dispersal effects are overcome by the aggregative effects. Thus an initially uniform field of cells becomes unstable as the mechanical properties change, through aging for example, and the homogeneous mass of cells breaks up into spatial patterns of cell aggregations, each with its own recruitment zone from which it attracts cells. The size of the parameters, in practice experimentally measurable, is involved in determining the existence and nature of the pattern. Mathematical analyses of the model equations quantify this notion and highlight certain parameter groupings which show how equivalent effects can be obtained by varying seemingly quite different biological parameters. Below I describe some of the surprising predicted results and phenomena all of which, importantly, have been verified experimentally.

Evolution and morphogenetic rules in cartilage formation in the vertebrate limb and why there are no 3–headed monsters

One major application of our theory was to limb cartilage development the results of which we also put into an evolutionary context. Since the limb is one of the most morphologically diversified of the vertebrate organs, and one of the more easily studied developmental systems experimentally, it is not surprising it is so important in both embryology and evolutionary biology where there is such a rich fossil record documenting the evolution of limb diversification.

Although morphogenesis appears deterministic on a macroscopic scale, on a microscopic scale cellular activities during the formation of the limb involve considerable randomness. Order emerges as an average outcome with some high probability. An important feature of morphogenetic patterns, particularly limbs, is that they are often laid down sequentially. In the developing forelimb, for example, the femur is formed first, followed by the tibia and fibula. We showed that certain morphogenetic events are extremely unlikely, in reality impossible, such as trifurcations from a single chondrogenic (cartilage) condensation. Mathematically, of course, they are not strictly forbidden by the pattern formation process but are developmentally impossible in fact, since they correspond to a very delicate choice of conditions and parameter tuning which are never found in embryonic development. This is an experimentally verified example of a *developmental constraint*. The '*morphogenetic rules*' for limb cartilage patterning we discovered are summarized and explained in the following figure and below in some figures of real limbs together with experiments which confirmed our predictions.

Morphogenic (biological developmental) rules

Referring to the figures below, the three basic cell condensations (which result in bone formation) which the mathematical model showed are possible are: (a) a single condensation F; (b) a branching bifurcation, B; and (c) a segmental condensation, S. Complicated cartilage patterns are formed solely by a combination of these basic bifurcations, as shown in (d) below: it is just one example of the complex morphogenesis and digitations of the forelimb of the salamander (*Ambystoma mecicanum*) which was studied experimentally following our theoretical predictions. The limb diagram in (d) in the following page, shows the standard names of the limb patterning: H(humerus), R(radius), U(ulna), C(condensation) with I–V the limb's digit numbering. The limb diagram (e) shows the sequential development of the limb with only B and S, namely the basic pattern formations in (b) and (c).

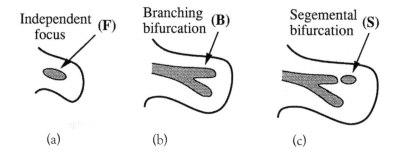

Independent focus **(F)**	Branching bifurcation **(B)**	Segemental bifurcation **(S)**
(a)	(b)	(c)

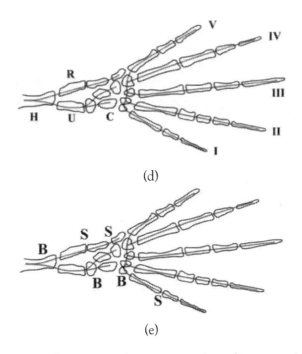

(d)

(e)

The theory initiated a series of experimental studies, organised by our colleague, Professor Pere Alberch, which confirmed our predictions and the developmental laws we had discovered. A variety of limb buds were treated with a mitotic inhibitor called colchicine.[8] This chemical reduces the dimensions of the limb by reducing cell proliferation. We predicted, from the mathematical model, that such a reduction in tissue size would reduce the number of bifurcation events and result in a limb with fewer digits and cartilage patterning.

The following figures quantitatively show the experimental results of the mitotic inhibitor, colchicine, on the limb cartilage growth of just two of the species studied experimentally, namely a salamander (*Ambystoma mexicanum*) and a frog (*Xenopus laevis*). The inhibitor reduced the number of cell aggregation patterns in the limb and hence the final size and cartilage skeletal elements as predicted by our theory.

---

[8] G.F. Oster, N. Shubin, J.D. Murray, and P. Alberch. Evolution and morphogenetic rules: the shape of the vertebrate limb in ontogeny and phylogeny. *Evolution* 42: 862–884, 1988.

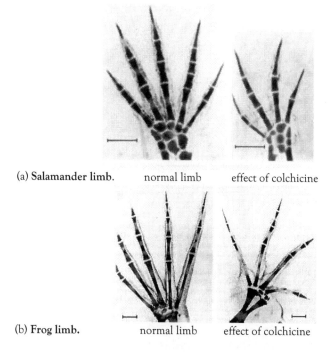

(a) **Salamander limb.**   normal limb   effect of colchicine

(b) **Frog limb.**   normal limb   effect of colchicine

The limb of the salamander on the left in (a) is the normal right limb while the one on its right is the left limb which had been treated with the cartilage formation inhibitor colchicine. In the case of figure (b) of the frog embryonic limb, the one on the left is the normal left limb with the one on the right the frog's right limb which was treated with, colchicine. Importantly the sequential development of all of the cartilage elements of the limbs only used the three basic rules described above which confirmed our theory and hypotheses. This research importantly helps to explain the stable developmental process in limb cartilage formation.

Using these basic rules of cartilage pattern formation a series of comparative experimental studies were carried out with examples from amphibians, reptiles, birds and mammals, which confirmed the mathematical model's predictions, and confirmed the hypothesis, namely that tetrapod limb development consists only of iterations of the processes of focal condensation, segmentation and branching. The experimental results supported the theoretical conclusion that branching, segmentation and *de novo* condensation events are reflections of the basic cellular properties of cartilage forming tissue which we discovered.

The effect of treating the developing foot, for example of a salamander *Ambystoma mexicanum*, with the mitotic inhibitor colchicine is to reduce the number of skeletal elements as predicted by our theory. In early evolution salamander limbs had fewer cartilage limb elements, as is the case with many species, so we came up with the idea of how to make evolution move backward. It is clearly possible when we consider evolution of form as simply variations in the morphogenetic parameters in the patterning mechanism during development. The following figure quantitatively shows the consequence of the inhibitor on limb cartilage growth and how it relates to natural evolutionary development of the limb. The two figures on the upper right are from fossil records while those on the lower right are from experimental use of colchicine which reduced the number of cartilage elements as predicted by the mathematical model. The comparison between the evolutionary development and the experimental manipulation of cartilage cell reduction is striking. The normal limb cartilage pattern is the single figure on the left.

The figure is an unequivocal example where moving "evolution" backwards has happened solely through changing the basic parameters of the morphogenetic processes. The tragic effect of thalidomide is another example of how the presence of a chemical, which inhibited chondrogenic cell aggregation and division, affected the final chondrogenic patterns in humans.

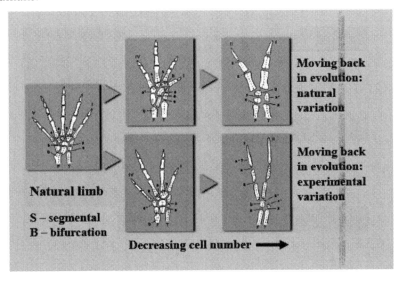

The study of these theoretical mechanical models for pattern formation in biological development showed that there are considerable restrictions as to the possible patterns of chondrogenesis (as well as other developmental aspects). From the morphogenetic laws we discovered it is highly unlikely, impossible in fact, that a trifurcation can occur; that is, a branching of *one* element into *three* elements. There are numerous examples of two-headed snakes and other reptiles, conjoined twins and so on. Although there is sometimes an appearance of a 1-to-3 splitting, the theory shows that all branchings are initially binary. This is because a trifurcation is possible only under such a very narrow set of parameter values and conditions which are essentially impossible to occur in nature. Including even the most minute asymmetries makes it impossible. The conclusion of the unlikelihood of trifurcations is the reason we never see any three-headed monsters. The figures below show two examples of human branching.

Very few three-headed monsters have been reported, and of these the veracity is always highly questionable. If we come back to the limited bifurcations shown by the developmental laws above, and specifically that a trifurcation is so highly unlikely, we can see how a three-headed monster can arise, namely, via a bifurcation of the body axis, such as we see in the skeleton in (a), followed by a further bifurcation of one of the branches: this is clear in the example in (b).

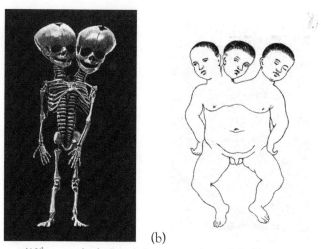

(a)   (b)

(a) Skeleton (19th century) of a *Dicephalus*, a young boy, while (b) is an example, (19th century) of a *Tricephalus* which is generated by sequential bifurcations.

In mythology, of course, there are many 3-headed and 7-headed monsters. Cerberus, the dog which guards the gate for Hades, is usually 3-headed, as well as mythical snakes. There are some marvellous descriptions of monsters in the literature, often by the clergy such as the one by William Turner (MA, Oxford 1675) 1653-1701, Vicar of the village Walberton in England who wrote a book on them in 1697. The title is incredibly long, typical of titles at the time, and so I have left out large parts of it and kept the original spelling and grammar:

A Compleat History Of the Most Remarkable Providences, both of Judgement and Mercy,........To which is Added. Whatever is Curious in the Works of Nature.........The author recommends it 'as useful to minister in Furnishing Topicks of Reproof and Exhortation........

In the book there is a description of a 3-headed monster:

"*a Child, terrible to behold, with flaming and shining Eyes; the Mouth and Nostrils were like those of an Ox; it had long horns, and a Back Hairy like a Dog's It had the Faces of Apes in the Breast where Teats should stand; it had Cats Eyes under the Navel, fasten'd to the Hypogastrium, and they looked hideously. It had the Heads of Dogs upon both Elbows, and at the White-Bones of each Knee, looking forwards. It was Splay-footed and Splay-handed; the Feet like Swans Feet, and a Tail turn'd upwards, that crook'd up backwards about half an Ell long. It lived four Hours from its Birth; and near its Death, it spake thus "Watch for the Lord your God comes*".

In a biography of the author by John Dunton, a contemporary, Turner is described as "*a man of wonderful moderation, and, of great piety.*"

Teratology highlights some of the most fundamental questions in evolution, namely, why do we not get certain forms in nature. The developmental process embodies various systems of constraint which bias the evolution of the system. Teratologies, among other things, provide an excellent source of information on the potential of developmental processes. They also suggest which monstrosities are possible and which are not. It is interesting that specific morphologies are found in quite different species suggesting a certain common developmental process for part of their development, not unlike the process of animal coat patterns in a wide diversity of species.

Along with one of my Oxford doctoral students, Daniel Bentil, I applied the theory to the formation of human fingerprints since it involves mechanical processes during development. Among other things the research clearly shows why all fingerprint patterns are unique. Various ridge patterns such as whorls, arches, loops, spirals, bifurcating lines, and so on, such as in the human fingerprint example in the figure below, can all be obtained by the model mechanism we proposed.

Human fingerprint, courtesy of an English criminal.

Much of the theory, practical biological extensions and original applications were further developed together with my former graduate and post-doctoral student Philip Maini. I have collaborated and written more research articles with Philip than with any other colleague in my caareer, and we have been close friends since he started his doctorate with me in 1982. In 1998 he succeeded me as Professor of Mathematical Biology in the University of Oxford and as the Director of the *Centre for Mathematical Biology*, now called the *Wolfson Centre for Mathematical Biology* because of an enormous donation. Philip is now one of the internationally renowned figures in the field: he was elected a Fellow of the prestigious Royal Society (FRS) in 2015.

There was an important, purely chance consequence of this research, which is another example of the academic benefits of the Oxford college system of visitors regularly being invited as dinner guests. In the late 1980s I had been collaborating with Professor Mark Ferguson in the School of Biological Sciences at the University of Manchester (he is now an Honorary Professor), on a problem related to the stripes on the backs of alligators. He is an internationally renowned scientist and one of his many areas of international recognition expertise is on the *crocodilia*. We also later collaborated on alligator teeth formation. Mark asked me at the dinner, in Corpus Christi College, what I was working on now and I said it was a problem on limb cartilage development and more recently on wound healing. With regard to the latter he asked what kind of experiments were done so I described some of the interesting graft experimental research my friend Professor Lewis Wolpert had done on chick limb development. I told him of the surprising fact that a wound made on the embryonic limb bud healed without scarring while those on the limb bud after hatching did not. This intrigued Mark and he started to try and find out experimentally why no scarring occurred on the embryo. Impressively, he discovered why and developed a product which prevents scarring and accelerates wound healing. Among other things he demonstrated its remarkable success on children in Africa who had keloids which normally give rise to large appalling scars. Mark is now Chief Scientific Adviser to the Government of Ireland and Director General of the Science Foundation Ireland, a national foundation involved in investment in scientific and engineering innovation.

3. Prostate cancer and PSA (prostate specific antigen) tests anomaly

This section could have one of the most important effects on life expectancy for some of the men who read it. I have discussed the importance of such tests with many friends some of whom, as a result have increased their life expectancy by many years and sadly has shown several others that their life expectancy was very much less than they had ever expected since an undetected prostate cancer had already metastasized. Particularly in the UK when I ask friends and colleagues if they have had a PSA (prostate specific antigen) blood test: most have never heard of PSA.

Approximately 1 in 6 men will get prostate cancer. This compares with approximately 1 in 8 women who will get breast cancer. There is an almost constant debate as to whether or not men should have a PSA test. PSA is the number obtained from a routine blood test which is associated with the prostate and it is widely believed in the medical profession that a high number is probably associated with prostate cancer. The *US Preventive Services Task Force* (USPSTF) in 2012 made the following recommendation (and it has been reiterated since):

"Prostate cancer is a serious health problem that affects thousands of men and their families. But before getting a PSA test, all men deserve to know what the science tells us about PSA screening: there is a very small potential benefit and significant potential harms. We encourage clinicians to consider this evidence and not screen their patients with a PSA test unless the individual being screened understands what is known about PSA screening and makes the personal decision that even a small possibility of benefit outweighs the known risk of harms."

I show below that this is an outrageous recommendation as well as being medically wrong. The recommendation of the *National Health Service* in the UK is no better.

The *National Health Service* in the UK, Medicare in the US, and many other public and private medical insurances, do not pay for routine PSA tests unless specifically recommended by a patient's medical practitioner.

XIV. Mathematics in the Real World – from Animal Coat Patterns to Brain Tumours, Divorce Prediction and Others

The cost is minute. Government medical committees recommend that if a test is carried out it should only be for men over 50 and the acceptable PSA level should be less than 4.0ng/mL (nanograms/cubic centimetre: one nanogram =10^{-9} gram). The problem with many in the medical profession, not only many of those who sit on such government committees, is that they are often completely unaware of the important research literature in areas in which they presume to give advice. From my experience with several such government bodies, including the *National Science Foundation*, the professionals who sit on such bodies are not always the best qualified, nor even above average, in their field but it is often felt that sitting on such a committee enhances their reputation. In this section I describe how a very simple realistic mathematical model, verified by experiment and published in a major medical journal, shows that the recommendation is not only wrong it is one of the worst I have known to come from recent medical committees and probably has, resulted in a large number of lost lives which could have been saved, and could be in the future if the USPFTS recommendation is continued to be generally observed. I should add that there is a similar view currently being expressed about not recommending mammograms for women below a certain age, a recommendation which is equally outrageous.

Using the USPFTS recommended PSA level of 4.0ng/mL as the cut off a clinical trial was carried out over a 7-year period of 9,459 men all of whom had a PSA of less than 4. Of these 2,950 concluded the trial and underwent biopsies of the prostate to determine whether or not they had prostate cancer. The results, published in 2004[9] in the prestigious widely read medical journal, showed that 428, that is 14% of the men, had prostate cancer. It is also known that many men have a PSA level much higher than 4 and do not have prostate cancer.

In another study conducted in eight European countries, the *European Randomized Study of Screening for Prostate Cancer*, 182,160 men between 50 and 74 years started the study. After a follow up, eleven years after, in the core age group the relative reduction in the risk of death was 21%: see also

---

[9] Ian M. Thompson *et al.* Prevalence of Prostate Cancer among Men with a Prostate-Specific Antigen Level ≤4.0ng per millilitre *New England J. Med.* 350:2239-2246, 2004.

the follow up article[10] on the study with an additional two years. The article also summarises the results of the original study.

The important question is how do we explain this anomaly scientifically and what are the medical implications. Together with a friend and medical colleague Dr. Larry True and several medical colleagues and a Ph.D. student of mine, we published an invited editorial research paper in a major medical journal in 2001[11] which describes our basic mathematical model and tumour injected mice experiments which explained the clinical study conclusions and resolved the medical anomaly using the predictions of the model which were medically confirmed.

Basically, what are the key parameters and symptoms in determining whether or not there probably is a carcinoma and also which parameters determine its growth? To understand how we developed a model you first have to know the basic medical facts. PSA is produced by normal prostate cells and also by prostate cancer cells. PSA usually increases with age and the size of the prostate. The widespread presumption is that PSA levels in men with prostate cancer are generally, but not always, higher than those without a carcinoma. There is, in fact, a large variance of PSA with cancer volume. Various modifications have been proposed to refine the diagnosis such as age-specific ranges, the molecular form of the PSA, the PSA density, which is the PSA divided by the prostate volume. These have had little effect on improving diagnosis.

The basic model for PSA and prostate cancer growth which we proposed is based on the accepted facts that the change in PSA depends on the PSA production. We proposed that the key elements in the model of how the PSA changes with time can be quantified from the simple word equation:

The rate of change of PSA = PSA production by normal cells

+ PSA production by cancer cell

– clearance (death) of cancer cells

---

[10] Fritz H. Schroder *et al.* Prostate-Cancer Mortality at 11 years Follow-up. *New England J. Med.* 366:981–990, 2012.

[11] Kristin R. Swanson, J. D. Murray, D. Lin, L. True, K. Buhler, R. Vassella. A quantitative model for the dynamics of serum prostate specific antigen as a marker for cancerous growth: an explanation of a medical anomaly. *Amer. J. Pathol.*, 158(6):2195–2199, 2001 (Invited editorial).

The mathematical equation[12] for this is, in a sense, a shorthand way of writing it, but importantly it has, imbedded in the equation, quantitative terms which let you obtain the solution of the equation which gives important individual quantitative prediction. By making some assumptions based on typical patient data, we postulated, correctly, that PSA is produced by normal prostate cells, that the cancer cells grow exponentially with a measurable parameter, a(per unit of time); that the PSA decays exponentially with a measurable parameter, r(per unit of time), and that the volume of the non-cancerous prostate cells is constant. This can all be quantified in what is called an ordinary differential equation the solution of which can easily be obtained by an advanced final year school or first year university level student in mathematics. The key number, we donate by μ, is the ratio

μ = decay rate of PSA / growth rate of the cancer

The main conclusion of the study is that the PSA and the tumour may or may **not** grow in synchrony and depends primarily on the value of this parameter μ. This has crucially important medical implications as I describe below.

Let us take two examples of typical tumour growth as shown in the figures below. In the first figure the tumour volume and the PSA level grow in synchrony while in the second figure they do not. It simply depends on the size of the ratio, μ, that is the ratio of the decay rate of PSA to the growth rate of the cancer. This explains the clinical trial anomaly of those men who had prostate cancer and had a low PSA: this gives a low value of the ratio of μ.

The figures below show the effect of a high and low ratio, μ, of the decay rate of PSA to the growth rate of the cancer. A low value of μ implies that the PSA and cancer volume do not grow in synchrony.

So, what major medical insights have we gained from this very simple but very practical PSA growth model?

1. Importantly the PSA dynamic model shows that PSA levels are related to tumour **growth** and not just size.

---

[12] For those with some mathematical background and curiosity about the equation and its solution, they are given and briefly described at the end of this chapter.

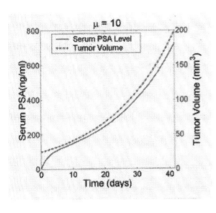 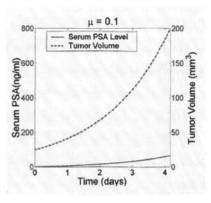

2. It shows that the clinically recommended significant PSA = 4ng/mL is totally arbitrary. Since tumour growth and prostate size is variable the model shows that there can be a large difference in relative tumour size when using **only one** PSA screening.

3. The medical advisory boards have not asked the right question nor, apparently, have they read the relevant literature. (If they have read it their recommendation is even more outrageous.)

4. There can be a delay between tumour growth and PSA production characterised by the ratio μ = PSA decay rate /tumour growth rate.

5. PSA screening should be routine irrespective of the PSA level. If there is a continuing **increase** in PSA over a period of roughly 1-2 years a biopsy should be carried out.

For a few years I gave an undergraduate lecture on this specific topic in a biology course in Princeton University to a class of around 170 students in which there was always a significant number, the majority of the class in fact, of premedical students. I described the situation and presented the government recommendations. For discussion among themselves and for homework questions requiring written answers I posed the following two questions:

1. The USPSTF (*US Preventive Service Task Force*) set an acceptable limit of 4.0ng/ml for PSA in a blood test screening. However many men have higher levels and do not have prostate cancer while many with lower PSA levels do. Can you give any explanation for this phenomenon?

2. What are the main parameters in determining the growth of a prostate carcinoma?

Typical reasonable answers are:
If the prostate is small the PSA production is smaller than for a larger prostate and so an equally serious carcinoma can exist at a smaller PSA level. A large prostate produces much more PSA which does not necessarily indicate the presence of a carcinoma.
Key measurable parameters are:
1. Cancer growth rate (cancer cell doubling time)
2. Decay rate and production rate of the PSA
3. Prostate size
4. Cancer cell death rate
Impressively 95% of the class essentially got the right answers. One year I asked the class: "So what should we do about the medical committee members of the *US Preventive Service Task Force?*" one of the students shouted: "*Fire them!*" which got loud applause from the whole class.

So, personally, what should one do about this? A major problem is that many in the family medical practice community are, as mentioned, unaware of crucial practical life preserving medical research. The more arrogant assume that non-medically qualified, albeit highly qualified researchers, do not know enough to make any recommendations. Prostate cancer, if caught early enough and it has not metastasized outside the prostate, can often be removed completely. So, you should ask your family doctor if he (or she) recommends you have a PSA test. If your doctor says "No", change your doctor! Alternatively you can ask if he has had a PSA test, or if it is a woman doctor, whether or not she recommends, a mammograms since, as mentioned, there are currently (2015) similar serious moves to discourage women from such examinations for related erroneous reasons in both the US and the UK, at least until they reach a certain age. Those on national committees tend to list the potential dangers of prostate biopsies. They would be better addressing the problem of infections in hospitals which would be much more important than trying to save money on tests, particularly the PSA one which costs so little. I also strongly recommend that PSA tests should start around 40 years old and the patient, himself, should keep track of his PSA so that any continual increase would more likely be noted and proper tests followed up. It is true that old men sometimes have slow growing prostate cancers and they may die from other causes first but that is a gamble the individual should decide. Biopsies can be a little uncomfortable (briefly) and, with incompetent doctors, very very occasionally causing infection, but if a man was asked whether he would rather have a biopsy to know if he has cancer or take the risk and perhaps shorten his life by many many years I think the answer is, or should be, obvious. In the case of women and mammograms the answer is even clearer since they have no risk of infection from the procedure.

4. Brain Tumours: Enhancing Imaging Techniques, Quantifying Therapy Efficacy and Estimating Patient Life Expectancy

As described in Chapter 12, shortly after moving to the University of Washington in the early 1990s the Chairman of Neuropathology, Dr. Ellsworth C. Alvord (always known as Buster) in the medical school got in touch with me to see if I would be interested in trying to model the growth and control of brain tumours, specifically high grade ones called gliomablastomas (gliomas), with a view to predicting growth, life expectancy and quantifying the effect of current treatments. It sounded a fascinating, challenging, and certainly an important research project which, if successful, would be extremely useful and important medically. Buster had worked on brain tumours, his speciality, for almost 40 years. It was the start of a long, very successful, very warm friendly collaboration which continued until he died in January 2010 at the age of 86. As usual I liked to get some of my graduate students and post-doctorals involved so they could get some experience outside of their main doctoral or post-doctoral research to help broaden their perspective. Quite soon we had developed a very simple but, as it turned out, highly relevant mathematical model, described below. Our first medical article was published in 1995[13], and as a first practical application, we used the model to quantify the effect of chemotherapy on the tumour growth.[14] The early work clearly showed the importance of cancer cell diffusion (that is spatial dispersal of the cancer), a major component in glioma growth which had been effectively ignored until that time, and certainly not understood. From then on I published, along with Buster and some of my collaborators, research papers mostly in

[13] G.C. Cruywagen, D.E. Woodward, P. Tracqui, G.T. Bartoo, J.D. Murray, E.C. Alvord Jr, The modelling of diffusive tumors. *J. Biol. Systems* **3** (1995): 937-945.
[14] P.K. Burgess, P.M. Kulesa, J.D. Murray, E.C. Alvord Jr, The interaction of growth rates and diffusion coefficients in a three-dimensional mathematical model of gliomas. *J. Neuropathol. Exp. Neurol.* **56** (1997): 704-713.

medical journals, refining and extending the model for anatomically correct brains and developing its practical medical use for patients with such brain tumours. The model procedures and predictions are now being used on a large number of patients in hospitals and medical centres on the west coast and mid-west of America who agreed to participate and from whom we obtain comparative data. This research, and also the above on prostate cancer, is somewhat different to most of my research in that its primary purpose is to help to predict the subsequent growth of a tumour, explain certain medical anomalies and highlight medical treatment deficiencies rather than to try and understand the underlying biological processes going on.

The aims of the initial research were, and still are, to (i) link the mathematical modelling with clinical research and practice; (ii) enhance imaging techniques; (iii) highlight limitations and inadequacies of current therapies and imaging; (iv) estimate life expectancy from detection; (v) estimate when and where the tumour started; (vi) importantly, quantify patient treatment efficacies **prior** to their use: such treatments include surgical removal (called resection), chemotherapy and radiation; (vii) explain why some patients live longer than others with the same treatment; (viii) help in designing clinical trials. With the model and its practical application using patient brain scans we have been able to contribute to all of these aims. A widely accepted medical belief is that gliomas are unpredictable: we also showed that this is not at all the case – the contrary in fact. As always it seems with the medical profession, getting the professionals in a specific area to read the relevant medical research literature, even in medical journals, is not easy.

High-grade glioblastoma brain tumours are the most aggressive brain tumours: they are always fatal with an approximate median life expectancy of 9–12 months. In spite of increasing accuracy of the brain imaging techniques, they still cannot remotely detect cancer cell densities sufficiently accurately as clearly illustrated in the figures below. Gliomas make up around half of all primary brain tumours. Typical treatments are mentioned below although, very encouragingly, there are increasing signs of possible genetic treatments albeit still very much in their infancy.

Brain tissue consists of grey and white matter: cancer cells migrate more quickly in white matter than in grey matter. The original practical model, which we proposed in 1995, is basically the same as is currently in use but now applied to anatomically correct brains. It encompasses two

477

key properties in the growth of glioblastoma brain tumours, namely the invasive diffusive (that is migratory) properties of the cancer cells in the brain tissue and their multiplication rate.

Tumours are spatially highly irregular but from two brain scans of the patient we can calculate the diffusion rate of tumour cells and how quickly they multiply for that patient. These are the cancer cell duplication (proliferation) rate which is exponential, and is denoted by r (/month), which means that the cancer cell doubles every (log2)/r months (that is about 0.7/r months) and the other, the diffusion (cell motility) denoted by D (mm²/month), which quantifies the invasiveness of the cancer cells. The cancer cell density is denoted by c (cells/mm³) which varies in the tumour and increases with time, denoted by t (months). The model is simply and intuitively described in words by the word equation:

Rate of change of tumour cell density at a position in the brain = Diffusion (motility) of tumour cells into that area

+ Proliferation of tumour cells at that position

The mathematical model equation simply quantifies what is said in words, using the various parameters.[15] The solutions of the basic mathematical equation are actually easy to obtain (first year university courses in mathematics) and provides some interesting and highly relevant information from a patient point of view and hopefully for the doctor. I am much less confident about the latter, particularly with neurosurgeons, most of whom feel they always know best even though many, most rather, do not keep up with new developments in the relevant medical literature.[16]

Using the model, together with the key parameters, namely the

[15] For those interested in the very basic mathematical details a very brief description is given at the end of this chapter. A more technical detailed discussion is given in various research papers in medical journals of which the following has relevant references: Glioblastoma brain tumours: estimating the time from brain tumour initiation and resolution of a patient survival anomaly after similar treatment protocols (J. D. Murray) J. Biol. Dyn. 6:sup2, 118–127, 2012.DOI:10.1080/17513758.2012.678392,2012.
http://dx.doi.org/10.1080/17513758.2012.678392
[16] *"Do you know the difference between a neurosurgeon and God?"* The answer is: *"God doesn't think he's a neurosurgeon."*

diffusion, D, and the cell growth rate, r, we can then predict the growth of the tumour and importantly estimate key aspects of the tumour's growth and the patient's response to different treatment protocols **prior** to their use. The figure below of a brain tumour is a computed solution of the model equation in an anatomically correct brain: it shows the detectable tumour at death and also the spread of the tumour cells beyond what can be detected by the most accurate and sophisticated current imaging techniques. Simulations of the model thus greatly enhance current imaging to whatever level of cancer cell density is required. Among other things the mathematical model solution shows how fast the tumour grows and, importantly, where in the brain it has reached. The limitations of current imaging techniques are clear.

This medically realistic model has been used to mimic various accepted medical treatments, specifically radiation, surgical resection (removal) and chemotherapy. We also showed that only those tumours with a low diffusion (that is spreading) rate could benefit from wide surgical resection although eventually there will be multifocal recurrence, as found clinically, and which we also explain using the model. It is clear from the figures below why surgery can never ever be successful. It can sometimes extend survival a few months but the key question is what kind of life will it be after the surgery. A close friend, some years ago, who had such a brain tumour and had read some of our research articles, was pressured by his family (and his neurosurgeon) to have surgery, even though he knew it could not be successful. Three weeks before he died he emailed me to say goodbye and said how much he wished he had never had the surgery and had passed the last months of his life as normally as possible without the dreadful medical problems which ensued as a consequence of the surgery. Sometimes surgery can be helpful to relieve specific problems but much more often not. At the reception after I gave a lecture, at which there were several neurosurgeons in the audience, I asked one: *"Why do you do surgery when you know it can't help?"* to which he replied: *"If I don't do it somebody else will."*

With the model, the informative procedure is to calculate the two key parameters for the patient from their enhanced CT (computer tomography) and MRI (*Magnetic Resonance Imaging*) brain scans and then calculate where in the brain the tumour has reached to whatever tumour density is required. The solutions of the mathematical gliomablastoma tumour model, shown in the figure below, with typical patient parameter values for the growth and dispersal in a three dimensional anatomically accurate brain, give cross section views of the virtual human brain through the site where the tumour started (the dark spot in the figures). In the figures below the left images in each is the tumour at diagnosis with currently available brain scans while the right images are of the same tumour at the time of death. The thick black contour shows the limit edge of the tumour which can be detected by enhanced CT (computer tomography) scans. The light contours outside this thick black line represent lines of constant cancer cell densities peripheral to the imaging limits and which can not be detected except by use of our model. For the tumour in grey matter the time from diagnosis to death is typically around 9 months while that in white matter it is around 5 months.

The mathematical analysis and the surgical procedure simulations, in the group of figures below, clearly show why surgery can never be successful for such tumours. With resection (that is surgical removal) the

Detection   Death

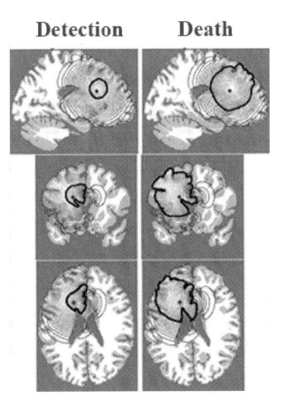

surgeon usually removes a slightly larger volume of the tumour which is seen with scans. The cancer which exists far beyond the scan volume, but which cannot be detected by scans, then inevitably and always diffuses back into the excised volume. This is why "recurrence" is described by surgeons as **unpredictable, as it would appear to be without medical the** understanding described here and why it has been wrongly described medically as a multifocal recurrence. The cross sectional figures below show, on the left, what a scan can detect while those on the right show, much more accurately, where the cancer has grown and why it appears multifocal after surgery but in fact it is simply regrowth into the resected area.

What can also be calculated from the patient's tumour parameters, and which are currently used for patients, are, for example, to: (i) estimate life expectancy both with, and without, treatments; (ii) explain why some patients with the same treatment live longer than others (particularly children); (iii) estimate when the tumour started, and (iv) show how fast the tumour volume grows. Regarding (i), with the scans we estimate the tumour volume and calculate the diameter of an equivalent sphere with the same volume. The mathematical analysis of the model equation then

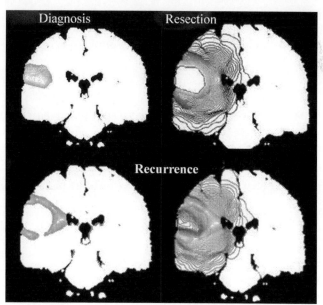

Tumour visible from brain scans.   Tumour visible using the
                                    mathematical model.

481

showed that the 'diameter' of a tumour would grow proportional to the time (t) from detection multiplied by the square root of the diffusion coefficient (D) times the cancer cell duplication rate (r). That is we showed that the equivalent spherical diameter growth of the patient's tumour is given by $4t\sqrt{Dr}$. In other words the tumour volume grows linearly with time. This prediction was confirmed by patient data. Typically a tumour is detected when it has approximately the equivalent volume of a sphere of 3cm in diameter with death occurring on average when it is equivalent to a sphere of 6cm in diameter. With the patient's two parameters associated with the tumour the approximate survival time can then be simply calculated. The predictions are in general agreement with published patient data as shown in the figure below.

To compare these survival model predictions with patient data we calculated the life expectancy using typical patient parameter values representing the least and most aggressive tumours in different parts of the brain: the mathematical model predictions are the clear light circles in the figure below. For comparison the results of two medical patient studies from 1993 and 2010[17], in the upper right of the figure below, are the triangles and the asterisks. For such a basic mathematical model the comparison was surprisingly accurate and very encouraging in being able to predict patient survival time.

Number (iii) above, which estimates when the tumour started (but is generally undetectable), I believe will no doubt be crucial when the connection to brain tumours as a result of the ever increasing use of cell phones used close to the head is finally universally recognized, not just medically. Experimental evidence is increasing that the radiation from the close proximity of a cell phone to the ear is resulting in non–normal effects, such as the increase in glucose levels in the brain. Recent research suggests that certain acids in the brain associated with nerve cell response are elevated giving rise to such things as anxiety and tiredness although after a nine-week behavioural therapy the brains in young people in the

[17] Ramakrishna, R. *et al.* Imaging features of invasion and preoperative and postoperative tumor burden in previously untreated gliomablastomas: Correlation with survival. *Surg. Neurol. Int.* 1:40-51, 2010.
Kreth, F.W. *et al.* Surgical resection and radiation therapy versus biopsy & radiation therapy in the treatment of Glioblastoma multiforme. *J. Neurosurg.* 78, 762-766, 1993.

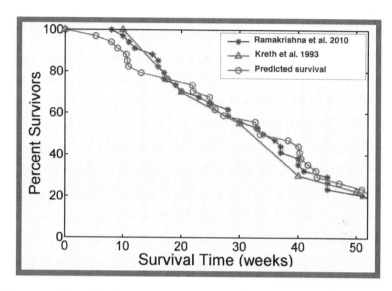

study seemed to be back to normal. The use of earpieces or remote microphones and headsets remove this danger. Associated with the effects of cell phone radiation, a friend in France, Professor Michel Thellier (a Member of the *French Academy*) and his botanist collaborators subjected growing plants to only two hours of a cell phone radiation the result of which were gross distortions in the grown plants. There is increasing experimental evidence of potentially serious medical problems from such cell phone use close to the head – and possibly even carried in a pocket close to the body.

With regard to (ii), for example, the model shows that a patient whose relevant parameters are such that the ratio D/r (that is how fast the cancer cells diffuse divided by the cancer cell growth rate) of the patient's tumour is small will live longer (by several months) than one with a larger value. As mentioned these parameters are determined from scans through the use of this model. This prediction has also recently been confirmed clinically. This ratio is also generally smaller in children with such tumours.

The results from the mathematical modelling described here show that the predicted spatial spread of brain tumours agrees with data from patients. The efficacy of specific treatments prior to their use and the increased life expectancy are also in good agreement with patient data. For all of these the model requires only 2 MRI (*Magnetic Resonance Imaging*) pre-treatment scans to estimate the two key parameters (diffusion/motility, D, and cancer cell replication rate, r) which we use to predict the expected course for the tumour growth in the brain of the patient. As mentioned the mathematical analysis and its predictions described here are now being used on a large number of patients in several hospitals around the USA.

So, what else have we gained from the mathematical modelling? Importantly it has suggested new ways to study gliomablastoma tumours. It suggests appropriate timing for serial scanning imaging follow-up. *In vivo* and *in vitro* studies of dispersal and invasion are now more quantifiable. Importantly, effects of individual treatments can be quantified and separated from individual patient side-effects *prior* to their use.

Unfortunately several experiences I, and some of my friends, have had with surgeons and doctors have added to my basic, generally less than positive, view of much of the medical profession. This is not new of course. Arguably the most famous and practical surgeon of the middle ages was Henri de Mondeville (c1260–c1320) who wrote a book, *Chirurgie* (Surgery), in 1316 (unfinished unfortunately): it was written in Latin and later translated into French. Like its author it is forthright, sharp-tongued and outspoken. He had no patience with ignorant colleagues. He also argued against the outdated Galen, still viewed as a god. He said: "*God surely did not exhaust all His creative powers in making Galen.*" de Mondeville felt surgery was the supreme discipline and that the surgeons of his day were totally disreputable. He described them as "*barbiers, fraters, aventuriers, vagabonds, ribauds et ribaudes, rufians et maquerelles*" (barbers, fellow travellers, adventurers, vagabonds, lascivious (men and women), ruffians and brothel keepers). He also said: "*Surgery is both a science and an art. Surgery is surer, more preferable, noble, perfect, necessary and lucrative.*" Mondeville, who was the doctor to two kings, Philipp Le Bel and his successor, Louis X, had very different views to most of the medical practices at the time. One example was pouring wine on a wound rather than mud. He was also a practical doctor of his times and, for example, had several ways of simulating virginity when it was crucial before a wedding.

Although the prognosis for patient survival with a gliomabalstoma tumour is bleak, there is an increasing number of novel, some bizarre, new approaches to non-surgical treatments. Some of these have increased life expectancy but, sadly, to date none have provided a cure.

5. Marital interaction and divorce prediction

Just before retiring a few years early from the University of Oxford in 1992 to go to the University of Washington in Seattle, to start a group in mathematical biology and medicine, I received a letter from a psychologist, Professor John Gottman, in the University of Washington, inviting me to come to the university and give a lecture. He added that he would also particularly like to talk with me about possibly collaborating on trying to model marital interaction with the aim of predicting divorce, among other things, specifically for newly married couples. I replied saying that I was, in fact, moving to the university in the autumn and we could meet then. I felt I should mention my scepticism about the practicality of such a mathematical model. Shortly after moving to Seattle we had lunch together and, to my surprise, I was hooked. It was such a novel potential use of practical mathematical modelling.

Out of curiosity I asked John Gottman how he had heard of me and my kind of practical mathematical research since we were in such different academic fields. It was by pure chance, he said. He belonged to the national science book club and one month had forgotten to return the card saying he did not want the book for that month because it had "mathematical" in the title and was probably pure mathematical, therefore useless. It turned out, unknown to me, my book *Mathematical Biology* had been adopted by the book club and so he was sent my book by default. He had studied mathematics at MIT as an undergraduate. He decided to read it and felt I had a highly original, very realistic and practical view of interdisciplinary research using mathematics in a wide spectrum of areas, and which he found he could understand. He felt I was the one person to contact who might be interested in working with him on problems in psychology and particularly this novel problem on marital interaction. He was right.

The rise in divorce rates in developed countries is widespread, and important, but a poorly understood, phenomenon. What makes some marriages happy but others miserable? Previous attempts at predicting marriage dissolution tended to be based on a variety of non–quantitative concepts such as mismatches in the couple's personality or areas of disagreement and many others: these have not been very successful. Some years later, after giving a public lecture on the topic in the Royal Society in London, the BBC interviewed me, the result of which is that I'll never give a BBC interview again. They sent me the interview which I thought was not unreasonable. It was when I later heard the full radio programme they had made that I learned they had also talked to someone who advised couples based on tea-leaf patterns in a cup, and another who read palms. The whole programme had become totally trivialised. I should certainly have been informed beforehand but then with so much of this trivialisation on BBC programmes for so long now I suppose it was just the norm.

Once again I got a few of my University of Washington graduate students involved and we all became fascinated with the possibility of constructing a realistic model: we published our first major research paper which describes the modelling in detail in 1995.[18] We developed a simple, but surprisingly accurate predictive mathematical model. Its remarkable success is based on following, over a period of nearly ten years, 700 newly married, or about to be married, couples who had agreed to participate in the study. The basic idea was to try and quantify how a couple interacted and influenced each other during a discussion of a topic of contention in their relationship and then use it to predict the future of the marriage. To get the data, couples, who had applied for a marriage license in King County in Washington State in the USA, were invited to participate in the study incentivised by a free holiday weekend in a departmental apartment. Each couple was filmed for 15 minutes while they discussed a topic of contention, which they chose. It could be on any subject, for example, money, housing, sex, in-laws, food; in fact any topic about which they did not agree and about which they felt strongly. The 15-minute interaction was filmed and then scored by two independent observers according to an accepted scoring system, called the SPAFF (*Specific Affect Coding System*) described below. The couple, of course, knew they were being observed but it was clear that after about the first minute or so they completely ignored the filming. With the data, the mathematical model, also described below, and the mathematical analysis of the data, it was possible to identify patterns predictive as to whether the couple would divorce or stay married; happily or unhappily.

After giving the Royal Society *Bakerian Public Lecture* in 2009 in which I described this work, as well as the brain research described above, there

---

[18] J. Cook, R. Tyson, K.A.J. White, R. Rushe, J. Gottman and J.D. Murray. Mathematics of marital conflict: Qualitative dynamic mathematical modelling of marital interaction. *J. Family Psychology* 9(2): 110-130, 1995.

was a large amount of international press attention and numerous interviews. Associated with an article about my lecture in the *Sydney Morning Herald* (27 March 2009) there was the cartoon below.

Based on the hypothesis that without a theoretical understanding of the processes related to marital relationship, stability and dissolution, it is difficult to design and evaluate effective relationship therapies. We used a psychological coding system to "score" each partner in a conflict conversation. The resultant time series can visually describe the ebb and flow of the interaction for a conversation. The SPAFF system we used

Sydney Morning Herald 27 March 2009. Reproduced
with the kind permission of the cartoonist, Cathy Cox.

consists of scoring each comment according to what the tone and so on implies: the following describes it. During the couple's discussion of the topic of contention, an integer number between +4 and –4 is given according to the sentiment expressed in each turn of speech. The basic system has specific numbers (positive or negative) given to each comment and expression. There were five positive codes, such as affection (+4), humour (+4), excitement (+4), interest (+2) and validation (+4) while the ten negative numbers are sadness (–1), anger (–1), contempt (–4), whining (–1), belligerence (–2), disgust (–3), defensiveness (–2), stonewalling (–2), domineering (–1) and for a neutral affect (+0.1). We only used the 16-code version. There was a continual scoring of the conversation during the 15-minute discussion.

Using the film, each time one of the couple spoke the observers counted up the total number of positive numbers then subtracted the total number from the negative answers and obtained a single number which was noted. Initially I was surprised how close the agreement was by the observers (often a couple of graduate psychology students). There is also a related 14 facial expression system which helps to identify the emotion. Later out of curiosity I showed several of the facial expression photos to one of our granddaughters, Eloise, admittedly a particularly clever and observant one, when she was about 5 and asked her how she thought the people felt. She got them all right very easily.

The cumulative positive minus the negative numbers for each partner were plotted on a graph with the horizontal axis the number denoting the order each spoke. The results give a kind of "Dow Jones" graph of the conversation using the positive minus the negative scores for each turn of speech. The figures below are two examples from actual couples. In the low divorce risk couple as the discussion proceeds there is almost always a higher positive to negative number as each partner speaks and a general increase as the discussion proceeds. In the couple with the high risk of divorce, on the other hand, the discussion deteriorates with the positive to negative ratio decreasing as the discussion proceeds. These are respectively very strong indications of a stable and an unstable marriage.

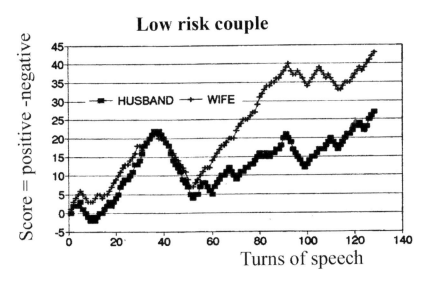

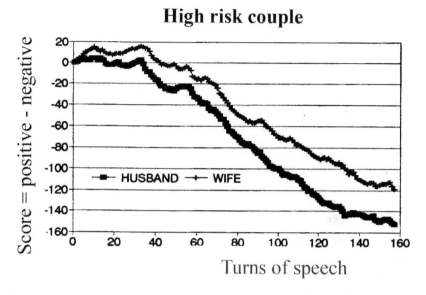

In the low risk couple discussion the ratio of positive to negative ratio as each speaks was approximately 5 to 1 whereas in the high–risk couple it was approximately 0.8 to 1.

Although this data gives a fairly good prediction of marriage stability the mathematical model using this data is much more accurate in its predictions. The model consists of an equation of how the wife reacts after the husband speaks as reflected in the score of positive minus negative numbers. The model equation we developed is, in words:

Wife's score of what she replies after the husband speaks =

> **How the wife generally feels about the marriage (quantified by parameter, a)**

> + **How easy it is for the wife to change her attitude from when she last spoke (quantified by a parameter, r_1)**

> + **How the husband influences the wife**

There is a similar equation for the husband. These are then quantified by two mathematical equations which are, in effect, simply a shorthand way of writing the equations, one for the wife (W) and one for the husband (H) namely:

$$W_{t+1} = a + r_1 W_t + I_{HW}(H_t), \quad H_{t+1} = b + r_2 H_t + I_{WH}(W_t)$$

where W_t and H_t are the scores of the wife and husband obtained from what they said at time t. To understand what the equations mean, consider, for example, the first equation, the wife's. The influence the husband (H) has on the wife (W) as a function of his score when he speaks at time t is $I_{HW}(H_t)$ and it reflects the influence he has when the wife replies namely at time t+1: her score then is denoted by W_{t+1}. The parameter r_1 is an inertia parameter, which quantifies how willing the wife is to change her attitude as reflected in her score the last time she spoke, namely W_t, at time t. For example, if r_1 is small the wife is not fixed on what she last said since this term is small which implies she is more willing to change her view than if it were larger. The parameter, a, reflects how the wife feels about the marriage when the husband is not influencing her, that is when $I_{HW}(H_t)$ is effectively zero.

All we had to make a prediction of the marriage were the data from the discussion, namely the data of which two examples are shown in the above two figures. With the data we were able to calculate a value for each of the parameters, a, b, r_1 and r_2 and what the influence of each on the other, as quantified in the influence functions $I_{HW}(H_t)$ (the influence of what the husband says on his wife) and $I_{WH}(W_t)$ (the influence of what the wife says on her husband) when each speaks. Basically the couple's data in the graph of their interaction are the solutions of the equations and from it we have to determine the form of the various terms in the equations. Intuitively it is like being given two numbers and asked to derive the quadratic equation which gives these as solutions – admittedly it is rather more difficult to do than that.

Although every couple has a unique relationship quantified by their own characteristic model parameters, in an analysis of the longitudinal study of these several hundred couples we found only five dominant couple behavioural styles. These are primarily based on the husband and wife influence functions obtained from the data, namely (i) validating, (ii) volatile, (iii) conflict-avoiding, (v) hostile and (v) hostile–detached. Only two of these styles, (i) and (iii), indicate a stable marriage, typically resulting in a long–term relationship. With S denoting a stable marriage and **U** an unstable one, which is generally predictive of divorce, the five types we found are:

Validating (S) – calmer, intimate, value companionate marriage, shared experience rather than individuality
Volatile (S/U) – romantic, passionate, have heated arguments with cycles of fights and sex
Avoiders (S) – avoid confrontation and conflict, interact only in positive range of their emotions
Hostile (U) – (mixed) conflict–avoiding wife, validating husband
Hostile–Detached (U) – (mixed) volatile husband, validating wife

For each of the more than 700 couples who took part in the long-term study during 1992-1994 we predicted that the couple would: (i) divorce, or (ii) stay married (a) happily, or (b) unhappily. Every one to two years, up to 2004, each couple was asked to complete a questionnaire (one from the wife and one from the husband) assessing their marriage. We compared these with our predictions. Of course, the couples were not informed of our predictions. Our prediction as to which couples would definitely get divorced was, astonishingly, 100% accurate, but some couples we predicted would stay married, but unhappily, in fact got divorced so our overall predictions of which couples would get divorced was 94% accurate. Of those who got divorced most got divorced within 4 years. As I watched some of the tape recordings I felt like telling some couples they might as well get divorced right away or for those not yet married to forget about it.

The ability to predict the longitudinal course of marital relationships, using this research procedure, has now been reported in the laboratories in four separate longitudinal studies as described in the book[19] we wrote together with some graduate students[20]. In the book the model has been

---

[19] *The Mathematics of Marriage: Dynamic Nonlinear Models.* J. Gottman, J. D. Murray, C. Swanson, R. Tyson, K. Swanson. MIT Press, Cambridge (2002). See also, *Mathematical Biology: I. An Introduction.* J. D. Murray. Springer, New York 2002.

[20] Two of the authors (Kristin Swanson and Rebecca Tyson) I got involved in the research were doctoral students of mine whose Ph.D. theses were totally unrelated to this research.

extended, for example, to incorporate the effect of a baby on marriages and also to cohabiting gay male and lesbian relationships.

So, what have we gained from the mathematics? We now have: (i) a new language for describing marital interaction and social influence and a rationale for the marital interaction experiments, (ii) the new concept that marriages can be classified into one of only 5 types of marriage depending on the couple's interaction style, and (iii) that stable marriages have matched interaction styles and unstable marriages have mismatched interaction styles.

From a practical point of view, it provides a rational scientific process for marital therapy which is now used in practice. In the therapy the couple is shown the videotape of their interaction and, after it is analysed, they are told what the model's predictions are for their marriage. They are then counselled how to effect "repair" as suggested by the parameter values and the steady states of their marriage derived from their data using the model together with its predictions. It is all very intuitive and easily explained. For the first couple who had therapy in the late 1990s it proved immensely successful and they went on to have two children in the early 2000s. The therapy procedure proved so successful that my colleague and friend, John Gottman, retired early from the University of Washington to start a marital therapy clinic and to run workshops for interested marital therapists and psychologists.

I am still astonished that human emotions can be incorporated so easily and intuitively into a mathematical model and that such accurate predictions can be made as to marital stability, particularly newly married couples. What also surprised me was that a discussion, sometimes highly charged and emotional, could so easily and usefully be encapsulated in such a basic mathematical model of a couple's interaction. I am now in no doubt that practical mathematical modelling can, and will be, extremely useful in the social and psychological sciences. In 2015 an applied mathematician on the faculty in University College London, Dr. Hannah Fry, published an interesting book on *The Mathematics of Love* where she successfully applies mathematical modelling to such things as optimising web dating and so on.

Robert Burton 1577-1640

It is perhaps appropriate to conclude this section with an exact quotation about a stable couple from the classic book published in 1621 (and several more times) by Robert Burton.

The Anatomy of Melancholy. *What it is, with all kinds, causes, symptoms, prognostics & several cures of it........... Philisophically, Medicinally, Historically Opened and Cut up.*

"*Every Lover admires his mistris though she bee very deformed of her selfe, ill favored, wrinkled, pimpled, pale, red, yellow, tan'd, tallow–faced .... be crooked, dry, bald, goggle–eyed, bleare–eyed, or with staring eyes, she looks like a squiz'd cat .... a nose like a promontory, gubber–tushed, rotten teeth, black, uneven browne teeth, beetle browed, a Witches beard ....*"

It goes on for another 20 lines!

Mathematical epilogue

This chapter has described only a very few examples of the many and diverse biological, medical and psychological problems I have found fascinating and have worked on in my academic career. For me, an essential criterion for any research is that it has to be of direct relevance in the real world and, if possible, verifiable experimentally as in those described in detail above. Often in science there is a deferred gratification of any new theory so it is encouraging that increasingly more experimental data and confirmation of our modelling predictions have been found.

Much of the research I have done, and its predictions, encouragingly have been a stimulant for guiding critical experiments which have resulted in significant discoveries. This, of course, should be the aim of any mathematical modelling, namely to stimulate in any way whatsoever any endeavour which results in furthering our understanding of biology, medicine, psychology and other fields. There is, of course, a vast amount – ever increasing in fact – of research still to be done. I have been immensely fortunate in that I did not have to restrict my interests to one specific area, which is increasingly the norm.

Although with the major developments in the past 30 years we now know a lot more about biological pattern development. Many of the rich

493

spectrum of spatial patterns observed evolve from a homogeneous mass of cells which are orchestrated by genes which initiate and control the pattern formation mechanisms: genes themselves are not involved in the actual physical process of pattern generation. My basic philosophy behind practical modelling in biology and medicine has been to try to incorporate the physicochemical events, which from observation and experiment appear to be going on during development, within a mechanistic model framework which can then be studied mathematically and, importantly, the results related back to the practical experimental science. These morphogenetic models, for example, provide the embryologist with possible scenarios as to how, and when, pattern is laid down, how elements in the embryo might be created and what constraints on possible patterns are imposed by realistic models.

Both the mechanochemical models and reaction–diffusion models have been fruitfully applied to a vast range of biological problems not only in morphogenesis but elsewhere, such as feather primordia arrangement, wound healing mentioned above, wound scarring, shell and mollusc patterns and many many others. The explosion in biochemical techniques over the last several decades has led to a still larger increase in our biological knowledge, but has partially eclipsed the study of the intermediate mechanisms which translate gene influence into chemicals, into gradients, and into pattern and form. As a result, there is still so very much to be done in this area, both experimentally and theoretically.

I have clearly only scratched the surface of a huge, immensely important and ever expanding interdisciplinary world. Biology, in its broadest sense including medicine, ecology and more, is clearly still *the* science of the foreseeable future. What is also clear is that the application of mathematical modelling in these biological, medical, ecological, psychological and social sciences, is going to play an increasingly important role in future major discoveries as well as epidemiological, population control and survival, ecological strategies and others. There is an ever increasing number of areas where theoretical modelling is important such as social behaviour, adaption to habitat changes, climate change and so on. In the case of zebras, for example, by unravelling how species adapt to specific environmental changes, such as land use. For example, of two types of zebra in the same environment, the Grévy's zebra (*Equus grevyi*) is nearing extinction while another, the Plains zebra (*Equus burchelli*) has adapted its behaviour to survive. Behavioural ecology is a large field of study and another ever expanding area of research. How bird flocks, schools of fish and so on, reach community decisions is another fascinating relatively new area. Locusts, for example, swarm and move in part because of cannibalism: each locust tries to eat the one in front!

I also worked on some of the benefits of cannibalism, albeit not now in humans. There is however, a major benefit as a consequence of ancient human cannibalism which resulted in a very small number of deaths (just over 100 in Britain) from Creutzfeldt Jacob disease (mad cow disease) compared with the number predicted (more than 250,000) in the outbreak in Europe in the late 1990s. The reason for this is that human cannibalism in the past caused prion diseases, such as, more recently (up to around the 1960s), kuru among the Fore in Papua New Guinea. DNA evidence suggests that a protective polymorphism arose more than 500,000 years ago indicating prion diseases were widespread in early human history. Cannibalism is a likely cause of these diseases. Selection favoured those with a polymorphism which protected against such prion diseases, of which Creutzfeldt Jacob disease is one. In data obtained from 30 women in Papua New Guinea who practiced mortuary cannibalism from around 1920 to the 1960's practically all had the protective polymorphism. With the Creuzfeld Jacob scare instead of the thousands erroneously predicted to die from the disease in Britain only 134 did: blood tests showed that none of them had the protective gene.

Cannibalism is not as rare as generally imagined. In 2015, it has been scientifically confirmed that the settlers in the first English settlement, James Fort in Virginia, under constant siege by the indigenous Indian population, practiced cannibalism in the terrible winter of 1609-10, known as the "starving time". Only around 60 of the original 300 survived.

Mathematical Biology, now also known by other names such as Systems Biology or Theoretical Biology, now has active researchers, numbering in the thousands, in practically all of the biomedical sciences and increasingly so in the social sciences, another growth area. One example of their involvement is the theoretical model we developed for the large trial study on marital interaction and divorce prediction which I described above and is proving so highly successful. Some other examples were described briefly in Chapter 9.

Any practical mathematical or theoretical biological and medical research must have genuine interdisciplinary content. There is no way mathematical modelling can solve major interdisciplinary problems on its own. On the other hand it is highly unlikely that even a reasonably complete understanding could come solely from experiment. All the examples I discussed in this chapter are included, along with many others, in the book I wrote, called *Mathematical Biology*, first published in 1989 (now in its 3rd edition in two volumes) and translated into several languages. Although much of it requires a certain mathematical knowledge, practically all the chapters have a non-technical description of both the problem and its practical implications. The covers of the latest edition are below with lovely photos of leopards.

I feel immensely privileged to have been able to do research in whatever field and whatever topic interested me. If I were to start my research career afresh the main thing I would change would be to work as an applied mathematician in the biomedical, ecological and evolutionary sciences from the very beginning. It is an absorbing and fascinating world the understanding of which we have essentially only scratched the surface.

Perhaps the last word in this chapter, though, should be that which is attributed to Alphonso X, King of Castile León and Galicia (1221-1284):

"If the Lord Almighty had consulted me before embarking on creation I should have recommended something simpler."

Mathematical appendices

Mathematical model for PSA (prostate specific antigen) and prostate cancer growth

The model word equation of the model given in the above section is:

Rate of change of PSA = PSA production by normal cells

+ PSA production by cancer cells

– clearance/death of cancer cells

The mathematical differential equation used to quantify this word equation is:

$$\frac{dp}{dt} = \beta_b V_b + \beta_c V_c - \gamma p, \quad p(t) = \text{PSA level}, \, p(0) = p_0$$

where V_b, V_c are the volumes of benign and cancerous cells respectively, β_b, β_c are the PSA production parameters associated with normal cells and cancerous cells and γ is the clearance rate of PSA. Since cancer cells produce more PSA than normal prostate cells the parameter $\beta_b \ll \beta_c$. We assume the volume of non–cancerous cells V_b is constant and that cancer grows at a constant rate, ρ, which implies $V_c = V_0 e^{\rho t}$. Substitution into the above differential equation gives the approximate governing PSA equation and, if the initial PSA value is p_0, then

$$\frac{dp}{dt} = \beta_c V_0 e^{\rho t} - \gamma p \Rightarrow p(t) = p_0 e^{-\gamma t} + \frac{\beta_c V_0}{\rho} e^{\rho t}$$

The solution, depending on the relative sizes of γ and ρ, gives different values for the ratio $\mu = \gamma/\rho$ which results in synchronous or non-synchronous tumour growth typically shown in the two figures in the PSA section described above in this chapter.

This model can easily be adapted to include medical treatments such as radiation and chemotherapy and to quantify their efficacy within the prostate.

Mathematical model for brain tumour growth

The model used is a basic linear diffusion model with only two parameters to be determined. The model used is, in words:

Rate of change of tumour cell density at a point in the brain =

Diffusion (motility) of tumour cells in that area

+ Net duplication of the tumour cells in that area

The mathematical equation, a partial differential equation, is

$$\frac{\partial c}{\partial t} = \nabla.(D(\mathbf{x})\nabla c) + rc$$

where c(**x**,t) denotes the tumour density at the position **x** in the brain and t denotes the time, r denotes the duplication rate of the cancer cells, which with this form implies the cells grow exponentially and quantified by the parameter r. D(**x**) denotes the diffusion rate at position **x**. The diffusion is greater in white matter than in grey matter. The solution and graphical results, as shown in the figures in the brain tumour section above, requires computer generated numerical solutions of this model equation together with the values of r and D(**x**) calculated from the patient's two brains scans.

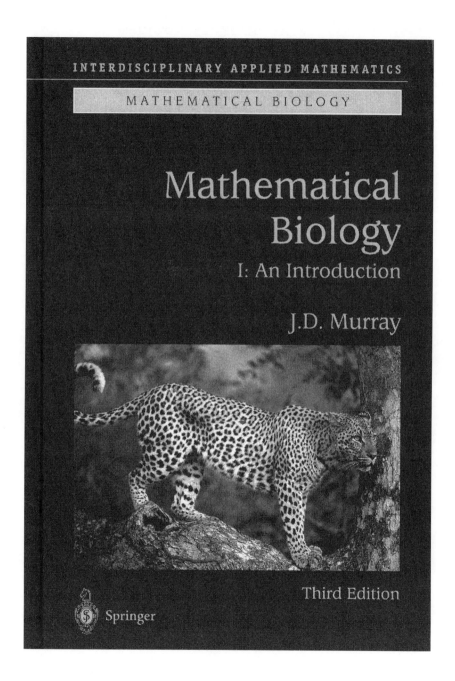

INTERDISCIPLINARY APPLIED MATHEMATICS

MATHEMATICAL BIOLOGY

Mathematical Biology

II: Spatial Models and
Biomedical Applications

J.D. Murray

Third Edition

Springer

Epilogue

Looking back on my life and serendipitous journey from the small world of a poor working class family in an isolated very small town in rural Scotland to the international world of university academia I feel immensely fortunate. It has been an ever-changing life of immense pleasure and fascination. The most important events which stand out, way beyond all the others, are fortunately contracting polio which launched me into a totally different world and resulted in the most important event of my life, meeting Sheila and having been able to spend almost 60 years together. When I return home from the university, or any time necessarily spent away for any reason, the sight of her still fills me with a warmth and happiness which has been, and still is, by far the most important part of my life. We have always dearly loved our children Mark and Sara whose kindness and concern for us have given us such pleasure and warmth all their lives, but they know, and have always known, without the slightest feeling of resentment, how much Sheila and I mean to each other.

Our daughter Sara, JDM, our son, Mark and Sheila, sitting on our old antique stone roller at our Oxford home, *Pinsgrove* in the winter c1983. My soft moose jacket was given to me by a cousin of my grandfather when I was 9: he got it in the Klondike in the 19th century.

Sheila and I have also been blessed with such lovely, lively, kind and considerate grandchildren, Sara's daughters, Mazowe, Neroli and Eloise. Mazowe graduates from college this year, Neroli is off on a gap year and for a term taught young children in rural Bali while Eloise, a high school freshman is the intellectual star of her school in Hawaii and is a natural mathematician.

Sheila and JDM in *La Combe,* our house in France, c1993.

Sheila and JDM in our Litchfield (Connecticut) home 2010.

Were I religious I would daily give thanks to God: instead I am daily grateful to Sheila and give thanks for the wonderful, warm and loving life she has given me and which we have had together for so many years.

Index

Index

Printed in Great Britain
by Amazon